Proud to be Deaf

Ministry, Saintliness and the History of the Catholic Deaf Community in South Africa, 1874–1994

Mark James

UJ Press

Proud to be Deaf:
Ministry, Saintliness and the History of the Catholic Deaf Community in South Africa, 1874–1994

Published by UJ Press
University of Johannesburg
Library
Auckland Park Kingsway Campus
PO Box 524
Auckland Park
2006
https://ujpress.uj.ac.za/

Compilation © Mark James 2025
Chapters © Author(s) 2025
Published Edition © Mark James 2025

First published 2025

https://doi.org/10.36615/9780906785546
978-0-906785-53-9 (Paperback)
978-0-906785-54-6 (PDF)
978-0-906785-55-3 (EPUB)
978-0-906785-56-0 (XML)

This publication had been submitted to a rigorous double-blind peer-review process prior to publication and all recommendations by the reviewers were considered and implemented before publication.

Proofreading: Louis Botes
Cover design: Hester Roets, UJ Graphic Design Studio
Typeset in 9/13pt Merriweather Light

Contents

Acknowledgements i

List of Abbreviations iii

Foreword v

Part I: Introductory Chapters 1

Chapter 1: Deaf Culture and Saintliness:
Countering Audism and Phonocentrism 3

Chapter 2: Reading from Infinity:
Proximity, Discourse and Deaf People as Teacher 41

Chapter 3: Epistemological, Methodological and
Ethical Considerations 73

Chapter 4: A Historical Survey of Catholic Ministry
to the Deaf Community 99

**Part II: A History of Deaf Education in Catholic Schools
for the Deaf in South Africa, 1874–1994** 153

Chapter 5: Pioneering Beginnings: Establishing Schools
for the Deaf, 1874–1920 155

Chapter 6: Acting in Good Conscience:
The Triumph of the Oral Method of Deaf Education,
1922–1937 169

Chapter 7: Totality and the Oral Method of Deaf Education in White and Coloured Catholic Schools for the Deaf, 1928–1969 185

Chapter 8: Catholic Schools for the Deaf and Apartheid, 1948–1968 225

Chapter 9: Total Communication, Bad Conscience and Shifts in Deaf Education, 1969–1981 263

Chapter 10: The Use of Sign Language in Catholic Schools for the Deaf, 1982-1994 291

Part III: Deaf Saintliness and Prophetic Witness 313

Chapter 11: Deaf Saintliness 315

Chapter 12: Robert Simmons: Doctor in Neurobiology and a Deaf Activist 317

Chapter 13: Father Cyril Axelrod (1942–): Compassionate Minister Instilling Dignity 327

Chapter 14: Ruben Xulu (1942–1985): Africanising Church Art 359

Chapter 15: Lindsay Moeletsi Dunn (1959–): Black Consciousness and Challenging Racism and Audism in a Catholic School for the Deaf 375

Chapter 16: Fr John Turner CMM (1945–2013): Pastor and Teacher 393

Chapter 17: The Deaf Community of Cape Town: Sign-Deaf Space as Breathing Spaces for Prophetic Ministry 401

Part IV: Conclusion and the Way Forward 417

Chapter 18: Conclusion 419

Bibliography 429

Endorsements

Mark James' book constitutes a substantive original contribution to the history of Deaf ministry in the Catholic Church in South Africa from 1874-1994. James, through careful archival research, provides a Catholic perspective which will become an invaluable resource for ministers (Deaf and Hearing) throughout the world. The book is also demanding and provocative because it is a spiritual witness to the giftedness of the Deaf community inspiring hope. Employing the philosophy of Emmanuel Levinas, James awakes the consciousness of the reader to put the conscience into question to think otherwise about the different abilities of Catholic Deaf community in South Africa. Accordingly, the book inspires newness, boldness, and resilience in ministry to approach the Kingdom of God and encounter the face of Christ crucified (crucified by the forces of phonocentrism and audism). There are many lessons to be learnt that gives voice and appeal to what Ruben Xulu's image evokes: "Christ was Africa crucified". In sum, the book pronounces words of blessing to remember and sign "a new journey" together from the heart.

Associate Professor Glenn Morrison,
School of Philosophy and Theology at the
University of Notre Dame, Fremantle, Australia.

James' inspiring work describes the history of the Catholic Church's ministry to Catholic Deaf people in South Africa, highlighting its achievements and shortcomings. This book resonates with Pope Francis' challenge that the Church become the merciful face of Christ in the world. This entails being passionate about meeting people who, like the Deaf community, are different and marginalised. It is to engage in a process of conversion, where we overcome our indifference by learning sign language so that Deaf people can feel more at home in the

Church. In so doing, we witness to a more authentic encounter with the Risen Christ.

Archbishop Dabula Mpako
Archdiocese of Pretoria,
Head of the Office of Ministry to the Deaf Community.

In this highly original piece of research, the author traces the history of the Catholic Deaf community in South Africa and links this to the changing understanding of being Deaf arising from a new cultural frame of reference that prioritizes dignity and autonomy over conformity to a norm as the distinguishing criteria of being human. This new frame is deepened through the philosophy of Emmanuel Levinas, a set of ideas that in turn is interpretive of 'being religious' in a new way. There is a kind of symphonic structure to the book, with the final movement sketching a number of examples of 'saintliness' in the community of Deaf people in South Africa, lifting the whole narrative to a higher and more inspiring level.

Professor Patrick Giddy,
Senior Research Associate in Philosophy and Religion,
University of KwaZulu-Natal,
author of *Aristotle in Africa* (UJ Press, 2025).

Dedication

*I dedicate this book to the Catholic Deaf communities in
South Africa, Eswatini and Lesotho
for your commitment to your faith
and breathing new life into mine.*

*You taught me the meaning of
the responsibility that arises
from proximity.*

*In loving remembrance of my Deaf grandparents,
Joseph and Eunice Hirst,
and my hearing parents, Ken and Margaret James.*

Acknowledgements

I wish to express my thanks and appreciation to all the people who provided the support and encouragement needed to help me complete this book.

I am indebted to all the Catholic Deaf community members who assisted me in my research, most especially those who agreed to be interviewed. The witness of your lives is truly inspirational. I also want to thank the hearing participants who were interviewed and who, through their lives, have displayed a selfless dedication to serving God and Deaf people.

A generous thanks goes to Fr Cyril Axelrod CSsR for writing the foreword to this book. He continues to inspire by his selfless love, commitment and service to the Deaf and Deaf-Blind communities across the world for the past 53 years.

My thanks extend to the late Bernard Connor OP who introduced me to the writings of Emmanuel Levinas as a student and whose life embodied being-for-the-Other.

I thank Professor Glenn Morrison from the Notre Dame Catholic University, Fremantle, Australia who helped me to read history through Levinasian eyes.

Deep gratitude to Philippe Denis OP for his friendship, encouragement and support that kept me motivated to publish my doctoral dissertation as a book.

I am thankful to all the archivists and librarians who assisted me in locating the material I needed. I thank Sr Christa Bucher OP and Anne Tangney from the King William's Town Dominican Sisters Archive for their invaluable assistance. I thank Catherine Paige and Bro Rex Harrison OMI for their help at the Catholic History Bureau in Johannesburg; Günther Simmermacher, editor of *The Southern Cross* in Cape Town; Sr Francis Krige OP who helped scan and photocopy material for me at the Cabra Dominican Sisters' Archive; Norma Oosthuizen from the Archive of the Archdiocese of Durban; Helena Glanville from the Archive of the Diocese of Port Elizabeth; Fr Sandile Mswane from the Archives of the Catholic Diocese of Manzini in Eswatini; the late Zofia Solej, previously archivist at the Historical Papers Archive in the William Cullen Library at the University of the Witwatersrand Library in Johannesburg and Janet Zambri, who has retired as head librarian, but who helped me enormously in finding articles and books for my research.

I would also like to acknowledge the help of my sister Brenda Smit-James who proofread my text on numerous occasions and edited it. Thank you for your invaluable assistance. With deep appreciation, I also thank Debbie French and Terence Creamer for their invaluable comments and editing skills that have helped me produce a book that, I hope, is both scholarly and accessible to the layperson.

Finally, I thank Bishop José Luis Ponce de Léon and the priests of the Diocese of Manzini for their help and support for my work with the Deaf community in Eswatini and for allowing me the time to edit my dissertation and transform it into a book.

Mark James
7 February 2025
Anniversary for deceased parents of Dominicans

List of Abbreviations

AAD	Archive of the Archdiocese of Durban
AACT	Archive of the Archdiocese of Cape Town
ACDM	Archive of the Catholic Diocese of Manzini
ADPE	Archive of the Diocese of Port Elizabeth
ANC	African National Congress
ASL	American Sign Language
BSL	British Sign Language
CDSA	Cabra Dominican Sisters' Archive
CHB	Catholic History Bureau
CM	Congregation for the Mission
CMM	Congregation of Mariannhill Missionaries
CODESA	Convention for a Democratic South Africa
CODA	Child(ren) of Deaf Adults
CSsR	Congregation of the Most Holy Redeemer
DCCT	Deaf Community of Cape Town
DeafSA	Deaf Federation of South Africa
DEAF	Deaf Equal Awareness Foundation
DET	Department of Education and Training
HSRC	Human Sciences Research Council
KDSA	King William's Town Dominican Sisters' Archive
NGO	Non-governmental organisation
OMI	Oblates of Mary Immaculate
OP	Order of Preachers (also known as the Dominicans)
OSD	Order of St Dominic
OSM	Order of the Servants of Mary

PAC	Pan-Africanist Congress
RA	Redemptorist Archive
SACBC	Southern African Catholic Bishops' Conference
SAIRR	South African Institute of Race Relations
SANCD	South African National Council for the Deaf
SASL	South African Sign Language
SASO	South African Students' Organisation
STJI	St Joseph's Theological Institute Archive
SLED	Sign Language Education and Development
SPM	Sound Perception Method
UDF	United Democratic Front
UWA	The University of the Witwatersrand Archive at the William Cullen Library

Foreword

It would have been impossible for me to read the entire book line by line on my braille device, but I was able to read the summary Mark James sent me. Well done, it is wonderful indeed. He frames the whole picture of Catholic Deaf Education and ministry with deaf people. It is true today that the gifts of deaf persons have been shared with many people in our country and in the world. As deaf people have become successful members of society, they have played roles in which they have served and benefitted both the hearing and the Deaf communities.

I cannot imagine how deaf people, who attended Catholic schools for the deaf, could have achieved what they have if it was not for the education provided by the Dominican sisters. Putting to one side the debate between education through the system of sign language or oralism, we must say that the Dominican sisters, through their goodness, availed themselves to teach the deaf children. The deaf children gained the benefit of improving their education whether it was through sign language or oralism. The sisters dedicated their lives to working for the betterment of deaf lives and endeavoured for their success.

In this respect, I agree with Emmanuel Levinas' understanding of saintliness. The Dominican sisters gave themselves fully to educating deaf children out of their own goodness and for the goodness of the deaf children. They were 'saintly' in their efforts. They deserve the appreciation and gratitude of the Deaf community. In this way, I still owe a great debt to the Dominican sisters who inspired me to give my life in loving service to and in ministry with Deaf people. For myself, I affirm the goodness of both sign language and oralism which has offered me access to communication with the Deaf and with hearing people in a broad sense.

I also appreciate Levinas' philosophy based on a person as a being a self as well as a person responsible to others. This frames a perfect and true charity of God in the realism of humanism. Human beings tend to read life like English from left to right, from self to the other. Levinas reminds us that we need to read life like Hebrew from right to left, from the other to the self. We are reciprocally responsible for one another.

I must say that Mark James makes a clear point about Deaf education given by the Cabra and the King William's Town Dominican Sisters, but he has not neglected their flaws and failures either. In many cases, they failed by not allowing deaf children and adults to express the value of sign language as a gift from God.

Initially, the Cabra Sisters did allow deaf children to learn sign language at school. They allowed for what Levinas would understand as reading from right to left. In contrast, the King William's Town Dominican sisters insisted on and only used the single oral method. However, even the Cabra Sisters eventually adopted oralism and abandoned education through sign language.

Many of the sisters were influenced and trained at an Institute for the Deaf in the Netherlands. The priest in charge was known to trample sign language firmly under his foot without considering the many variables that affect deaf children like mental health, or physical conditions such as cerebral palsy – to say nothing of the possibility of deafblindness, where touch is the only medium of communication. He was only interested in promoting oralism.

In 1976, I was invited to visit this Institute. I thought that I was invited as a friend but later I came to realise that I was treated as a guinea pig. He made an experiment on me and my language acquisition. I was extremely disgusted by the way he treated me. I could not believe how he made me feel inferior. On the last day there, I spoke openly with him saying that sign language, too, comes from God as it brings an awareness of God's boundless mercy and love for deaf children and deaf adults, enabling them to believe in God's immense love.

After saying this, I was shunned by him and, to some extent, by his followers. Of course, I realise that our humanity has successes and failures. A person might feel convinced that just because they have a profession, like being a teacher, one has nothing to learn from others. The failure in humanity is the lack of accountability from professional persons to the people they serve or educate. In this way, the professional person does not acknowledge any benefit from their peers like the deaf children and adults. I suspect Levinas would concur.

In my years of ministry, I have often met Deaf people who, like me, have been hurt and scarred by the strict and exclusive oral training they received at school. I often tell them the story of the lesson I learnt from my father.

At school, I would receive corporal punishment for using sign language. On one occasion, I was not beaten but was locked in the classroom during the tea break as a punishment for signing. I struggled to hold my bladder as I waited for a sister to open the door after the break. This experience added to my grievances against the sisters' policy of oralism.

In the evening, I shared the terrible experience with my father. He listened to my story. His answer was simple. It was: 'Forgive her for she does not understand what she is doing.' It put me in my place.

Later in the year, he bought several pairs of black stockings as a Christmas present for each sister who was my teacher. I was aghast and stood with my backhand over my forehead, shaking my head negatively. He said to me: 'Forgive them as they struggle with their shortcomings.'

It gave me a chance to think about what it meant for me. I slowly realised that it was a good way to forgive the sisters for the corporal punishments. Then I asked myself what my own shortcomings were. This released me from holding on to my grievance against the sisters. My father set the best example of forgiveness. It was how I grew up with the sense of forgiveness. I thank my father as a good Jew for teaching me the power of forgiveness for all the hurts I received from others and, also, to be aware of my shortcomings towards them.

As a priest, I used to use this experience in my sermons to the Deaf community. I encouraged them to liberate their grievance against the sisters for the corporal punishments received at school. I also encouraged them to reflect on their shortcomings as well as the shortcomings of the sisters. The Deaf community was deeply touched by the words I shared with them.

Despite some of these shortcomings and failings, I admit that I feel so blessed with both sign language and oralism as, together, they offer me greater accessibility to communication with deaf people as well as hearing people. Were I to use sign language only, I would never have thought of entering a seminary! Learning a spoken language offered me the encouragement of keeping my heart and mind open to the hearing world along with using sign language in the Deaf world. Nevertheless, I defend sign language as the more beneficial communication for hearing persons to learn in their encounters with the Deaf.

Reading parts of Mark James' book, I was reminded of other Deaf people who promoted the use of sign language, like my friend Robert Simmons. I, for one, will never allow oralism to have the last word. Sign language is what it is all about, as we have seen in the witness of those who sought to attend to the needs of the Deaf community by establishing the Deaf Community of Cape Town (DCCT), people like Stephen and Suzanne Lombard, Faith Cronwright and Wilma Newhoudt. They too have shown the saintliness of which Levinas speaks through the personal witness of their lives of service to the Deaf community.

Fr Cyril Axelrod CSsR OBE

Part I

Introductory Chapters

Chapter 1

Deaf Culture and Saintliness: Countering Audism and Phonocentrism

The title for this book *Proud to be Deaf* comes from a talk given in 1985 by Dr Robert Simmons, at that time a senior lecturer in anatomy at the University of the Witwatersrand in Johannesburg.[1] Simmons was giving a talk to the school-leaving pupils at St Vincent School for the Deaf and encouraging them to hold up their heads high as Deaf people as they leave school and face the challenges of life in a wider world. Simmons was himself a past pupil of St Vincent's[2] and had achieved extraordinary academic heights for a Deaf person at that time. He encouraged them not to see themselves as second-class human beings but to always strive to reach their true potential as Deaf human beings. He challenged these school leavers, not to be ashamed of being deaf, but rather 'Proud to be Deaf.'[3] Simmons wanted them to value their language and culture as it was central to their being. They should not just conform to the demands of the hearing world around them. Simmons challenged the young Deaf people to shape their future for themselves rather than limit themselves to perspectives that they needed to adapt to the demands of the hearing world around them.[4] Implicit in Simmons' appeal to the Deaf school-leavers was a critique of the education system that had formed him and them.

This book will attempt to detail and reflect upon the radical shift in Deaf people's consciousness of themselves within

---

[1] 'An address given by Dr Robert Simmons (past pupil of the school) at the Annual Prize Giving, December 1981,' *St Vincent School Magazine*, June 1982, 44–49. Box: Cyril Axelrod's Papers, File 2: Magazines, Redemptorist Archives, Cape Town.
[2] St Vincent's refers to St Vincent School for the Deaf in Melrose, Johannesburg. I will often use St Vincent's in the text because it is commonly used.
[3] 'An address given by Dr Robert Simmons,' 47.
[4] Ibid.

3

the context of the ministry that the Catholic Church offered to deaf people in South Africa from 1874 to 1994. It will also draw out certain figures within the Catholic Deaf community who responded, and sometimes reacted, to the ministry offered by the Church. This book is a revised version of my doctoral dissertation and I have used both archival and oral sources in conducting my research.[5]

Before venturing into the historical narrative of this contribution, it is necessary to clarify the terms and concepts prevalent within the Deaf world. It is also necessary to explain who Emmanuel Levinas is, what he meant by 'saintliness', and how it is used in this book.

Deafness and being Deaf

Since the modern period, there has been a major shift in thinking about deafness and how deaf people are perceived. Originally, thinking about deafness was informed by a natural law ethical perspective which emphasised deafness as a lack or defect that deaf people suffered in their being human. From this perspective, deafness is merely the physiological description of a person's lack of the ability to hear. For philosophers like Aristotle, this was a sign that they did not fully measure up to the standard of a human being imbued with reason. Deaf people were more akin to women and children who also did not qualify as being fully human.[6] This way of thinking saw no space for deaf people within the human community. At first, they were just ignored and treated as imbeciles who were incapable of being educated. The only solution was for the person to be saved through a miraculous healing.

In the modern period, after the Enlightenment, philosophers like Kant, Voltaire and Rousseau placed greater

---

5   I express my appreciation to the University of KwaZulu-Natal for granting permission to publish this book which is a revised version of my doctoral dissertation, 'Deaf as Other: A History of the Catholic Church's ministry to the Deaf Community in South Africa from 1948 to 1994,' PhD diss. (University of Kwazulu-Natal, Pietermaritzburg, 2019). I also thank Professor Philippe Denis, my supervisor, who accompanied me throughout the process of researching and writing the dissertation.
6   This will be explored more extensively in Chapter 4.

emphasis on the dignity of the individual and their human rights. The shift involved an appreciation of 'who' Deaf people are, rather than 'what' they are.[7] The dignity of deaf people was first recognised with attempts to educate members of the Deaf community starting in the sixteenth and seventeenth centuries. This was an enormous breakthrough for deaf people. The education of deaf people was seen as vital for their inclusion within society and two different methods of education were developed that were perceived, at the time, as mutually exclusive. The two competing methodologies were known as manualism and oralism.[8]

The manual method of Deaf education sought to educate deaf people by employing methodical signs and fingerspelling.[9] As deaf people were being educated and were together in schools for the deaf, they began to experience themselves as bonded together as a distinctive cultural and linguistic community, especially those who used sign language.

The oral or aural method of deaf education, in contrast, adopted the view that the best way to liberate deaf people from their prisons of silence was to teach deaf children to lip-read and vocalise a spoken language. This method utilises modern technology like hearing aids and later cochlear implants to help deaf children cope and function more effectively with hearing people. After 1880, more schools for the deaf adopted the oral method of deaf education as it was seen to be the most effective instrument to enable deaf people to enter the job market. These dynamics will be explored further in Chapter 5.

---

7 See Emmanuel Levinas, *Totality and Infinity: An Essay on Exteriority* (Pittsburgh: Duquesne University Press, 1969), 177.
8 Manualism as we have seen refers to the use of methodical signs (not necessarily natural sign language), fingerspelling (the whole alphabet has an equivalent hand sign) and encouraging writing in a spoken language whereas oralism refers to use of lip-reading and vocalisation of spoken languages in schools for the deaf. These two approaches were vigorously debated throughout the 19th and early 20th centuries. Oralism triumphed because many governments across the world adopted this approach as the only legitimate one.
9 This method was popularised by Abbe l'Epee in the 18th century. It will be explained more fully in Chapter 4.

The method of education shifted slightly in the 1970s with the introduction of Total Communication. Total Communication was the simultaneous use of signs alongside the English language. It is also known as the Combined Method. Another name for this methodology is Signed English. In Chapter 6, we will explore how Total Communication was promoted as a way out of the binary opposition of the manual and oral methodologies. However, more importantly, it opened the door to the acceptance of sign language as a legitimate language for the classroom.

Total Communication was later superseded by natural sign languages themselves. For example, bilingualism seeks to teach Deaf children through the means of South African Sign Language (SASL) but also to write in a spoken language like English, Afrikaans, Zulu or Sesotho. These developments point to a different perspective among Deaf people, in recognising that dignity is not just based on asserting one's rights but finding creative ways of being in the world with others. We will look at this and its implications for the education of the deaf in South Africa in Chapter 10.

Encountering Deaf terminology

When venturing into the reality of Deaf people's lives, it is important to recognise that one needs to set aside one's assumptions and be open to a different way of thinking, understanding and behaving. Simmons' talk to the school leavers has already highlighted some areas of contestation between hearing assumptions of deaf people and how Deaf people see and think about themselves. This has already been alluded to in the spelling of the words deaf and Deaf.

People who physiologically lack adequate hearing are referred to as deaf with a lowercase 'd'. In contrast, Deaf with a capitalised 'D' refers to those Deaf people who identify themselves culturally and linguistically as Deaf because they identify with a culturally distinct community of people who use sign language as their first language. They also lack the ability to hear. In some of the literature, the term 'd/Deaf' is used to delineate people who are both physiologically deaf and who also culturally identify as being Deaf.[10] Due to the awkward nature of d/Deaf, this book uses the lower-case d for the deaf who were trained in the oral method of deaf education and never learnt sign language nor identified with the Deaf community and the upper-case spelling D for those Deaf people who even though they went to oral schools for the deaf chose to communicate in sign language and asserted their Deaf cultural identity and dignity as members of a Deaf community. In this book, I will use the capitalised D to refer to those deaf people who use sign language and who assert their identity and dignity as being Deaf not deaf.

Arising from this struggle for the dignity of Deaf people, it is understood that being Deaf is a cultural and linguistic identity that Deaf people adopt. Instead of focusing on what deaf people lack or on their physiological inability to hear like a hearing person, being Deaf is the way Deaf people reframe themselves more positively. It is the conscious way that Deaf people choose to be in the world. By communicating with each other through sign language and belonging to a community of people formed by a Deaf culture and way of life, they shape their way of being in the world. This more positive outlook has meant that instead of feeling inferior to hearing people, Deaf people take pride in themselves. Like hearing people, they too, have their language and culture. As a result of this, Deaf people assert their identity as Deaf, rather than deaf, and challenge hearing people to learn sign language or make use of sign language interpreters when communicating with them.

From this linguistic-cultural perspective of being Deaf, forcing Deaf children and adults to conform to the assumptions of the hearing world, operating from a natural law ethical perspective is called audism.

Audism

In 1975, Tom Humphries, an academic from the United States, created the neologism 'audism' to refer to 'the notion that one is superior based on one's ability to hear or behave in the manner

---

10   See Richard J. Senghas and Leila Monaghan, 'Signs of Their Times: Deaf Communities and the Culture of Language,' *Annual Review of Anthropology* 31 (2002): 71–72.

of one who hears.'[11] This concept highlighted the injustices committed by hearing people's misplaced assumptions about the Deaf community and which have had a devastating effect on the lives of deaf people.

Harlan Lane, an American psychologist, developed this concept by arguing that audism was structural and institutionalised in society. Consequently, the concept of audism was expanded to include:

> the corporate institution for dealing with deaf people, dealing with them by making statements about them, authorizing views of them, describing them, teaching about them, governing where they go to school, and, in some cases where they live; in short, audism is the hearing way of dominating, restructuring and exercising authority over the deaf community.[12]

Deaf people experienced this misuse of power by hearing people when they went to various institutions like hospitals, schools, churches and government offices. The hearing people working in these institutions often determined that deaf people were 'deficient', 'not normal' or 'deviant' due to their 'handicap' and their inability to hear. This negative understanding of being deaf led the medical profession to seek ways to fix and remedy deaf people's deafness. The solution was to provide hearing aids and cochlear implants, and the educational solution was to send deaf children to schools that used the oral method of education where deaf children had to learn to speak and lip-read. 'Pupils were not encouraged to use sign language.'[13] In fact, the use of sign

---

11   Tom Humphries, 'Audism: The Making of a Word.' Unpublished paper, 1975. Quoted by H-D. Bauman, 'Introduction: Listening to Deaf Studies,' in *Open Your Eyes: Deaf Studies Talking*, ed. H-Dirkson Bauman (Minneapolis/London: University of Minnesota Press, 2008), 13, 30.
12   Harlan Lane, *The Mask of Benevolence: Disabling the Deaf Community* (San Diego, Dawn Sign Press, 1989), 43.
13   Jacinta Teixeira, interview conducted by Mark James, 13 July 2016, 455 in Mark James, 'Deaf as Other: A Levinasian Reading of the History of Deaf Ministry in the Catholic Church in South Africa from 1948 to 1994.' PhD diss. (University of KwaZulu-Natal, Pietermaritzburg, 2019).

language was actively discouraged through corporal punishment if deaf children were seen signing at school. This was all done, in good conscience, to ensure that the deaf person's 'imprisoned spirit would find liberation'[14] when 'the sound barrier had been broken'[15] and they could lead 'a normal life.'[16]

Harlan Lane has argued that audism is veiled by what he called the 'mask of benevolence'[17] where hearing people see themselves acting in altruistic and caring ways towards deaf people, or as acting in 'good conscience.'[18] For Lane, hearing people and their institutions appear to be altruistic in their care for deaf people but in effect, they dominate deaf people's lives by making decisions for them and treating them in paternalistic and oppressive ways.[19] This power continues to be exercised by hearing people over deaf people through various institutions under their control like hospitals, schools, churches and government offices, although in some institutions it may not be as prevalent as before.

Audism functions like racism, not only because of attitudes of superiority of one group over another but also due to the institutionalisation of these attitudes. Through the oral method of education in schools and the provision of hearing aids and cochlear implants to deaf children, hearing people seek to train deaf people to function in, what they call, the 'hearing world.' These audist agendas, under 'the guise of benevolent care for the Deaf community, are hostile to the Deaf community, their language, their identity and their self-understanding.'[20] Education systems, the medical profession, government policies and even church missions operated on audist assumptions and paid little regard to the opinions and thinking of Deaf people themselves. Many Deaf people reject audism and the natural law

---

14 'At St. Vincent's Her Spirit Found Liberation,' *The Star*, Wednesday 15 July 1964, 33.
15 'At St. Vincent's,' 33.
16 Ibid.
17 Lane, *The Mask of Benevolence*, 43.
18 Emmanuel Levinas, *Collected Philosophical Papers*, (Dordrecht, Kluwer Academic Publishers, 1993), 31. This understanding of 'good conscience' which will be elaborated upon in Chapter 9.
19 See Lane, *The Mask of Benevolence*, 69-72.
20 See Lane, *The Mask of Benevolence*, 43.

assumptions from which many biological and medical definitions of deafness have arisen.

For many centuries too, it was believed and understood that only spoken languages were truly languages. Sign language was disparaged as mere gesture and viewed as primitive, closer to the way animals communicate rather than human beings. In 1960, William Stokoe both argued for and demonstrated the linguistic structures of sign languages. In so doing, he overturned centuries of misconceptions.[21] Sign language is a language utilising space rather than sound as its medium of communication, relying on sight and the visual rather than hearing and the audiological. This awareness has broadened our understanding of language and even what constitutes being human.

Part II attempts to demonstrate why the structural injustices of audism have become increasingly understood as a form of cultural and linguistic colonialism,[22] where deaf children in schools for the deaf were denied access to their language and culture. For example, often deaf children were coerced by schools for the deaf to learn to speak spoken languages and punished if they were found signing. Deaf teachers were effectively purged from schools for the deaf and were not considered good enough to teach deaf children. They were relegated to being the hearing teachers' assistants. This oppression was perpetrated not just as prejudice against deaf people but was the institutionalised result of policies propagated by governments, taught in universities, perpetrated by the medical profession under the guise of care for the deaf and forced upon defenceless deaf children in schools for the deaf. For Lane, the hearing are the colonisers who imposed their language, culture and value system on the Deaf oppressed, in ways similar to what European colonisers perpetrated against African people in the nineteenth century.[23]

---

21   See William Stokoe, 'Sign Language Structure,' *Studies in Linguistics Occasional Papers* 8 (1960) and *Semiotics and Human Sign Languages* (The Hague: Mouton, 1972).
22   Paddy Ladd, *Understanding Deaf Culture: In Search of Deafhood* (Clevedon, UK: Multilingual Matters, 2003), 81–83.
23   Lane, *The Mask of Benevolence*, 74.

Phonocentrism

According to H-Dirksen Bauman, underpinning audism is the historical misconception of phonocentrism. The term 'phonocentrism' was coined by Jacques Derrida who understood it to be the limiting of language to speech and the use of the voice and vocalisation.[24] In so doing, other ways of communicating are ignored. Derrida focused primarily on the written means of communication.

H-Dirksen Bauman used Derrida's idea and applied it to the experience of the Deaf community. He argued that phonocentrism privileged speech by overemphasising the 'maniacal obsession' with the human voice over sign language.[25] Consequently, it has been a major foundational factor in contributing to audism. For centuries, sound has been mistakenly privileged over sign as the only legitimate indicator of language. These ideas will be explored and elaborated upon in Chapter 4.

In contrast to audism and phonocentrism, Deaf people have sought to develop more liberating perspectives of themselves as expressed in concepts like Deafhood, bilingualism in Deaf education, being DeaF, and Deaf Gain.

Deafhood

To counter what Deaf people perceive to be the colonising and oppressive system of audism and phonocentrism, they promoted the importance of cultivating Deafhood instead. Paddy Ladd, a British academic and Deaf himself, proposed the idea of 'Deafhood' as an alternative to the audist understanding of deafness. Deafhood is the Deaf 'way of being in the world, of conceiving the world and their place within it in both potentiality and actuality.'[26] Therefore, Deaf people have a common and equal human dignity with hearing people. Deaf people were not

---

24 See H-Dirksen Bauman, 'Listening to Phonocentrism with Deaf Eyes: Derrida's Mute Philosophy of (Sign) Language,' *Essays in Philosophy* 9, 1 (2008): 1. Accessed 7 September 2018, http://www.commons.pacific.edu/eip/
25 Bauman, 'Listening to Phonocentrism,' 4.
26 Ladd, *Understanding Deaf Culture*, 81.

to be understood negatively as those who lack hearing but rather positively as those who share a common way of being in the world. Consequently, Ladd understood Deafhood to be

> [A] process by which Deaf individuals come to actualize their Deaf identity, positing that those individuals construct that identity around several differently ordered sets of priorities and principles, which are affected by various factors such as nation, era and class.'[27]

Deaf identity had arisen from a contestation between the medical approach to deafness, which focused on the biological lack of hearing and the medical remedies of this condition, and the cultural-linguistic way of being Deaf.[28] Linked to this is the idea that Deaf culture refers to the discourse that Deaf people historically have developed and maintained 'about themselves, their lives, their beliefs, their interpretation of the world, their needs, and their dreams.'[29]

Bilingual-bicultural approach to Deaf education

In South Africa, after the first democratic elections in 1994, the policy towards the education of deaf children shifted, in line with worldwide trends, to a greater reliance on the bilingual-bicultural approach.[30] This approach focused on two realities that deaf children learn more easily using a natural sign language like South African Sign Language (SASL) as their first language, and for writing purposes need learn a spoken language as second language. The two languages are considered distinct from each other and used for different purposes.

---

27 Ibid, xviii.
28 Ibid.
29 Tom Humphries, 'Talking Culture and Culture Talking,' in Bauman, *Open Your Eyes*, 35.
30 For a comprehensive review of the Bilingual-Bicultural approach in South Africa, see Philemon Akach, 'Application of South African Sign Language (SASL) in a Bilingual-Bicultural Approach in Education of the Deaf.' Unpublished PhD dissertation (University of the Free State, 2010).

Deaf children also often live in two cultures and, in the United States, more than 90% of deaf children live in hearing families.[31] Deaf children adapt their attitudes, behaviours and values in relation to these two different cultures. They also find creative ways to respond to these two cultures as they interact with both cultures.

> This approach therefore implies that deaf children do not per se require remedial teaching strategies, because the bilingual-bicultural programme provides a unique visual learning environment in their linguistic, cultural and social needs are met.[32]

Many Deaf children who are educated in schools using the bilingual-bicultural approach achieve not only a great degree of self-esteem, self-confidence and self-acceptance but also display increased literacy skills and academic achievement.[33] This approach has displaced the aural-oral method as one which is more respectful of Deaf people and their linguistic and cultural distinctiveness.

DeaF identity

Recent scholarship on Deaf identity has also challenged the polarising of Deaf identity as radically opposed to the hearing world. In 2005, Guy McIlroy, a Deaf lecturer in Deaf Education at the University of the Witwatersrand, suggested that perhaps Deaf identity is much more fluid than what has previously been suggested.

McIlroy proposed an alternative way to speak about Deaf people which takes this fluidity into account and to rather use the word 'DeaF'. In this formulation, the 'F' refers to the fluidity of

---

31 See National Association of the Deaf, Accessed 6 December 2024. http://nad.org/resources/early-intervention for-infants-and-toddlers/
32 Akach, 'Application of SASL,' 20.
33 Akach, 'Application of SASL,' 22.

identities, as Deaf people negotiate their place within and at the interface between the Deaf and hearing worlds.[34]

While doing research on Deaf children in hearing families, McIlroy and Storbeck investigated 'how a bicultural DeaF identity is assumed.'[35] They found that although all the participants were happy to identify with the Deaf community, this did not mean that they imposed 'a moratorium on dialogue with the hearing society.'[36] They were particularly concerned with strengthening the bonds they had with close family members and their hearing school teachers thereby displaying 'the fluid bicultural DeaF identity proposed by the researchers.'[37]

Deaf Gain

Deafhood, the bilingual-bicultural approach to Deaf education and DeaF are focused on appreciating and even celebrating the Deaf way of being in the world. Related to these concepts is Deaf Gain, which recognises and treasures human diversity. Deaf Gain reframes deafness from focusing on hearing loss or disability to celebrating what the whole of humanity stands to gain from the experiences of Deaf people. Deaf people can benefit society in ways that help us understand our humanity more fully. Deaf Gain is not so concerned about addressing audism as acknowledging the gifts that Deaf people bring to our understanding of what it means to be human.

> Deaf Gain is defined as a reframing of 'deaf' as a form of sensory and cognitive diversity that has the potential to contribute to the greater good of humanity. There are three different signs that we use to mean Deaf Gain. The first can

---

34 See Guy McIlroy, 'Deaf identities: A range of possibilities.' Paper presented at the Deafness and Mental Health Conference, Worcester, Cape Town, De La Bat Institute for the Deaf, August 2005.
35 Guy McIlroy and Claudine Storbeck, 'Development of Deaf Identity: An Ethnographic Study,' *Journal of Deaf Studies and Deaf Education* 16, 4 (Fall 2011): 497. Accessed 8 September 2018, DOI: 10.1093/deafed/enr017
36 McIlroy and Storbeck, 'Development of Deaf Identity,' 509.
37 Ibid.

be glossed as DEAF INCREASE, and it expresses the opposite notion of hearing 'loss'. It emphasizes that Deaf people have something of importance. The second sign can be glossed as DEAF BENEFIT, and it emphasizes that deafness is not just a loss but a benefit as well. The third sign can be glossed as DEAF CONTRIBUTE. This sign emphasizes the importance of considering all the ways that Deaf people contribute to humankind.[38]

Bauman and Murray list the number of ways in which Deaf people contribute to human diversity. The first way that deaf people have contributed is to 'the wholesale redefinition of language.'[39] The human brain is adaptable and can as easily learn a sign language as it does a spoken language. 'Language can take the form of speech but it does not have to; language can just as easily take the form of visual signs.'[40] An example of this is 'baby signing'[41] where hearing parents can communicate with their hearing children in sign language before the infants learn to speak.

Another way in which Deaf people benefit humanity is through their predominantly visual way of being in the world. Bauman and Murray point to the benefits that hearing people can gain by developing the enhanced visuospatial mental images, mental rotation skills, facial recognition skills, peripheral recognition skills and spatial cognition skills that Deaf people constantly employ.[42] It is not that deaf people see any better than hearing people but rather what they do with what they

---

[38] H-Dirksen L. Bauman and Joseph M. Murray, 'Reframing: From Hearing Loss to Deaf Gain,' trans. from ASL, Fallon Brizendine and Emily Schenker, *Deaf Studies Digital Journal* 1, (Fall 2009): 3. Accessed 30 November 2022, http://dsdj.gallaudet.edu

[39] H-Dirksen L. Bauman and Joseph J. Murray, 'Deaf Studies in the 21st Century: "Deaf-Gain" and the Future of Human Diversity,' in *The Oxford Handbook of Deaf Studies, Language, and Education*, vol 2, ed. Marc Marschark and Patricia Elizabeth Spencer (Oxford Handbooks Online, September 2012), 12. Accessed 30 November 2022, DOI: 10.1093/oxfordhb/9780195390032.013.0014

[40] H-Dirksen, L. Bauman, 'Reframing the Future of Deaf Education: From Hearing Loss to Deaf-Gain.' Talk given to the Canadian Hearing Society, 8. Accessed 30 November 2022, https://www.chs.ca/sites/default/files/uploads

[41] Bauman, 'Reframing the Future of Deaf Education,' 9.

[42] Bauman and Murray, 'Deaf Studies in the 21st Century,' 13.

see 'pushes the boundaries on traditional hearing practices of seeing.'[43] Hearing people, too, could benefit from a bilingual visual learning environment where they learn both auditory and visual learning skills.[44] Education systems need to recognise multiple intelligences and not just rely on IQ tests to determine the bandwidth of human knowing.[45]

When signing, Deaf people make use of skills similar to those used in the film industry by employing a 'constant tableau of close-up and distant shots, replete with camera movements and editing techniques.'[46] One area where there is a close affinity to film and signed languages is animation where they are both less constrained by time and space.[47] Bauman asked what innovations might Deaf filmmakers make to this industry if cinematic techniques were taught in schools for the deaf?[48] Or how teachers can explain the process of cell mitosis in sign language using visual presentations in their explanations.[49] Hearing children could benefit from this too because although spoken languages can describe the process, these descriptions may not help them to visualise it.

Deaf people could contribute to developing a different cultural aesthetic in architecture too. They would design buildings that conform more to the needs of Deaf people and that are more 'organic, curvilinear, and bathed in light.'[50] For example, tables would not be rectangular but round. This has implications for social behaviour and access because 'in a circle, everyone is invited to a communal conversation if they so wish.'[51]

Another contribution is that it is easier for Deaf people to communicate across national boundaries than is the case for hearing people. International meetings of Deaf people take place

---

43 Bauman, 'Reframing the Future of Deaf Education,' 12.
44 Bauman and Murray, 'Deaf Studies in the 21st Century,' 14.
45 Bauman, 'Reframing the Future of Deaf education,' 11.
46 Bauman and Murray, 'Deaf Studies in the 21st Century,' 15.
47 Bauman, 'Reframing the Future of Deaf Education,' 18.
48 Ibid.
49 Ibid.
50 Bauman and Murray, 'Deaf Studies in the 21st Century,' 16.
51 Bauman, 'Reframing the Future of Deaf Education,' 19.

in International Sign (IS).[52] It has a greater potential to be a global language than any spoken language and may take far less time to learn.

If education systems integrated the insights of Deaf Gain, both Deaf and hearing people would benefit enormously. Educationalists need to engage with the imaginative and creative thinking to which Deaf Gain points by taking seriously the insights of neuroscience, appreciating the importance of human intelligence and acknowledging the diverse ways of human knowing and being in a community. In short, Deaf Gain means human-gain.[53]

Purpose of this book

The purpose of this book is not to apportion blame or to scapegoat hearing people for the injustices committed to Deaf people. The purpose of writing it is not to wage war on behalf of the Deaf community or even to try to champion their rights. The purpose behind writing this book is to look at history through a reframing or contemplative lens. In this book, the focus is on how the hearing community can learn to listen to and be transformed by proximity to their Deaf neighbours.

Contemplation can be understood as reflecting on how to see in a radically new way that leads to a change of consciousness. From a Christian perspective, contemplation is a listening and learning from God that radically transforms our life and our way of seeing and of understanding our neighbour whose reality is different to ours. Contemplation can also never be separated from action. A truly transformative contemplative view always challenges us to a new praxis and way of living in relating to others and to creation. Our limited and misguided perspectives are placed under scrutiny. Adopting a more contemplative stance towards life and others means we begin to walk in their shoes and have our consciences chafed. We learn to stop trying to control others or make them like ourselves but rather recognise our responsibility to act justly towards them.

---

52   Bauman and Murray, 'Deaf Studies in the 21st Century,' 20.
53   Bauman, 'Reframing the Future of Deaf Education,' 25.

It is for this reason that I have chosen to use the philosophy of Emmanuel Levinas (1906-1995) to help us reflect on how to develop this reframing and contemplative stance towards the Deaf community. For Levinas, 'ethics is an optics':

> Ethics is not a corollary of the vision of God, it is that very vision. Ethics is an optics, such that everything I know of God and everything I hear of his Word and reasonably say to him must find an ethical expression ... To know God is to know what must be done. God is merciful means be merciful like him.[54]

This is the contemplative revolution we need to undergo if we are to live in peace as human beings. Levinas himself sought peace but also recognised that true peace must be based on a transformation in our ways of seeing and relating to others. True peace always involves justice for the neighbour. He wrote:

> My neighbour's face has an alterity which is not allergic but opens up the beyond. The Justice rendered to the Other, my neighbour, gives me an unpassable proximity to God. The pious man is the just man.[55]

Those who recognise their responsibility for the poor one or the marginalised neighbour can realise the eschatological or messianic peace. This search for peace means I undergo a revolution in self-understanding by acknowledging those who face me and who challenge me to put their needs before my own. The commitment to justice and peace is not just an optional extra but is truly the gospel message. For Levinas, those who can put the life of the suffering other before their own, understand holiness and saintliness.

> Prophets preoccupied themselves not with immortality of the soul, but with the poor, the widow, the orphan, the stranger.[56]

---

54 Emmanuel Levinas, *Difficult Freedom: Essays on Judaism* (Baltimore: The Johns Hopkins University Press, 1990), 17.
55 Levinas, *Difficult Freedom*, 18.
56 Ibid, 20.

Consequently, for Levinas, ethics is not only about a way of seeing but also a way of living 'otherwise than being' through a receptiveness to the communication or discourse of the other.

This book is about pointing to this prophetically contemplative and transformative stance which will be the lens through which we will critically read the history of the Catholic Church's ministry to the Deaf community as well as the significant contribution some Deaf people have made to this history themselves. Before elaborating further upon Levinas' philosophy, let us look at his life story.

Emmanuel Levinas (1906–1995)

Emmanuel Levinas was born in Kuanas, Lithuania on 12 January 1906. He was raised in an Orthodox Jewish family and his faith remained central to his identity and philosophy throughout his life.[57]

At the beginning of the First World War in 1914, Levinas' family fled Lithuania for Ukraine but returned to their home country six years later when it was safe again. In 1923, Levinas moved to France at the age of 17 to study at the University of Strasbourg.[58] Thereafter he went to the University of Freiburg and studied phenomenology under Edmund Husserl and Martin Heidegger.[59]

He returned to France in 1930 and taught at the École Normale Israélite Orientale in Paris. This was a school for Jewish students from an orthodox upbringing.[60] He began writing about Husserl and Heidegger at a time when they were not well-

---

57 This short biography has been previously published in a journal article 'Christian Ministry, the Philosophy of Emmanuel Levinas and the Deaf Community,' *Journal of Theology in Southern Africa* 167 (July 2000): 44–45. Reproduced with permission.
58 Peter Steinfels, 'Emmanuel Levinas, 90, French Ethical Philosopher,' *New York Times*, 27 December 1995, 1. Accessed 3 May 2019, www.nyti.ms/29iQumz
59 Anya Topolski, *Arendt, Levinas and a Politics of Relationality* (London: Rowman and Littlefield, 2015), 6.
60 Steinfels, 'Emmanuel Levinas,' 3.

known in France.[61] However, Levinas regretted his enthusiasm for Heidegger when, in 1933, Heidegger publicly announced his support for the Nazi Party in Germany. This proved to be a turning point in his life as a philosopher. Levinas began to challenge the starting point of phenomenology and all Western philosophy. He criticised its preoccupation with ontology and the egocentric self. Levinas began to regard himself as a post-phenomenologist[62] challenging what he saw as Heidegger's paganism. For Levinas, philosophy should not be oriented to Being and the Self but rather the marginalised Other, that is, the suffering neighbour. Using the Jewish tradition as his template, he developed a philosophy that sought to base true humanism on our willingness to accept our responsibility for the suffering of the neighbour. In his writings, Levinas saw himself as bringing the wisdom of the Bible, the Jewish world, to the wisdom of philosophy, the Greek world or as bringing Jerusalem to Athens. This approach Levinas saw 'as translating the Jewish sources into "Greek," Greek being his metaphor for the language Jews have in common with other inhabitants of the Western world.'[63]

During the Second World War, Levinas was captured as a French soldier and interned as a prisoner of war in a labour camp. This experience shaped his philosophy and the imagery he used in his writing. Many of his family from Lithuania died in the Shoah. However, his wife Raisa and his daughter Simone survived due to the help of friends, particularly Louis Blanchot and his wife, who were both Catholics. They arranged with a community of Catholic nuns to hide Levinas' wife and daughter in their convent for the duration of the war.[64]

After the war, Levinas returned to his teaching post in Paris where he remained until taking up a post at the Nanterre branch of the University of Paris in 1967 and then the Sorbonne in 1973.[65]

---

61 Colin Davis, *Levinas: An Introduction* (Cambridge: Polity Press, 1996), 1.
62 Topolski, *Arendt, Levinas and a Politics of Relationality*, 6–7.
63 Annette Aronowicz, 'Translator's Introduction,' in Emmanuel Levinas, *Nine Talmudic Readings* (Bloomington and Indianapolis: Indiana University Press, 1990), ix.
64 Ibid, 8.
65 Steinfels, 'Emmanuel Levinas,' 3.

He retired from teaching in 1973. He continued writing many books and articles until his death on 25 December 1995.[66] His most celebrated works were *Totality and Infinity* (1961) and *Otherwise than Being* (1974).

Terry Veling, an Australian theologian, puts it very succinctly when he says that Levinas in his philosophical writing:

> is trying to read life otherwise, 'otherwise than being,' to read against the all-powerful desire of the ego to be and to secure its presence in the world. He is trying to read in a counter-directional way that begins from the other side, from the other point of view … He is reading from right to left, across the grain of a prevalent Western philosophy and culture.[67]

Levinas' body of writing in enormous. For the purpose of this book, the next section focuses on Levinas' understanding of holiness and saintliness.

Levinas' understanding of holiness and saintliness

For Levinas, holiness is separateness. God is absolutely transcendent and separate from us. For a faithful Jew, there is no possibility of union. Jews believe that the only union possible with God is obedience to the Torah, the revealed Word of God. The Torah teaches how to separate oneself from sin and to keep oneself holy. Thus, for Levinas, keeping the Torah means cultivating holiness, a holiness that is synonymous with the practice of justice and compassion towards suffering neighbours.

So instead of focusing on a transcendent God we cannot know, Levinas says the Torah calls us to recognise God's transcendent presence as an authority, not a force, that is recognisable in the vulnerable face of the marginalised and suffering other that commands us to responsibility.[68] The

---

66   Ibid.
67   Terry Veling, *For You Alone: Emmanuel Levinas and the Answerable Life* (Eugene, Oregon: Cascade Books, 2014), 11.
68   See Tamra Wright, Peter Hughes and Alison Ainley, 'The Paradox of Morality: An Interview with Emmanuel Levinas,' in *The*

other approaches us from a transcendent height in his or her vulnerability and it is their suffering that commands our response.[69] This command constitutes our humanity. To be fully human is to understand that we are held hostage to the demand of their face, their vulnerability and suffering. When we accept responsibility and in passivity say: 'Here I am' (*hineni*), we express our freedom.[70]

> The being that expresses itself imposes itself, but does so precisely by appealing to me with its destitution and nudity – its hunger – without my being able to be deaf to that appeal. Thus in expression the being that imposes itself does not limit but promotes my freedom, by arousing my goodness. [71]

We act freely not when we do what we like but when we overcome our complacency and self-sufficiency and respond generously to the needs of the suffering and marginalised. Proximity challenges us to transcend self-interest and to open up our lives, in passivity, to the other by offering them hospitality and acting justly towards the neighbour.[72]

For Levinas, the self's response-ability to the suffering neighbour is the way by which 'God comes to mind.'[73] It is when hospitality and justice towards the neighbour is practised that we can meaningfully speak about God, the ultimately transcendent, the wholly Other. For Levinas, religion, prayer and justice are truly one.[74] Our God language is always idolatry and a false religion if it is not deeply rooted in a way of life that is de-centred, passive and displays a kenotic self-giving relation to the other or the marginalised neighbour.

In fact, Levinas is critical of how Christians speak so glibly of God's immanence and how through contemplation, we can be

---

Provocation of Levinas: Rethinking the Other, ed. Robert Bernasconi and David Wood (London and New York: Routledge, 1988), 169.
69 Levinas, *Totality and Infinity*, 200.
70 Emmanuel Levinas, *Otherwise Than Being or Beyond Essence* (Pittsburgh: Duquesne University Press, 1998), 146.
71 Levinas, *Totality and Infinity*, 200.
72 Levinas, *Otherwise Than Being*, 77.
73 See 'Foreword' in Emmanuel Levinas, *Of God who Comes to Mind* (Stanford: Stanford University Press, 1998), xi–xv.
74 Levinas, *Difficult Freedom*, 18.

drawn into a mystical union with God. Mystical union with God for Levinas smacks of a problematic desire for interiority, consolation and self-satisfying sufficiency. This path neglects the importance of accepting responsibility for the suffering of other people. We open up to exteriority by becoming responsible for the other.

For Levinas, God is external to human interiority and experience. God is so external and transcendent that God can only be experienced as 'a trace or near-absence',[75] that is, footsteps already covered over and no longer even visible. The presence of God are the footsteps of the one who has already passed by (Exodus 33:21-23).[76] For Levinas, the exteriority of the suffering neighbour is the closest we can get to God. It is through the height and transcendence of the exterior neighbour who faces us with authority that our subjectivity and interiority are called into question. We are commanded by the face of the other to responsible action. Like God, the other or neighbour always eludes our grasp and our attempts to control them or use them for our own purposes.

You shall not kill

For Levinas, we are called to 'open up' to the one who faces us. We should refrain from trying to control them or even to attempt to grasp them intellectually. If we attempt this, we bring them into the ambit of our terms of reference. This contravenes the commandment: 'You shall not kill.' We thematise them into the categories of our own choosing and understanding, our worldview, and so we deny their radical alterity.

Levinas wrote that 'with the appearance of the human – and this is my entire philosophy – there is something more important than my life, and that is the life of the other.'[77] Thus Levinas can say that the saint is:

> the person who in his being is more attached to the being of the other than to his own. I believe that it is in saintliness

---

75 Davis, *Levinas*, 100.
76 Emmanuel Levinas, *Collected Philosophical Papers* (Dordrecht: Martinus Nijhoff Publishers, 1987), 106–107.
77 Wright, Hughes and Ainley, 'The Paradox of Morality,' 172.

that the human begins; not in the accomplishment of saintliness, but in the value. It is the first value, an undeniable value.[78]

For Levinas, saintliness is rooted in the Jewish Bible and not only in Christianity. Saintliness is inherent, not only in the sixth commandment 'Thou shalt not kill', but also in the injunction 'Love your neighbour' and 'Love the stranger.'[79] By living the course of our lives, we are inadvertently killing someone. This is not just true of individuals but, as we will see, in our institutions too. Levinas gave the example: 'When we sit down at the table in the morning and drink coffee, we kill an Ethiopian who doesn't have any coffee. It is in this sense that the commandment must be understood.'[80]

Loving your neighbour means therefore to be more concerned about the deaths of the suffering ones in our world. Their deaths are of greater concern than our own death. Consequently, the commandment 'Thou shalt not kill' and 'loving my neighbour' limit my personal freedom and concerns for my life. A different understanding of freedom is envisaged. Rather than just self-fulfilment, I, in an act of generosity, give my life as a gift, a free and gratuitous gift for the other. This is true charity or a commanding love. When we live our lives with great generosity and as a gift for others, we fulfil the commandment to love our neighbour and to love God. 'God is the one who says that one must love the other.'[81]

For Levinas, proximity or this encounter with the other or marginalised people like Deaf people, is a privileged moment. In this book, we reflect on how through our encounter with the Deaf community our lives are interrupted and disrupted. Deaf people exist in their own right – as different to and separate from the hearing community. They exist as alterity. Deaf people's alterity calls the hearing community into question by challenging our complacent and often misguided or even prejudiced ways

---

78   Ibid, 172–173.
79   Ibid,' 173.
80   Ibid.
81   Ibid, 177.

of understanding them. By our interactions with Deaf people, we the hearing, are challenged, if we are honest, to undergo a process of unlearning and being undone (what Levinas refers to as passivity) – so that our ways of understanding Deaf people can be renewed and refreshed. Our sense of well-being is disturbed and we are challenged to think again about how we are to relate in new ways to this person who faces us and how to be hospitable and compassionate towards them. For example, when a hearing person begins to learn sign language they relate towards a Deaf person with a transformed sense of hospitality. It is a recognition that we are called to live by a different ethic.

Ethics is the first philosophy

Levinas often said that ethics is the first metaphysics.[82] This insight is important for philosophy, ethics, spirituality and Christian living. For centuries, the metaphysics of Greek philosophers, like Aristotle, dominated Western philosophy and Christian theology.

Aristotelian thinking encouraged a virtue ethics that universalised moral behaviour for all human beings. It was derived from the idea that all human beings are united by what is their given human nature.[83] Our biological, rational and linguistic characteristics across the species show that human beings share a common nature. This is often referred to as natural law. As a result of this, it is possible to deduce an ethic that arises from the objective laws of our nature as rational and intelligent beings. For the English Dominican theologian, Herbert McCabe, the weakness of this way of thinking is:

> its too ready assumption that mankind [sic] as a unity exists 'by nature'. It seems to me that human unity is something towards which we move, a goal of history.

---

82 For further reading, see Adriann Peperzak, ed., *Ethics as First Philosophy: The Significance of Emmanuel Levinas for Philosophy, Literature and Religion* (New York and London: Routledge, 1995).
83 See Herbert McCabe, *Law, Love and Language* (London: Sheed and Ward, 1968), 35–67.

The early formulations of natural law had the negative effect that those human beings who deviated from these 'laws of nature', like the blind, deaf, women or slaves, were considered as having a defect in their human nature. Consequently, they were often ignored and marginalised within society. This will be explored further in Chapter 4.

During the Enlightenment and the modern period, with philosophers like Kant and Descartes, we see a greater emphasis placed on the dignity of the human subject. Ethics became linked to loving the person as an autonomous individual and recognising that they shared equal rights with other human beings. This finally became embodied in the Universal Declaration of Human Rights established by the United Nations in 1948. During this period, we see how for the Deaf community, schools for the deaf emerge. Two different methods of deaf education were advocated, either through the means of the oral approach or in sign language. Being educated meant that deaf adults were able to find employment and participate more fully within society. Deaf people were increasingly appreciated as human beings endowed with dignity after centuries of this being denied. However, there were limitations with this modern conceptualisation.

In the postmodern period, ethics is understood within the context of language and communication. As McCabe pointed out: 'ethics has to do with communication, with the fact that human animals make use of conventional signs and symbols.'[84] So human beings through language are self-creative in their communication with each other. Human beings can participate in a community of people and be influenced by them, even to the extent of remaking themselves. For McCabe, 'communication disturbs our present world, lays it open to influence from others, which may involve revolutionary change.'[85] Even the language of God as revealed in the Word of God can be learned and can transform our relations with each other.

Levinas also focused on language and communication by challenging Western philosophical thinking. Instead of starting

---

84   McCabe, *Law, Love and Language*, 2.
85   Ibid, 101.

with the subject or the self as Descartes did coining the maxim – I think therefore I am – Levinas attempted to read life as otherwise than being. By this, Levinas advocated that one should separate 'oneself from a whole philosophical tradition that sought the foundations of the self in the self.'[86] Instead of being-for-self, he understood true humanity as those who become being-for-the-other. This being-for-the-other challenged the more ontological understanding of being-for-self. The emphasis was placed more on intersubjectivity rather than subjectivity, on alterity rather than unity, and singularity rather than universality. This is evident in his thinking about the face of the other.

Levinas' understanding of the face or the neighbour

Levinas emphasised the radical alterity of the other so the encounter with the face of other is not just another way of speaking about the difference in class, race, ethnicity or nationality. Levinas was adamant that his ethical philosophy should not be confused with identity politics. He said that the best way to recognise the face or the neighbour is 'not to notice the colour of their eyes.'[87] So, strictly speaking, the neighbour is not to be easily identified as either Ethiopian[88] or as Deaf. For Levinas, the face is not to be represented because the representation of the other is dangerous. It can equally lead to freedom or oppression. Diane Perpich pointed out that 'singularity expresses ethical resistance to the misappropriations that come with representation.'[89] It is a way of classifying and even controlling the person represented and people are always more than how we are represented or with which we seek to identify or classify them, as Perpich wrote: 'I am this but not only this.'[90]

---

86 Levinas, *Totality and Infinity*, 88.
87 Emmanuel Levinas, *Ethics and Infinity*, (Pittsburgh: Duquesne University Press, 1985), 85.
88 Wright, Hughes and Ainley, 'The Paradox of Morality,' 173. In discussing the matter of saintliness, Levinas says it refers to the sixth commandment. 'Thou shalt not kill'.
89 Diane Perpich, 'Levinas, Feminism and Identity Politics,' in *Radicalizing Levinas*, ed. Peter Atterton and Matthew Calarco (Albany NY: SUNY Press, 2010), 34.
90 Perpich, 'Levinas, Feminism and Identity Politics,' 33.

But Levinas' understanding of the singularity of the face goes further than warning us against the dangers of representation of the other. Levinas wrote: 'The oneself is a singularity prior to the distinction between the particular and the universal.'[91] Lisa Guenther explained this to mean that 'before I am conscious of having committed myself to anyone – before I am even conscious of being a self – I am already responsible for the Other in a way that both interrupts my identity and also singles me out as a unique one: irreducibly myself because I am inescapably for the Other.'[92] In this respect, the self is responsible for the other even before the self has a name and it is this that constitutes its selfhood.

Individual identity or representation is secondary to discovering one's true human identity as for-the-other. For Guenther this means that singularity means that 'anyone is responsible for any Other.'[93] So it no longer matters who the Other is, 'what matters is that s/he faces me, and that a face, any face, commands me.'[94] This does not mean that the particular differences between people do not matter. They do matter enormously, especially when deciding how to respond in any given situation.

In this respect, Levinas speaks of the ethical juxtaposition of 'the Saying' and 'the said'. 'The Saying' is the ethical 'impulse' or first philosophy that challenges all human interactions at the level of 'the said', the daily practice of politics, economics, culture and religion. One will act differently to one who is an aggressor or a victim, but central to our true human identity is that we are responsible for all those who face us. In each singular face that we encounter in proximity, we are challenged to react ethically.[95] Each person and each situation is different and cannot be measured by a universal response – based on natural law or

---

[91] Levinas, *Otherwise Than Being*, 108.
[92] Lisa Guenther, '"Nameless Singularity": Levinas on Individuation and Ethical Singularity,' *Epoché: A Journal for the History of Philosophy* 14, 1 (Fall 2009): 178.
[93] Guenther, 'Nameless Singularity,' 170.
[94] Ibid, 182.
[95] Ibid.

human rights – because a universal measure may not adequately lead to an ethical response to the one who faces us.

In this book, the politics of difference forms an integral part of the historical narrative being recounted. However, Levinas' philosophy is being used as a necessary counterweight to this history of identity. Levinas' philosophy is a reminder that we are not just describing a contest of identities but ultimately trying to learn from the neighbour, or the other, so that we can move towards living together in a more just way and cultivate a new ethic between hearing and Deaf communities. Levinas' understanding of the singularity of the face is partially expressed in the concept of 'DeaF' that we highlighted earlier, which is a move beyond a rigid representation and fixed identities of Deaf versus hearing. For Levinas, we are always on a trajectory of seeking greater justice[96] and enabling a new world to break into the presently flawed reality. The challenges have not stopped but keep on developing and evolving. Greater relationality and appreciation for intersubjectivity and alterity may mean hearing people will be more willing to interact with Deaf people and be more appreciative of, and willing to, learn sign language and so improve their relationality. This is what Levinas refers to as hospitality or saintliness.

Saintly or prophetic ministry as hospitality

Levinas says true religion, holiness and saintliness is living an answerable life, that is, a life where one accepts responsibility for one's neighbour. When one gives one's life in faithful and loving service of one's neighbour regardless of the cost to oneself. This is living a spirituality of holiness or saintliness. In his book *Alterity and Transcendence*, Levinas wrote:

> Responsibility for the other, the 'dis-interested' for-the-other of saintliness. I'm not saying men [sic] are saints, or moving towards saintliness. I'm only saying that the vocation of saintliness is recognized by all human beings as a value and that this recognition defines the human. The

---

[96] Wright, Hughes and Ainley, 'The Paradox of Morality,' 177.

human has pierced through imperturbable being; even if no social organization, nor any institution can, in the name of purely ontological necessities, ensure, or even produce saintliness. There have been saints.[97]

For Levinas, to be human is to be saintly, that is, concerned for the other. Central to his philosophy is the idea that to be human is to have:

already heard and understood the commandment of saintliness in the face of the other man [sic]. Even when it is said that at the origin there are altruistic instincts, there is the recognition that God has already spoken. He began to speak very early.[98]

True religion is not about cultivating a spirituality or a practice of life imbued with the desire for personal salvation or mystical union with the divine. Rather it is recognising the infinite in the face of the vulnerable face of the neighbour which commands us to say, 'Here I am' and respond to their suffering and marginalisation. In the terminology of spirituality, it is a kenotic process of decentring self and giving oneself as bread for the suffering neighbour. When we encounter the neighbour, we are standing on holy ground. Levinas saw the face of the vulnerable neighbour as having great height and authority because it is an epiphany or a holiness, a trace of the wholly Other.

When hearing people begin to learn sign language and the laws of countries are changed to allow for the education of deaf children in sign language, we get an idea of what Levinas meant by hospitality. Hospitality means opening up to the world of the other and welcoming their difference and alterity. Bauman and Murray's concept of Deaf Gain, which we outlined earlier, accords with Levinas' understanding of alterity and hospitality. This is honouring the face of the other and recognising that one is one's 'brother's' keeper. Hospitality is also becoming conscious of the

---

[97] Emmanuel Levinas, *Alterity and Transcendence* (London: The Athlone Press, 1999), 171.
[98] Levinas, *Alterity and Transcendence*, 180.

other's struggles. It is to 'haemorrhage for the wounds of the other' even to the point of substitution.

Substitution is responsibility for our neighbour and doing what we can for the good of this neighbour even to the extent of giving away the food that was destined for our own mouth.[99] This is an act of utmost freedom of holiness and saintliness and is the way that God comes to mind. The saints are those holy ones who put justice and peace for the neighbour into practice.

Levinas' idea of saintliness was developed by Edith Wyschogrod, who made this concept central to developing a post-modern ethics.

Saintliness and hagiography: The contribution of Edith Wyschogrod

Edith Wyschogrod (1936–2009) was an American postmodernist philosopher who was immensely influenced by Levinas' thought. She used his philosophy to attempt to lay the foundations for post-modern ethics. For Wyschogrod, this involved a shift from the development of intricate moral theories to narrating or writing hagiography. This surprising perspective highlighted the importance of the witness value of the individuals who are engaged in responding to the suffering and nameless ones, not only by their words and fanciful theories but more importantly by their praxis.

For Wyschogrod, moral theories are limited because a particular moral argument is often not accepted by those who stand outside the hermeneutical thought that developed it. Secondly, the formulation of a moral theory does not guarantee that it will be put into practice.[100] In contrast, the selfless actions of the saints speak more powerfully than any theory. Implicit in this praxis is a 'command' to emulate these saintly actions in one's

---

99 Levinas, *Otherwise Than Being*, xxviii.
100 See Edith Wyschogrod, *Saints and Postmodernism: Revisioning Moral Philosophy* (Chicago: Chicago University Press, 1990), xvi and xxv. For further commentary, see Merold Westphal, 'The Empty Suitcase as Rainbow,' in *Saintly Influence: Edith Wyschogrod and the Possibilities of Philosophy of Religion*, ed. Eric Boynton and Martin Kavka (New York: Fordham University Press, 2009), 48-62.

own life. For Wyschogrod, post-modern ethics and morality is about this shift from theory to praxis.

For Wyschogrod, a saint or a saintly life is characterised as:

> One whose adult life in its entirety is devoted to the alleviation of sorrow (the psychological suffering) and pain (the physical suffering) that afflicts other persons without distinction of rank or group or, alternatively, that afflicts sentient beings, whatever the cost to the saint in pain or sorrow.[101]

In short, this means that the saint (or the ethical person) is one whose life is characterised by living a life of compassion and mercy by responding to the suffering neighbour without counting the cost to oneself. In this respect, Wyschogrod and Levinas concur.

Wyschogrod goes further than Levinas arguing that this moral praxis is transmitted through hagiography. For her, hagiographies are those narratives or histories that seek to ensure that the reader is swept up by its 'imperative force' and also in which the reader is challenged 'to extend and elaborate [this narrative] with her/his own life.'[102]

For Wyschogrod, hagiographies are histories that challenge people to live more ethically. These saintly men and women incarnate the word in their bodily existence by negating their self-interest and so are freer to respond to the suffering and needs of their neighbour. As a result of doing this, they share in the glory of the glory of the infinite.[103] Their saintly lives become a test and a

---

[101] Wyschogrod, *Saints and Postmodernism*, 34.
[102] Wyschogrod, *Saints and Postmodernism*, xxiii.
[103] 'I would appeal to a revivified notion of glory, one attested in the broken body of the other, both that of the victim and that of the one who is willing to substitute her/himself for the other ... Look out for the creation of suffering in order to suffer, for pride in one's own strength to withstand vicissitude. But the language of glory can be used to describe the suspension of the *conatus* to know or to do, as becoming pure passivity before the need of the other. The one who does so, says in effect, '"*me voici*, here I am" bears witness to and is chastened by the glory of the infinite and in so doing is glorified.' See Edith Wyschogrod and Carl Raschke, 'Heterological History: A Conversation,' *Journal for Cultural and*

testament to others of how living ethically means to show concern for the suffering of others, and how it takes precedence over *conatus*, that is self-interest and self-preservation.

This book is an attempt at hagiography in Wyschogrod's understanding of the term. How are we to live more ethically, more justly, more compassionately and lovingly towards the Deaf neighbour among us? How can we honour the God we worship and profess by reaching out more generously and hospitably to the Deaf neighbour in our midst? The Deaf neighbour does not exhaust the other but, in this book, will provide the basis for the ethical life required for responding to the countless others in our world. This opening up and accepting responsibility for the other is sacred work. This sacred work involves becoming a de-centred, kenotic and self-giving self who, in proximity to the Other, is obsessed with seeking better justice for all peoples. This is an opening up or passivity to all of humanity, creating breathing spaces for all unrecognised Others.

The challenge to Christian theology

Levinas' and Wyschogrod's understanding of saintliness is not that foreign to Christian perspectives. There are parallels in the Johannine and Jamesian injunctions of 'How can you say you love the God you do not see when you do not love your neighbour whom you do see?' (1 Jn 4:20)[104] or 'I will show you my faith by my deeds' (Jam 2:14-26) through the practice of justice and peace. For Christians, kenotic[105] or self-emptying and self-giving example of Jesus Christ on the cross is the one who calls God to mind. We are called to emulate Christ's example as did the saints and to share in Christ's glory. By sharing in Christ's kenotic love and compassion for our suffering neighbour by taking up our cross, we are drawn into the community of divine self-emptying love of the Holy Trinity.

Religious Theory 1, 2 (2000): 2. Accessed 2 May 2019, www.jcrt.org/archives/01.2/wyschogrod_raschke.shtml

104 Scriptural quotations throughout the book follow the New Revised Standard Version (NRSV).

105 From the Greek word *kenóō* meaning empty out, pour out or deplete.

Saints in the Catholic tradition

In the Catholic tradition, the desire for holiness and sanctity is embodied in the lives of the saints. The saints are upheld as model Christians, especially those who are officially canonised by the Church. They are canonised because they lived a life of holiness and continue to inspire us, the present-day faithful, to emulate them and to embody or incarnate in our lives their generous acts of loving charity, virtue and faith in God.

The martyrs and saints have been part of the Catholic tradition since the New Testament was written. However, the Church's understanding of saints and holiness has changed and developed over the years. In the writing of St Paul, the saints are understood as the believing Christians who, through baptism and a life of striving for virtue, separate themselves from the world around them. The Church is the community of those who are separated from the values of this world. Like the martyrs, those saints who in a time of persecution gave their lives for Christ were considered the true role models of the Christian faith. In the fourth century and later, when Christianity became the state religion of the Roman Empire under Emperor Constantine, sanctity was seen in those people who renounced the world of power, status and marriage and lived as monks or hermits. Alongside these shifts in understanding of saints and holiness, the Popes declared certain Christians as canonised saints and established criteria for the acceptance of saints in the Church.

At the Second Vatican Council from 1962–1965, the bishops of the world accepted the document *Lumen Gentium*, which promoted the universal call to holiness for all believing Christians and not just for the select few. It is the responsibility of all the baptised to strive for holiness and sanctity, in other words, seek to become a saint. The feast of All Saints is an important feast day in the life of the Church. This feast celebrates the universal call to holiness and reminds all Christians each year that they are striving to become saints. Answering the universal call to holiness and saintliness is summed up in the injunction to become perfect (holy) and compassionate like our heavenly Father is perfect (holy) and compassionate (Lev 17:1; Mt 5:48; Lk 6:36).

In our Christian understanding we are called to be holy as our heavenly Father is holy (Mt 5:48). James Cyfko says that holiness in our Christian thinking has come to mean 'growing in a share of the life of God'[106] empowered by the Holy Spirit and emulating the self-emptying of the crucified Christ. We hear in John's Gospel, Jesus saying to the disciples: 'Those who love me will keep my word, and my Father will love them, and we will come to them and make our home with them' (Jn 14:23). To become holy is to share in the divine life of God, Father, Son and Holy Spirit. Even in our Christian tradition, we have come to understand spiritual growth as arising from a contemplation that is purgative, illuminative and unitive.

Levinas and Wyschogrod's understanding of saintliness offers new possibilities for Christian mission and evangelisation in today's postmodern world. The truth of the Christian faith is determined by its doctrines and its praxis. Using the philosophy of Levinas and the theology of Hans Urs von Balthasar, Glenn Morrison, an Australian Catholic theologian, describes the living of the Christian faith as a coming to God by way of a personal encounter with Jesus Christ and the Other in Christ. If the self is created in the image and likeness of God so this likeness diminishes as self-interest takes centre stage. But the self that accepts responsibility for the Other, through an ethical transcendence of self, becomes more closely drawn into a greater likeness with God. Levinas called this holiness or saintliness. Morrison refers to this ethical transcendence as Trinitarian praxis.[107]

It is a Christian life and practice that is self-emptying and kenotic, just as the Trinity is the outpouring of the Father for the Son, the Son of the Father, bounded by the love of the Holy Spirit. It is this self-giving and kenotic love that boils over and pours itself in love into creation. For the Christian, this overflowing and self-giving love is revealed in Christ's death on the cross. The

---

[106] James Cyfko, 'Levinas and the Significance of Passivity in the Christian Religious Experience,' *Open Theology* 4 (2018): 515. Accessed 15 May 2019, https://doi.org/10.1515/opth-2018-0040

[107] Glenn Morrison, *A Theology of Alterity. Levinas, von Balthasar, and Trinitarian Praxis* (Pittsburgh: Duquesne University Press, 2013), 210ff.

Christian life is about embracing in one's own life the mind of Christ (Phil 2:5) emulating his kenotic love for suffering humanity.

It involves a similar path of kenosis, 'haemorrhaging', dying-for-the-other, martyrdom and witness to a Kingdom of a non-thematisable God. Saintliness means accepting responsibility for the Other and thereby anticipating an eschatology of messianic peace, the reign of God that is always new and beyond our grasp and understanding.[108] In this book, I hope to show that Levinas' thinking is not contrary to traditional Catholic understandings of holiness and sanctity. Levinas' approach can help us appreciate the contribution of those we will meet in this book, who were courageous enough to live in a saintly way.

Structure of the book

The first part of this book comprises four introductory chapters, the first chapter explains the concepts used in the book, the second one focuses on Levinas' thinking, and the third focuses on how Levinas' philosophy both challenges traditional historical research and how it can help to shape a new approach to history. Chapter 4 looks at the Catholic Church's ministry to the Deaf community from Biblical times to the beginning of the twentieth century.

The second part of the book discusses the Catholic Church's contribution to the education of deaf children in Catholic schools for the deaf in South Africa from 1874 to 1994. This section focuses primarily on two separate congregations of Dominican sisters. The first congregation to establish a school for the deaf in Cape Town in 1874 was the Congregation of Dominican Sisters of our Lady of the Rosary and St Catherine of Siena who came from Cabra, Dublin in Ireland. The second Catholic school for the deaf was established by the Congregation of Dominican Sisters of St Catharine of Siena who started their school in King William's Town, now known as Qonce, in the Eastern Cape in 1884.

These Dominican sisters were inspired by St Dominic, but particularly St Catherine of Siena (1347–1380), a fourteenth-

---

108 Levinas, *Otherwise than Being*, 52.

century laywoman and Dominican, to give themselves in loving service to their neighbour. Levinas and Wyschogrod's understanding of saintliness as disinterested love and concern for the neighbour to the point of substitution is evident in the writings of Catherine of Siena. After spending three years praying and living a contemplative life in the alcove in her parents' home in Siena, she had a revelation that God was calling her beyond a life of prayer and contemplation to an apostolic life. She was not to remain in her alcove but to venture into the world to proclaim Christ and the love of God to the world. In his hagiographical biography of Catherine, Raymond of Capua, her spiritual director, wrote that she had a vision of God saying to her: 'It is on two feet you must walk my way, it is on two wings that you will fly to heaven. Love of God and love of neighbour.'[109]

In her *Dialogue*, where Catherine described a conversation between God and herself, she wrote:

> I ask you to love me with the same love with which I love you. But for me, you cannot do this, for I loved you without being loved. Whatever love you have for me you owe me, so you love me not gratuitously but out of duty, while I love you not out of duty but gratuitously. So you cannot give me the kind of love I ask of you. This is why I have put you among your neighbours: so that you can do for them what you cannot do for me – that is, love them without any concern for thanks and without looking for any profit for yourself. And whatever you do for them I will consider done for me.[110]

From the time of this personal revelation, Catherine engaged in a public and prophetic ministry that was uncharacteristic for women of her time.

These Dominican women were among the early pioneers of Deaf education in South Africa and they broke new ground in the nineteenth and early twentieth centuries when the prevailing

---

109   Raymond of Capua, *The Biography of St Catharine of Sienna* (Dublin: James Duffy and Co, n.d.), 62.
110   Catherine of Siena, *The Dialogue* (London: SPCK, 1980), 121.

wisdom arising from phonocentric bias was that deaf children could not be educated. This account shows that despite their prophetic and saintly efforts to educate deaf children, the Dominican sisters' mission was compromised by the prejudices and blindspots, both racial and audist, that prevailed during British colonial rule and later under apartheid.

Alongside the Catholic schools for the deaf, some chaplains ministered to the deaf children at school or deaf adults in the parish. These chaplains were priests appointed by the local bishop for this specific ministry. This section also discusses these chaplains.

The third part of the book focuses on Catholic Deaf individuals and organisations that made a significant contribution to overcoming audism and challenging Deaf people to assume their rightful and dignified place within the Church and society. Robert Simmons was not the only one to promote the dignity of Deaf people and this book will try to highlight the other Deaf 'saints' like Bridget Lyne, Fr Cyril Axelrod CSsR, Ruben Xulu, Lindsay Moeletsi Dunn, Fr John Turner CMM and members of the Deaf Community of Cape Town.

Part IV summarises and concludes the book with a chapter on the power of saintly witness to a new world. Finally, the chapter proposes 'the way forward'.

It is important to re-emphasise that this book is an attempt to write an interruptive and ethical, or in the words of Edith Wyschogrod, a heterological history. In these pages, I hope to record how the institutional Church's approach to deaf ministry both served and failed Deaf people. It will also be hagiography in Wyschogrod's sense of promoting learning and imitation.

I have used Levinas' philosophy to clarify and deepen our appreciation of Vatican II's call to holiness for each baptised Christian. Levinas' ideas help us to move beyond a pietistic faith to ask deep and searching questions about our faith and spirituality and how we can integrate a life of contemplation with Christian or Trinitarian praxis. Authentic faith requires authentic witness which undergoes constant de-centring and an outpouring of self for the sake of the suffering and marginalised other.

In our daily lives, we stumble over or upon the wounds of others, even unexpectedly. Living by the Levinasian saintly ethic means not to pass them by, but to rather respond readily with a concern for justice, comforting words, a challenge, a loving gesture or an act of generosity. It is in these moments that a new world is made manifest as well as in dramatic acts of political or economic self-sacrifice and transformation. A new world breaks into the present broken world when transformative acts of generosity, justice and good, hopefully uncontaminated by self-interest, are manifested in the daily choices of individuals, activists and even governments.

Chapter 2

Reading from Infinity: Proximity, Discourse and Deaf People as Teacher[1]

The American anthropologists, John and Jean Comaroff, have argued that early missionaries in South Africa did not sufficiently distinguish the gospel message from the civilising and dominating mission of colonialism. Many missionaries failed to appreciate the difference between universal salvation and their own cultural identity.

> Consequently, conversion required not only that would-be Christians accept the gospel, but that they discard all marks of degeneracy and primitivism ... The coupling of salvation to civilization would complicate the meaning of redemption – and, with it, the practical theology of mission.[2]

This conflation was injurious and oppressive to the indigenous cultures and traditions of African people. In this book, we reflect on how deaf people have suffered because of similar insensitive practices within the Catholic Church in South Africa, especially regarding the education of deaf children.

In the previous chapter we highlighted the importance of ethics as optics or a way to view our relations with others, that

---

[1] This chapter was previously published in a slightly different form and entitled 'Christian Ministry, the Philosophy of Emmanuel Levinas and the Deaf Community,' *Journal of Theology for Southern Africa* 167 (July 2020): 43–61. It is reproduced with permission. The chapter was also part of my doctoral dissertation 'Deaf as Other: A Levinasian Reading of the History of Deaf Ministry in the Catholic Church in South Africa from 1948 to 1994.' PhD diss. (University of KwaZulu-Natal, Pietermaritzburg, 2019), 41-68.

[2] Jean and John Comaroff, *Of Revelation and Revolution: Christianity, Colonialism and Consciousness in South Africa* (Chicago: Chicago University Press, 1991), 1, 64.

is, with the neighbour. In this chapter, we seek to deepen our understanding of Levinas' philosophy. Throughout this chapter, we will expand upon his philosophical thinking and how this reading 'otherwise' or from infinity, reading from right to left affects the relationship between the deaf child and the teacher in the classroom. Levinas' understanding of education was not that it should be self-referential, which is his criticism of the Socratic maieutic system of education, but that education must be truly teaching where the self is opened up to the new in the encounter with the other. This has implications for Christian mission today.

Travelling in a foreign and strange land

When reading the works of the philosopher Emmanuel Levinas, especially his two major works, *Totality and Infinity* (1961) and *Otherwise than Being* (1974), it is vital to realise that one is venturing into a different and foreign land, wandering into alterity. Levinas wrote and used words that are commonplace in ordinary life and religious language. However, he constantly changed their meaning, so radically at times, that they often carry a specific meaning contrary to the ordinary sense of the word. His works are very complex to read and without a clear logical structure. This is because Levinas wrote in a style more akin to poetry with the extensive use of hyperbole to make his point.[3]

Intentionally, Levinas wanted his reader to identify with Abraham, who left his hometown Ur and travelled to Israel, an unknown, distant and foreign land. In contrast to Abraham's journey, Odysseus or Ulysses' journey led him back to the familiarity of his hometown in Ithaca.[4] This Abrahamic stepping into the unknown,[5] means that Levinas is constantly unsettling the reader, confusing them and at times mystifying them with

---

[3] For more information on Levinas' use of hyperbole, see Nathan David Bonney, *A Figure of Rhetoric: Holiness, Hyperbole and Embodied Subjectivity in the Later Writings of Emmanuel Levinas*, PhD diss. (University of Toronto, Canada, 2020).

[4] Stephen Minister, *De-facing the Other: Reason, Ethics, and Politics after Difference* (Milwaukee: Marquette University Press, 2012), 73.

[5] Colin Davis, *Levinas: An Introduction* (Cambridge: Polity Press, 1996), 35.

Chapter 2

what he is saying. Just when you think that you are beginning to grasp what Levinas is saying or arguing, he trips you up and makes you feel unsure that you understand the text before you. His texts are intentionally designed, according to Davis, to give one the experience of the encounter with the Other, with alterity and with difference.[6] For example, Levinas wrote that the encounter with the other is:

> a movement going forth from a world that is familiar to us ... from an 'at home' ['*chez soi*'] which we inhabit, toward an alien outside-of-oneself ['*hors-de-soi*'], toward a yonder.[7]

Consequently, Davis pointed out that:

> Alterity turns out to be not only the *theme* of Levinas' text, but also the key to its complex textual performance ... aiming at exposure to alterity rather than exposition of it.[8]

Within Levinas' writings, there is an ongoing struggle to wrest the other from traditional understandings, to show dissatisfaction and 'dis-ease' at the language being used. The Other is different from who we think they are, and so the most honest response in relation to the Other, for Levinas, is to recognise our ignorance and admit that we do not know them.

Levinas also used language in a double-edged way, continually adapting grammar and punctuation to make a point.[9] In the spelling of 'other' and 'Other', he distinguished between two different ways of relating to the external world. The word 'other' was used to refer to all those things and elements of life, like food, which can be assimilated into one's body, for one's sense of enjoyment of the world. He used the capitalised 'Other' to speak about the relation of alterity where other human beings call us to accept ethical responsibility.

South African educationalist, Hilary Janks, has written about the importance of understanding the meaning of language

---

6   Davis, *Levinas*, 55–56.
7   Levinas, *Totality and Infinity*, 33.
8   Ibid, 56.
9   Levinas, *Totality and Infinity*, 57.

in texts: 'If one takes a sentence in a text and makes different linguistic choices, one can ask students to explain what the change does to the meaning.'[10] Similarly, for Levinas, the one who faces us is not just any other but the Other, the one who points to infinity. Changing a word's spelling or a sentence's punctuation gives the word or sentence a different meaning. In the same way, Levinas spelled the French word *désinteressement* as dés-inter-esse-ment (English translation dis-interestedness) to show the break with being (*esse*).[11]

Some commentators on Levinas distinguish between his secular and religious writings, but in many instances when one reads Levinas' religious commentaries one gains insight into his so-called 'secular' writings. His understanding of the Jewish approach to exegesis of scripture is a case in point. In discussing revelation, Levinas highlighted how in understanding the Biblical text one moves beyond the plain meaning. This meaning is valid one, but in Biblical exegesis, one needs to go back to the Hebrew text.

> It is by going back to the Hebrew text from the translations of the Old Testament from the translations, venerable as they may be, that the strange or mysterious ambiguity or polysemy authorized by the Hebrew syntax is revealed: words coexist rather than immediately being co-ordinated or subordinated with and to one another, contrary to what is predominant in the languages that are said to be developed and functional.[12]

Levinas typified Jewish exegesis as recognising the difference between the plain meaning and the meaning that needs to be uncovered. One word or even verse of the Old Testament can open up a whole world that at first was unexpected, but which

---

10   Hilary Janks, 'Language and the Design of Texts,' *English Teaching: Practice and Critique* 4, 3 (December 2005), 109. Accessed 4 May 2019, http://education.waikoto.ac.nz/research/files/etpc/2005v4n3art6.pdf
11   See Morrison, *A Theology of Alterity*, 133.
12   Emmanuel Levinas, *Beyond the Verse: Talmudic Readings and Lectures* (Bloomington, Indiana: Indiana University Press, 1994), 132.

uncovers 'new and penetrating readings,'[13] that reveal a plurality of renewing and even 'cleansed' meanings[14] within the Word of God.[15] Levinas quotes Psalm 62:11, 'Once God has spoken, twice have I heard'.[16]

Levinas' 'double vision' is central to his writings.[17] He regularly referred to the contrasts between the ethical and the political; between totality and infinity; between the saying and the said. The naive and plain meaning of a text is that which arises from the perspective of the political, from totality, from the said. Uncovering the ethical reading of the text means deconstructing these plain or totalising readings. An ethical reading unlocks an understanding from infinity or transcendence and that is what he called a renewed or cleansed reading. The cleansed reading reflects 'the Saying' rather than 'the said'. A plain reading can perpetuate violence against the Other whereas a cleansed reading encourages responsibility for the Other, a responsibility that is non-violent and which promotes justice and peacebuilding. The one is a reading from an imperialism of the same, whereas the Other opens one up to the infinity of alterity and difference. Transcendence, face, height, infinity, and proximity are Levinas' terms that point to a relation with the Other which is just and open to discourse.

A plain reading: Liberating imprisoned spirits

As a pedagogic tool and to embark on both the plain and cleansed readings of the text, I have chosen to use a newspaper article and photograph that appeared in the Johannesburg newspaper *The Star* on Wednesday 15 July 1964. In doing so, I hope to explain how I am making use of Levinas' philosophy for understanding the Deaf Other. Levinas often reiterated that the Other was not to be

---

13 Levinas, *Beyond the Verse*, 133.
14 Davis, *Levinas*, 56.
15 This way of reading scripture is referred to as Midrash. See Levinas, *Beyond the Verse*, 132–133.
16 Levinas, *Beyond the Verse*, 132.
17 See Robert Eaglestone, 'Postcolonial Thought and Levinas' Double Vision,' in *Radicalizing Levinas*, ed. Peter Atterton and Matthew Calarco (Albany: SUNY Press, 2010), 57–68.

too readily identified with specific human faces[18] even though he often described the Other as neighbour, or even as the poor, or the widow, orphan and foreigner.[19] The face reveals the infinity of the Other and so can not to be limited to one representation or another.

The newspaper article (Figure 1) and a detail of the photograph (Figure 2) will be utilised for pedagogic purposes:

In the article and accompanying photograph (see Figure 1), entitled: 'At St. Vincent's her spirit found liberation,' there is a reference made to two different deaf children. The article refers to an interview with May and the photograph depicts the experiences of Linda. Both article and photograph appeared on 15 July 1964 on the Charities Page of *The Star*. The article intended to praise the work that the Dominican sisters of King William's Town were doing for deaf children at St Vincent School. The sisters' work and ministry are portrayed as noble and charitable.

The left-hand column of the article describes how a young deaf woman referred to as May was living a normal life. This was due to the education she had received at St Vincent School. Originally, she had resented and resisted having to come to school at the age of four, but she was not to know that it would be at this school that 'her imprisoned spirit would find liberation.'[20] This liberation was precisely the education and training she received by being taught to lip-read and to use her voice for speech. 'Henceforth pointing and gestures were replaced with oral communication.'[21] She learnt how to express her wishes and needs as well as understand what others were saying to her by learning to speak. Even though she was profoundly deaf and could not benefit from the use of a hearing aid or acoustic training, nevertheless she remained 'a pure oralist and one of its most fervent devotees.'[22]

---

18 Emmanuel Levinas, *Ethics and Infinity: Conversations with Philippe Nemo* (Pittsburgh: Duquesne University Press, 1985), 85–86.
19 Levinas, *Ethics and Infinity*, 142.
20 See Robin Hood, 'At St. Vincent's Her Spirit Found Liberation,' *The Johannesburg Star*, Wednesday 15 July 1964, 33.
21 Hood, 'At St. Vincent's,' 33.
22 Ibid.

Chapter 2

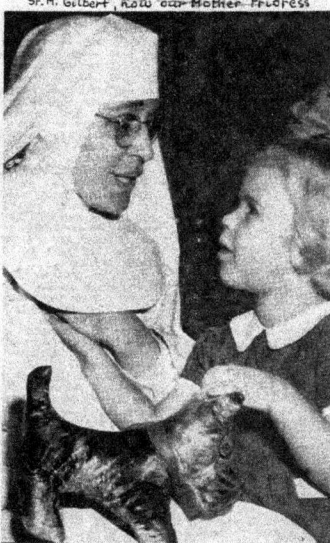

Figure 1: Extract from *The Star*, 15 July 1964

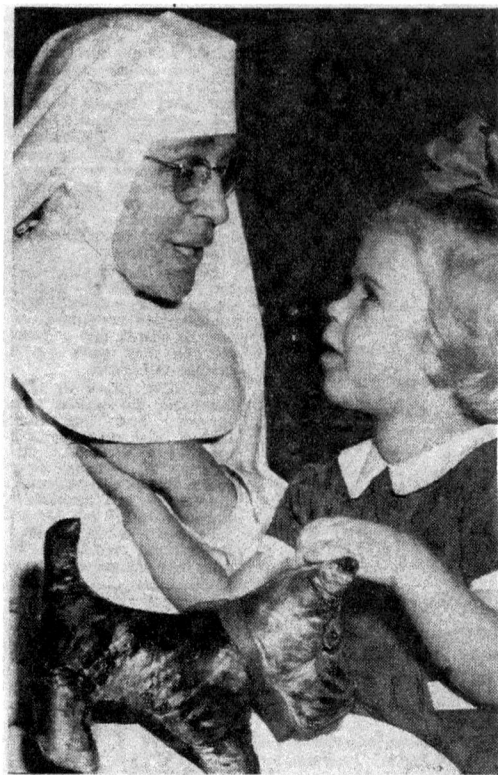

The age of miracles is not past. They are being performed daily at St. Vincent's School for the Deaf at Melrose. One of them is described in the accompanying article. Another is shown above: Linda, aged three, is being taught lip-reading and voice production. Having no idea of sound, Linda is shown to place her hand on the sister's chest to enable her to feel that something goes on inside when the sister talks. Linda, who was born deaf, was being taught to vocalize the word "dog." The lesson is made easier by the presence of a toy dog.

Figure 2: Detail of the photograph in Figure 1

'She becomes indignant at the mere mention of gestures or signs with which at times, deaf people help themselves.'[23]

The article outlined how she had many hearing friends due to her having received an oral education. She had also become a leader among her deaf friends. May was liberated from the prison of deafness. She was able to live a normal life, with normal (hearing) friends and a normal job. After she matriculated, she

---

23   Ibid.

found employment in dress design and commercial art. The article ended by congratulating her: 'May deserves to be congratulated on the courage and determination with which she overcame her handicap.'[24]

In the accompanying photograph (Figure 2) we see a picture of a young girl, Linda, who is three years old. She is being taught the basics of lip-reading and voice production by an unnamed Dominican sister. The deaf girl's hand is directed to the sister's throat where she can feel the vibrations produced by the sister's larynx. She is being taught how to vocalise the word 'dog.' The caption reminded the readers that what they are seeing is a miracle in the making. A deaf child is taught how to speak.

The picture's composition was intended to be informative. It revealed an intimate face-to-face encounter between a teacher and a learner. It was presented as a caring and benevolent relationship. The teacher commands height by imparting knowledge and skills by drawing out of the learner skills that she was not aware she possessed. This has equipped the learner to function in a hearing world and thereby transcend her handicap and disability. The teacher of the deaf children is portrayed as a miracle-maker by empowering them and giving them an education through which they learn to communicate in a spoken language, using lip-reading, voice production and concept formation. In a grateful response, the learner looks at her teacher with a responsive gaze of wonder, appreciation and even perhaps adoration. The Dominican sister appeared to be the gateway to the numinous, opening the child to her deepest dignity.

The idea that the deaf school, through its dedicated teachers, was liberating deaf children from their prisons of silence was a way of representing and celebrating the work being done by means of the oral method of education. This was the method that St Vincent School for the Deaf in Melrose, Johannesburg had adopted since it started in 1934.[25]

---

24   Ibid.
25   'History/Development of St Vincent School,' *St Vincent School Magazine*, 1999, 5.

Underlying this perspective was the view that deafness is the lack of the physiological ability to hear sound. This limited the child's ability to communicate and so to function adequately in the hearing world. The task of the teacher was to teach the child how to speak and communicate. Without these abilities, the child was condemned to be forever imprisoned in a world of silence.

This narrative seems right and self-evident. It is only natural that deaf people be incorporated into a hearing world. It seemed the compassionate thing to do.

A plain reading is an argument from totality and the same

Levinas can assist in deconstructing this reading of the image and the narrative in the newspaper article. In returning to the photograph, we can see that the perspectives expressed in the caption and photograph give very little, if any, consideration to the otherness of the deaf child. She has the name Linda. The photographer, more than likely, wanted us to see Linda as the recipient of the teacher's benevolence and skill. Linda is deaf and handicapped. The teacher is hearing and empowered. The one is the adult and the other is the dependent child. What the picture and the narrative depict is familiar. It is what we understand as the relationship between teacher and learner but within the family also the relationship between parent and child, and so by implication the relationship between hearing and deaf. The hearing are the adults and teachers and the deaf are the children and the learners.

For Levinas, this is a reading of the same and the Other from the perspective of what he calls totality. By totality, Levinas means a way of viewing and understanding the world from a subject's or self's comprehension of the world. When a person tries to grasp and understand the world of another person through means of their subjective lenses (in this case, from the perspective of the hearing Dominican sister), often it is done with little or no regard or respect for the alterity of the Other. In effect, the Other's 'alterity is thereby reabsorbed into my own identity as a thinker or a possessor.'[26]

For Levinas, this pointed to a disturbing defect within Western philosophy and the Western way of life in general. Western rationality that emanated from Greek philosophers like Socrates, Plato and Aristotle are philosophies which start from totality. Levinas criticised Western rationality as thinking that operated from the perspective that all knowledge is anamnesis, recollection or maieutics.[27] The Socratic method was based on the idea that knowledge and truth were innate to all people so that when a teacher like Socrates asked the right questions, those being taught would remember or recollect the knowledge that they latently had within themselves all along.[28] Consequently, the teacher is the midwife of the truth and knowledge that a person already possessed.

Even though the Socratic method acknowledges the subjectivity of the other, Levinas found this way of understanding teaching extremely problematic. Norman Wirbza explained: 'The student engaged in philosophical exploration is finally alone, is a law unto him or herself (*autos-nomos*).'[29] Perhaps the student is not alone in the physical sense because Socrates and other teachers are present to ask questions and challenge the student's thinking. Rather, the problem is that the student does not receive any teaching. The student does not receive anything from anyone else, it is all self-referential. In Levinas' understanding, the student is never put into question. 'Being questioned and being put into question is not the same thing.'[30]

In the maieutic method, all thinking, knowledge and truth are processed by the self – it must make sense to me. Even if this knowledge is challenged by another person's questions, it does this only in respect to my previous understanding. I see and

---

26   Levinas, *Totality and Infinity*, 33.
27   See Levinas, *Totality and Infinity*, 43.
28   For further discussion on maieutics, see Stephen Minister, *De-facing the Other*, 145–150.
29   Norman Wirzba, 'From Maieutics to Metanoia: Levinas's Understanding of the Philosophical Task,' *Man and World* 28 (1995): 131.
30   Wirzba, 'From Maieutics to Metanoia,' 131.

understand the point the other is making, only with reference to my previous understanding. As Wirzba wrote: 'Philosophical exploration, on the autonomous model, thus depends on the possibility of reality conforming to a pre-established frame of reference.'[31] This leads to the modern distrust of authority and exteriority which is troubling. For Levinas, this means that nothing new can be learnt.

> In the welcoming of the face, the will opens to reason. Language is not limited to the maieutic awakening of thoughts common to beings. It does not accelerate the inward maturation of a reason common to all; it teaches and introduces the new into a thought. The introduction of the new into a thought, the idea of infinity, is the very work of reason. The absolutely new is the Other.[32]

Engaging with the Other in discourse puts the autonomous self into question and non-violently challenges the self to think anew, to think as being-for-the-other rather than being-for-itself. It is an ethical challenge to recognise responsibility for the other, for the infinite, the Good beyond being. The self is no longer to understand itself as an explorer because like Ulysses this brings the self 'home' to itself in interiority. Rather true teaching happens when the self is opened up to a new land beyond the self in exteriority. My encounter with the Other does not fit comfortably or easily with the knowledge that previously had meaning and sense for me. Rather I encounter utter otherness and recognise that there is a distance and wide abyss between my thoughts, my experience and that of the Other. It is this wide abyss or transcendence that puts 'my world' into question and calls forth a transformed response compared to my usual one of incorporating the other into my way of thinking. As Wirzba highlighted:

> The Other came and went without having to fit into my world. My only sense that the Other has come is the sense that my world has been disturbed by something of which I

---
31 Ibid.
32 Levinas, *Totality and Infinity*, 219.

am not entirely sure. Autonomy has, in other words, been shaken, been put into question.[33]

The ethical relation with the Other is true teaching because it unsettles us. The problem with maieutics is that it makes us comfortable with ourselves and our present way of thinking and living without regard to the face of the Other. Rather than the usual autonomous response, the self is challenged to develop a heteronomous response because the Other exceeds my grasp and:

> [P]uts into question the whole machinery and process by which I would comprehend him or her. For the first time I discover that I am not a law unto myself, that I am already handed over to the other who reveals the injustice of my law.[34]

For Levinas, the difference of the Other teaches the self through the 'infinity of exteriority'[35] or what Wirzba described as 'the insufficiency and the injustice of the autonomous life.'[36]

The plain or maieutic reading is ontological and violent

For Levinas, all attempts by a self to comprehend the Other are to be dismissed as ontology. 'Ontology is Levinas' general term for any relation to otherness that is reducible to comprehension or understanding.'[37] It is a type of rationality that colonises and does not allow the Other any independence outside the same's conceptualisations. This is a perspective from totality. In our example, it would be the teacher's view of the child that we have described. Any attempt to grasp the Other within the framework of one's own view and perspective, Levinas called 'thematization and

---

33 Wirzba, 'From Maieutics to Metanoia,' 139.
34 Ibid.
35 Levinas, *Totality and Infinity*, 185.
36 Wirzba, 'From Maieutics to Metanoia,' 140.
37 Simon Critchley and Robert Bernasconi, eds, *The Cambridge Companion to Levinas* (Cambridge: Cambridge University Press, 2004), 11.

conceptualization.'[38] Conceptualising or thematising the Other in relation to the categories of the same, Levinas understood, is similar to the work of the hand in grasping something and thereby possessing it. 'Possession is pre-eminently the form in which the other becomes the same, by becoming mine.'[39]

In possessing the Other, the Other loses independence and loses what Levinas called their singularity or that which makes them unique and different from every other person. These grasping, possessing, assimilatory tendencies, Levinas referred to as 'the imperialism of the same.'[40] Otherness is ignored, overlooked or negated because the Other is comprehended within my frame of reference which is not theirs.

Another way of expressing this is to say that the self treats the Other as an object and not a subject, as a 'what' and not a 'who'.[41] The Other becomes an instrument in the hand of the self-same who incorporates the Other into the self's world and frames of reference. Consequently, the self assimilates the Other to his purposes and to satisfy his own needs, as a relation of master to a servant or a factory owner to his workers. The Other exists in relation to the same as a use-value and not a person in their own right.[42]

> To be sure, most of the time the *who* is a *what*. We ask, 'Who is Mr. X?' and we answer: 'He is President of the State Council,' or 'He is Mr. So-and-so.' The answer presents itself as a quiddity.[43]

Treating someone as a what rather than as a who is, for Levinas, an act of violence against the Other. He understood that violence:

---

[38] Levinas, *Totality and Infinity*, 46.
[39] Ibid.
[40] Levinas, *Totality and Infinity*, 39.
[41] Ibid, 177.
[42] Diane Perpich, 'Levinas, Feminism and Identity Politics,' in *Radicalizing Levinas*, ed. Peter Atterton and Matthew Calarco (Albany: SUNY Press, 2010), 30.
[43] Levinas, *Totality and Infinity*, 177.

is to be found in any action in which one acts as if one were alone to act: as if the rest of the universe were there only to receive the action; violence is consequently also any action which we endure without at every point collaborating in it.[44]

Even though the Other is recognised in their distinctiveness, nevertheless they are partially negated[45] because they are seen as a possession, an object and at the perpetrator's disposal.[46] This partial negation takes place when a perpetrator denies the Other any opportunity to shape their own lives. This is what Levinas referred to as 'appropriation and power'[47] exerted over and against the Other.

Totality as an unjust reading

For Levinas, totality is not just about describing the unjust relations between people but also how people begin to transcend totality and embody the infinity of an ethical relation. For him, human beings are embodied beings who act from totality by arranging life to satisfy their needs. We consume food and drink to nourish and enjoy ourselves in life. But we can extend this idea in relation to Others. They exist for the self, to become part of me, to make my life better and more comfortable.

> Nourishment, as a means of invigoration, is the transmutation of the other into the same, which is the essence of enjoyment: an energy that is other, recognized as other, recognized, we will see, as sustaining the very act that is directed upon it, becomes, in enjoyment, my own energy, my strength, me. All enjoyment is in this sense alimentation.[48]

---

44 Emmanuel Levinas, *Difficult Freedom: Essays on Judaism* (Baltimore: The Johns Hopkins University Press, 1990), 6.
45 Emmanuel Levinas, *Entre Nous* (New York: Columbia University Press, 1998), 9.
46 Minister, *De-facing the Other*, 152.
47 Levinas, *Collected Philosophical Papers*, 50.
48 Levinas, *Totality and Infinity*, 111.

This approach to life is a subjective one where our world negates alterity. The human ego, my ego, stands at the centre. I am focused on myself and not the Other.

> In enjoyment, I am absolutely for myself. Egoist without reference to the Other, I am alone without solitude, innocently egoist and alone. Not against the Others, not 'as for me' ... but entirely deaf to the Other, outside of all communication and all refusal to communicate – without ears, like a hungry stomach.[49]

My economy or the 'world I constitute nourishes me and bathes me'[50] and so 'in enjoyment throbs egoist being.'[51] This is what living life means – finding enjoyment and satisfying our needs. Therefore, 'we act according to enjoyment in the construction of our economy, that is, the structures – practical, intellectual, moral, religious – we employ so that we can be at-home in the world.'[52] This means we have a concern for our happiness and well-being. This could be a healthy self-love and need not be an immoral egotism. But it does illustrate that 'my personal existence is characterised by self-interest.'[53]

The danger is that because 'one is entangled in a struggle for life'[54] – a struggle to be – one could assume that this way of being is my own unique possession. Stephen Minister, an American philosopher and commentator on Levinas' writings, explained that:

> The power of reason thus serves the goal of intellectually conquering the world in order always to remain in control and at-home in the world, feeling justified in one's 'own way of life.' Reason thus functions to help us sleep well at

---

49 Ibid, 134.
50 Ibid, 129.
51 Ibid, 147.
52 Minister, *De-facing the Other*, 69.
53 Linus Vanlaere, Roger Burggraeve and Laetus Lategan, *Vulnerable Responsibility: Small Vices for Caregivers* (Bloemfontein: Sun Media, 2019), 113.
54 Vanlaere, Burggraeve and Lategan, *Vulnerable Responsibility*, 113.

> night, feeling secure, comfortable, and in-the-know, able to remain at-home with oneself.[55]

Topolski related this to the Jewish understanding of *yetzer ra*, which describes a certain egoism or selfishness that can be good because it from this selfishness one builds a house for your family and works hard to provide for them. However, it is negative when one disregards the needs of one's poor neighbours – looking only at one's own good and neglecting theirs.[56]

Transcendence takes place, and the ethical relation begins, when the self recognises the Other as a 'who' – a person and a neighbour – and not a 'what', like food and drink. The Jewish concern for the neighbour and their good is known as the *yetzer tov*,[57] which lies at the heart of what Levinas meant by Desire.

Desire

Levinas developed a critique of economy by distinguishing between our needs that lead to our being-at-home in the world, and 'Desire.'[58] Transcendence occurs for Levinas when a person shifts focus from an economy of fulfilling their needs to developing 'Desire for Infinity.'[59] Gibbs pointed out that 'transcendence occurs in this world not by ecstatically pulling me out to some other world but by changing what it means to be in this world.'[60] Consequently, Desire is desire for the good of the Other, my neighbour. It transcends the economy of my needs and my being at home-with-myself.

---

55 Minister, *De-facing the Other*, 147.
56 Topolski, *Arendt, Levinas and a politics of relationality*, 138–140.
57 Ibid, 195–196.
58 Levinas referred to Desire with a capital D to distinguish it from the normal usage of the word desire. See *Totality and Infinity*, 33–35.
59 Levinas, *Totality and Infinity*, 50.
60 Robert Gibbs, 'Jewish Dimensions of Radical Ethics,' in *Ethics as First Philosophy: The Significance of Emmanuel Levinas for Philosophy, Literature and Religion*, ed. Adriaan T. Peperzak (New York and London: Routledge, 1995), 14.

> Desire is not interested in satisfaction or exchange; it does not assimilate or integrate, because it is not oriented toward enrichment or expansion.[61]

While Desire transcends and challenges us to move beyond the economy of enjoyment, it does not deny it. Peperzak explained that 'transcendence does not condemn the joys of life, but it prevents them from becoming absolute; it despises idolatry.'[62] By being-at-home-with- myself I can offer hospitality to the Other. This is the beginning of a change in relation. I am still inviting people into my world, relating to them from the comfort of my place in the world but I start to extend a hand of friendship to the Other. It can be the beginning of the discovery of alterity.

> Desire transcends economy by desiring the other – not for satisfaction or consolation, not as a partner in love, but as the one whose face orients my life and thereby grants it significance. In desire I discover that I am not enclosed within myself, because I am 'always already' to and for the Other, responsible, hostage, substitute.[63]

In this sense, being at-home-with-myself is not just a selfish experience but one which can begin the transition to discovering the Other through the offer of hospitality. This made it possible to develop a cleansed or changed understanding of the Other and the self that is not possessive, grasping or egoist but rather becoming open to and responsible for the Other. This is the beginning of a different vantage point and the self's opening up to an ethical relation with the Other.

Singularity of each person

For Levinas, this shift comes with a renewed and a cleansed view of rationality. He held out hope for the liberation of philosophy

---

61 Adriaan Peperzak, 'Transcendence,' in *Ethics as First Philosophy: The Significance of Emmanuel Levinas for Philosophy, Literature and Religion*, ed. Adriaan T. Peperzak (New York and London: Routledge, 1995), 189.
62 Peperzak, 'Transcendence,' 190.
63 Peperzak, 'Transcendence,' 190.

from the pursuit of autonomy and a narrow reading from one's own economy.[64] As we have already argued, some approaches to philosophy and reason, especially those that emphasise autonomous ways of thinking, can be opposed to ethics because they are essentially violent. They strip people of their humanity in a violence that

> does not consist so much in injuring or annihilating persons as in interrupting their continuity, making them play roles in which they no longer recognize themselves, making them betray not only commitments but their own substance.[65]

Our humanity is not determined by the unifying characteristics of the universalisation of the human, those things that make us all the same and equal with one another, as expressed in the human rights debate or derived from natural law. Rather, it is to be found in the singularity of each person, those things which make us different from each other, that is, the irreducible differences that make us unique. It is through relating to one another in our uniqueness and not in our sameness, that we discover the mystery and wonder of being human. It is in recognising their singular specificity and alterity that we discover the gift and wonder of human intersubjectivity.

> Singularity expresses the idea that each human being is a unique, irreplaceable self, irreducible to any of the attributes or qualities that could be used to describe her and that would inevitably reduce her to what she has in common with others.[66]

Appreciating the Other's alterity as singularity is not about gaining a greater comprehension, understanding and knowledge of 'them' as different or binary opposites, or even our being a unique person.[67] For Levinas, all these attempts reduce alterity or

---

64 See Minister, *De-facing the Other*, 156.
65 Levinas, *Totality and Infinity*, 21.
66 Perpich, 'Levinas, Feminism and Identity Politics,' 29.
67 See Perpich, 'Levinas, Feminism and Identity Politics,' 29. Perpich pointed out that 'difference can be determined only by

singularity to an ontological category instead than an ethical one. Rather, it is the realisation that one does not know and cannot fully grasp the Other. To try to grasp or comprehend the Other is violent because it treats the Other as a *what*, an object of power or knowledge and so denies that the Other is a *who*, a face whose 'eyes look at you.'[68]

The one who faces me is the Other who puts the self under question. As Guenther argued 'singularity arises through the ethical event of facing and/or substitution, whereby I become myself in being commanded to unique responsibility for you.'[69] The face that confronts me needs to be related to 'as a unique, irreducible and unrepeatable Other.'[70] But it is not just that the Other exists as a unique individual but also in the Other's singularising command: '*Anyone* is responsible for *any Other*.'[71]

In using the word 'any' instead of 'all', Guenther emphasised Levinas' concern to avoid seeing ethical responsibility as a way of thinking in relation to categories or groups of people who are responsible (the rich or the hearing) and another group or totality of recipients of this hospitality (the poor or Deaf people). Understanding responsibility in this way means falling into ontological ways of thinking where responsibility becomes a universalised understanding of subjectivity.[72] Rather Levinas' understanding of singularity is that any self 'as a singularly responsible subject, [is] commanded in this or that particular situation by a singular Other.'[73] Therefore, Guenther concluded singularity is not about 'who this Other *is*; what matters is *that* s/he faces me, and that *a* face, any face, commands me.'[74] The particular circumstances in which we find ourselves and the face that commands me become vitally important in deciding how

---

starting from the subject or the same.'
68 Levinas, *Totality and Infinity*, 178.
69 Lisa Guenther, '"Nameless Singularity": Levinas on Individuation and Ethical Subjectivity,' *Epoché: A Journal for the History of Philosophy* 14, 1 (Fall 2009): 169.
70 Ibid.
71 Ibid, 170.
72 Ibid.
73 Ibid, 170–171.
74 Ibid, 182.

we have to respond in any particular situation. Whether the one facing us is a victim or perpetrator will affect our response.[75]

In this sense, the Other is truly incomprehensible, a mystery and a trace of infinity.[76] Each situation has a uniqueness that defies universalisation but rather is deeply dependent upon context and the reality of the one who faces us. This is why Levinas referred to the encounter with the one who faces us as transcendence and infinity.

The face of the Other commands from height and vulnerability

What the self encounters is the face of the Other as a transcendent alterity that calls the self to responsibility. Levinas referred to the encounter with the Other as proximity or as a 'relation without relation.'[77] This means that it is not a relation where we can assume any common ground or mutuality. When one describes the relation with the Other as a relationship of equals one is talking from a totalising perspective where the self and the Other are perceived to share common ground. The consequence of doing this is that 'the Other becomes just another version of the Same.'[78]

Levinas even went so far as to suggest that no encounter takes place because there is no mutuality or anything in common between the same and the Other. The Other is a stranger, a foreigner to the self and there is a vast distance 'an absolute separation'[79] between the two. They are never on the same page. For Levinas, it is better to describe the relation between the self and the Other as an asymmetrical one.

In an asymmetrical relation, the Other is free if they are separate from me and beyond my physical and mental control.[80] If they are not separate then they fall under my dominating,

---

75 Ibid, 184, footnote 7.
76 Levinas, *Time and the Other* (Pittsburgh: Duquesne University Press, 1987), 75.
77 Levinas, *Totality and Infinity*, 80.
78 Davis, *Levinas*, 45.
79 Brian Schroeder, *Altared Ground: Levinas, History and Violence* (New York/London: Routledge, 1996), 15.
80 Gibbs, 'Jewish Dimensions of Radical Ethics,' 14.

assimilatory and totalising attempts to grasp, to know and possess them. This separation is what Levinas referred to as height.

> The other person appears higher than I ... His height is the transcendence beyond my here, my grasp – but the asymmetry is that I cannot say that his here is similarly displaced. His looking down at me, therefore, is not my looking up at him. We have a disparity, an asymmetry in the spatial field that happens vertically and not horizontally.[81]

Proximity or the encounter with the face of the Other disrupts and breaks into the self's complacent world and questions it from a stance of both 'great height and humility.'[82] For Levinas, the height is not a power relation, but rather height as encountered in 'the other person's poverty, destitution and most importantly humility.'[83] It is both a plea and a command.[84] While the face is vulnerable and naked, it commands the self from a great height and calls it to responsibility. The face of the Other in their vulnerability and humility disturbs one's being at home with oneself. It overturns and disrupts one's own economy of comfort and sense of well-being in the world. The Other also has height in ethically resisting the self's efforts to include them in the self's own economy. The face displays great vulnerability in saying: 'Thou shall not kill me.' In doing so, the face challenges and resists the self's grasping, comprehending and totalising efforts.

The Other who is 'vulnerable, nude and fragile and in need of welcome'[85] commands a height way above me. It is for me to recognise that I am responsible for the Other and that my relation needs to be an ethical one. This height is an ethical demand that questions my life and shows me that I am unjust in relation to the Other, to my neighbour.

---

81   Ibid, 14–15.
82   Minister, *De-facing the Other*, 77.
83   Levinas, *Totality and Infinity*, 200.
84   Michael Morgan, *The Cambridge Introduction to Emmanuel Levinas* (Cambridge: Cambridge University Press, 2011), 67.
85   Minister, *De-facing the Other*, 77.

The ethical relation as epiphany and election

When I realise that I am unjust in relation to the Other then I recognise that I need to act justly in relation to them. In changing from a self-for-itself to a moral or ethical self-for-the-other, the self recognises that the needs of the Other take priority over the self's needs. To act justly means that I have an ethical and moral responsibility to put their lives ahead of my own. For Levinas, this means that I need to go to the extent of giving them the food that was destined for my own mouth, food I received for my own survival.[86] I am obliged to ensure that my existence is not the violent cause of the Other's suffering. Consequently, the face of the Other holds me accountable and responsible, just as Cain was responsible for his brother Abel (Gen 4:9–10). According to Levinas: 'Morality begins when freedom instead of being justified by itself, feels itself to be arbitrary and violent.'[87]

When the self goes beyond self-interest, realising that the world is not my possession but a place I share with the Other, an epiphany takes place. The self listens and hears the voice of the Other and undergoes a transformation. No longer does the self attempt to comprehend the Other, but rather sees that it is called to respond to the Other in a morally and ethically responsible way.[88] For Levinas, this is a true expression of freedom, where the self responds to the need of the neighbour in solidarity.

> Man [sic] is not only responsible for himself and for his acts before others, he is responsible for others in such a way that he loses his innocence when he looks at them. He becomes really human when he is ready to answer, 'Here I am' ("*Hinneni*") to the call of the other.[89]

---

86 Levinas, *Otherwise than Being*, 74.
87 Levinas, *Totality and Infinity*, 84.
88 Minister, *De-facing the Other*, 85.
89 Catherine Chalier, 'Levinas and the Hebraic Tradition,' in *Ethics as First Philosophy: The Significance of Emmanuel Levinas for Philosophy, Literature and Religion*, ed. Adriaan T. Peperzak (New York and London: Routledge, 1995), 8.

Responding by answering this call to responsibility for the Other is what Levinas called 'election.'[90] Election is accepting responsibility for the Other. In relation to Deaf people, it is important that hearing people recognise that they have been acting unjustly in relation to them. They are being challenged to accept the call to change and become for-the-Deaf-Other. The ethical relation is a call to set aside their convictions regarding what is good for Deaf people and stand in responsible solidarity with their Deaf neighbour. Doing this means recognising that one accepts election and the call to act justly and responsibly in relation to the Other.

Discourse and teaching

Levinas said that 'the manifestation of the face is discourse.'[91] Discourse is to recognise that one is in relationship with the Other even before any conversation has started. One is in relationship even before a word is uttered. Discourse is about the interhuman relationship between the self and the Other. Discourse is 'the Saying' before there is any 'Said', the ethical relation that exists before any speech taking place between them. The self engages in a discourse which is separate from and exterior to the self's world and its familiar frames of reference. Discourse is a teaching from the Other that the self could never have discovered or understood on its own. It comes to the self from without, as an epiphany or revelation from the Other. 'The face is a revelation, an unforeseen and unforeseeable breach within what is known and knowable. It entails the production of new, unexpected meanings rather than the communication of what is already familiar.'[92]

As a result of this, a new meaning which is beyond the self's own experience is produced. It is a good that emerges from beyond the self's usual frames of reference and thereby exceeds its own ability to be rational and good.[93] For this reason, Levinas talked about the good that is beyond being, or otherwise than being.

---

90 Levinas, *Otherwise than Being*, 122.
91 Levinas, *Totality and Infinity*, 66.
92 Davis, *Levinas: An Introduction*, 47.
93 Levinas, *Totality and Infinity*, 69–70.

How the self responds to the discourse initiated by the face of the Other is thus vitally important.

> Face and discourse are tied. The face speaks. It speaks, it is in this that it renders possible and begins all discourse. I have just refused the notion of vision to describe the authentic relationship with the Other; it is discourse and, more exactly, response or responsibility which is the authentic relationship.[94]

The ethical relation presents the self with a choice. The self can choose to ignore this command and even reject the call. The self can go on to reduce or assimilate the Other to some of 'the socio-historically mediated meanings through which I interpret the world.'[95] Or the self can respond to the face's call and accept its moral or ethical responsibility towards the Other. The self can engage in discourse and dialogue with the Other and become open to their teaching. By accepting this teaching, the self accepts responsibility to live justly and non-violently in relation to the Other.[96]

Throughout his writings, Levinas sought to promote relations that were just and not violent or oppressive. He argued that the only truly human response is one which accepts 'the irreducible ethical proximity of one human being to another, morality, and through that encounter a relation to all others, justice.'[97]

The practice of just relations between the self and the Other is the ethical relation.[98] It is how we discover our humanity and the humanity of the Other.[99] Not even if I choose to kill or murder the Other, can I deny that I am in an ethical relationship with the

---

94 Levinas, *Ethics and Infinity*, 87–88.
95 Minister, *De-facing the Other*, 75.
96 See Levinas, *Totality and Infinity*, 203–4.
97 Richard Cohen, 'Foreword' to Emmanuel Levinas, *Otherwise Than Being or Beyond Essence* (Pittsburgh: Duquesne University Press, 1998), xi.
98 See in Levinas, *Collected Philosophical Papers*, 149: Levinas wrote that: 'The free man (sic) is pledged to his neighbour.'
99 See Lewis, *Deaf Liberation Theology*, 3.

murdered Other.[100] Murder is an unjust choice of action in relation to the face of the Other.[101]

For this reason, Levinas argued that the ethical relation is pre-original, that is, it pre-exists any relation between the same and the Other. It is a moral or ethical prerogative that exists prior to or anterior to any interaction with the Other. Unlike the violent discourse of a tyrant who undermines people's freedom, the face engaged in discourse is essentially non-violent and grants the self the freedom to respond ethically or to turn away in hatred or indifference.

The transformed understanding of rationality

If ethical responsibility challenged the subject to a different way of understanding the self as essentially an intersubjective or inter-relational way of being human,[102] then reason and knowledge can be reconceptualised.[103] Levinas proposed that we start with alterity rather than the self. Instead of the maieutical approach, where reason is self-referential or an internal monologue with the self, it should be discourse or the dialogical response to the Other by an ethical subject. Then it is teaching because something new is learnt. Teaching is not concerned with the overthrow of autonomy or its annihilation, but rather its redirection, its opening up to the new.[104]

Thereby reason undergoes metanoia[105] or a radical transformation, an acknowledgement of having got it wrong, and so the self learns the ethical, the new. In this encounter, the self

---

100 Levinas, *Totality and Infinity*, 198.
101 Robert Eaglestone, 'Postcolonial Thought and Levinas' Double Vision,' in *Radicalizing Levinas*, ed. Peter Atterton and Matthew Calarco (Albany, NY: SUNY Press, 2010), 61.
102 Minister, *De-facing the Other*, 157.
103 Levinas, *Totality and Infinity*, 44.
104 Wirzba, 'From Maieutics to Metanoia,' 141.
105 Wirzba says that this is not a word that Levinas uses but it does capture a sense of what Levinas is pointing to. Levinas avoided theological terms in his philosophical writings as he was afraid of being misunderstood. Wirzba uses metanoia to mean 'repentance, the acknowledgement of wrongdoing, in face of a power beyond myself.' See Wirzba, 'From Maieutics to Metanoia,' 140.

is redirected from interiority to exteriority. A transformed reason calls the subject into question and invites them to practice justice in relation to the Other.[106] It is only a subject, already concerned with others and their perspectives, who can recognise the need to go beyond their limited perspectives and accept the validity of the Other's experiences.[107] It is overcoming the narrowness of a self-referential life in the pursuit of knowledge as an interior act of recollection to investing one's freedom by inspiring being by putting one 'on a new path of responsibility to a law beyond myself.'[108]

Then reason can be reconceptualised 'as an ongoing, honest, open, reason-giving dialogue an ethical subject has with others.'[109] So instead of seeing reason as the way to win an argument, or that one alone possesses the truth, rather, reason needs to be seen as a way of encountering the Other, listening to their perspectives, being open and receptive to their worldview and insights. In doing so, we also get an opportunity to share why we act and think in the way we do. Central to listening to others is not to 'listen only when their views make sense to us, but also and especially when they do not.'[110] So it is vitally important to develop a way of 'reasoning with others.'[111] By this means, we can become open to the perspectives and criticisms of others which then 'teaches and introduces the new into thought.'[112] 'Rational dialogue presupposes a plurality of perspectives, which it makes no guarantee of overcoming.'[113]

Reason and thought open us to alterity and singularity and thereby also to polysemic readings of reality and experience. As a teacher, the Other does not necessarily open us up to new content but frees us to embark on an adventure, where like Abraham, the security and comfort of an autonomous life are left behind, and we

---

106 Levinas, *Totality and Infinity*, 88.
107 Minister, *De-facing the Other*, 157.
108 Wirbza, 'From Maieutics to Metanoia,' 141.
109 Minister, *De-facing the Other*, 165.
110 Ibid, 166.
111 Ibid.
112 Levinas, *Totality and Infinity*, 219.
113 Minister, *De-facing the Other*, 167.

are led into a new land, a new rationality, beyond our established and autonomous worldviews.[114]

In this regard, it is necessary to return to our reading of the newspaper article and the photograph and see how we can understand it afresh not from the perspective of totality but rather infinity.

A cleansed and 'metanoic' reading from infinity or reading otherwise than being

From the perspective of the hearing Dominican sister who taught deaf children, her mission was to overcome the disadvantages that the deaf child experienced in life, in not being able to hear, and to give her a better chance of making it in the world and to find her 'place in the sun.'[115] The deaf child had to find her place in a predominantly hearing world and so for her to succeed she would need to be well-equipped to find her rightful place. This required, therefore, that the child learn how to lip-read, how to vocalise and to have a skill which she could use to find gainful employment. In referring to May, the article explained how she 'deserves to be congratulated on the courage and determination with which she overcame her handicap.'[116] She has made it in the hearing world, she matriculated from school 'without claiming any concessions,'[117] she completed a course in dress-design and commercial art, she persevered in her first job and her efficiency at doing office work contributed towards her being promoted and receiving salary increases. She is a success story because she can flourish in normal life. She can 'hold her own in a normal conversation where her wit and repartee are outstanding.'[118]

---

114   See Wirzba, 'From Maieutics to Metanoia,' 141.
115   Blaise Pascal, *Pensées and Other Writings*, trans. Honor Levi, (Oxford: Oxford University Press, 1995), 25. Levinas' uses this quote from Pascal: '"That is my place in the sun." That is how the usurpation of the whole world began' in his list of quotations before the Contents page in *Otherwise Than Being*.
116   Hood, 'At St. Vincent's,' 33.
117   Ibid.
118   Ibid.

Underlying what is presented in the article and supported by the photograph, is an assumption that being hearing is the norm and deafness is an unfortunate deviation from that norm. Those who deviate will only thrive if they are brought into alignment with the majority and conform to what is normal, with what is the same. Deafness is seen as a handicap or a disability that needs to be rectified and rehabilitated. Consequently, from a hearing perspective, the deaf child, being deficient in hearing, needs to be trained and educated to fit and function in a hearing world. These are the lenses through which the hearing Dominican sister (ironically wearing spectacles) read into the experience of the deaf child.

This eisegetical[119] reading of the Other is what needs to be problematised. It is a totalising reading of the deaf experience by the hearing. Not only is it paternalistic because hearing people assume that they know what is best for Deaf people, but it is also colonising and imperialistic. It is hearing people who then determine how the deaf child should be trained and educated without any reference to deaf children's preferences or that of the adult Deaf community . The experience of the deaf child is ignored. There is no dialogue with or input from Deaf people themselves. There is little consideration in this article for the world of the Other.

When we refer back to our photograph, we can see that reading it from a Levinasian perspective, calls into question the view – which the article presents – that puts the Dominican sister, as teacher and representative of the divine and infinity, at the heart of the discourse. In sharp contrast, with a renewed or cleansed reading, it is the 'teacher' who is called into question by the deaf child. It is not the teacher who comes 'from the position of height and transcendence'[120] but rather the little girl, Linda. She commands great height but also vulnerability. She knows the

---

119 'Eisegesis' in contrast to 'exegesis' is the reading of one's own subjective understanding and interpretation into a biblical text rather than reading the text in its historical context and drawing its meaning from the intention of the author. See 'How do Exegesis and Eisegesis Differ,' www.compellingtruth.org/exegesis-eisegesis.html
120 Levinas, *Totality and Infinity*, 86–87.

experience of being Deaf from the inside contrary to the sister who can only imagine and project her hearing understanding onto the deaf child. The sister may feel compassionate and loving towards the child evident in the intimacy of the teaching relation. Nevertheless, her service, compassion and love are expressed from within her hearing economy. It is likely that the sister does not recognise the need for discourse or to receive teaching from the Deaf child.

This putting under question would include questions like: What do Deaf people have to say or teach the hearing about what it means to be human, about human agency, about language, about developing a liberating education of Deaf people, their community life and culture? If the teacher opened up and recognised the need to be a learner and allow the face of the Other to disturb and disrupt her economy and her being a self-at-home-with-herself, maybe something new could have emerged. The egoity of the audist teacher triumphs because she knows best. Consequently, hearing people, as we will see in the chapters that follow, imposed their hearing solutions on deaf people, creating in the process social structures that did them a disservice and were often detrimental to their well-being.

When the hearing presume that they can shape the lives of the deaf without regard for Deaf people's views and self-understanding, then the hearing can be justly accused of acting in a totalising and violent way. This is referred to as audism where the hearing are the knowledgeable ones and the deaf are ignorant.

Conclusion

When approaching Levinas' writings, it is as if one is entering a foreign country. Levinas can be confounding to read and difficult to understand. This is because he wrote in an extensively hyperbolic and poetic way to challenge, and at times even to shock the reader into a new way of seeing and thinking.

By using a newspaper article as a heuristic device, it has been possible to reflect on the writings of Emmanuel Levinas. It also helps us understand the model of education for deaf children practised in Catholic schools for the deaf. This model was known as the oral method of deaf education and its basic tenet was liberating the deaf from a world of silence. Using Levinas' philosophy, it was possible to deconstruct 'the plain reading' of the deaf experience as a projection of hearing attitudes and assumptions onto the deaf experience. A Levinasian reading challenges all philosophies, theologies and ideologies to critical self-awareness as to whether they are merely self-referential egologies or do they seriously consider the alterity of the marginalised Other.

In this chapter, we have tried to show that a plain reading is a reading from totality which does violence to the experience of deaf people or all people being evangelised. Hearing people assumed that they knew what was best for the Deaf community without regard for the views of Deaf people themselves. This violent relation between hearing and deaf, as we saw in the first chapter, is referred to as audism. In contrast to audism and the plain reading of the deaf experience, Levinas' philosophy can assist in providing a cleansed reading from the perspective of the Deaf community which we will explore further in Part III of this book.

Chapter 3

Epistemological, Methodological and Ethical Considerations

As we saw in the previous chapter, the philosophy of Emmanuel Levinas will be utilised to throw light on the situation in which deaf Catholics in South Africa found themselves from 1874 to 1994. In this chapter, we focus on how Levinas' philosophy both challenges traditional historical research and how it can help shape a new approach to history. I will also look reflexively at my position in relation to the Deaf community. The chapter closes with a short explanation about the archival and oral history methodologies employed in researching this book. I conclude by highlighting some of the ethical challenges in doing this research.

The role of theory in historical research

Historians are divided in their opinions regarding the value of theory in historical research. Some historians have pointed out that history is essentially a study which moves from the particular to the general and so trying to find facts to fit the theory undermines the whole historical research process.

The historical process identifies the 'uniqueness', complexity and particularity of events, as well as the power of human agency.[1] From this perspective, history is understood as getting to the truth of the past by focusing on the facts and the evidence that can be uncovered from archival documents. The use of theory could also encourage determinism, giving the impression of a certain inevitability of the historical process.[2] All events detailed in history inevitably are marshalled to support the theory.

---

1   John Tosh, *The Pursuit of History: Aims, Methods and New Directions in the Study of Modern History*, 2nd ed. (London/New York: Longman, 1991), 158.
2   Tosh, *The Pursuit of History*, 158.

John Tosh, a historian who has reflected on the role of theory in history, has pointed out that there are theories that do not fall into determinism, but which take the relationship between human agency and social structure seriously.[3] The questions these historians asked questioned whether human beings were the protagonists of history or whether human history was not shaped and at times deformed by the structures of society. In South African historiography, the debates between liberal and Marxist or structuralist historians have borne testament to this.[4] In more recent times, the post-modern and post-colonial approaches to history also continue to emphasise structuralist approaches to history.

In contrast, Levinas' philosophy of alterity offers another vantage point on history as ethical. Like many structuralist approaches, it alerts the historian to the needs and struggles of the vulnerable and marginalised people in society. Levinas' emphasis on the 'face of the Other' as accusing, traumatising and disrupting the self, is language employed to unsettle, to disturb the comfortable and those at home in their own economies. Yet it also calls people to personal responsibility and an ethical response to the suffering Other. It is not a historical theory but a challenge to praxis. Levinas' approach is more akin to a pair of new shoes which are never a perfect fit, but which constantly chafe one's feet.[5] These shoes chafe our conscience, helping us recognise our bad conscience, that we have not done enough to respond to the suffering, the marginalisation or the exclusion of our neighbour

---

[3] Tosh, *The Pursuit of History*, 161.
[4] For more on these debates, see Christopher Saunders, *The Making of the South African Past: Major Historians on Race and Class* (Cape Town: David Philip, 1988).
[5] For the image of shoes, I am indebted to Glenn Morrison. See his article 'Practical Theology from the Heart: Becoming Children of God,' *Compass: A Review of Topical Theology* (Spring, September 2016): 30–34. Morrison compares practical theology with well-worn shoes which he said carry the memories of our daily lives. I have changed the image slightly by referring to Levinas' philosophy as new shoes. These shoes chafe our consciences and make us aware of our responsibility to the suffering neighbour or the Other.

or the Other. David Tracy referred to this view of history as interruptive and ambiguous.⁶

> History is not only contingent; history is interruptive. Western history is, through and through, an interruptive narrative with no single theme and no controlling plot. To be American, for example, is to live with pride by participating in a noble experiment of freedom and plurality. But to be a white American is also to belong to a history that encompasses the near destruction of one people (the North American Indians, the true native Americans) and the enslavement of another people (the blacks) ... To cherish the Christian scriptures as a charter document of liberation is entirely right. Yet we must also face its anti-Judaic strands, ... centuries of Christian 'teaching of contempt' for the Jews [as well as its] subjection of women in Christian history.⁷

Levinas reminded us that the face of the Other calls one to responsibility; to breach totality and to move from being a self for-itself to becoming a self for-the-other. Edith Wyschogrod referred to this task of the historian as heterological.⁸ The heterological historian studies Otherness or alterity in history.⁹ This means that the historian has the ethical responsibility or obligation and liability to tell the truth about the past of the marginalised, and often, nameless others of history.

For Wyschogrod, all history is apophatic, an absent presence where 'the past itself is inscrutable and thus always

---

6   For Tracy, 'the Holocaust is a searing interruption of all the traditions of Western culture ... We must recognize that Western humanist history includes all the guards at Auschwitz who read Goethe and listened to Bach and Mozart in their "spare time"'. See David Tracy, *Plurality and Ambiguity: Hermeneutics, Religion and Hope* (Chicago: University of Chicago Press, 1987), 68–74.
7   Tracy, *Plurality and Ambiguity*, 68–69.
8   Edith Wyschogrod, *An Ethics of Remembering: History, Heterology and the Nameless Others* (Chicago & London: The University of Chicago Press, 1998), 38.
9   See Edith Wyschogrod and Carl Raschke, 'Heterological History: A Conversation,' *Journal for Cultural and Religious Theory* 1, 2 (2000). Accessed 2 May 2019. www.jcrt.org/archives/01.2/wyschogrod_raschke.shtml

an unsurpassable negation.'[10] History can only be recovered as a trace. So rather than only focusing on truth as correspondence with the evidence as 'facts', the heterological historian also finds truth in memory and remembrance. According to Robert Eaglestone, it is not the 'facts of history' that bring the other to the fore, but the relationship with the other that allows the 'facts of history' to emerge.[11]

Memories expose us to the other person and their world. 'They open up a world that is not ours.'[12] Memories lay bare the existential ethical truth of a person, a community, a people or even a nation. In every person or community, there are the hidden or shadow elements of a personality, a community or a nation which people repress or conveniently forget about. Memory performs the function of uncovering that which has been covered over in forgetfulness or pushed to the margins of society. Memory and the ethical relation with the Other uncover the lives and experiences of those who remain 'invisible'[13] to history and often written out of history, that is, the forgotten or unrecognised Other.

Doing theology with Levinas

Memory is also a powerful Biblical motif through which believing Jews and Christians are called to deeper faith and experience of God's redeeming work in history. The Jewish people are constantly reminded that God led them out of Egypt when they were slaves and brought them to the Promised Land. God also released them from exile in Babylon and instructed them to rebuild the Temple. The Gospel accounts recount the dangerous memory of Jesus' life, death and resurrection which is remembered and celebrated in the Eucharist. Memory functions to remind people of God's love for them and their need to respond in love towards their suffering neighbour.

Levinas' language unsettles the researcher, the historian and the theologian. Levinas' philosophy questions our intentions.

---

10 Wyschogrod and Raschke, 'Heterological History,' 1.
11 Robert Eaglestone, *The Holocaust and the Postmodern* (Oxford: Oxford University Press, 2004), 178.
12 Eaglestone, *The Holocaust and the Postmodern*, 158.
13 Emmanuel Levinas, *Totality and Infinity*, 243.

What is our starting point? Are we motivated for personal gain and self-interest? Are we willing to open ourselves to being unsettled by proximity to the Other? If we are to become heterological or ethical historians or theologians, we need to be conscious and sensitive to the marginalisation of others by our language, thinking, social systems and Church institutions.[14] The researcher, historian or theologian, in the writing the history of Christian mission, is challenged to aim for greater humility in approaching their research, to be self-critical as well as reflexive. Researchers can never claim that they know or fully understand. The alterity of the Other always calls researchers to move beyond their present knowledge and preconceptions. The marginalised and suffering Other calls one's existence into question. The German philosopher Heidegger understood the self's existence as *Dasein*, literally 'there being.' But this 'there being' is always *miteinandersein*, being-with-others.[15] Authentic existence for Heidegger was becoming your own person and individuating out from the group and realising one's potential in the world.

For Levinas, alterity undermines this project of the self in its attempts to realise itself. Alterity challenges the self's egoist pursuit and presents a call to act with compassion and mercy to the suffering Other even to the extent of self-sacrifice. For Levinas, this willingness to respond in compassion to the pain of the Other is what constitutes our being human, a subject. Subjectivity is always intersubjectivity in alterity. The failure to respond is merely a continuation of our long history of

---

14 See Davis, *Levinas: An Introduction*, 45: Colin Davis summed up the problem when he wrote: 'The difficulty in describing the encounter with alterity lies in the constant danger of transforming the Other, however unwittingly or unwillingly, into a reflection or projection of the Same. If the Other becomes an object of knowledge or experience (my knowledge, my experience), then immediately its alterity has been overwhelmed … Even to describe the relationship with the Other as a relationship implies a totalizing perspective from which both self and Other are seen to share common ground, which has the consequence that the Other becomes another version of the Same.'

15 See Lauren Bialystok, 'Being Your Self: Identity, Metaphysics, and the Search for Authenticity.' Unpublished doctoral diss., University of Toronto, Canada, 2009, 147–148.

inhumanity and our lack of subjectivity. The true human being is always a self-for-the-other.

Becoming a subject is always a work in progress. Morrison described this as 'the (im)possibilities of Levinas' philosophy for Christian theology.'[16]

> Doing theology with Levinas is both possible and impossible. It is largely possible because Levinas' thought is like a treasury of keys to unlock the mysteries of personhood, prayer and ethics. Yet, we also face a sense of the impossible as the language of alterity itself beckons a whole eternity to be proclaimed. We seem to be always late for the other and find it so hard to welcome our neighbour with a heart and a smile.[17]

In reading Levinas, Morrison understood that the living of the Christian faith is coming to God by way of ethical transcendence or what he called Trinitarian praxis.[18] Trinitarian praxis, in the language of alterity, is a Christian life and practice that is self-emptying, kenotic and passive. In passivity, 'the self may encounter new possibilities and new ways of seeing and hearing the truth of the Other.'[19] The Church in its ministry to the Deaf stands accused of ignoring the face, and at times, repressing the 'signs'[20] of the Deaf Other.

This study is an attempt to write an interruptive and heterological history to record how the institutional Church's

---

16 See Glenn Morrison, 'The (Im)possibilities of Levinas for Christian Theology: The Search for a Language of Alterity,' in *Responsibility, God and Society: Theological Ethics in Dialogue: Festschrift Roger Burggraeve*, ed. J. de Tavernier, et al. (Leuven: Peters, 2008), 103–122. I share with Morrison an interest in the relation of Levinas' philosophy with theology but more specifically its relevance for the history of Christianity.
17 Morrison, 'The (Im)possibilities of Levinas for Christian Theology,' 106.
18 Morrison, 'The (Im)possibilities of Levinas for Christian Theology,' 105.
19 Glenn Morrison, *A Theology of Alterity: Levinas, von Balthasar, and Trinitarian Praxis* (Pittsburgh: Duquesne University Press, 2013), 69.
20 I have used 'signs' rather than voice.

approach to deaf ministry both served and failed the Deaf Other. Using a Levinasian lens, it will be necessary to gauge the extent to which Catholic deaf education and ministry were experienced by Deaf people as totalising and oppressive; and the extent to which it empowered some Deaf people to transform and shape their lives in a more liberating way.

Reflexity in research

Engaging in historical research means also being conscious of reflexivity. Reflexivity is a self-critical awareness that researchers adopt knowing that they can't be completely objective or stand 'outside of the research field'[21] and therefore they try to integrate and 'incorporate that knowledge creatively and effectively'[22] into their research.

In this research, I recognise that I am a hearing person reflecting on the experience of Deaf people. My experience of the Deaf world is primarily from my maternal grandparents who were both deaf. This experience has made me very sympathetic to the challenges that deaf people experience.

As we discussed in the previous section, Levinas' philosophy is a challenge to the researcher to recognise one's worldview or being-at-home-with-oneself and to put oneself under question. Being a white[23], hearing, South African-born male, a Catholic priest and a chaplain for the Deaf community affects the way I see and understand the world and so it will also affect my epistemological assumptions when approaching a subject like Deaf ministry. I cannot position myself as an objective outsider.

My life history has been influenced by growing up with deaf grandparents and my mother being a child of deaf adults (CODA). I remember being impressed with my grandfather's excellent lip-reading ability. He had been trained by the Dominican sisters at

---

21 John Swinton and Harriet Mowat, *Practical Theology and Qualitative Research*, 2nd ed. (London: SCM Press, 2016), 57.
22 Ibid.
23 This reference is pertinent because in later chapters I will be dealing with the challenges of being Deaf within the context of apartheid South Africa.

the Sacred Heart School for the Deaf in King William's Town in the 1920s. This made it easier for me, as the hearing grandson, to communicate with him. He seemed to adjust well to the challenges of working and functioning in a hearing world. He had excelled at sport all his life.[24] My grandmother was the opposite. She was profoundly deaf and relied on sign language, she was not as proficient at lip-reading. Her voice production, for me as her grandson, had much to be desired. I battled to understand her.

Due to my grandparents both being deaf, I thought I had some idea about what being deaf meant. I had tried to learn a little sign language. However, my grandfather was orally trained and only used sign language when he was with other deaf people. Knowing that my grandfather had benefitted from his education at the school for the deaf in King William's Town, I had a very positive view of the oral method of deaf education.

In this sense, I had chosen sides in the debate, even though academically, I try to keep an open mind. I believe that we, as hearing people, have an enormous amount to learn from the experience of Deaf people and, like Mary of Bethany, we need to choose the better part and learn from their experience (Lk 10:42).

Since 2006, I have been involved with Deaf ministry in Johannesburg, Soweto and Eswatini.[25] My ability to sign has improved enormously due to my daily contact with Deaf people, although I am far from being completely fluent. Through contact with the various Deaf communities, my understanding of Deaf culture and Deaf identity has grown and developed. When I started, I incorrectly assumed, that I already had some insight into the lives of Deaf people because of my contact with my grandparents and that it would not be difficult for me to learn sign language.

---

24   Joseph Hirst played rugby for Transvaal from 1938–1942 earning 21 caps at fullback. He played in the Transvaal team that beat Western Province, captained by the famous Danie Craven, in the Currie Cup final at Ellis Park in 1939. This was the first time Transvaal won the Currie Cup. See 'Inspiring Sportsman Passes Away,' *The Springs and Brakpan Advertiser*, 25 May 2001.

25   In April 2018, King Mswati III announced that the name of the country had been changed from Swaziland to Eswatini.

Being in contact with the Deaf community has challenged me to undergo a conversion in my perspective and understanding of Deaf people. I shared the misconception of many hearing people that being deaf was an affliction. I was bowled over when I first heard a Deaf friend and congregant, Francois de Villiers, explain to me that he was happy and content with being Deaf. He felt enriched by being part of a Deaf community which shared a language that enabled them to communicate with each other.

For me, this was one of my first encounters with a Deaf person who put my life under question. The self-satisfied economy by which I had previously lived my life was questioned. I had approached deaf people primarily from a perspective of benevolence. A benevolence of feeling sorry for them and the predicament in which they found themselves. I wanted to help and put things right.

The transformation that I underwent made me realise that I have much to learn from the Deaf community. The first was to learn sign language. Previously I had not realised that sign language was a separate language from English with its own grammatical structure. Before this, I had assumed my signed English was sign language. By participating in courses in SASL run by Sign Language Education and Development (SLED), an NGO in Johannesburg, I was introduced to the fundamentals of SASL. With practice, I was able to improve my signing. I consider myself a second-language signer.

Another challenge was to revise how I looked at my ministry and mission. Previously, I saw myself as working for the deaf and even used that terminology. However, in conducting the research I received a brochure from DeafSA where the transformation of the organisation from the South African National Council of the Deaf (SANCD) to DeafSA was described as a shift from being an organisation working 'for' the deaf to being an organisation 'of' the Deaf community.[26] This change of preposition challenged my previous mindset.

---

26   Doreen Hayhurst, DeafSA, personal email to Mark James, 20 September 2014.

No longer did I work from the assumption that deaf people were victims of hearing loss but rather a community with agency that was bonded together through their use of sign language. Deaf people had skills and talents that could be included in ministry. I did not have a monopoly on skills. With my limited ability to sign, I realised that in this ministry it was I who was the one who was handicapped and not any Deaf person. This forced me to become humble in my approach to ministry.

I recognised that I had lots to learn from the Deaf community about ministry. I sought to discuss with members of the Catholic Deaf community the best way to minister in the Deaf environment. For example, Deaf people taught me that in the Eucharist it is important that everyone see what is being signed. This meant we agreed to change some of the customary practices of saying Mass. Hearing people normally stand at the reading of the Gospel out of respect for the Word of God, but during the signed Mass we sit so everyone has an unobstructed view of the person signing. Whenever possible we also turn the lectern a little to one side too so that the congregation can have a clearer view of the signer's hands.

Even though I have grown in my understanding of the Deaf community and my participation within it, nevertheless, I realise that I am not deaf/Deaf. As a hearing person, I am an outsider to the Deaf world, but I am nevertheless privileged to share in the life of the Deaf communities in which I minister. My experience is limited and it does not equip me to speak on behalf of Deaf people or think that I can understand what it means to be Deaf. I recognise that I am an outsider to the Deaf experience and this limits the scope of this study too.

Taking a cue from Steve Biko, who in the struggle against apartheid, was insistent that white people should not presume to know what black people think or feel or try to fight the struggle against apartheid on their behalf,[27] I have tried to do the same concerning the Deaf community. Similarly, I do not want to present myself as a champion for Deaf people's rights.

---

27 See Julian Brown, *The Road to Soweto: Resistance and the Uprising of 16 June 1976* (Johannesburg: Jacana Media, 2016), 42.

In the research, I have strived to allow Deaf people to speak for themselves. Consequently, I have resorted to quoting them as often as possible, rather than paraphrasing what they have said and advocated. British Deaf activist Paddy Ladd has said that 'Deafhood is a verb and not a noun.'[28] Deafhood is about the self-actualisation and empowerment of Deaf people, a movement and an action that they must embark upon themselves. Similarly, Biko also believed that black people would 'carve out their own destiny.'[29]

My intention in this book is primarily to address a hearing audience. I call on hearing people to have 'open minds, open hearts'[30] to the struggles of Deaf people in our midst. As hearing people there is much to learn from Deaf people about what it means to be human. Sign language also broadens our horizons about what constitutes language and human communication. Deaf discourse is a teaching from which hearing people need to learn. Hearing people need to learn the local sign language of their country as they continue to meet more Deaf people in the shops, as bank tellers and in the workplace.

A more extensive history of Deaf organisations and movements in South Africa like DeafSA and the contributions made by Deaf people from other churches still needs to be written. It is a rich history and one which needs further research. In writing this history, I attempt to bring to the fore Deaf perspectives from a historical perspective that shows how Deaf people, like Black people, have come to understand themselves anew. In doing so, I hope that this research will contribute towards a greater appreciation of the contribution made by the Deaf community to the life of the Catholic Church in South Africa.

---

28 Ladd, *Understanding Deaf Culture*, 448.
29 It is the sub-title for Chapter 2 on the South African Students' Organisation (SASO) in Brown, *The Road to Soweto*, 40.
30 I have intentionally chosen this phrasing in tribute to a book written by a team of writers, hearing and Deaf, laypeople and Dominican Sisters, with Sarah Fitzgerald, a lay Catholic Deaf woman, as narrator. The book describes and details the experiences of Catholic Deaf people in Australia from 1875 to 1995. See Sarah Fitzgerald and Janice Andrew, eds, *Open Minds Open Hearts: Stories of the Australian Catholic Deaf Community*, (Lidcombe, NSW: CCOD, 1999).

Methodology

In collecting data for this research, I invariably use the qualitative rather than the quantitative approach. The qualitative approach involves the accumulation of data from archival research which means, firstly, the uncovering of the primary sources through archival research; secondly, complementing archival research with oral history research through interviewing individuals who actively participated in the historical events under study or who are knowledgeable about these matters; and thirdly, through reading of secondary literature of a historical, philosophical and sociological nature.

Archival research

Archival research is integral to historical research. McKemmish and Gilliland pointed out that until the mid-1990s, the archive was seen 'as an institution that systematically promotes, preserves and makes accessible memory, culture and identity in the form of bureaucratic and social evidence.'[31] The archive was the place where the facts about the past were stored. In uncovering this evidence in texts and documents from the past, it was presumed that the past could be brought back to life. This was also my approach when I first started consulting various archives.

For material on St Vincent School for the Deaf and St Thomas School for the Deaf in Woodlands in the Eastern Cape, the King William's Town Dominican Sisters Archive (KDSA) in Johannesburg was incredibly valuable. There is a near-complete collection of the St Vincent School magazine which was incredibly instructive in understanding the method of deaf education employed at the school from 1948 until 1994. The archive also had extensive information on the foundation of St Thomas School for the Deaf in Woodlands in the Eastern Cape. There was a limited

---

[31] Sue McKemmish and Anne Gilliland, 'Archival and Recordkeeping Research: Past, Present and Future,' in *Research Methods: Information, Systems, and Context*, ed. K. Williamson and G. Johanson (Prahan, Victoria: Tilde Publishing, 2013), 84. Accessed 3 May 2019, www.uzk.unizd.hr/rams/wp-content/uploads/2013/04/Chapter4.ResearchMethods-WilliamsonJohanson-2.pdf

amount of information on KwaThintwa school in Inchanga with which some of the sisters had been involved. The Cabra Dominican Sisters' Archive (CDSA) in Cape Town had extensive information on the Dominican-Grimley School, the Wittebome School and the Hammanskraal School that were established by the Cabra Dominicans.

Much of the work on the Deaf chaplaincies was accessed from newspaper articles in *The Southern Cross*. The Catholic History Bureau (CHB) in Victory Park, Johannesburg was very helpful in this respect as it houses all the copies of *The Southern Cross* newspaper from 1921 to 2013. I also had the opportunity to consult *The Southern Cross* Archive in Cape Town.

The Archive of the Archdiocese of Durban (AAD) had extensive information on the establishment and development of the KwaThintwa School for the Deaf in the Archbishop Hurley Archives collection. However, this collection has now been moved over to the Denis E. Hurley Library at St Joseph's Theological Institute at Cedara, near Pietermaritzburg. The Archive of the Diocesan of Port Elizabeth (ADPE) had useful information on St Thomas School for the Deaf in Woodlands and information on the work of Bishop Ernest Green. The Archive of the Archdiocese of Cape Town (AACT) at the Chancery in Cape Town had a limited amount of information on the two schools for the deaf in the Archdiocese. Unfortunately, there was virtually no information on the work of Fr Ernest Green before he went to Port Elizabeth, or after his retirement as bishop and his return to Cape Town as a chaplain to the deaf.

The Archive of DeafSA agreed to email to me all the electronic copies of *The Silent Messenger* from 1935 to 1995. This was the magazine of DeafSA's predecessor and the now defunct organisation called the SANCD. This proved incredibly helpful in supplying background information about work with the Deaf community in South Africa during the period under study. Unfortunately, much of the information was from a hearing perspective but occasionally there were valuable articles written by deaf authors.

The University of the Witwatersrand Archive at the William Cullen Library (UWA) helped find information regarding Rev. Arthur Blaxall, an Anglican priest and co-founder of the SANCD.

However, I began to recognise that most of the archival material was written from the perspective of the Dominican sisters who taught in the school or the priests who worked with the deaf and not the deaf people themselves. In the case of the Church archives, they often reflected the history of the schools or parishes that they represented. What was considered worthy of inclusion were the thoughts, reports and comments of the school principals, teachers, the Board of Governors and Boards of Management. Even *The Southern Cross* newspaper reflected the thoughts and opinions of various Church authorities like the popes, cardinals, archbishops, bishops, chaplains of the deaf, religious sisters and principals of schools rather than the opinions of the Deaf people themselves.

A notable exception was the Redemptorist archive which had an excellent collection of accounts of Fr Cyril Axelrod's life, some of his papers and letters, and journal and newspaper articles on him. He was also a contributor to *The Southern Cross*. The Archive of the South African Province of the Redemptorists (RA) in Cape Town also had extensive information on Fr Axelrod and his life and ministry in South Africa.

Taking on board, Edith Wyschogrod's idea of reading history from a heterological historical perspective, it became more apparent to me that no archive can be accepted uncritically as value-free and objective.

> Increasingly the Archive is being explored as a contested, political space, a societal concept associated with the promotion of asymmetrical power, grand narratives, nationalism, surveillance, and the omission, dimunition or silencing of alternative narratives.[32]

---

32 McKemmish and Gilliland, 'Archival and Recordkeeping,' 86.

Archives are spaces of power which allow narratives to be told through voices that can be heard and recorded.[33] This power of the archive, however, is selective because often only some narratives and some voices are permitted. This is because the archive is a record of those narratives that the archivists consider to be valuable and important. The documents collected in the archive represent the perspectives of what the archivists consider to be of historical value and worth keeping for posterity's sake. The archive is, therefore, a social construct and it contains 'the information and social values of the rulers, governments, businesses, associations, and individuals who establish and maintain them.[34]

In the Church context, the archive reflects the interests of the organisation or Church community that maintains the archive and at times the interests and thoughts of individual archivists, who in the Church environment are not trained historians or archivists.

The archive is also a place of silence where some voices are missing.[35] However, the 'voice' of the ordinary deaf school pupil or the deaf adult in the Church was ostensibly absent from this archival record. They were truly an 'absent presence' referred to in the third person but seldom in their own 'voice' or in sign. There is also a dearth of information available on the history of the Deaf Community of Cape Town (DCCT). Very little has been recorded or documented in any significant way even by the organisation itself. Similarly, the Archive of the Congregation of Mariannhill Missionaries (ACMM) in Mariannhill, has almost nothing on the life and work of Fr John Turner CMM. An archivist there once explained to me that 'Fr John's work was not typically the work

---

33 Rodney G.S. Carter, 'Of Things Said and Unsaid: Power, Archival Silences, and Power in Silence,' *Archivaria* 61 (Spring 2006): 215–233. This is paraphrase of thoughts on page 216. Accessed 3 May 2019, www.archivaria.ca/archivar/index.php/archivaria/article/view/12341
34 Joan M. Schwartz and Terry Cook, 'Archives, Records and Power: The Making of Modern Memory,' *Archival Science* 2, 1–19 (2002): 3. Accessed 3 May 2019, www.nyu.edu/classes/bkg/methods/schwartz.pdf
35 Carter, 'Of Things Said and Unsaid,' 217.

of a Mariannhill priest!' Nothing was kept when he passed away in 2013.

For Carter, these 'archival silences, however they occur, have a potentially disastrous impact on marginalised groups,'[36] like the Catholic Deaf community. These memories can be easily lost. Silence can mean that societal and ecclesial memory is compromised.[37] For these reasons, the oral history approach was also employed to recover and record some of these Deaf memories or what Carter called 'finding voices in silence.'[38]

Oral history research

Due to the silences in the archival research, it was necessary to complement it with oral history research. Introducing an oral history research component to this study was necessary because of the large gaps in the archival material. Equally important, the archival material reflected the interests and concerns of the hearing principals, management boards and teachers. These documents also record the attitudes of the bishops, priests, sisters and hearing laity. Seldom ever were Deaf people's perspectives recorded in the archival material. In this respect, oral history functioned as a way of uncovering the Deaf perspective.

> Oral history can provide a corrective to the bias of the written sources. Social history aspires to treat the history of society as a whole, not just the rich and the articulate.[39]

Oral history assisted in uncovering the stories of the deaf children in the schools and the deaf adults in the church pews. Many of the stories related have not been recorded before.

> Oral history is a history built around people. It thrusts life into history itself and widens its scope. It allows heroes not just from the leaders, but from the unknown majority of the people … It brings history into, and out of, the community.

---
36 Ibid, 220.
37 Ibid.
38 Ibid, 222–224.
39 In this case, 'the hearing and the articulate.' See Tosh, *The Pursuit of History*, 210.

> It helps the less privileged, and especially the old, towards dignity and self-confidence. It makes for contact – and thence understanding – between social classes and between generations.[40]

I used the oral history approach to try to capture the perspectives and self-understanding of Deaf people themselves, rather than having someone speak on their behalf. The experience of the Deaf community members themselves needed to be expressed. However, I did not restrict interviews to the Deaf community. I also interviewed some hearing people, especially retired principals and teachers to clarify some details that I did not find in the archival material. Nevertheless, I interviewed six Deaf and four hearing people.

At the beginning of the interview process, my view of oral history concurred with Kros and Ulrich's definition as 'history that has been passed down through word of mouth.'[41] They distinguished between two different approaches. There is the first-hand oral testimony or eyewitness accounts of the events which the person interviewed experienced and the second is oral testimony based on oral tradition, stories, praise songs or narratives passed from one generation to the next.[42] In this study, oral history has been applied firstly as eyewitness accounts.

I conducted interviews with those who had attended or taught in schools for the deaf in South Africa or had participated in pastoral ministry in the Deaf community. This included both hearing and Deaf laity, priests and religious sisters and Deaf pupils. The choice of those interviewed was conducted by the snowball approach to data collection. This sampling approach is also known as the network, chain referral or reputational method. Like a snowball, it usually starts with one or a few people and then

---

40 Paul Thompson, *The Voice of the Past: Oral history*. 3rd ed. (Oxford: Oxford University Press, 2000), 23.
41 Cynthia Kros and Nicole Ulrich, 'The Truth of Tales: Oral Testimony and Teaching History in Schools,' in *Oral History in a Wounded Country: Interactive Interviewing in South Africa*, ed. Philippe Denis and Radikobo Ntsimane. (Scottsville: University of KwaZulu-Natal, 2008), 91.
42 Kros and Ulrich, "The Truth of Tales,' 91.

spreads out to others using the links or connections of people to each other.[43]

In 2014, I conducted my first interview with Fr Cyril Axelrod CSsR, a deaf-blind priest, who ministered extensively throughout South Africa during my period of research. It was invaluable in validating and confirming various events and developments among deaf people. It was my first time to interview a deaf-blind person. As I signed, Axelrod who read my signing with his hands. He felt the signs I was making with my hands. When I fingerspelled I did so by using the deaf-blind alphabet on the palm of his left hand. When Fr Cyril responded, he primarily voiced his responses, but used signs on occasion, so that I could capture what he was saying on video.

I chose to interview Fr Axelrod first and in discussion with him, I identified other key people to interview. Through this, I identified members of DCCT who had attended either the Dominican-Grimley School or the School for the Deaf in Wittebome. I interviewed them in the following order for no other reason than that it was convenient for them: First, I interviewed Jennifer Gillespie had been a pupil at Dominican-Grimley School in Cape Town; then Carmen Kuscus, Suzanne Lombard and Faith Cronwright who attended the Wittebome School. Thereafter, I interviewed my first hearing person, Sr Liguori Töns, a King William's Town Dominican sister, who taught at both the St Vincent School in Johannesburg and the St Thomas School at Woodlands in the Eastern Cape. Then was the turn of Sisters Macrina Donoghue, Siobhan Murphy and Jacinta Texeira, Cabra Dominican sisters each involved in a different Cabra school. Sr Macrina taught at Dominican-Grimley, Sr Siobhan was at Hammanskraal and Sr Jacinta at Wittebome. The last person I interviewed was Francois de Villiers, a previous pupil from St Vincent School.

I used my computer camera to film seven of the interviews. I would position the computer in such a way that it could record

---

[43] See W. Lawrence Neuman, *Social Research Methods: Qualitative and Quantitative Approaches*, 4th ed. (Boston: Allyn and Bacon, 2000), 199–200.

both people and record our signing to each other. I transcribed the interviews from the video footage as transcriptions are much easier to use as documented history in a written text than visual data. Permission to record these interviews was sought from each interviewee, however, all of the Deaf people agreed to be filmed. This made the interview process much easier as I could not take notes and watch the person's signing at the same time. After transcribing the interviews, I sent them to the interviewees to verify their veracity.

I am proficient in SASL (NQF level 5), even though I am not completely fluent, and I transcribed the interviews myself. Signing can differ from one region to another in South Africa. Even in one city, deaf people can sign differently because the signing one learnt was influenced by the school for the deaf one attended. When it was difficult to interpret some of the material or when I was not familiar with some of the signs being used, I requested the assistance of a Deaf signer, Faith Cronwright, to check the accuracy of my transcriptions.

Three hearing interviewees refused to allow the filming or taping of the interview. I had to write down notes during the interview and then, from the notes and memory, write up the interview. I then sent the transcripts back to those interviewed for their comments and corrections. We finalised the documents together to their satisfaction.

Two separate interview schedules were developed: one for hearing interviewees and another for Deaf interviewees. It is not the purpose of the study to delve into any psychological or traumatic experiences and in the letter explaining the purpose of the interview given to each interviewee before the interview took place, it was made clear that the interviewee could refuse to answer a question or even terminate the interview at any point.

I had been apprehensive before the interviews with some of the hearing teachers at the schools for the deaf that they may have resisted participating in the research. Some of them have given their whole lives to teaching deaf children and I was afraid that they may take exception to the focus of the study. However, this fear proved to be unfounded as all the hearing participants were happy to be interviewed and explain the methods employed in the schools. What was particularly helpful about the hearing teachers and principals interviewed was that they helped give important background information about the oral method of deaf education.

The Deaf people were willing interviewees too. The research focused on the role played by Deaf people in shaping their own faith experience. While many found the interview questions affirmed their experiences of school and church life as Deaf people, there were some instances when an interview question brought to mind a hurtful experience suffered by the interviewee. These included derogatory attitudes held against Deaf people by hearing people, incidents of racial intolerance or audist impositions.

Care was given to explain to each Deaf interviewee in sign, before the interview taking place, that what they disclosed in the interview would be kept confidential. It was also explained that they had the right to refuse to answer any questions during the interview. And that they could refuse to be quoted by name in the research. They could also stop the interview at any point.

Two respondents replied to questions via email. The first was Fr Cyril Axelrod who sent me a timeline of his work in South Africa and other chaplains who preceded him and those who were his successors. This helped when interviewing him later.

Lindsay Moeletsi Dunn, the second respondent, lives in the United States. It was not possible to interview him due to distance and my limited budget and he agreed to share his experiences of deaf education at Wittebome school via email. He sent me two separate emails detailing his experiences at Wittebome School in 1976. He did all this while engaged in full-time lecturing and marking at Gallaudet University in Washington DC.

A third respondent, Nigel Pickford, gave me a copy of a talk he had prepared for the 50th anniversary of St Vincent School for the Deaf detailing his experiences at the school.

One of the problems I experienced when engaging in the interview process was that occasionally when interviewing a Deaf person, my question did not always come across clearly enough. I would have to repeat the question and express it differently way so that the person could get a better idea of what I was asking. I think that this was partly due to my limited signing ability and partly due to not formulating the question well enough. It is one thing to formulate the question in English and write it down, but when it comes to expressing it in sign language, it needs to follow a sign language structure. Signing is not just using the English grammatical structure but rather finding a way to translate words and sounds into signs and space. It needed careful preparation before the interview but often questions would arise spontaneously in the interview process and it was not possible to prepare these spontaneous questions.

But more significantly, during the interviewing process, I noticed the difficulties interviewees sometimes had in remembering the past. They made mistakes or shaped events in a specific way. I began to realise that the memories of those I interviewed were not flawless and not always accurate.

> Memory is a dynamic process. When we remember, we select, organise, omit and sometimes invent aspects of our past experiences according to what we need, feel and believe in the present moment. The memories of the past are fluid.[44]

More than 'inaccurate' and fluid, their memories were also very personal. The responses were always tempered with their own standpoints and perspectives on the ministry offered and received. While their contributions added a personal perspective to what they narrated, as well as clarified events from the archival evidence, they were often expressed subjectively.

Robert Grele, an American oral historian, has written extensively on memory and subjectivity in the interview process.[45]

44　Philippe Denis, 'Memory and Commemoration as a Subject of Enquiry for African Christianity Scholars,' *Studia Historiae Ecclesiasticae* 41, 3 (2015): 7.
45　Ronald J. Grele, 'Reflections on the Practice of Oral History: Retrieving What We Can From an Earlier Critique,' *Suomen Antropologi: Journal of the Finnish Anthropological Society* 32, 4 (Winter 2007): 11–23.

He defined oral history as 'a conversational narrative created by the interaction of the interviewer and the interviewee and determined by linguistic, social and ideological structures.'[46]

Grele argued that there has been a shift in oral history from seeing the interview as a document revealing the truth about the past to one where the interview is understood as a text that was constructed through dialogue. 'This was a basic epistemological shift from a concern with accuracy to a concern with narrative construction.'[47] Previously, interviews were done to provide the historian with facts and information about the past. The truth lay in facts that the historian could uncover through the interviewing process. The concern with memory was in relation to its accuracy as a true reflection of the past without bias.

However, memory and remembering the past is understood as much more complex when one begins to understand the interview as a text constructed through dialogue. Firstly, Grele pointed out that the role of the interviewer is much more important than what was thought before. 'Among documents used by historians, oral histories were created by the interest of the historian.'[48] Oral histories are not just documents that tell stories about the past. They are documents that record the present time too. They reveal how the past continues in the present. Consequently, Grele believed that 'if historians were to build an interpretation upon their own interviews they needed to be very clear about their position in the process of creation.'[49]

Secondly, Grele said 'the person interviewed was no longer simply a source but a key creator and interpreter of a history.'[50] The interviewee shapes the past by what they experienced, perceived and understood. The interview becomes a place where there is a conversation, a dialogue and even where, at times, a negotiation takes place between the interviewer and the interviewee. Often the two have very different positions or understandings of the past: the one because they lived in that past, and the other because of

---

46 Grele, 'Reflections on the Practice of Oral History, 1, 16–17.
47 Grele,'Reflections on the Practice of Oral History,' 13.
48 Grele, 'Reflections on the Practice of Oral History,' 13.
49 Ibid.
50 Ibid.

what they have read about this past. For Grele, the historian is 'no longer a collector of observations but a co-creator of verbal texts.'[51] The historian shares 'interpretative rights'[52] with the interviewee. This allows the interviewee the right to their own perspective of the past, even though the historian may disagree.

Thirdly, there is the question about memory. People live through the same events but remember them differently. This is often due to the complex interplay between individual and collective memory, where individual memories are affected by various religious, economic, political, social and cultural influences. Also, it is not just a question about the interviewee, but also the interviewer. Grele said that an understanding of the interview as dialogic means that the historian needs to be aware of their own memories and ideological perspectives that they also bring to the interview.[53]

This new understanding of oral history as conversation and dialogue means that the oral historian needs to consider the ethics involved in researching to ensure that those who volunteer to be interviewed, especially the Deaf people, do not come to any harm in the interview process.

The ethical challenges

A major ethical issue in historical research, especially one which involves oral history, is the preservation of the oral history archive. As outlined in a previous section on research methodology, the interviews done in this research have been placed on a memory stick and will be kept in the Archive of the Vice-Province of Order of Preachers in Southern Africa in Springs, South Africa. Transcribed versions of some interviews form the appendix of the PhD dissertation and are held at the University of KwaZulu-Natal. In contrast to interviews done by sociologists and journalists, historical researchers understand that 'the main purpose of an interview is to collect oral information for future

---

51 Ibid.
52 Ibid.
53 Grele, 'Reflections on the Practice of Oral History,' 15.

use.'[54] It is vitally important to keep a record of the experiences of Deaf people so that their history and memories are not forgotten or silenced. Those interviewed have signed a form permitting the interview to remain part of the oral archive and that their names can used in the research. In this respect, Denis says, the oral historian 'always doubles up as an archivist.'[55]

The research was conducted with the four basic ethical principles in mind: respect for people's dignity and autonomy; non-maleficence; beneficence and justice.[56] In the interviewing process it is vital to respect the dignity of each person interviewed but greater sensitivity needs to be paid to the Deaf participants. Deaf people have been unfairly treated by hearing people in the past and without proper respect. Hearing people often assumed that being deaf was equated with having an intellectual disability too. It still happens that hearing people often speak in the company of Deaf people, without interpreting what they are saying to the person. This makes the Deaf person feel left out of the conversation and excluded. Deaf people feel offended by this treatment. Sometimes hearing people will even speak about a Deaf person in his or her presence knowing that the person will not hear what is said. In these cases, Deaf people feel slighted and disrespected.

At times, hearing people will also take it upon themselves to tell Deaf people what to do without explaining the process of what is expected or happening. Again, Deaf people feel they are being treated differently to the way a hearing person would have been treated. The dignity of the Deaf person needs to be taken seriously, especially relating to behaviour which respects the Deaf person's culture and what is considered acceptable modes of behaviour.

So that the autonomy and identity of respondents were protected, each interviewee received and signed an informed consent form before the interview was conducted. The contents

---

54 Philippe Denis, 'The Ethics of Oral History,' in *Oral History in a Wounded Country: Interactive Interviewing in South Africa,*' ed. Philippe Denis and Radikobo Ntsimane, (Scottsville: University of KwaZulu-Natal Press, 2008), 65.
55 Denis, 'The Ethics of Oral History,' 65.
56 See Denis, 'The Ethics of Oral History,' 67–70.

of the consent form stated that each Deaf interviewee had the right to refuse to do the interview; that they could also refuse to answer any question which they considered problematic; and that they had the right to anonymity. They were also informed that they could refuse this request. For Deaf respondents, this was explained to them in sign language.

The ethical principle of non-maleficence is concerned with ensuring 'that any harm resulting from the interview process is kept to an absolute minimum.'[57] On one occasion, during an interview with a respondent, answering one of the interview questions recalled a particularly painful moment in his life when he felt rejected or unappreciated. He paused a little and then decided not to continue relating the story indicating that if I wanted more information about what transpired, I should contact a third person whose name he gave me. It would have been completely unethical of me at this point to pursue this question or to pressurise him in any way to reveal what he was not willing to divulge.

The principle of beneficence means that those people who were interviewed need to benefit from the interview process. Each person interviewed agreed knowing that there was to be no financial benefit. After the interview, each person interviewed was given a copy of the interview transcript. Denis argued that justice 'requires that those who stand to benefit from the research should bear the burdens of the research.'[58] To this end, I ensured that those interviewed did not have to incur any expenses. We conducted the interviews in places which were convenient for the interviewees. I paid for my transport costs to get to the places of their choosing to conduct the interviews. Most often, I conducted the interviews in people's homes. However, while I was in Cape Town, I interviewed a few of the Deaf participants at their place of work, which was at the DCCT offices. I was given a separate room in which to interview the participants.

---

57   Denis, 'The Ethics of Oral History,' 69.
58   Ibid, 70.

All these safeguards were put in place to ensure that the interview process caused no offence or any harm to those who volunteered to participate in the research for this book.

Conclusion

The epistemological, methodological and ethical challenges in writing this book have been outlined. The research for this book has been drawn from an epistemological approach in Levinas' philosophy that opens up a more sympathetic reading of the history of Catholic Deaf people in South Africa. The use of both archival and oral historical methodologies as sources has added greater depth to the research. While conducting the research some ethical challenges were encountered but I have outlined how they were dealt with so as not to cause any further offence or harm. In the next chapter, I present a brief history on the history of the relations between the hearing and Deaf communities starting from the early Greek philosophers until about 1948, before moving on to the results of the historical research undertaken.

Chapter 4

A Historical Survey of Catholic Ministry to the Deaf Community

The purpose of this chapter is to reflect on the historical influence of audism and phonocentrism on Catholic ministry to the Deaf community. Down the ages, deaf people have been subjected to the disparaging or pitiful gaze of the Church and society. Deafness has been considered a handicap or a defect that distinguishes deaf people from the hearing majority. Being deaf made them different but it also marginalised them. To find oneself as the Other of history is to discover oneself to be ignored, treated with contempt and denied human dignity. It is to find oneself trampled underfoot in, what Wyschogrod has called, the 'mud of history.'[1]

In this chapter we employ Levinas' philosophy to assist in firstly, reflecting on the ecclesial encounter with the face of the Deaf people as representative of the Other; secondly, critiquing Catholic ministerial praxis for the times when it lacked vigilance of this face and acted in totalising ways; thirdly, acknowledging the occasions when hospitality was offered to the Deaf Other, and fourthly, recognising the saintly efforts of both hearing and deaf people in shaping a new vision for Deaf people. In doing so, we will hopefully see how Catholic ministry has been both a totalising and liberatory praxis.

At the outset, we need to briefly recall what was highlighted in Chapter 1. This history needs to be read in light of the different perspectives of how human people were understood. The perspective of natural law inherited from the Greek philosophers had its limitations because it contributed extensively to marginalising deaf people for many centuries. During the modern

---

[1] Edith Wyschogrod and Carl Raschke, 'Heterological History: A Conversation,' *Journal for Cultural and Religious Theory*, 1, 2 (2000): 2. Accessed 2 May 2019, www.jcrt.org/archives/01.2/wyschogrod_raschke.shtml

period with its emphasis on the dignity of each human being, this alienation was alleviated to some extent because it was recognised that deaf people had the right to education as any other human being. But this modernist perspective also had its shortcomings. Levinas' post-modern philosophical approach will help to show how modernism itself was not sufficiently open to the challenge of alterity and the Other. Christian ministry was affected by all these philosophical perspectives.

Christian ministry to deaf people has biblical roots in Jesus' ministry. However, the only response envisaged was the miraculous cure. Discourse about deaf people was primarily focused on deafness as a symbol of the lack of faith in God or even the inability to have faith. Consequently, the first period will include the biblical and patristic [2]approaches to the deaf. The second period will look briefly at the Middle Ages. Both these periods can be typified, notwithstanding some exceptions, as a neglect of ministry to deaf people. The third period starts with a look at the Renaissance period, and the beginnings of deaf education and pastoral ministry to the deaf. The fourth period focuses on the Enlightenment until the second half of the nineteenth century. During this period, there was increasing institutionalisation of the ministry to the deaf through schools and chaplaincies, which was influenced by the method of education debate. The fifth period, from the first Education Conference of Milan in 1880 until 1951, was the period of oralism's triumph over the manual method and the promotion of modern scientific methods in Deaf education. However, new ways of thinking about the relationship between the hearing and Deaf communities were also coming to birth. This led to the establishment of organisations to assert Deaf rights, challenge injustices and envisage a new identity beyond hearing stereotypes.

---

2   The patristic period is considered to have commenced after the New Testament period (100 AD) and to end with the Second Council of Nicaea in 787

The beginnings of the 'Ministry to the Deaf'

The first reference to ministry for the deaf, or at least to those without speech, goes back to the First Council of Orange in AD 441. The bishops of South Gaul called this Council prior to the collapse of Roman Imperial rule in the West in AD 476. During the period AD 314–506, the bishops called approximately twenty-three Councils to discuss dogma and disciplinary questions.[3] The task included developing local and regional laws for the smooth running of the Church in this region, especially with the decline in the influence of the Imperial authority in Rome.

The first Council of Orange focused entirely on disciplinary questions. It was presided over by St Hilary of Arles with 17 bishops in attendance. Thirty canons or Church laws were produced. In this regard, Broesterhuizen pointed out that this Council permitted that pertaining to the sacraments 'Deaf persons who were able to indicate using clear signs that they understood their meaning were admitted to the sacraments.'[4] This practice is maintained to the present day where Canon Law permits deaf people to contract marriage using signs.[5] However, Canon 12 of the 1983 Code of Canon Law directed that:

> Persons suddenly deprived of the power of speech shall be reconciled or baptised if they give, or shall have given beforehand, a sign that they wish it.[6]

This formulation highlighted two important points which are pertinent to the Catholic Church's approach to deaf ministry. First, the text spoke of those who are without speech and second, it acknowledged the use of signs as being a valid way of showing comprehension and consent for the receiving of the sacraments.

---

3 Michael Edward Moore, 'The Spirit of the Gallican Councils, AD 314–506,' *Annarium Historiae Conciliorum* 39 (January 2007): 10. Accessed 8 September 2018,
4 Marcel Broesterhuizen, 'Faith in Deaf culture,' *Theological Studies* 66, 2 (June 2005): 307.
5 Michael Edward Moore, 'The Spirit of the Gallican Councils, AD 314–506,' *Annarium Historiae Conciliorum* 39 (January 2007): 10. Accessed 8 September 2018,.
6 Edward Landon, *A Manual of Councils of the Holy Catholic Church*, vol. II (Edinburgh: John Grant, 1909), 1.

While this shows, as Broesterhuizen has argued, that from the earliest centuries, the Church embarked upon the ministry to the deaf,[7] it also highlighted the tension, even the contradiction that has existed in the Catholic ministry to the deaf from its beginnings. This is the tension between the preference for a speech-centred understanding of deafness and the secondary acceptance of signing. This tension is still present in Catholic deaf ministry today. It is important to outline the nature of this tension and its effects on Catholic ministry.

Being deprived of speech

The origin of this speech-centred approach to deafness dates back to the Greek period. The Hippocratic physicians in the fifth century BC were the first to make the connection between deafness and speechlessness. A question to ask is why was this emphasis on speechlessness considered so important in relation to the deaf in Greek society?

In Greece, speech was considered a sign of rationality. In his dialogue with Theaetetus, about knowledge and its attainment, Plato had Socrates say that true knowledge was to hold the right opinion and to be able to define or explain it rationally. This was manifested when thought was expressed through speech. Socrates said: 'And everyone who is not born deaf or dumb is able sooner or later to manifest what he thinks of anything.'[8] Speech was a manifestation of rationality and the ability to think. The philosopher most influential in this regard was Aristotle. In a similar vein, Aristotle made the connection between hearing, speech and intelligence, remarking that:

> It is hearing that contributes most to the growth of intelligence. For rational discourse is a cause of instruction in virtue of its being audible ... Accordingly, of persons destitute from birth of either sense, the blind are more intelligent than the deaf and dumb.[9]

---

7   Broesterhuizen, 'Faith in Deaf Culture,' 307.
8   Plato, *Theaetetus*, 206d.
9   Quoted in Bonnie Gracer, 'What the Rabbis heard: Deafness in the Mishnah,' in *Jewish Perspectives on Theology and the Human*

Speech results from the vocalising of words that make sense. Aristotle argued that it was through the spoken word, namely language, that people expressed rationality. The spoken word was crucial in distinguishing between human beings and animals.[10] While animals make sounds, and use voice, they do it without recourse to *logos* or reason.[11]

Logos is both intelligence or discursive reasoning but also the 'principle within us that enables us to understand and govern ourselves.'[12] As a result of this, it is possible to deduce an ethic based on virtues that arise from the objective laws of our nature as rational and intelligent beings. His view was that the person imbued with *logos*, who can reason, make conscious, deliberate choices and perform virtuous actions was fully human and contributed to the good life of the city-state. Aristotle contributed enormously to what is now called natural law that all human beings are united by *logos* and that it constitutes their human nature.

However, as it was the *logos* that defined a human being, Aristotle also argued that human beings were not all equal. Some were more able to attain the full stature of becoming fully human whereas others were excluded because they had 'deficient souls.'[13] Predictably, it was only those who were indigenous Greek free males, part of the well-born and educated elite, like Aristotle himself, who could truly aspire to full humanity. Among the excluded were women, children, those born with deformities or disabilities and natural slaves who included all the barbarian or non-Greek nations.

Experience of Disability, ed. Judith Abrams (Binghamton, NY: Haworth Press, 2006), 89.

10   'Voice is a certain sound of ensouled beings and belongs only to ensouled beings,' Aristotle, *De Anima*, 420b 5–7 in *The Basic Works of Aristotle*, ed. Richard McKeon (New York: Random House, 1941), 572.

11   Aristotle, *De Anima*, 420b 34. Book II, Chapter 8 in *The Basic Works*, 573.

12   Jean Vanier, *Made for Happiness: Discovering the Meaning of Life with Aristotle* (London: Darton, Longman and Todd, 2001), 18.

13   See Tim Christiaens, 'Aristotle's Anthropological Machine and Slavery: An Agambenian Interpretation,' *Epoché: A Journal for the History of Philosophy* 23,1 (Fall 2018): 239–262.

British philosopher Malcolm Heath asked whether having deficient souls meant that Aristotle thought that women, children, the disabled or natural slaves lacked *logos* or autonomous rationality?[14] Heath argued that Aristotle would have known that foreigners were human because they were able to reason. However, it is important to note that Aristotle differentiated between different kinds of rationality. While the foreigners, or natural slaves, were able to reason technically by building elaborate buildings and to reason theoretically by understanding mathematics, they were incapable of making autonomous and deliberative choices directed to good ends that ensured that they could live a truly virtuous life or *eudaimonia*. 'Deliberation is reasoning back from a goal to the action required to implement that goal.'[15] Due to their incapacity for autonomous practical rationality, they were naturally fit to be slaves.[16] Slaves were the property of their masters and so they were incapable of autonomous reasoning or making deliberative choices as they had to do the bidding of the master. Slaves were dependent on their masters for all decision-making. Slaves were mere implements in the hands of the master. They were not able to deliberate independently of the master. Slaves were also only able to realise a limited happiness as servants in the family. They had to accept their station in life.

Similarly for Aristotle, women were also 'imperfectly formed'[17] or misbegotten males and were only able to realise their humanity and happiness in the family context by performing their duty of procreation and child-raising. Women were inferior like slaves but not in the same way. For Aristotle, the non-Greeks treat their wives like slaves but the husband-wife relationship among Greeks was not despotic but rather aristocratic. Women have entitlements in being wives and the raising of children which husbands should not usurp. Relationships between husband and

---

14 Malcolm Heath, 'Aristotle on Natural Slavery,' *Phronesis: A Journal for Ancient Philosophy*' 53, 3 (2008): 243–270.
15 Heath, 'Aristotle on Natural Slavery,' 5.
16 Ibid, 244.
17 Ibid, 256.

wives should therefore be regulated by justice which does not apply to slaves.[18]

Children, in sharp contrast to slaves, were more akin to animals because they were incapable of causal reasoning. However, they differed from animals because children 'grow out of this incapacity'[19] by developing this capacity as adults through being educated. Consequently, Greek society had no problem with the practice of infanticide. Children, especially those born with deformities or handicaps, were left to die next to a statue and to be consumed by dogs or wild beasts. Prominent philosophers like Plato (427–347 BC) and Aristotle (384–322 BC) argued in favour of the practice that unhealthy and defective children should be left to die. Aristotle wrote: 'With regard to the choice between abandoning an infant or rearing it, let there be a law that no crippled child be reared.[20]

This applied to deaf children too and not only those with physical or mental disabilities. Despite this practice, many deaf children survived because deafness was often identified only later in the infant's life when a lack of spoken language development became noticeable.

When we look at scripture, and particularly the New Testament, we see a similar priority given to speech and speechlessness.

Scripture and 'ministry to the deaf'

At the heart of Christian ministry is the desire to be faithful disciples of Jesus Christ. Scripture is the starting point for ministry and mission. Christ served and ministered to people in his life by preaching the coming reign of God, teaching people, healing the sick and the disabled, and exorcising demons. Faithful disciples are called to take heed of Jesus' words: 'I have set you an example, that you should also do as I have done for you' (Jn 13:15).

---

18   Ibid, 256–257.
19   Ibid, 247.
20   Aristotle, *Politics*, 7, 1335b, 20–26, in *The Basic Works of Aristotle*, ed. Richard McKeon (New York: Random House, 1941), 1302.

Salvation for deaf people as miraculous healing

Catholic ministry to the deaf through the ages has been greatly influenced by three gospel passages, namely, Matthew 11:5, Mark 7:32–37 and Mark 9:17–27. In Matthew 11:5, Jesus responded to the question set to him by John the Baptist: 'Are you the one who is to come, or are we to wait for another?' Jesus answered by pointing to the eschatological signs that were being made manifest through his ministry: 'the blind receive their sight, the lame walk, the lepers are cleansed, the deaf hear, the dead are raised, and the poor have good news brought to them (Mt 11:5). God's power breaks into the world through the ministry of Jesus. This theme is one taken over from the Jewish scriptures, especially Isaiah 29:18–19 and 61:1–2. In these passages, it is emphasised that on the day when the Lord God will deliver his people from bondage, not only will the fortunes of Israel be reversed, but also those of the poor, the deaf, the blind, the lame and even the dead.

Similarly, Mark's accounts of Jesus healing the man who is deaf and has a speech impediment (7:31–37) and the boy possessed by a demon that made him speechless (9:17–27) highlighted Jesus' heavenly power to cure the sick and possessed. The emphasis was on Jesus' power to heal and cure the deaf and those with various disabilities. Jesus' miracles were signs of God overturning the disorder of the world and restoring the natural order, the order of being hearing, sighted and able-bodied. Healing the bodily defect was, therefore, equated with sanctity, as following the example of Christ and being close to God.

Healing was not a new theme introduced by Christianity. The earliest medical reference to attempts to cure deafness dates back to the Egyptian Ebers papyrus which was written in 1500 BC. In this papyrus, reference is made to the ancient writings of Imhotep, an Egyptian physician, who lived around 3000 BC.[21] His treatments for deafness included a varied list of injections of olive

---

21 Regi Theodore Enerstvedt, *The Legacy of the Past II: The Development of Education for the Deaf*, (Dronninglund: Nord Press, 1996), 4. Accessed 28 June 2015, www.folk.uio.no/regie/litteratur/index.htm

oil, red lead, bat's wings, ant eggs or goat's urine into the deaf person's ear.

Deafness as a lack of faith or inability to have faith

Another New Testament approach, which also has roots in the Hebrew Bible, is to understand deafness and the deaf metaphorically. Being deaf or blind is used to infer people's lack of faith or their unwillingness to respond to the word of God. It is first used to show Israel's lack of faith in God. Israel's hardness of heart and unwillingness to follow God's law is described in many passages as being deaf to God's commands.

Similarly, in the New Testament writings, the disciples are often described as deaf or blind, meaning that they too lack faith. This is a hearing way of speaking but it impacts negatively on deaf and blind people. John Hull has argued in relation to blindness that these passages have hindered blind people (and the same could be said of the deaf) reading their experience in the scriptures.[22]

Although this displays insensitivity to the Deaf community and those with disabilities, fortunately, it inherited a positive Jewish tradition too.

Law to protect the deaf

The Hebrew Scriptures, in Exodus 4:11, understood disability and deafness as a way of being human. The Lord said to Moses: 'Who gives speech to mortals? Who makes them mute or deaf, seeing or blind? Is it not I, the Lord?' The book of Leviticus provides the first legal provision for the protection of deaf people. 'You shall not revile the deaf or put a stumbling block before the blind; you shall fear your God: I am the Lord (Lev 19:14).' The Hebrew Bible was based on a tradition of protecting the vulnerable and marginalised because the Jewish people were themselves slaves in Egypt who were led out of oppression into greater freedom. They were

---

[22] John M. Hull, 'Open Letter from a Blind Disciple to a Sighted Saviour,' in *Boundaries, Borders and the Bible*, ed. Martin O'Kane (London/New York: Sheffield Academic Press, 2002), 154–177.

excluded, however, from being members of the Temple priests and a Levite.

Except for the exclusion from belonging to the Levites and becoming priests in the Temple, the attitude towards deaf people was 'optimistic, empathetic and positive – deaf people are not cursed, damned or shunted aside; they are to be treated with the respect due to all manifestations of the divine plan.'[23] They were protected by the Torah. Consequently, the Jewish understanding of disability and deafness placed less emphasis on healing and focused rather on the need to provide them with benevolent and compassionate protection.

In this tradition, the vulnerability of the suffering one is acknowledged and respected. It informed Levinas' understanding that the encounter with or the epiphany of the face of the Other was both a plea and a command from height and vulnerability. Levinas wrote:

> The being that expresses itself imposes itself but does so precisely by appealing to me with its destitution and nudity – its hunger – without my being able to be deaf to that appeal.[24]

For Levinas, there is an obligation on the self to respond to the suffering of the vulnerable Other by being hospitable. As we have seen, to act accordingly is, for Levinas, to be saintly and to initiate the ethical relation, where the self is de-centred and responsibility for the marginalised Other is accepted.

The Christian perspective was also littered with other confusions relating to the Deaf community that hindered the development of a more hospitable praxis. We turn to St Paul and St Augustine to reflect further on the Church's ministerial praxis.

---

23 John V. van Cleve and Barry A. Crouch, *A Place of Their Own: Creating the Deaf Community in America*, (Washington DC: Gallaudet University Press, 1989), 2.
24 Levinas, *Totality and Infinity*, 200.

Faith comes from hearing

The early Greek understanding of speech influenced the New Testament. One of the most controversial texts that has affected the deaf negatively is St Paul's saying in Romans 10:17 that 'faith comes from what is heard.' It is worthwhile to read this in the context of the whole quotation: 'So faith comes from what is heard, and what is heard comes through the word of Christ.'

Similarly, in Galatians 3:2 Paul asked the Galatian community if they had received the Holy Spirit through adherence to the Law or through 'the hearing of faith.' Faith is the kind of hearing that internalised and grasped the meaning of the proclaimed word and lived it out. 'Hearing the faith' is a metaphor referring to the faith that came to people through the acceptance of the proclamation and living it out rather than an adherence to following a law or a duty.

Unfortunately, for deaf people, the literal interpretation of Paul's writing in Romans 10:17 that 'faith comes from what is heard' meant that, for many centuries, deaf people were treated as if they were incapable of faith. The source of this misapprehension of St Paul has often been attributed to the writings of St Augustine.

St Augustine (354–430)

St Augustine, the bishop of Carthage in North Africa, was one of the greatest theologians of the Latin Church. He was a convert from Manichaeism and wrote extensively on Christian theology. In his writings, Augustine referred to the deaf twice. The first occasion was to reaffirm the teaching of St Paul that faith comes through hearing (Rom 10:17). In doing so, Lewis pointed out, Augustine seemingly supported the view that deaf people could not become believers.[25]

However, if Augustine's text 'Against Julian' is scrutinised more closely it becomes apparent that this was not his intention. He wrote:

---

25   Hannah Lewis, *Deaf Liberation Theology*, 78.

> You say: 'At the beginning of life, human nature is adorned with the gift of innocence.' We agree wholeheartedly, so far as personal sins are concerned. But, since you also deny that an infant is subject to original sin, you must answer why such great innocence is sometimes born blind; sometimes deaf. Deafness is a hindrance to faith itself, as the Apostle says: 'Faith is from hearing' (Rom 10:17)'.[26]

A closer and more faithful reading of Augustine's text shows that this comment was made in the context of Augustine's polemical debate against the heresy of Pelagianism.[27] Augustine used the example of blindness, deafness and other disabilities to argue against the Pelagianists who held that infants were born without original sin. For Augustine, deafness, blindness and other disabilities in infants were to be understood as not arising from personal sin but rather from being born into a disordered damaged world, one tainted with sin. Baptism was required to ensure that these infants could be saved. Deafness or any disability did not prevent the acquisition of a faith, it only hindered it.

While the text stated that 'deafness was a hindrance to faith,' some commentators interpreted this to mean that the deaf were either incapable of attaining faith or could only be educated using a spoken language and the use of the oral method of deaf education. The corollary to this was to also dismiss the usefulness of sign language, especially in the field of education and Christian worship.

When we consider the other text that Augustine wrote about deaf people and signing, he is very positive about the power of signs.

The second text is much more important: in it, Augustine acknowledged that deaf people used sign language as a means of communication and that they were able to marry and have

---

26 St Augustine, 'Against Julian,' Book 3, Chapter 4, paragraph 10, in *The Fathers of the Church*, vol. 35, ed. Roy Joseph Deferrari (New York: Fathers of the Church, 1957), 115.
27 See E.A.F 'What Did St Augustine Say?' *American Annals of the Deaf* 57, 1 (January 1912): 108–120.

children. In *De quantitate animae* (The magnitude of the soul)[28] written in about 388, Augustine asked Evodius his friend the question:[29] How could a deaf married couple, if they lived in an isolated place, communicate with their hearing son? Evodius responded that they would communicate in sign because both speaking and signing pertain to the soul.[30] Augustine's approval of Evodius' response is significant because it means that communication between people, and not the physical ability to hear and speak, was for Augustine, a determinant of being human. This means that communication by signing was on par with speaking as a determinant of a way to express one's humanity.

This insight is significant especially if seen in conjunction with Augustine's teaching in some of his other writings where he distinguished between natural and intentionally given signs. In *De Doctrina*[31] Augustine distinguished between 'natural signs' and 'given signs.' The natural signs are the audible words we use when we communicate that correspond to what they refer to. When these signs are used in a language for the communication then they become given signs, that is, signs which are intentionally given for the sake of communication. Spoken words are natural signs but a spoken language is a given sign. It is the intentional giving and receiving of signs for communication. For Augustine, even non-verbal forms of communication which take place between people and which are expressed through gestures, like nods of the head, coughs and facial expressions are given signs.

---

28   St Augustine, 'The Magnitude of the Soul (*De quantitate animae*),' in *The Fathers of the Church*, vol. 4, ed. Hermigild Dressler (Washington DC: The Catholic University of America Press, 1947), 51–152.

29   Evodius and Augustine met in Milan when Augustine still lived there. Evodius was already a Christian believer. He agreed to join Augustine in returning to Thagaste in North Africa to start a lay Christian community there. He later became a priest and was made bishop of Uzalis, a town near Carthage.

30   St Augustine, *De quantitate animae*, chapter 18, paragraph 31, 92–93. Also see Lorraine Leeson and Haaris Sheikh, *Experiencing Deafhood: A Snapshot of Five Nations* (Dublin: Interesource Group Publishing, 2010), 90.

31   St Augustine, 'Christian Instruction (*De doctrina Christiana*),' in *The Fathers of the Church*, vol. 2, ed. Roy Joseph Deferrari (Washington DC: The Catholic University of America Press, 1947), 3–235.

Consequently, in Augustine's understanding communication can be realised either through the hearing of spoken words or by the seeing of gestures.

> When we nod, we are giving a sign only to the eyes of the person whom we desire through this sign to make a sharer of our will. Some express ever so much by the movements of the hands. Actors by the motions of their limbs give certain signs to those who understand and, in a certain sense, speak to their eyes ... All these signs are like visible words [*verba visibilia*].[32]

Augustine's theory of signs[33] can be applied to sign language. Augustine's penetrating insight is that signs or gestures can be understood as visible 'words' *verba visibilia*. This is another way of communication rather than just audible words [*verba audibile*]. If Augustine had applied this distinction to a discussion about sign language, it could have opened doors to a healthy appreciation of sign language because signing is itself an intentional giving and receiving of signs for communication. The only difference between spoken languages and sign language is that signing is based on sight rather than on hearing. While Augustine was not thinking of sign language as a *verba visibilia*, it is, nevertheless, compatible with his argument.

Augustine's idea that communication is at the heart of our humanity is a point that has been developed by postmodern philosophers like Levinas and Derrida. We will take a detour, to reflect on Levinas' and Derrida's understanding of language, so that they might help us understand how the Church missed an opportunity in Augustine's statements concerning communication, language, deafness and faith.

---

32 St Augustine, '*De Doctrina Christiana*', Book 2, Chapter 3, paragraph 4, in, *The Fathers of the Church*, vol. 2, ed. Roy Joseph Deferrari, 63.

33 For more information on Augustine's theory of signs, see B. Darrell Jackson, 'The Theory of Signs in St Augustine's *De doctina christiana*,' *Revue d'Etudes Augustiniennes et Patristiques* 15, 1-2 (1969): 9-49.

Levinas' understanding of language and speech

Unlike Aristotle, Emmanuel Levinas' understanding of language and speech is rooted in the interpersonal capacity to communicate and engage in conversation and to dialogue. Levinas pays no attention to the voice or the vocalisation of speech. In his second major work, *Otherwise than Being* (1974), Levinas distinguished between 'the Saying' which existed prior to any linguistic concepts and the content of what can be articulated, which is 'the Said'. How are we to understand this distinction?

When commenting on this distinction between 'the Saying and the Said', Simmons said that it was best understood when compared with the traditional understanding of language.[34] We usually assume that language originates with the speaker who, intending to speak, first formulates thoughts into words and then expresses them. In this traditional formulation, the speaker, or the self, is pre-eminent and the focus is on what the speaker says.[35] In contrast, by emphasising 'the Saying', Levinas began not with the self speaking but rather with the one addressed. He shifted the emphasis from the self to the Other.[36] This shift changed the focus from what was said – the content of communication or what Levinas called 'the Said' – to the encounter with the Other. This encounter happened before anything being said. Before any act of speech, there was always the approach or the encounter with the Other first. Even before any word was uttered, the self was exposed to the Other. The epiphany with the Other happened before any passing on of a message.

> The saying includes not only the content of speech, but the process itself which includes the Thou who is addressed and the speaker as attendant to the spoken word.[37]

This 'Saying', the approach and encounter with the Other, which happened prior to speech, is what Levinas also referred to as

---

[34] William Paul Simmons, 'The Third: Levinas' Theoretical Move from An Archical Ethics to the Realm of Justice and Politics,' *Philosophy and Social Criticism* 25, 6 (1999): 88.
[35] Simmons, 'The Third,' 88.
[36] Ibid.
[37] Ibid.

'proximity'. Proximity is the encounter with the face. The face as the vulnerable one, the suffering one, the oppressed one, the stranger, the widow and the orphan. Proximity to the face or the neighbour called the self into question. The self discovered itself to be unjust. 'The Saying' de-posed, de-centralised and de-situated the self.[38] In Levinas' terminology, the an-archical, the anterior ethical relation or 'the Saying' was otherwise than Being. This new non-ontological foundation of 'the Saying' allowed Levinas to reassert and extol a responsibility that is concrete, infinite and asymmetrical. Before any intentional actions, the self through proximity to the Other was ethically responsible for the Other.

Levinas' understanding of 'the Saying and the Said' highlighted that this encounter exists before anything that is said between the interlocutors. This encounter initiates a conversation where, even without speaking, the Other calls the self, cocooned in its own economy, to accountability. Language is the ethical language and a signification of transcendence and infinity.

> Conversation, from the very fact that it maintains the distance between me and the Other, the radical separation asserted in transcendence which prevents the reconstitution of totality, cannot renounce the egoism of its existence; but the very fact of being in a conversation consists in recognizing in the Other a *right* over this egoism, and hence in justifying itself. Apology, in which the I at the same time asserts itself and inclines before the transcendent, belongs to the essence of conversation.[39]

In and through facing the Other, the self comes to understand language. Language is not discourse, if by discourse, one means the communicating of meaning and the expressing of words between interlocutors. Rather, for Levinas, language is primarily the encounter and the ethical relation between the self and the Other.

This is an asymmetrical relation between the interlocutors, where the self is called to respond to the ethical demand of the

---

38   Ibid, 89.
39   Levinas, *Totality and Infinity*, 40.

face.[40] In this exchange and conversation, the two interlocutors remain independent of each other. The Other approaches the self from a height and infinity that transcends the world of the self. The Other cannot be murdered, that is to be contained or assimilated into the world of the self. The Other is infinite, has a dignity, a transcendence that resists any attempt of the self to grasp or control them. Any attempt by the self to use language to grasp or understand the Other exposes the self's violence. Rather in the encounter with the face, the self is passive.

Rather than assimilate the Other, the self needs to learn from the Other, to listen and engage in discussion. It is important to recognise the error, the injustices committed against the Other, and the prejudices perpetrated against the Other. There is a need to apologise but also to move from being a solitary ego to recognising that it is in a conversation and dialogue with the Other. Hereby the Other is the teacher and the self the learner. When this happens, communication takes place which goes beyond the words spoken. This movement can also involve finding a new land like Abraham, where the differences between the self and the Other can be acknowledged and appreciated. It is not about welcoming the Other into one's own economy, but travelling to a new land, perhaps even the Other's land. For the hearing person, accepting responsibility towards the Deaf Other, would mean accepting the need to learn sign language.

Even though Levinas did not understand language as vocalised discourse, he confusingly used language and speech interchangeably in his writings. In so doing, we showed that he still assumed that language involved a spoken language. In this regard, Jacques Derrida's concept of 'phonocentrism' is a critique that can be applied to Levinas too.

Phonocentrism

The privileging of speech and the vocalisation of sound over other forms of communication, going as far back as Aristotle, has been identified by the French philosopher Jacques Derrida as

---

40   Ibid.

'the most original and powerful ethnocentrism.'[41] For Derrida, phonocentrism is the limiting of language to speech, and thus to the use of the voice and vocalisation, and ignoring other ways of communicating. Language has alterity and so goes beyond merely speech and vocalisation. For Derrida, language can also be expressed through the written word.

H-Dirksen Bauman has applied Derrida's concept of phonocentrism in relation to sign language. He argued that phonocentrism, that is the privileging of speech and orality over sign language, is the main contributing factor to audism.[42]

Derrida saw that the language of the interlocutors does not necessarily need to be a spoken language. The writings of Derrida and Levinas support the idea that Augustine had, that communication is more than what is spoken and heard. It is more than speech. It is about communication between people and learning from the Other. Signs themselves are a form of communication and so 'Sign'[43] is itself a language through which people communicate.

Unfortunately, later theologians never developed Augustine's insights into the world of the deaf in relation to sign language. Augustine was not rooted in the experience of the Deaf community and, so, a golden opportunity to appreciate the value of sign language and to positively influence deaf ministry within the Christian tradition went unnoticed. Hence, the tension and contradiction between speech and sign remained unresolved in Catholic ministry for many centuries.

---

41 Jacques Derrida, *Of Grammatology* (Baltimore: Johns Hopkins University Press, 1976), 3.
42 See H-Dirksen Bauman, 'Listening to Phonocentrism with Deaf Eyes: Derrida's Mute Philosophy of (Sign) Language,' *Essays in Philosophy* 9,1 (2008): 2. Accessed 7 September 2018, http://www.commons.pacific.edu/eip/
43 Sign is capitalised to refer to signed language and to distinguish it from other uses of the word sign. See Oliver Sacks, *Seeing Voices: A Journey into the World of the Deaf* (London: Picador, 1990), xi.

Chapter 4

The Middle Ages (476–1400)

The Middle Ages continued the New Testament's emphases on the healing of the deaf as miraculous and as a metaphor. In this respect, the Middle Ages maintained a totalising attitude towards the deaf person. The pastoral needs of the deaf were largely ignored and a miraculous healing was the only benefit they could receive from the Church. Nevertheless, there were two pockets of hope: firstly, the introduction of the idea that the deaf could be educated, even though little education was done, and secondly, the use of sign language in the monasteries.

St John of Beverley

As we have seen, healing was the primary paradigm for Christian responses to the deaf and disabled communities. This perspective was often tainted with both audist and phonocentric assumptions. For example, St John of Beverley (d. 751), a bishop in Northumbria in England, was remembered for his miraculous healing of a deaf boy. Bede the Venerable described the account of this miraculous healing, in his book *The Ecclesiastical History of England*, but interestingly, placed the emphasis, not on the miraculous powers of healing, but on how St John of Beverley painstakingly taught the young boy how to speak.[44]

Despite the concern for healing something new is being hinted at by St John of Beverley's miraculous cure. This is the education motif. Educating the deaf boy was perceived to be a miracle. This indicated a shift in mentality and consciousness because before this deaf people were thought to be ineducable. The least one can say is that it was not recorded before this time. In this shift, St John of Beverley anticipated the oral method of Deaf education by almost a thousand years.

St Vincent Ferrer (1350–1419)

Another saint in the Middle Ages recognised for his healing ministry was Vincent Ferrer. There were many deaf, blind, lame

---

[44] See Mike Gulliver, 'Bede's St John Less a Healer More a Teacher?' Accessed 7 September 2018, https://mikegulliver.com/2016/10/21/bedes-st-john-less-a-healer-more-a-teacher

and people with other disabilities that Vincent is claimed to have healed. All the healings were attributed to his powerful prayer and intercession. On 29 March 1418, Vincent healed Guillaume de Villiers, a youth stricken dumb as a child, in the presence of the King of Spain[45] Unlike St John of Beverley, Ferrer's contribution remained within the framework of the miraculous. No reference is made to any attempt to educate the child.

Unfortunately, during the Middle Ages, the biblical motif of healing was linked to deafness as a metaphor for faithlessness. This compounded prejudices against the Deaf community.

Being deaf as a metaphor

Theologians, like St Gregory the Great (540–604), used deafness as a metaphor for sin and the deaf as a metaphor for the sinner's lack of faith. In his sermon on Mark 7:31–37, Gregory spoke about sinners as the spiritually deaf and dumb, 'who do not, because they will not, hear those things that belong to their great and eternal interest.'[46] Distinguishing between the corporally deaf and the spiritually deaf, Gregory said:

> To be corporally deaf, so as not to hear what is said, is a very great misfortune and deserves compassion, though there is nothing criminal in it. But a wilfully spiritual deafness, and an obstinate refusing to hearken to what is said, is more than a misfortune: it is a voluntary crime.[47]

Gregory spoke about remedies that needed to be put in place to cure the spiritually deaf and dumb with regular recourse to the sacrament of penance. It is there that Jesus will put his fingers in their ears and touch their tongue and say the powerful words: *Ephphetha*, be opened. Even though Gregory the Great had the

---

45 See Stanislaus Hogan, *Saint Vincent Ferrer OP* (London/New York: Longmans, Green and Company, 1911), 80–81.
46 Pope Gregory the Great, 'Homily on Mark 7:31–37.' Accessed 8 September 2018, https://thedivinelamp.wordpress.com/2011/08/22/sunday-august-28-pope-st-gregory-the-greats-homily-on-mark-731-37/
47 Pope Gregory the Great, 'Homily on Mark 7:31–37.'

best of intentions in using deafness as a metaphor, the negative connection between deaf as sinner was unfortunately reinforced.

Within a hearing context, however, gestures and even a form of sign language were used in the monasteries. This was another pocket of hope where the Church could discover a deeper appreciation for the natural sign language of deaf people too.

Monastic sign languages

The Rule of St Benedict called upon monks who took vows of poverty, chastity and obedience to live in silence. The monastic silence was maintained to emphasise that prayer depends on an interior attitude of silence. It was not to show that speech was wrong but rather witness to how speech, like wealth, sexuality, power and self-determination, can be misused or abused.

Under the Cluniac reform of the Benedictine monasticism established at Cluny in France in 910, the monks developed a system of manual signs for both communicating with each other and maintaining monastic silence.[48] By 1100, the Cluniac signs had spread to other monasteries throughout France, southern England and Germany.

Monastic sign language was taken over by the Cistercians, with the establishment of their reformed Benedictine monasteries. In 1152, the Cistercian General Chapter listed the punishments to be meted out to those who chose words over signs during meals. The novice master had to instruct novices in sign language too.[49] While they borrowed Cluniac signs, they also developed their own.

> By the thirteenth century, the use of manual signs in place of spoken words had become a common aspect of monastic discipline in Cistercian abbeys and remained so until the end of the Middle Ages and beyond.[50]

---

48 Scott Bruce, 'The Origins of Cistercian Sign Language,' *Cîteaux: Commetarii cistercienses* 52 (2001): 199.
49 Bruce, 'The Origins of Cistercian Sign Language,' 203.
50 Ibid, 208.

While the monks used these signs in their monasteries, speech was still privileged over natural sign languages. The phonocentric bias was never questioned even by the monks themselves who lived in monasteries where sign language was accepted and used daily. Nevertheless, some Deaf women and men like Teresa de Cartegena and El Mudo did reflect on being Deaf and possibly even learn sign language while living in monasteries.

Teresa de Cartegena: Being deaf as a spiritual grace

The first known expression of the gift of being deaf was articulated by Teresa de Cartegena (b. circa 1415). Little is known about Teresa except that she was born into a 'Judeo-conversio' family, the de Cartegena/Santa Maria family from Burgos. Her grandfather converted to Christianity from Judaism in about 1390 and later he became bishop of Cartegena in 1402 and bishop of Burgos ten years later.

Teresa and her brothers were all well-educated, probably at home as one may expect in a wealthy family. Teresa says she was educated at the University of Salamanca before becoming deaf. More than likely she stayed in a convent and was tutored by someone from the university – as women were not usually allowed to study at university – a privilege at that time reserved for men only.

The most transformative experience of her life was her going deaf. Twenty years after becoming deaf, she wrote her first treatise called the *Grove of the Infirm*. In this book, she described the traumatic experience she underwent in being cut off from the hearing world around her and being enveloped in a world of silence and solitude. At first, it felt like an exile from the world she knew and the family she loved, but gradually she realised it was a school in how to distance oneself from worldly chatter and the preoccupation with worldly cares. It was a school of spirituality and prayer.

Through her suffering, Teresa saw herself being led by God to himself and released from all worldly distractions. She was invited and led by God, who tugging on her mantle, led her to a rich supper – the marriage supper of the Lamb (Rev 19:9).[51] Her deafness, she began to experience was God's gentle tugging at her mantle was a call to recognise that it is given for her good, enabling her to find the path of virtue.[52] This awareness effected a complete transformation of her self-understanding and relationship with God, a metanoia. This was to enable her to accept and embrace her being deaf as a gift and find peace within herself. Thus, the second half of her treatise to devoted to the virtue of patience. She elaborates on the patience required to suffer with prudence. It is by cultivating of patience that one grows in the prudence required to live a holy life.

Teresa's second treatise, *Wonder at the Works of God*, was written to challenge those people who doubted that she wrote the *Grove of the Infirm*. They believed that only men knew how to write books so she could not have written this book herself. She contradicted them saying those who think that a woman is incapable of writing a book doubt God's grace and generosity. She wrote:

> People marvel at what I wrote in the treatise and I marvel at what, in fact, I kept quiet, but I do not marvel doubting nor do I insist on my wonder. For my experience makes me sure, and God of truth knows that I had no other master or consulted with any other learned authority nor translated from other books, as some people with malicious wonder are wont to say. Rather, this alone is the truth: that God of all knowledge, Lord of all virtues, Father of mercy, God of every consolation, He who consoles us all in our tribulation, He alone taught me, He alone read (to) me.[53]

In this second treatise, Teresa challenged the prejudices of her time and argued that if God can work through the gifts of men, so too God's grace can work through the writings of a woman, even a deaf woman. This extraordinary woman of the fifteenth century

---

51   Teresa de Cartegena, 'Grove of the Infirm,' in *The Writings of Teresa de Cartegena*, ed. Dayle Seidenspinner-Nunez (Cambridge: DS Brewer, 1998), 39.
52   Teresa de Cartegena, 'Grove of the Infirm,' 45.
53   Teresa de Cartegena, 'Wonder at the Works of God,' 102-103.

was able to articulate a theology of being deaf and give courage and hope to others similarly afflicted. While Teresa operated from a theology of deafness as an affliction, she never prayed for healing. Instead, she counselled the need to accept being deaf and see it as a 'gift' from God who used her deafness to lead her to deeper spiritual insight and self-appreciation.

While Teresa de Cartegena was educated before going deaf, her experience points to a shift happening at the time. There was a greater realisation that deaf people could be educated. She stands at a turning point from a natural law perspective to a more modern one, where human beings should be appreciated for their gifted individuality and be instilled with dignity even though they may be deaf or a woman. This new perspective was to have enormous long-term benefits for the Deaf community.

The Renaissance period (1450–1700)

The Renaissance marked the period of the re-birth of interest in classical culture among artists and scientists from the mid-fifteenth century until the end of the seventeenth century. It was also the period within which the beginnings of Deaf education emerged in Europe.

Girolamo Cardano (1501–1576)

During the Renaissance, Girolamo Cardano, an Italian physicist and mathematician, was the first person to lobby for the education of deaf people. He wrote that the deaf person 'when reading, hears, and when writing, speaks.'[54] This was a vital shift away from healing to education. The formal education of deaf people began to be envisaged. One of the first beneficiaries of this new type of thinking was possibly a deaf Spanish artist known as El Mudo (The Mute).

---

54 Savino Castiglione, 'Deaf People in the World: Between the Past and the Present,' *Dolentium Hominum* 73 (2010): 14.

El Mudo (1526–1579)

There is no indication that Cardano's views had influenced the monks of Spain who taught a deaf man known as El Mudo, or the mute. His baptismal name was Juan Fernandez Navarette. In sixteenth-century Spain, he was appointed as the court artist to Philip II of Spain.[55] He knew sign language but could also read, as well as write, and he knew history and Scripture. It is not clear where he learnt all of this. It could well have been in a monastery, as from an early age he had lived in the monastery of La Estella at Logroño in Spain. These monks were from the enclosed Order of St Jerome, also known as the Hieronymites, and kept a life of silence.

It was most certainly in the monastery that he was educated and learnt to draw and paint. He was trained by one of the monks, Vicente de Santo Domingo. He went to Italy to study art and was greatly influenced by the works of Titian and Bassano. He spent over 20 years there before returning to Spain in 1568, where he was appointed the court painter for Philip II. Juan Fernandez Navarette or El Mudo was a well-educated deaf person, who knew how to sign but not speak. Due to the monastery being one where silence is a primary value the monks probably tended to sign rather than speak and so El Mudo signed rather than spoke.

Surprisingly, sign language was making much more impact on a small island off the United States' coast, which was an example of Deaf Gain and the value of sign language. This had no relation to the Catholic Church but it was an example of what was possible when there is proximity to the face.

Martha's Vineyard

In the United States in 1640 an island called Martha's Vineyard was inhabited by Protestant immigrants from Kent in south-east England. What is particularly striking about this community is that it was comprised of a high percentage of Deaf people. The net effect was that virtually everyone on the island became bilingual. Islanders knew how to both speak English and to sign. Many of the signs used originated from Kent which meant that there was

---

55   Leeson and Sheik, *Experiencing Deafhood*, 26.

a strong affinity between British Sign Language (BSL) and the version used on the island.[56] Sometimes hearing people were seen signing to each other and not only in their interactions with a Deaf person. It is significant that 'when both hearing and Deaf are able to sign together, no-one is handicapped at all.'[57]

This is the first recorded account of a community of hearing and deaf people who used sign language without prejudice, without phonocentric and audistic attitudes. A new relationship between the hearing and the deaf existed where totality was breached and the ethical relation honoured.

Within the Catholic Church, education was to prove to be both an obstacle and a boon to deaf people. It opened up the door to limited empowerment of the deaf and was certainly a positive move away from the Aristotelian neglect of deaf people.

Pedro Ponce de Leon OSB (1520–1584)

Spanish Benedictine monk, Pedro Ponce de Leon tried to systematise the education of wealthy deaf individuals. This was to have serious implications for the pastoral practice of the Church in the following centuries when many schools for the deaf were established.

Pedro Ponce de Leon was born in Valladolid in Spain and was educated in Salamanca. He became a Benedictine monk at the monastery at Oña, near Burgos in northern Spain. Ponce de Leon taught the sons of noble families in Spain how to speak, read and write. This was required so that they would be able to receive their inheritance. According to the Justinian legal code that had influenced Spanish law, those who were deaf and were unable to speak were limited in their legal rights.[58] Only deaf people

---

56   Ladd, *Understanding Deaf Culture*, 101.
57   Ladd, *Understanding Deaf Culture*, 102.
58   In 530 AD, the Roman Emperor Justinian classified the legal rights of deaf people through laws he passed. These laws have become known as the Justinian Code. In these laws, speechlessness was considered an impediment to citizenship. The Code, therefore, distinguished between three different groups of deaf people. Firstly, it identified those born deaf and dumb and who had no legal rights or any obligations whatsoever. Guardians were to be appointed to control their affairs. Secondly, there were those who became deaf

who could speak had full legal rights. For example, if the family heir was deaf and unable to speak, the family then risked losing its estates.[59]

Ponce de Leon's first students were two brothers, Francisco and Pedro de Velasco. He began by teaching them how to write the names of various objects. From there he taught them how to articulate these written words. In this way, they were able to acquire the Spanish language. There is no evidence of his using a manual alphabet, but there is an indication that he used signs with which to communicate with his deaf pupils. As previously discussed, the Benedictine and Cistercian monks used signs in their monasteries to communicate with each other so that they would not break the solemn silence necessary for a contemplative life. In Oña, a fifteenth-century manuscript shows that the community used about 360 signs.[60] This would indicate that Pedro Ponce de Leon was familiar with the use of signs. However, the weight for Ponce de Leon lay heavier on the side of speech than sign.

Ponce de Leon is credited with being the first teacher of the deaf and the founder of the oral method of education. However, a distinction needs to be made between education and the teaching of speech. Ponce de Leon was more interested in the teaching of speech and not necessarily providing education of the deaf. However, Leeson and Sheikh acknowledged that despite some reservations, there was a definite shift in attitude. They maintain that 'this shift recognises that deaf people have the same intellectual abilities as hearing people.'[61]

---

and dumb after birth and who had learnt how to write. They were permitted to marry and to conduct their own affairs through the means of writing. Thirdly, there were those who were deaf from birth but not dumb. Included in this category were those who became deaf while being born but were not dumb. These were assumed to have the use of language and, therefore, had no legal restrictions placed upon them. They were treated just like hearing people who could not speak. They had all the rights of hearing people. For more information, see Leeson and Skeikh, *Experiencing Deafhood*, 89–90.

59 Leeson and Sheikh, *Experiencing Deafhood*, 25.
60 Ibid, 26.
61 Ibid, 27.

Ponce de Leon's work was ground-breaking at the time. However, it remained tied to phonocentric thinking and audism. Deaf people's alterity was not recognised but this was a move in a better direction. They were taught to speak and were educated to a limited degree. They were enabled at least to inherit property and were not condemned to a life of poverty and dependency on the welfare of others.

Recent research has raised the possibility that Pedro de Velasco may have been ordained a priest. Portolano has argued that research focused more on Ponce de Leon's educational methods rather than whether Pedro de Velasco did get ordained. 'Certainly, the educational methods are important, but just as important – and a great deal more surprising – would be any indication that a congenitally deaf man became a priest in the sixteenth century.'[62]

Ponce de Leon's work inspired others to teach the deaf. One of these was another Spaniard, Juan Pablo Bonet.

Juan Pablo Bonet (c. 1573–1633)

Juan Pablo Bonet published the first book on how to teach speech to deaf pupils. He sought to teach deaf people how they could learn a spoken language using various means like fingerspelling – also known as dactylology – the use of signs or gestures, as well as reading and writing. His method included teaching the sounds of each letter of the alphabet. Thereafter, his pupils were encouraged to develop a vocabulary of nouns, verbs, conjunctions, adverbs and prepositions. It was his idea that deaf people needed to develop the use of a spoken language so that they could develop intellectually. He also encouraged lip-reading.

He influenced several educationalists such as Sir Kenelm Digby, John Bulwer and John Wallis who began to employ his methods in England.[63] Most of the deaf people who received an education throughout the seventeenth century were the sons of

---

62 Portolano, *Be Opened!*, 25. For more detailed discussion on Pedro de Velasco, see Portolano, *Be Opened!*, 23–26.
63 See Kenneth W Hodgson, *The Deaf and Their Problems: A Study in Special Education* (London: Watts and Co, 1953), 95–104.

the wealthy. This was to change later in the eighteenth century. In the Catholic Church, another saint was continuing where St John of Beverley left off in the eighth century, namely, St Francis de Sales.

St Francis de Sales (1567–1622)

Francis de Sales was considered the protector of the deaf because he was regarded to have healed a young deaf boy called Martin in 1605. In fact, Francis de Sales was involved in catechising the boy more than in healing him. They communicated with each other in sign language. De Sales did not teach him to speak a spoken language but learnt sign language. Portolano pointed out it was very likely 'that de Sales learnt Martin's natural sign language and then, in the process of communication, expanded it with new religious signs to teach him the mysteries of faith. Within a year, Martin had learned enough to receive his first Holy Communion, and after two years he was confirmed.'[64]

After his canonisation by Pope Pius XII, St Francis de Sales was made the patron saint for pastoral care of the Deaf community. However, unlike Ponce de Leon and Bonet, De Sales never developed a system of education. This development emerged in the following century and was a major shift in the emancipation of all deaf people, not just the rich.

The Enlightenment period (1700–1815)

The Enlightenment is marked by the shift in human consciousness that was ushered in by the thinking of René Descartes. Descartes believed that all human beings were distinctive individuals with their own self-awareness and conscience. In the Western world, people became aware that they were 'more than just a cog in the machine.'[65] They were individuals imbued with dignity with their own inner life and giftedness.

For many thinkers of the enlightenment, education and schools were important institutions for bringing light to darkened

---

64 Portolano, *Be Opened!*, 41.
65 Broesterhuizen, 'Pastoral Ministry With the Deaf,' 2.

minds. A major shift was that it was not just restricted to the wealthy and middle class, even the poor needed to be educated. Education was salvation.

This had an important impact on Catholic and Christian understandings of ministry. According to Marcel Broesterhuizen, this awareness of people's individuality made it:

> unbearable that in Christian communities and villages, there were persons baptised who were not able to receive the Christian message and the sacraments: outsiders not only in the hearing society but also in the hearing church.[66]

There was a pastoral goal to Deaf education and that was to ensure that the Christian message and the sacramental life of the Catholic Church were accessible to deaf people. Again, the tension between speech and sign was evident and intensified. It centred around two Christian pastors, one a French Catholic priest Abbé de l'Épée and the other, a German Lutheran pastor, Samuel Heinecke.

Abbé de l'Épée (1712–1789) and manualism

Charles-Michel de l'Épée was born at Versailles in France. After receiving his education, he desired to become a priest. However, he was not accepted for ordination because he was a Jansenist, an ascetic theology based on the writings of the Dutch theologian Cornelius Jansen. He tried studying law but did not find this inspiring. He returned to the idea of being a priest and recanted his adherence to Jansenism. The Bishop of Troyes ordained him.

During his pastoral ministry, he met two young girls whom he greeted and with whom he attempted to speak, but they did not answer. The mother explained that the girls were deaf and had been receiving tuition from another priest, Père Vanin. Unfortunately, this priest had died and so their education had been halted. Abbé de l'Épée decided to teach them himself. Instead of using Vanin's method of teaching using pictures, de l'Épée decided to use signs and the manual alphabet. He was concerned that the children also did not know their catechism and were not

---

66   Ibid.

educated in their faith. He wanted to ensure that they were not only educated but also catechised.

De l'Épée established the first school for the deaf in Paris for deaf children from poor families. It was called the Institute for Deaf-mutes. He took on 60 children and often provided for these children from his own pocket. Teachers prior to him emphasised speech but de l'Épée emphasised the importance of a good education through the medium of his methodical signs. De l'Épée developed his methodical signs from those used by a deaf child but his signs were not strictly speaking a natural sign language. He changed the signs to what he called methodical signs and used them along the grammatical structure of French rather than using the grammatical structure inherent in sign language itself. He did this because he wanted the deaf children to be able to write in good French. De l'Épée used an oral-based sign language which could be called a version of Signed French.

De l'Épée's ministry was a breakthrough for Catholic Deaf education. For the first time, there was an attempt to minister to deaf people who were not just from wealthy families. De l'Épée was able to recognise deaf people in their alterity, as no one had before him. He was able to devise an educational system in methodical signs, which changed the face of Deaf education. Although he was not able to move beyond phonocentrism, de l'Épée's achievements were remarkable for his time. His life marked a new chapter in Catholic deaf ministry and one where the experience of deaf people was taken seriously. De l'Épée is revered for being the founder of the manual approach to Deaf education.

We now move to the work of a Protestant pastor, Samuel Heinecke, who became known as the founder of the oral method of Deaf education.

Samuel Heinicke and oralism (1727–1790)

Samuel Heinicke was born on 14 April 1727 in Nautschütz in the Electorate of Saxony in the eastern part of Germany. He began tutoring students in 1754 to earn a living. One of his students was a young deaf boy. Heinicke used a manual alphabet to teach his deaf pupil. By 1768, he was teaching other deaf children in Eppendorf and he became well-known as a successful teacher of the deaf. His methodology was to use writing and signing at the beginning until the pupil understood German. He was greatly influenced by the Swiss teacher of the deaf, Amman. As a result, he encouraged the use of lip-reading and taught pupils how to speak. He taught them to speak by having them feel the vibrations in the throat. He was adamant that it was having access to a spoken language that enabled deaf children to be educated properly.

Samuel Heinicke was in regular contact with Abbé Charles de l'Épée and corresponded with him by letter.[67] These letters reveal the controversy which has become known as the methods debate: manualism versus oralism.[68] Heinicke was very critical of the manual approach and 'insisted on the transcendent significance of sound.'[69] He even claimed that people dream in sound and through a spoken language, and so he denounced signs as useless and proclaimed oral methods as the only means by which to instruct deaf pupils.[70]

In 1777, Heinicke opened the first oral school for the deaf in Leipzig. Its original name was the 'Electoral Saxon Institute for Mutes and Other Persons Afflicted with Speech Defects'. The school exists to this day and is known as the Samuel Heinicke School for the Deaf.[71]

It was after the French Revolution that the educational revolution among the deaf really expanded rapidly.

The emergence of the Deaf community and their culture after the French Revolution

With the French Revolution, came the flourishing of Enlightenment ideas. De l'Épée died in 1789 at the beginning of the Revolution. During the Revolution, many loyal Catholics were persecuted for their faith because they were seen as royalists and

---

[67] Hodgson, *The Deaf and Their Problems*, 136.
[68] Enverstedt, *The Legacy of the Past*, 58.
[69] Ibid.
[70] Ibid.
[71] Jamie Berke, 'Samuel Heinicke, Father of Oral Education.' Accessed 11 February 2018, https://www.verywell.com/samuel-heinicke-oral-education-1046549

against the Revolution. Abbé Sicard, one of de l'Épée's disciples, was not one of these. In 1790, the revolutionary Commission of the Academy appointed Sicard to succeed de l'Épée at the Paris Institute. He was given a government grant for the expenses of the school and was excused from taking an oath of allegiance to the Civil Constitution.[72] However, in 1792, Sicard ran into trouble with the authorities and was arrested with two other priests. He managed to escape but the other two did not and were executed. Massieu, one of Sicard's deaf pupils, petitioned the National Assembly to have Sicard pardoned. This was granted and Sicard went back to teaching his deaf pupils.[73]

The Revolution inspired Deaf people to grow in dignity and gave them the space and freedom to experiment. Many of the new developments that transpired after the Revolution, happened outside the influence of the Church. Hearing artists trained these deaf artists who were able to exhibit their art in public. One Deaf artist, Claude Deseine, became famous and was commissioned to do busts of Voltaire, Rousseau, Mirabeau, Danton and Robespierre.[74]

Some Deaf people wrote popular political pamphlets[75] and were soldiers in the Revolutionary Army. This showed that Deaf people were becoming politically aware and active in advancing the ideals of the Revolution. Consequently, France became the first country to recognise Deaf people as 'children of the nation' and started the first publicly funded school for the deaf.[76]

In 1834, Berthier established the first Deaf national organisation called the *Societe Centrale des Sourds-Muets*. This society met every year on Abbé de l'Épée's birthday for a banquet to celebrate sign language.[77]

The flourishing of education for the deaf in both its manual and oral forms continued to grow and develop throughout the

---

72 Hodgson, *The Deaf and Their Problems*, 133.
73 Ibid, 134.
74 Ladd, *Understanding Deaf Culture*, 106.
75 Ibid, 108. Ladd refers to Pierre Desloges who composed the first Deaf text in 1779. He was a devoted Jacobin.
76 Ladd, *Understanding Deaf Culture*, 106.
77 Lewis, *Deaf Liberation Theology*, 22.

nineteenth century and many schools for the deaf, both manual and oral, were established throughout the world.

The flourishing of Deaf education (1815–1880)

While de l'Épée was enormously influential in France, his ideas and methods spread to North America, as well as to Italy, the Netherlands, and to Ireland. From Ireland, de l'Épée's methods reached the shores of South Africa and Australia.

Deaf education in the United States[78]

One of the most influential families involved in Deaf education in the United States was a Protestant family, the Gallaudet family.[79] They were of French Huguenot descent.[80] In 1815, Thomas Hopkins Gallaudet came to France to study Deaf education under Abbé Sicard at the Paris Institute. There he met Laurent Clerc, a Deaf Catholic teacher, and the two of them returned to the United States. On the boat trip back, Clerc taught Gallaudet sign language and Gallaudet taught Clerc English.[81]

With the assistance of Laurent Clerc, who had worked with Abbé Sicard, Thomas Gallaudet went to Hartford in 1817 and started a deaf school there called the American School for the Deaf.[82] This school promoted the education of deaf pupils through sign language.

Thomas Gallaudet's son, Edward Miner Gallaudet established the first Deaf college in the United States. When it was established on 8 April 1864, it was called the 'Columbia Institution for the Deaf and Dumb and the Blind.'[83] The combined method of instruction was used. This included signing and fingerspelling

---

78   For a comprehensive history of Deaf education in the United States, see Harlan Lane, *When the Mind Hears: A History of the Deaf* (New York: Random House, 1984).
79   Enverstedt, *The Legacy of the Past II*, 67.
80   Hodgson, *The Deaf and Their Problems*, 181.
81   Enverstedt, *The Legacy of the Past II*, 68.
82   The school was originally known as the American Asylum for the Education and Instruction of Deaf and Dumb Persons. See Enverstedt, *The Legacy of the Past II*, 68.
83   Enverstedt, *The Legacy of the Past II*, 70.

with speech and lip-reading. However, the name was changed in 1894 to the Gallaudet College. Today, it is known as Gallaudet University. It remains the only deaf university in the world. The manual approach to Deaf education was dominant in the United States until the establishment of the Lexington School in New York and the Clarke School in Northampton, Massachusetts in 1867. These were both purely oral schools.[84]

The first Catholic school for the deaf started in the United States was the St Joseph's Institute for the Deaf in St Louis, Missouri in 1837. The Sisters of St Joseph of Carondolet started it.[85] This school used the oral method of Deaf education.

Catholic Deaf education

Besides the United States, de l'Épée's method influenced the establishment of many Catholic schools for the deaf throughout Europe. Among them were schools for the deaf established in Italy, the Sint-Michielsgested Institute for the Deaf in the Netherlands, and in Ireland, St Mary's School for the Deaf in Dublin, run by the Cabra Dominican Sisters.

Catholic Deaf education in Italy

The Catholic Church was integral to the development of Deaf education in Italy. The first school for the deaf in Italy was established in 1784 in Rome by Abbate Silvestri who trained under de l'Épée. In 1828, another priest Tommaso Pendola started a deaf school in Siena also using the manual approach.

In 1867, Abba Serfino Balestra (1834–86), a deaf teacher in Como, visited a deaf school in Rotterdam in the Netherlands that used the oral method.[86] He returned to Italy a convert to oralism. Another priest in Milan, Abba Giulio Tarra, also became a convinced oralist through growing sense of dissatisfaction with the combined method of signs and speech that he had been

---

84 Enverstedt, *The Legacy of the Past II*, 69.
85 For more information, visit www.csjcarondelet.org/educational-institutions/
86 Hodgson, *The Deaf and Their Problems*, 241.

using. In 1870, he decided to abandon signing and focused only on speech and lip-reading.

Unlike the practice in France, most of the schools for the deaf in Italy used the oral method of Deaf education.

Catholic Deaf education in the Netherlands[87]

The Dutch priest Martinus van Beek, with the encouragement of his bishop, Den Dubbelden, began the Institute for the Deaf in Sint-Michielsgested in 1840.[88] Until then, the only school for the deaf in the country was the Guyot Institute in Groningen, a liberal Protestant school.

Van Beek wanted the Catholic deaf children to be educated and know the basic tenets of their Catholic faith. He decided to start a Catholic deaf school along the lines of de l'Epée's school in Paris. Later the school became strongly oralist under Fr Antonio van Uden.

Catholic Deaf education in Ireland[89]

An Irish Vincentian priest, Fr Thomas McNamara CM, was concerned about the lack of religious instruction for deaf Irish children. He wrote to the bishops of Ireland in 1845 requesting support for the establishment of a school for the deaf. It took six years to raise the necessary funds to run the school. He had also asked the Dominican nuns in Cabra to take over the school. These nuns were a Second Order or contemplative congregation of the Dominican sisters. They agreed and sent two nuns and two deaf pupils to a school for the deaf in Caen in Normandy to study their approach to Deaf education. They set out on 11 January 1846. This school in Caen had been started by Abbé Jamet in 1816. Jamet had trained with Abbé Sicard at the Paris Institute for the Deaf.

---

87 For a comprehensive summary of Deaf education in the Netherlands in the nineteenth century, see Corrie Tijsseling and Agnes Tellings, 'The Christian's Duty Toward the Deaf: Differing Christian View on Deaf Schooling and Education in 19th Century Dutch Society,' *American Annals of the Deaf* 154, 1 (2009): 36–49.
88 Tijsseling and Tellings, 'The Christian's Duty Toward the Deaf,' 39–42.
89 The information for this section was taken from Fitzgerald and Andrew, *Open Minds Open Hearts*, 37–42.

The nuns and pupils returned in August 1846. There were already 15 pupils ready to start school in September 1846 at the new school that was given the name, St Mary's Institution for the Deaf and Dumb. By 1850, the school had already grown to 50 pupils. The method of education in the school was strictly in Irish Sign Language (ISL) and Signed English.

The Cabra Dominican nuns sent sisters to South Africa and Australia. These nuns started the first Catholic schools for the deaf in both these countries. Two students from St Mary's, Ellen Hogan and Bridget Lyne, were to make an enormous contribution to Deaf education in Australia and South Africa respectively. The early beginnings in South Africa will be recounted in the next chapter.

Catholic Deaf education in Australia

In 1875, a Deaf Dominican sister, Sr Mary Gabriel Hogan was sent to Australia from Ireland to start the first Catholic school for the deaf in Maitland near Newcastle in New South Wales. This was an expression of great confidence in deaf people that Hogan could be entrusted with such an important task and mission.

Hogan was a previous pupil of St Mary's Institution for the Deaf and Dumb in Dublin.[90] Born as Ellen Hogan in Dublin, Ireland in 1842, she started school at St Mary's on 1 December 1851 at the age of 9. Due to scarlet fever, she became profoundly deaf at the age of seven. By this stage she was already proficient in written and spoken English. She remained at the school until 1864, becoming qualified as a teacher's assistant. Contrary to the dictates of the time, she was later able to become a qualified teacher which meant she became a choir sister and was not forced to be a lay sister. She entered the convent and was professed in 1867, the first Deaf woman to take this route with the Cabra Dominican nuns.

In 1875, Sr Hogan arrived in Australia to start up and teach at the Maitland school. Being deaf and starting a school for the deaf was not as unusual in the nineteenth century as it would seem. The first two schools for the deaf in Australia were founded by two deaf men. In 1860, Thomas Pattison started a school in

---

90   Fitzgerald and Andrew, *Open Minds Open Hearts*, 42–53.

Sydney and Frederick John Rose started one in Melbourne. Many schools in Europe and North America were also employing deaf teachers. Frederick John Rose had been trained at the Old Kent Road School for the Deaf in England where, between 1841 and 1842, there had been nine deaf teachers in the school and only three hearing teachers.[91]

Chaplaincies for the deaf

Except for Italy and the United States, most of the Catholic schools for the deaf took their inspiration from de l'Épée's Paris Institute. His influence during the nineteenth century was extensive although this was to change. The golden era of the flourishing of sign language and deaf teachers in schools for the deaf was to be reversed with the triumph of audism and phonocentrism. This was first noticeable in the chaplaincies for the deaf where hearing chaplains asserted their authority over their deaf flock and turned back the gains made by the deaf themselves.

St Francis de Sales and Abbé de l'Épée were pioneers in developing the deaf ministry beyond the school. They were concerned with the faith life of the deaf and not merely their education. They wanted to ensure that deaf children and adults have access to the sacramental life of the Church.

There is very little documentation of Catholic chaplaincies to the deaf in the Catholic Church during the nineteenth century. More extensive work has been done on the ministries in the Anglican Church[92] and Evangelical churches[93] in England. This research has demonstrated that the involvement of deaf people in establishing missions in Britain was much more extensive than previously thought.[94] The most striking account is of Charles Davis who started the Stoke-on-Trent mission in 1868.[95] He had been a cobbler but had developed his own shop into a meeting place

---

91 Branson and Miller, *Damned for Their Difference*, 142–143.
92 See Lewis, *Deaf Liberation Theology*, 39–60.
93 See Esme Cleall, '"Deaf to the Word": Gender, Deafness and Protestantism in Nineteenth-Century Britain and Ireland,' *Gender & History* 25, 3 (November 2013): 590–603.
94 Lewis, *Deaf Liberation Theology*, 43–49.
95 Ibid, 47.

for adult deaf people. He had a mission to find other deaf adults, teaching them sign language and knowledge of Christ. There were at least two other missions started by deaf people themselves.[96] Branson and Miller have typified this period as one of great flourishing for Deaf people and Deaf communities in many parts of the world with schools with deaf teachers and churches with deaf missioners.[97] This is particularly the case in the Anglican Church and the Evangelical churches.

> The early DEAF-CHURCH[98] of the mid-nineteenth century was largely non-denominational and a place where religious minded Deaf men were responsible for their own worship of God and preaching the Gospel to other Deaf people. It was a place where two Deaf men were heading for ordination in the 1880s and an all-Deaf management committee flourished. It was a place where Deaf people could meet together, use their language, and relax in their culture; the origin not only of DEAF-CHURCH but also of the adult community of the DEAF-WORLD itself. It was a place where some attempts were made to fight for the right of Deaf people to training and employment.[99]

It would be interesting to know what transpired within the Catholic Church where it is not as easy for lay people to start a church and deaf men were still excluded from ordination. Catholic Deaf communities existed but they would have been served by hearing priests, who signed. The extent to which they would have allowed Deaf initiative is still to be researched.

Nevertheless, even though Catholic chaplains knew sign language and used it extensively in ministry, as Broesterhuizen pointed out, they still were under the misconception that deafness was a defect. Deafness as a defect required a remedy and so this meant that deaf people were never seen as the equal of hearing

---
96 Ibid, 47.
97 Branson and Miller, *Damned for Their Difference*, 143–145.
98 Writing words in capitals like DEAF-CHURCH or DEAF-WORLD is a Deaf way of transcribing or writing down signs called 'Gloss'. When written in this manner it refers to a sign or a Deaf concept which is represented by a sign.
99 Lewis, *Deaf Liberation Theology*, 48.

people. Consequently, they saw the education of the deaf and ministry to the deaf as 'a work of mercy and charity.'[100] They were always seen as inferior to hearing people and in need of their mercy and charity. Broesterhuizen gave the example of a Deaf man, Antonius Megens, who taught sign language at Martinus van Beek's Institute for the Deaf in the Netherlands. In the school annals, Megens was praised for his intelligence and command of sign language and yet was also listed in the annals as a nursed patient, not a teacher.[101]

Lewis argued that prominent Anglican chaplains or missioners for the deaf held similar attitudes. The chaplaincies for the deaf in England were established by hearing people to ensure that deaf people were catechised and Christianised. For example, Rev. Samuel Smith, an Anglican missionary, started a mission to the deaf in 1851. He was concerned about the lack of faith among deaf people referring to 'the uneducated deaf and dumb as savages, atheists and heathens.'[102] Once they went to school, learnt to speak the English language and received some scriptural teaching, they were considered ready to attend church.

Despite the period of Deaf renaissance from the beginning to the mid-nineteenth century, a shift started happening in Church and society. There was a move against the use of sign language in education and therefore also the employment of deaf teachers. For example, in 1841, the Old Kent School in England had a predominance of deaf over hearing teachers, this predominance was to be reversed ten years later. By 1851, there were eight hearing teachers in the school and only four deaf teachers. What accounted for this shift?

Deaf education in the nineteenth century: Evolutionism and eugenics

The nineteenth century saw the flourishing of Deaf education in both its oral and manual forms throughout the world. Schools sprang up throughout Europe, North America, as well

---

100 Broesterhuizen, 'Pastoral Ministry With the Deaf,' 2.
101 Ibid.
102 Lewis, *Deaf Liberation Theology*, 41.

as in Australia and South Africa. In England, Ireland, Scotland, Germany, Finland, Italy, Spain and Sweden the debate raged on about which was the best methodology for Deaf education: oralism or manualism.

However, towards the end of the nineteenth century the Deaf people's sense of themselves that developed after the French Revolution came under threat. Branson and Miller attribute this change to Western society's move towards more professional and bureaucratic administration.[103] Lewis expressed this more bluntly saying that 'scientists and legislators attempted to categorize and control anyone who was not perceived as "normal" by the majority of society.'[104] The attitude among hearing people towards deaf people was greatly influenced by the 'scientific' and evolutionist thinking of the late nineteenth and early twentieth centuries.

The Milan Conference of 1880

Another turning point in the manual versus oral debate, or the methods debate, came when one hundred and sixty-four delegates, the majority of whom came from Italy and France, attended 'The Second International Congress of Teachers of Deaf Mutes' in Milan from 6 to 11 September 1880.[105] The outcome of the Milan Congress, as it became known, was a triumph for pure oralism over the manual approaches to Deaf education. While not a Church conference, it was chaired by a priest, who was also a devoted oralist, Giulio Tarra (1832–1889). Most of the delegates at the conference came from schools in Europe and the United States which promoted the oral method of education.

The deliberations of the congress were summed up by the dismissive comment made in English by a Sienese oral educator and Catholic priest, Padre Marchio who said: 'Come hear our

---

[103] Branson and Miller, *Damned for Their Difference*, 145.
[104] Lewis, *Deaf Liberation Theology*, 23.
[105] See Hodgson, *The Deaf and Their Problems*, 243: The First International Conference of Teachers of the Deaf was held in Paris in 1878. 'It was international in little but name, but it was a precedent, and agreement was reached there to hold a really international conference two years later in Milan.'

children!' Marchio sought to dismiss the arguments of the American, Thomas Gallaudet, who had argued in favour of using sign language in the education of the deaf.[106] Many of the Catholic priests at the Milan Conference were in favour of the oral approach as they considered it the most modern and scientific approach.

This conference in Milan was a triumph for those who supported the oral method of Deaf education and was a setback for those who favoured the manual method. Deaf teachers were the most affected by this conference as they lost their employment or were gradually phased out. Eight resolutions were passed which had wide-ranging ramifications for Deaf education worldwide.

The first resolution passed in Milan emphasised the superiority of speech over signs in enabling the deaf to integrate into hearing society and so concluded that the oral method of education should be preferred to that of a manual system of education. It was striking that at the Milan Congress, only two of the 164 delegates were deaf. Both deaf people voted against the oral method of education. It was a conference of the hearing to decide what is best for the deaf. The oral approach was the remedy to the ills of the deaf by enabling them to function more effectively in the 'normal' hearing world.

The second Milan resolution discouraged the use of sign language or combined methods in education because sign language adversely affected the ability of deaf children to develop speech and lip-reading skills. Therefore, an emphasis on a purely oral approach was recommended.

The third resolution encouraged State aid for Deaf education and for governments to play a greater role in the education of deaf children. At this time most of the schools for the deaf had been established and were run by churches.

The fourth resolution insisted that the methods used for the education of deaf children should be similar to those used in the education of hearing children. They had to know the grammatical

---

[106] See www.milan1880.com/daytodayproceedings. Accessed 25 March 2013

structure of a spoken language. They were to learn it first in its spoken form and then in its written form.

The fifth resolution promoted the publication of books by teachers of the oral system that would enhance the learning of language by deaf children.

The sixth resolution encouraged those deaf adults, who had already completed school, to continue using the oral method in different areas of life. They should not forget the lessons learnt at school.

The seventh resolution tried to set a standard for the admittance of deaf children into school from eight to ten years of age, the number of years recommended for school attendance was suggested to be at least seven years and class sizes should not be compromised of more than ten children. This was probably an improvement on existing practice at that time. Milan at least acknowledged that deaf children needed to be educated. However, considering that hearing children probably started school at an earlier age, it set the beginning of education very late and only allowed for seven years.

The eighth resolution suggested the prudent, gradual and progressive introduction of the oral method into schools where it was not yet applied. New pupils should be placed in a separate class where they would be taught in a spoken language; and kept from the corrupting influence of other pupils using the manual approach; and each year the manual approach was to be phased out.

This conference had a great impact throughout Europe and the United States as governments gradually insisted on the implementation of the oral method as the most scientific approach to Deaf education. In Britain, for example, the Royal Commission on the Blind, the Deaf and Dumb, in 1889, recommended that the oral system of education be utilised in British schools for the deaf.[107] By 1905, 96% of all schools in the United States were designated

---

107   Enverstedt, *The legacy of the Past II*, 87.

to be oral schools.[108] Sign language was considered a relic of the past and forbidden for use in these schools.

When governments changed their education policies in favour of the oral method of education, it had a negative impact on the training and employment of deaf teachers and education in sign language. Hearing teachers were preferred and therefore employed to teach the deaf how to speak.

The vast majority of those at Milan were in favour of the oral method of education, so the outcome was predetermined. This enthusiasm for the oral method was a triumph for audism and phonocentrism. It was bolstered by emerging theories of social Darwinism and the eugenics movement. It meant that those who favoured the manual method of education and the use of sign language suffered further setbacks.

Evolutionism

Branson and Miller pointed out that modern science has been particularly detrimental for deaf people as it pathologised deaf people as defective and deficient human beings.[109] Science in the nineteenth century reaffirmed the phonocentric view that human beings were those who could speak and sign language was not considered to be a language.

> Those without speech, thus, were labelled frequently as "mindless," as less than human. Those who were deaf were assumed to be incapable of learning language, incapable of human understanding.[110]

The evolutionist anthropologist Edward Tylor theorised about the origins of language. He dismissed sign language as a more primitive stage of language development. Gesture came first and was more primitive to the development of spoken languages.[111] Being primitive it had no place in an advanced civilised society.

---

108   Ibid, 80.
109   Branson and Miller, *Damned for Their Difference*, 16.
110   Ibid, 25.
111   Ibid, 150.

Subsequently, 'natural sign language was not seen as a viable medium for education.'[112]

These perspectives together with the desire to create an ordered society, out of inherently selfish and anarchical individuals – and evolutionism – created the conditions for the eventual pathologising of deaf people. The scientific theory of evolution promoted the idea of biological progress and supported the idea of the supremacy of human beings over other animals. 'For the Darwinists and the evolutionists, the laws of nature needed to be harnessed to ensure effective human development.'[113]

Linking the theory of evolution and society led to the development of social Darwinism, which provided an ideological justification for, and legitimacy to, colonialism. Europeans were evolutionarily more suited to rule over the more primitive peoples of the world.[114] Colonial governments saw themselves as bringing civilisation and modern progress to the natives. Racism emerged from this form of evolutionary thinking as did eugenics. 'Evolutionist control over the natural development of humans received explicit expression in eugenics.'[115] Eugenics was also used in relation to the Deaf community too.

The most serious of the assaults came from the Scottish-born American inventor of the telephone and the hearing aid - Alexander Graham Bell.

Alexander Graham Bell and the eugenics movement

Alexander Graham Bell was born in Edinburgh, Scotland on 3 March 1847 and immigrated to Canada in July 1870. He accepted a post to a school for the deaf in Boston in 1871. He met Mabel Hubbard, who had been a former pupil at the school, marrying her on 11 July 1877.

Bell was incredibly hostile to the use of sign language and Deaf culture and was involved in the eugenics movement. This movement 'focused on the development of social control

---

112 Ibid, 160.
113 Ibid, 151.
114 Ibid, 28.
115 Ibid, 151.

over human reproduction to engineer the physical and mental improvement of future generations.'[116] It was influenced by social Darwinism and debated on the best means to develop racial purity in the United States. Bell was obsessed with the idea that a separate deaf race would evolve if deaf people were permitted to continue marrying each other.

In 1883, Bell gave a talk entitled: 'Memoir upon the formation of a deaf variety of the human race.' In his talk, Bell argued that the marriage of deaf people held the risk of the emergence of a separate 'race' that would only communicate in sign language.[117] They would be isolated from the hearing world.

He recommended that deaf people should be more fully integrated into a hearing world through promoting the oral method of education. He believed that if this was done, then the intermarriage of deaf people would decrease and consequently fewer deaf children would be born. He hoped that over time the Deaf community would become extinct. This was futile because the majority of deaf children are born to hearing parents and not to deaf parents.

Chaplaincy in the twentieth century

The belief in the modern myth of scientific and evolutionary progress, linked with phonocentrism, meant the resurgence of audism affected the churches too. Subsequently, deaf people were still looked upon by hearing people, even the most sympathetic of hearing people, as defective human beings. This can account for why the achievements of the deaf after the French Revolution, as we described earlier, in becoming artists, sculptors, actors and writers were so easily reversed in favour of the oral method of education in schools for the deaf. Fewer and fewer Deaf teachers were trained and employed in schools for the deaf at the beginning of the twentieth century. While pure oralism predominated in the

---

[116] Ibid, 29.
[117] Alexander Graham Bell, 'Memoir upon the formation of a deaf variety of the human race.' Paper presented to the National Academy of Sciences, New Haven, Connecticut, 13 November 1883. Retrieved 20 February 2018, https://archive.org/details/cihm_08831

schools, sign language persisted in the Catholic deaf chaplaincies. These were often too under the control of hearing chaplains. In the Catholic Church, Canon Law forbade the ordination of any person with a physical defect.[118]

Lewis pointed to the attempts of the Anglican bishops to control the deaf missions, with the establishment of the Council of Church Missioners to the Deaf and Dumb (CCMDD) in 1905.[119] Deaf missioners began to be replaced by hearing ones because many of the Deaf missioners did not have enough English to participate in the training courses. The effect of these changes in the Anglican Church was that many of the Deaf churches run by Deaf people themselves were transformed into a church 'where the (usually hearing) missioner did everything for the deaf that attended and the focus shifted from a church where Deaf people could meet and worship in their own language to a place where the deaf came to obtain welfare assistance.'[120]

In the early twentieth century audism and phonocentrism or, in Levinas' terminology, the imperialism of the same had won out. The gains made by deaf people in relation to sign language, deaf culture, deaf employment and deaf leadership had been overturned. The situation was far worse for deaf people in Nazi Germany. The Nazis took eugenic thinking to an extremist conclusion.

The Nazis and deaf people

In January 1934, the Nazis passed a law that permitted the sterilisation of people who suffered 'from a hereditary disease.' The law led to the forced sterilisation of approximately 375 000

---

[118] Canon 984 § 2 of the 1917 Canon Law stated that 'the following persons are irregular *ex defectu*: 2. bodily defective men who, on account of debility cannot safely, or for reason of deformity with due dignity, engage in the sacred ministry of the altar;' See Stanislaus Woywod, *The New Canon Law: A Commentary and Summary of the New Code of Canon Law* (New York: Joseph F Wagner, 1918), 197.
[119] Lewis, *Deaf Liberation Theology*, 53–54.
[120] Ibid, 55.

German nationals.[121] It is estimated that about 17 000 deaf people were forcibly sterilised often without anaesthesia.[122]

During this period, the Nazi regime also implemented a euthanasia programme called Action T4 for the elimination of people with bodily and mental disabilities. It is estimated that between 1940 and 1941, about 100 000 disabled, deaf and psychiatric patients were murdered.[123] The deaf and disabled were also experimented upon by being injected with typhoid and by having their bodies tested for resilience to cold and pressure.

In 1941, the German Catholic Bishops protested against the Nazi euthanasia programme. Clement August von Galen, Bishop of Münster (1878–1946) preached against the euthanasia programme on 3 August 1941.[124] Amazingly, the Nazi leadership called the Action T4 programme to a halt. However, it more likely continued but not so openly. The Nazis did not prosecute von Galen either possibly because they were afraid that it might affect the war effort if they arrested and executed him for treason.[125] However, this action of the Catholic Bishops did not go unpunished. In retaliation, 37 priests of his diocese were deported to concentration camps and ten lost their lives.[126]

From Levinas' perspective, Bishop van Galen's courageous act could be understood as an example of accepting ethical responsibility for the other. Van Galen discovered that he was responsible to speak out for the nameless victims of Nazi brutality, those people who were being experimented upon and killed mercilessly. He felt obliged to speak out even though he himself was in danger of suffering at the hands of the Nazis. However, as it transpired, he was not touched, others were persecuted instead.

---

121 Branson and Miller, *Damned for their Difference*, 32.
122 Leeson and Sheikh, *Experiencing Deafhood*, 64.
123 Ibid, 64.
124 Gordon C. Zahn, *German Catholics and Hitler's Wars: A Study in Social Control* (New York: Sheed and Ward, 1962), 86–87.
125 'Three sermons in defiance of the Nazis by Bishop von Galen.' The Church in History Information Centre. Accessed 5 November 2018, www.churchinhistory.org/pages/booklets/vongalen(n).htm
126 Ibid.

Accusations against the Catholic Church

However, when it came to the genocide perpetrated against Jews, the Catholic Church has been accused of remaining silent. Neither Pope Pius XII nor the German Catholic Bishops raised any protest against the genocide against Jews being committed in the concentration camps.[127] One argument is that if they had raised their voices against anti-Semitism as they had against the injustice committed against those with disabilities, there is the possibility that the Shoah may have been avoided or curtailed. That they did not do so, opened them up to accusations of complicity with the Nazis.[128]

The Vatican has decided to open its secret archives for researchers to study accusations of Pope Pius XII's silence on the killing of Jews during the Shoah. This took place from 2 March 2020.[129] Despite this, Levinas' point would be that in persecution and being held hostage in compassion for the other, one always discovers that 'in approach I am first a servant of a neighbour, already late and guilty for being late.'[130] In the shuddering[131] and trembling before the Other and their suffering, one is always late on the scene and guilty of having done too little.

However, even in these desperate times some deaf people, or saints in Levinas' thinking, asserted their autonomy to choose their own destiny. This was going to set the trend for the twentieth century – deaf people coming into their own again.

---

127 Robert P. Ericksen, 'German Churches and the Holocaust: Assessing the Argument for Complicity,' The Raul Hilberg Memorial Lecture, The University of Vermont, 15 April 2013, 17. Accessed 29 October 2018, www.uvm.edu/sites/default/files/media/HilbergLectureEricksen.pdf
128 Ericksen, 'German Churches and the Holocaust,' 17–19.
129 Frances D' Emilio, 'Vatican to Open Archives on World War II-Era Pope Pius XII,' *Crux*, 4 March 2019. Accessed 23 May 2019, https://cruxnow.com/vatican/2019/03/04/vatican-to-open-archives-on-world-war-ii-era-pope-pius-xii/
130 Levinas, *Otherwise Than Being*, 87.
131 Ibid.

Deaf people in the Resistance

During the Warsaw Uprising against the Nazi occupation of Poland from 1 August until 2 October 1944, there was a platoon of about 29 deaf Poles, among them men, women and even children, who resisted the German occupation. They were led by a deaf man called Wieslaw Jablonski.[132]

During the 63 days of fighting during the uprising, over 16 000 Polish Home Army fighters were killed. Interestingly, none of the deaf people died even though some of them were involved in the heavy fighting. After the rebellion had been quelled by the Nazis, eleven deaf members of the uprising were sent to prisoner-of-war camps, including two minors.[133]

Deaf people showed their willingness to stand up against all forms of oppression and diminishment even to sacrificing their own lives for the common good.

Oralism predominates

After the Second World War, oralism became the predominant method of education in schools for the deaf. The major shift was due to the medicalisation of education. The school became seen as a clinic where vast amounts of time were expended in getting the deaf children to hear using hearing aids, and amplifiers, as well as giving them speech therapy.[134] Modern scientific technology was the saviour of the deaf and the modern world.

It was the modern myth that science and technology would eventually find a solution to all the world's problems. Modernism 'seeks to transcend the limitations of the everyday through heroic action, creativity, and extraordinary religious experience. Modernism is a kind of heroic romanticism.'[135] This heroic romanticism is challenged by post-modernist thinking in which science and technology have often not been able to fulfil their

---

132   See Leeson and Sheikh, *Experiencing Deafhood*, 65–66.
133   Ibid.
134   See Branson and Miller, *Damned for Their Difference*, 205–207.
135   Michael Morgan, *The Cambridge Introduction to Levinas* (Cambridge: Cambridge University Press, 2011), 86.

promises but have also caused untold harm and destruction in the name of progress.

The same can be said about the oral method of deaf education with its modernist agenda. While it brought some benefits to deaf people it was at the expense of sign language. Nevertheless, sign language continued to be used in Catholic chaplaincy work and, unfortunately, referred to as pastoral care for the hearing impaired.[136] It was often charitable work which kept the deaf people passive and dependent on the hearing chaplains. Little was done to empower deaf people themselves. However, this model was to be challenged and transformed in 1951.

The establishment of the World Federation of the Deaf

In 1951, the first international Deaf association was formed in Rome and was called the World Federation of the Deaf (WFD). The WFD seeks to promote the human rights of Deaf people across the globe and to celebrate Deaf culture and sign languages.[137] This marked the beginning of a whole emancipation movement for Deaf people which took off in the 1970s throughout the Deaf world. South Africa was no exception.

It took some time for the ideas of the WFD to influence Catholic Deaf ministry but influence, it did.

Conclusion

In this historical survey, I have tried to outline the reality of Catholic ministry to the deaf down the ages. This involved an encounter between a predominantly hearing church and clergy with the Deaf community. Levinas referred to this encounter as proximity. In proximity, the Church is a reluctant servant of the Deaf community and in its outreach to be 'already late and guilty for being late.'[138] The Church's reluctant ministry to

---

[136] Broesterhuizen, 'Pastoral Ministry with the Deaf,' 1.
[137] See https://www.wfdeaf.org/who-we-are/our philosophy/ Accessed 20 February 2018.
[138] Levinas, *Otherwise than Being*, 87.

the deaf was hampered by taking on board a flawed philosophy of the human person, as we saw in the discussion on Aristotle. Aristotle's phonocentric contributed towards a denial of deaf people's full human dignity. Audism became the model for the exclusion of Deaf people's right to their language and culture. Hearing people thought themselves to be superior to Deaf people and to act on their behalf rather than to learn from them. Catholic schools for the deaf and even church chaplaincies accepted this mistaken view.

The Church never fully linked the value of sign language used in the monasteries and the natural sign language of Deaf people. The Church missed an opportunity to learn from its proximity to the Deaf community. However, there were some saintly efforts to enable Deaf people to emerge from being trampled into the 'mud of history.'[139]

In this chapter, I have sought to highlight some of the transcendent moments or liberatory praxis that shifted thinking regarding the Church's ministry to deaf people. This happened firstly, through the saintly efforts of Teresa of Cartegena who saw in her deafness not an affliction but a gift from God. She challenged the perceptions of her time that deaf people and women could make significant contributions to theology and spirituality through the written word. Secondly, the insight that deaf people could be educated revolutionised life for the Deaf community. The saintly efforts of Pedro Ponce de Leon and Samuel Heinecke to teach deaf men to speak and educate them as well as de l'Épée's attempts to educate all classes of deaf people through methodical signs helped improve the lives of the Deaf community. After the French Revolution, De l'Épée was fêted by Deaf people for making sign language socially acceptable. His manual approach to Deaf education opened the way for deaf people to become teachers in schools for the deaf. Deaf people found a greater sense of self-confidence and self-belief after the Revolution. There was the flourishing of Deaf culture and art during this period too.

---

139 Wyschogrod, 'Heterological History,' 2.

However, during the nineteenth century the distorted phonocentric understanding of the human person as rational and speaking persisted. This happened despite the inroads Deaf people had made in overcoming prejudice against them in both Church and society after the French Revolution. Phonocentrism and audism were strengthened by the new scientific discoveries of evolution and the pseudo-science of eugenics. Hearing and able-bodied people, like Alexander Graham Bell, advocated for the oral method of deaf education rather than de l'Épée's manual method.

The culmination of the shift happened with the Milan Congress in 1880 which was a hearing-dominated conference where Deaf perspectives were ignored and side-lined. Hearing and able-bodied people never thought they had anything to learn from the deaf or the disabled. Many of the advocates for the oral method were Catholic priests from Italy who had started their schools for the deaf. The Catholic approach to deaf education shifted accordingly. We will take up this theme later when we will look at this shift within the South African context.

During the Second World War, the pseudo-science of eugenics led to the inhumanity and abuses of Jewish people but also the deaf and disabled. The Catholic Church raised its head above the parapet in condemning the Nazi excesses in experimenting upon, sterilising and murder of people with disabilities including deaf people. This was another moment of transcendence or liberatory praxis in relation to the Deaf Other. Bishop van Galen's act of bravery was not extended to all others, especially not to the Jewish population, who were the most affected by this brutality.

In Part II, we will deepen our understanding of the saintliness of those who contributed to Catholic schools for the deaf in South Africa where the ambivalence between oralism and sign language persisted. In Part III, we will look at those saintly Catholic Deaf people who contributed enormously to their emancipation.

Part II

A History of Deaf Education in Catholic Schools for the Deaf in South Africa, 1874–1994

Chapter 5

Pioneering Beginnings: Establishing Schools for the Deaf, 1874–1920

This chapter shows how the arrival of the Cabra Dominican sisters sparked off a series of events which earmarked a new era for deaf people in South Africa. It highlights how the education of the deaf started in South Africa and inspired the Dutch Reformed Church to begin its own schools for Afrikaans-speaking South Africans. It also shows how these initiatives highlighted a transition from indifference to the plight of deaf people in South Africa to making people aware that the education of the deaf was both possible and necessary.

The chapter shows how this transition can be understood in Levinasian terms as an overcoming of indifference to a practice of a more compassionate response even to the extent of employing deaf teachers in the Cape Town School for the Deaf. Nevertheless, tensions existed between hearing and deaf teachers, which highlights the difficulties in overcoming prejudices among the hearing towards deaf people. Despite this, the saintly influence of the hearing and deaf teachers in equipping a generation of children with education was a major step forward.

Early origins of the Cape Town School for the Deaf

Mother Dymphna Kinsella OP with five other Irish Dominican nuns came out to South Africa from Cabra, Dublin in 1863. Bishop Raymond Griffith, himself a Dominican and the first resident bishop of Cape Town, had invited them to come out to take on responsibility for the first Catholic school in South Africa. The school, established in 1860,[1] was being run by lay people but there were problems with its administration. By the time the Dominican

---

[1] The delay in getting Dominican Sisters to come from Cabra may have been the result of a conflict of jurisdiction that had existed between the Dominican men and women that had started in the

nuns arrived in the Cape, Griffith had died and the newly appointed Bishop Grimley welcomed them to Cape Town. The sisters immediately took over the administration of the school for the hearing settler children.[2]

By 1873, Kinsella became aware of the need to start a school for the deaf. She was herself a trained teacher of the deaf from the St Mary's School for the Deaf in Dublin where she taught before coming to Cape Town. St Mary's had been started 26 years previously, in 1846, and was the first Catholic school for the deaf started in Ireland.[3] As mentioned in the previous chapter, an Irish Vincentian priest, Fr Thomas McNamara CM, was concerned about the lack of religious instruction for deaf Irish children. He wrote to the bishops of Ireland in 1845 requesting support for establishing a school for the deaf. He had also asked the Dominican nuns in Cabra to take responsibility for the school. They agreed and, on 11 January 1846, they sent two nuns and two deaf pupils to a school for the deaf in Caen in Normandy, France to study Deaf education.

This school in Caen was only thirty years old and had been started by Abbé Jamet in 1816. Jamet had trained with Abbé Sicard at the Paris Institute for the Deaf,[4] the school that was founded by Abbé Charles de l'Épée, the founder of the manual approach to Deaf education.

St Mary's School for the Deaf, Dublin

The nuns and pupils returned to Dublin in August 1846. There were 15 pupils ready to start school in September 1846 at the new school that was given the name: St Mary's Institution for the Deaf and Dumb. By 1850, the school had already grown to 50 pupils. The method of education in the school was strictly in Irish Sign Language (ISL) and Signed English. Kinsella was one

---

1830s. See Kathleen Boner, *Dominican Women: A Time to Speak* (Pietermaritzburg: Cluster Publications, 2000), 32.

[2] Fr William Leeson, 'Pioneer Work for the Deaf: Nuns First in the Cape to Care for Mutes,' *The Southern Cross* (TSC), 25 March 1931, 12/260.

[3] Boner, *The Irish Dominicans and Education in the Western Cape*, 156.

[4] The information for this section was taken from Fitzgerald and Andrew, *Open Minds Open Hearts*, 37–42.

of those trained in this methodology before she was sent out to South Africa.

St Joseph's School for the Deaf, Cape Town

Mother Kinsella found it impossible to manage the task of running the school for deaf children on top of her other responsibilities[5] and so employed Bridget Lyne,[6] a young 24-year-old Irish Deaf teacher to assist. Lyne had been one of Kinsella's top pupils at the school for the deaf in Dublin before she came to South Africa. Shortly after Lyne's arrival in March 1874, St Joseph's School for the Deaf was opened in Cape Town.[7] Within the first year, there were six pupils.[8]

Lyne's work at the school was held in high esteem by no less than Father Frederick Charles Kolbe (1854–1936), a respected priest and a renowned educationist and commentator on South African political life at this time. He felt that she was a prime example of the invaluable contribution deaf people could make to society.

> The teacher of our school here, Miss Lyne, displays very high abilities indeed: besides English, she knows French very well, and some time ago, learning that the parents of two of her pupils could only speak Dutch and that therefore the lads' education was more or less useless at home, she set to work and taught herself Dutch that she might teach them.[9]

Frederick Kolbe was born in George, in 1854. He was a convert and the son of a Congregational and nonconformist[10] missionary who

---

5 Mother Dymphna Kinsella is the foundress of the Cabra Dominican Sisters in the Western Cape.
6 See Kathleen Boner, *Dominican Women*, 137 and 'Pioneer Work for the Deaf,' TSC, 12/260. Some publications spell her surname as Lynne.
7 Kathleen Boner, *Dr FC Kolbe*, 257.
8 Boner, *Dominican Women*, 138.
9 Quoted in Boner, *Dr FC Kolbe*, 259.
10 The nonconformist churches where those that dissented and did not conform to doctrines of the established church in England, the Anglican Church. Among these churches are the Baptist,

came to work in South Africa with the London Missionary Society. Kolbe was ordained in 1882 after completing his studies at the Gregorian University in Rome. In September that year, he returned to South Africa and started his ministry in Cape Town. However, in 1884, just two years after his ordination, both his hearing and his eyesight deteriorated.[11] His deafness and bad eyesight proved to be a great hindrance to doing parish ministry and he devoted himself more fully to the work of teaching and lecturing.

Fortuitously, his residence was next door to St Mary's school, as well as the school for the deaf in Cape Town. Consequently, Kolbe became increasingly aware of the needs of deaf children. He began to learn sign language from Bridget Lyne. He became so proficient in sign language that he was able to teach the deaf children their catechism and assist in the school, whenever required.[12] He was the first chaplain to the deaf in South Africa. At the time, many parents of deaf children were reluctant to have their children attend school because deafness was perceived to be 'a stigma on the family name or a sign of mental deficiency.'[13] He continued to have a lifelong devotion and concern for deaf children until he died in 1936.[14]

The dedication and abilities of Lyne, in collaboration with Mother Dympna Kinsella, impressed and inspired a Dutch Reformed Church minister, Dominee William Murray, to start a school for the deaf for Afrikaans-speaking children.

The De la Bat School for the Deaf

In 1881, William Murray was the minister of the Dutch Reformed Church in Worcester. His congregation included a family who had a deaf son called Piet de la Bat. Rather than send the child to the Cabra sisters' school in Cape Town, 112 miles away, Murray proposed to the Church Synod that he start a separate school for the deaf in Worcester. This school would be attached to a Dutch

---

Methodist, Presbyterian, Congregationalist churches and the Quakers.
11 Kathleen Boner, *Dr FC Kolbe*, 226.
12 Boner, *Dr FC Kolbe*, 260.
13 Ibid, 258.
14 Mary Singleton, 'Monsignor Kolbe,' *TSC*, 7 January 1948, 6.

Reformed school for the blind that had already been established by the Church in 1847.[15]

During the Synod's deliberations a few of the Dutch Reformed clergy raised fears that their deaf congregants could be won over to the Catholic faith if they were permitted to attend the Cabra Dominican School for the Deaf in Cape Town.[16] There had been a great deal of antagonism and suspicion between Calvinists and Catholics in South Africa, where Catholics looked upon Calvinists as heretics and Calvinists distrusted the '*Roomse gevaar*' or the Roman [Catholic] threat.[17]

The Synod voted overwhelmingly in favour of the proposal to start a school for the deaf in Worcester. They also agreed that the young boy's brother, Jan de la Bat, be appointed his teacher. Consequently, they decided to send Jan de la Bat to the Guyot School for the Deaf in Groningen, Holland for training.[18]

The Synod's decision proved to be a good one as Jan de la Bat worked tirelessly building up the school until his retirement as principal in December 1926. He gave 45 years of service to the school for the deaf in Worcester.

---

15 In the souvenir programme prepared for the visit of Helen Keller to South Africa in 1951, the following explanation is given for the establishment of the deaf school in Worcester. 'Naturally a minister of the Dutch Reformed Church in the country would be concerned to have a deaf member of his congregation educated in his own home language, so when the Rev. William Murray of Worcester found a deaf boy, Piet de la Bat by name, he did not arrange to send him to the school 112 miles away but convinced the Church Synod that they must have their own school.' 'Our Deaf and our Blind: A Brief Record of Work in South Africa,' AW Blaxall, *The Visit of Helen Keller to South Africa*, Souvenir Programme, 152/1104 12, KDSA, Johannesburg.
16 See Boner, *The Irish Dominicans and Education in the Western Cape*, 158.
17 See JG Strydom, *Die Roomse Gevaar en hoe om dit te Bestry* (Kaapstad: Nasionale Pers, 1937).
18 There appears to have been some collaboration with the Dominican Sisters in his training. In 1962, Desmond Hatton wrote: 'It is interesting to recall that Dr. J.B.G. de la Bat first learned sign language from Mother Dympna and later, after studying further, became the first principal of the Worcester School for the Deaf. This school was opened by the Dutch Reformed Church.' 'The Deaf to Hear …' *TSC*, 21 November 1962, 5/557.

The new school and Jan de la Bat's dedication in building it up impressed the Catholics. In 1883, Kolbe gave a lecture in Cape Town to raise awareness about the plight of deaf children but he also emphasised their potential. He argued, in an ecumenical spirit, that many deaf children were denied the advantage of an education at either St Joseph's School or the School for the De la Bat School for the Deaf in Worcester due to people's ignorance that there were schools for the deaf.[19] When we look at the lived experience of deaf people before to the establishment of schools for the deaf in South Africa, they had no prospects for development or improvement. They were usually kept at home and away from the eyes of others because they were an embarrassment to the family. Kolbe recognised this problem.

Levinas' *il y a* – existential indifference

Emmanuel Levinas can help us understand the situation in which deaf people found themselves before the establishment of schools for the deaf. Levinas speaks about living a life without hope of development or progress, a life stripped down to nothing. This is an example of what he refers to as anonymous Being, or the '*il y a*'. The words *il y a*, in French, literally mean 'There is.' Levinas describes the *il y a* as 'the muffled rustling of nothingness back into which the elements flow and are lost.'[20] Using a childhood image, 'one sleeps alone, the adults continue life; the child feels the silence of his bedroom as a "rumbling."'[21] It is also the original chaos or emptiness that existed before creation.[22] It is life without meaning or purpose. Life focused on survival and always under threat. It is not a human existence.

Some commentators believe that Levinas developed this understanding of existence during his period in a German prisoner-of-war camp. It also calls to mind descriptions of the experiences of Jewish people in the concentration camps, a life stripped of dignity and worth.[23] This sense of the anonymity of

---

19   Boner, *The Irish Dominicans and Education in the Western Cape*, 259.
20   Levinas, *Totality and Infinity*, 146.
21   Levinas, *Ethics and Infinity*, 48.
22   Ibid.
23   Terry Veling, *For You Alone*, 21.

being is akin to indifference. For Levinas, existence is indifferent to whether one lives or dies.

Many people who are marginalised, abandoned, neglected and forgotten live on this edge of existence, in a frightening non-existence. It is a sub-human life and existence without hope of change or transformation. Colloquially, we refer to this type of existence as a 'living hell.' This was the experience of deaf people, as we saw in Chapter 4, who were always looked upon as defective humans who lacked reason because they could not speak. They were mere 'brutes' and in early Greek society, deaf and disabled infants were left to die without food or sustenance. If they made it into adulthood, they were often not able to find a livelihood and lived depending on the generosity of their hearing families. They were often prevented from having a life independent of their families of birth.

The starting of schools for the deaf was a prophetic moment in the history of deaf people. Hearing people began to see that deaf people were more than just brutes but could communicate, learn and study. They could make a useful contribution to society. From a Levinasian perspective, this was a moment of insight, to recognise that hearing people were responsible for their deaf neighbours and could educate them. Human life begins with saintliness, that is, when people move towards the needs of their neighbour with compassion, mercy and love. For Levinas, this 'for-the-other of saintliness defines the human.'[24] With the opening of the schools, there is an overcoming of the *il y a* or indifference to the plight of the Deaf community and the establishment of more ethical and caring relations between hearing and deaf. This is what Levinas also referred to as the practice of non-indifference.[25] In this shift to the ethical, suffering and marginalised Deaf people had a place that gave hope and the possibility of a more humane future that they had never experienced before. Levinas referred to this shift as

---

24 Levinas, *Alterity and Transcendence*, 171.
25 Non-indifference refers to the response of the self to exposure to the other or neighbour, or proximity, in which the self feels obliged to accept responsibility for the neighbour even to the point of substitution. Levinas uses the term non-indifference in *Time and the Other*, 19 but is used much more extensively in his later work *Otherwise than Being*, 48,71, 91, 97, 123.

extending the hand of hospitality to the marginalised Other, as a sharing of our resources so that others may have life.

The relations between the St Joseph's and the Worcester schools for the deaf remained on a cordial basis. Both schools continued to grow steadily with the St Joseph's School taking in both white and coloured children even though they were taught in separate classrooms. However, tragic events took place at the Catholic school for the deaf, with Bridget Lyne's untimely death in 1887. She worked as the only teacher for thirteen years.[26] The sisters were at a loss to find another deaf teacher and Lyne was replaced by a hearing Dominican sister. The manual method remained the official medium of instruction in this school for 45 years and the school continued to employ Deaf teachers.

New events in the Catholic world of Deaf education were about to transpire when the King William's Town Dominican sisters decided to open a new school for the deaf in 1884. This school for the deaf was going to use the oral method of deaf education and so the manual-oral debate, which had been raging in Europe for 150 years, was introduced to South Africa.

The King William's Town Convent School for the Education of the Deaf

In 1884, a young deaf boy, called Tom Moore, was brought by his parents to the sisters in King William's Town in the hope that he could be educated. Sister Stephana Hanshuber was appointed to take on this responsibility. She had trained at the Institute for the Deaf and Dumb in Dillingen, Bavaria in Germany and arrived in South Africa two years previously. This institute was dedicated to training teachers in the oral method of deaf education.

A few others joined the school so that by 1888, the King William's Town Convent School for the Education of the Deaf was formally established.[27] This school adopted the oral method

---

26   Boner, *Dominican Women*, 138.
27   See 'Beginning and Development of the School,' 152/1104 43, KDSA. Also see Mariette Gouws, *All For God's People*, 207.

of deaf education from the outset, using the so-called German method developed by Samuel Heinecke.[28]

New developments in deaf education at that time

This section discusses early developments at the King William's Town School for the Deaf and at St Joseph's School for the Deaf in Cape Town.

New developments at the King William's Town and Cape Town schools

This section outlines developments at that time at the King William's Town and Cape Town schools.

King William's Town School for the Deaf

When Sr Stephana died on 9 October 1897,[29] Sr Gisella Greissl,[30] who had trained at Dillingen and Gmund in Germany, was already the school's new principal. She had taken over after her profession on 9 July 1895. In 1897, the school had ten deaf children.[31] Greissl taught art and commercial subjects. Among her pupils was the famous William Bevington, who won a bursary to study art at Rhodes University after he painted 'an outstanding portrait likeness of Cecil Rhodes.'[32] From there, he went to study art at the Royal College of Arts in London before returning to Cape Town and

---

28 Gouws, *All For God's People*, 35.
29 Sr M. Eleonora OSD, 'Sister Mary Stephana Hanshuber OSD,' 6–8., Box 1: Annals 1897–1903; 1905–1906 Book 18, 6–8. KWT Motherhouse, KDSA.
    'Sister Greissl,' 1.
30 Sister Gisella Greissl was born on 13 December 1865 in Pentenacker, Bavaria. At the age of 14, she started a teacher's diploma course in Kaufbeuren. In 1885, she passed her examination and went to work as principal of an oral deaf school in Ursberg. In July 1892, she entered the convent of St Ursula as a candidate. She arrived at the motherhouse in King William's Town in 1893. She died on 11 July 1957. See 'Sister M. Gisella Greissl OP,' 1. Box 19 Necrology, File 349 (19/349), KDSA. Also see 'Obituary: Sr Gisella Greissl,' *The Silver Star*, 1957, 130.
31 Sr M. Eleonora OSD, 'Sister Mary Stephana Hanshuber OSD,' 6–8.
32 'Sister Greissl,' 1.

becoming a professor of Fine Arts at the University of Cape Town. Bevington painted many landscapes, the most famous being one of the Victoria Falls. He lectured there until he died in 1953.

In 1917, during Sr Greissl's tenure as principal, the school was recognised by the Cape Department of Education and given a partial government grant. Before this, it had been a private Catholic school and did not receive any state aid. After receiving the government grant, the school was obliged to follow the Cape Department of Education's curriculum for schools for the deaf. Sr Greissl remained in charge of the school until her retirement in 1924.

Unlike the oral schools which only employed hearing teachers, and only Dominican sisters of the King William's Town congregation, the Cabra schools which used the manual method continued to employ Deaf teachers and laywomen.

New deaf teachers at St Joseph's School

In 1896, another Deaf teacher Anne Marsh was brought from Ireland to help teach in St Joseph's School for the Deaf. The school was still small and in financial difficulties and there was talk about closing it down.[33] Marsh had originally come out to be an assistant teacher. However, she discovered on arrival that she was the school's only teacher and was appointed principal of the school in 1900. She needed an assistant and so recommended that one of the pupils be trained as a pupil-teacher. In October 1902 a suitable candidate was found in Alice Collins. She was appointed at the young age of 15.[34] It is not clear how long she worked as a teacher.

Around the same time, Marsh trained another young Deaf South African woman as a teacher. Mrs F.E. Hugo came to the school as a pupil in 1890 at the age of four. She stayed until 1897, when at the age of 12, she went to the Exeter School for the Deaf in England to continue her education for a further three years. On her return to Cape Town, and at the tender age of fifteen, she began to teach at the school. She received coaching from Marsh. She taught

---

33 Boner, *Dominican Women*, 144.
34 Boner, *Dominican Women*, 144–145.

handiwork subjects like fretwork, chip-carving and basketwork.[35] Hugo worked at the school until her retirement, 35 years later, in December 1936.[36]

In December 1902, Marsh was given a term's notice by Mother Pius McLaughlin, the prioress of St Mary's community, that her services at the school for the deaf were no longer required. Marsh was incensed by such unfair treatment as she felt that there was no valid reason for the dismissal. She had increased the number of pupils to forty since taking over and in her eyes had saved the school from closure. No reason is given as to why the decision was later rescinded but the conflict must have been resolved because Marsh continued teaching at the school.

Fr Kolbe continued his work with the school, also assisting Marsh where needed.[37] This cooperation and collaboration between a school for the deaf and a Catholic chaplain laid the foundation and model for future Catholic Deaf ministry in South Africa. The school provided education while the chaplain was responsible for the pastoral and catechetical needs of the deaf children and the deaf adults. This collaboration between the school and the chaplain was reinforced with Sr Techilde Kolbe, Fr Kolbe's sister, when she became principal of the school.[38]

The school for the deaf continued to expand so that by 1906, another Deaf teacher, Hannah Farrell, came out from Ireland to teach.[39] She taught in sign language and was the fifth Deaf teacher to have joined the school staff.

In 1908, Farrell, like Marsh before her, came into conflict with the hearing principal. Farrell claimed that the principal was ineffective as a teacher because she had no grasp of sign language.[40] Farrell was not going to keep quiet when she saw an injustice at play. She insisted that she had the interests of the deaf children

---

35 '35 years' Work for Deaf: Retirement of Mrs. F. E. Hugo,' TSC, 13 January 1937, 2/18.
36 Mrs Hugo was the last Deaf teacher to be employed at a Catholic Deaf school until the 1970s.
37 Boner, Dominican Women, 147.
38 Ibid, 147.
39 Ibid, 146.
40 Ibid, 146-149.

at heart and wanted them to receive the best education that could be offered. Sr Techilde was affronted by Farrell's outspokenness and demanded that Farrell be summarily dismissed and sent back to Ireland. This all blew over and Farrell continued to teach at the school until her untimely death in 1919 from tuberculosis.

Putting aside considerations of personal clashes, or resentment from Farrell towards Sr Techilde for not being appointed principal, the clash between them arose because Sr Techilde was appointed as school principal even though she did not have a good command of sign language. Farrell was aggrieved and angry that the real needs of the deaf children were not being properly addressed.

Marsh and Farrell's anger and moral indignation can be viewed as part of a broader contestation between hearing and deaf teachers of deaf children. Mother Dymphna's vision in establishing the school was to ensure that the school employed the manual methods of Deaf education. For this reason, she employed a deaf teacher in Bridget Lyne to teach the children. There appears to be a shift in emphasis with the appointment of hearing principals. Perhaps the deaf teachers thought themselves more competent in determining how the deaf children should be taught but the hearing principals were asserting that it was their school. These incidents show an underlying mistrust between hearing and deaf, as well as showing where the true relations of power in the school lay.

From these conflicts, it is apparent that, even though the deaf were employed in the school, they were no longer entrusted with holding the reins of power in the school. The hearing and not the deaf had the final say. The empowerment of deaf people in the school had clear limits. Authority was ultimately in the hands of the hearing Dominican sisters. It also pointed to a fundamental problem in the way that hearing people thought about deaf people, which goes back to the time of the philosopher Aristotle who privileged speech and the voice over other forms of communication.

Conclusion

This chapter demonstrated how the work of the schools for the deaf gave new purpose and meaning to the lives of many of the deaf children who came through these schools. We have already heard the names of Tom Moore, Piet de la Bat, William Bevington and Mrs F. E. Hugo. Many others remained unnamed and anonymous. These deaf people's lives were transformed by the education they received in these schools for the deaf.

It is a recognition by the hearing that they have a responsibility to share what they have with their suffering neighbour. This non-indifference and responsibility for the other is displayed in the lives of Mother Dymphna Kinsella, Bridget Lyne, Dominee William Murray, Jan de la Bat, Sr Stephana Hanshuber, Sr Gisella Greisll, not to mention the deaf teachers like Anne Marsh, Mrs Hugo and Hannah Farrell. They gave their lives in dedicated service for the good of the excluded and neglected deaf neighbour.

For Levinas, this is the meaning he gives to holiness and sanctity – people who find themselves dedicated to the good of the other even to the point of substitution, who haemorrhage for the sake of the other, or as he says elsewhere, who are 'willing to give the bread destined for one's own mouth, for one's own existence.' For him these are people who display non-indifference to the suffering of others whom he called saintly or what Wyschogrod refers to as having saintly influence. They display what it means to be holy, that is, to be a human being who recognises the responsibility to live ethically, prophetically and messianically to alleviate the suffering of the other.

But it is not only the hearing who exert saintly influence. In St Joseph's School for the Deaf, the manual method of Deaf education meant that Deaf teachers and staff members were employed. These Deaf adults provided 'saintly' role models for the Deaf children they taught. The Deaf children were accustomed to seeing intelligent, competent, efficient and responsible hearing adults. It must have been incredibly ennobling for them to encounter an equally or even more intelligent deaf person like Bridget Lyne. Even Fr Frederick Kolbe was enthusiastic about her intelligence and abilities. The employing of Deaf teachers was another truly prophetic inspiration. Bridget Lyne, Anne Marsh, Mrs F.E. Hugo and Hannah Farrell also need to be counted among the saintly as they too dedicated themselves to selfless service to improve the lives of the deaf children they served and inspired.

For Levinas, hospitality or compassion is also the practice of justice. To act with responsibility for the good of the neighbour is to be just. Yet justice is not attained once and for all. Justice is always a work in progress as we saw in the conflict between Hannah Farrell and Sr Techilde Kolbe OP.

Both of these methods of Deaf education had an influence on the history of South African schools for the deaf.

Chapter 6

Acting in Good Conscience: The Triumph of the Oral Method of Deaf Education, 1922–1937

The previous chapter illustrated, how the conflict between Sr Techilde Kolbe and Hannah Farrell revealed a discrepancy in power between the hearing Dominican sisters and the Deaf staff members. In this chapter, we will show how the oral method of deaf education became the dominant method of deaf education in Catholic schools for the deaf. We will highlight how this led to the extinction of deaf teachers and that all new schools for the deaf over this period adopted the oral method. Education through the medium of sign language was gradually eliminated but not entirely because the chaplains for deaf adults, particularly in Cape Town, ministered in sign language.

While the Cape Town school for the deaf was originally started with a deaf teacher Bridget Lyne, we see how by 1908, it was firmly under the control of the Dominican sisters. This power discrepancy became more acute in 1922 when Sr Berchmans Cotter became the provincial of the Cabra Dominican sisters. She decided to send Sr Alacoque Broderick to the Dominican School for the Deaf in King William's Town to learn the oral method of educating the deaf.[1] Cotter did this because, as Boner pointed out, although the Cabra school for the deaf in Cape Town was getting good results, the school lagged behind the other schools for the deaf in South Africa.[2]

In 1926, the Union government's Department of Education took over the administration of all the schools for the deaf. The government was in favour of the oral approach to deaf education as it was understood to be the modern and scientific approach

---

1   'Pioneer Work for the Deaf,' *TSC*, 25 March 1931, 16/260.
2   Boner, *Dominican Women*, 149.

to deaf education. In 1928, Parliament in Cape Town passed the Vocational Training and Special Schools Act, No. 29. This Act ensured that all special schools fell directly under the Union Education Department.

After her time in King William's Town, Sr Alacoque became a convert to the oral method. Gradually, the Cabra Dominican sisters changed their approach to deaf education for all their South African schools for the deaf.[3] A devastating implication of this shift, from manual to oral schools, meant that many Deaf teachers lost their jobs or were excluded from the education field.

The King William's Town School for the Deaf

The King William's Town School for the Deaf also fell under the authority of the Union government. In January 1925, Sr Cyrilla Hötzl[4] and Sr Verena Huber[5] took over the reins at the school. They were both trained at the Yale School for the Deaf, also known as the Clark School in Northampton, Massachusetts in the United States. When these two sisters took over the school, there were 16 girls and 10 boys.[6] Despite the small number of pupils, the school

---

3   See Boner, *Dominican Women*, 138–149 and 'Jubilarian Taught Deaf for 44 years,' TSC, 19 September 1962, 9/453. A similar process happened in St Mary's School for the Deaf in Cabra, Ireland. Dominican Sisters, like Sr Nicholas Griffey OP, became exponents of the oral method of education.

4   Sister Cyrilla Hötzl was born on 5 December 1883 at Dengling. After leaving school she worked at an orphanage in Kaufbeuren until she entered the King William's Town Congregation in Schlehdorf in 1905. She was professed in the King William's Town convent chapel on 17 October 1908. She started work at the deaf school in 1925. She died on 27 September 1959. 'Sister M Cyrilla Hötzl Died 27th September 1959,' 1. 20/376, KDSA.

5   Sr Verena Huber was born on 14 November 1889, the first-born of 12 children. She grew up in Mazing near Osterhofen, Bavaria. She entered the convent at Schlehdorf in 1912 and arrived in South Africa in March 1914. She was professed on 10 October 1915. She started teaching at the King William's Town deaf school in 1925. She continued teaching at St Vincent School in 1934 until 1948. She continued teaching in hearing schools until her retirement in 1972. She died on 6 June 1978. 'Sr Verena Huber OP (Katarina),' 1. 26/606, KDSA.

6   My maternal grandfather Joseph Hirst, and his two brothers – Edward Hirst and Barney Hirst – attended the King William's Town school in the 1920s.

had a good reputation in the country. It continued as an oral school for the deaf.

The school continued in King William's Town until the end of 1933. It later moved to Johannesburg in 1934 as most of the pupils came from the Reef area. This move was a logical step forward.

De la Bat School for the Deaf, Worcester

The Dutch Reformed school in Worcester, like the Cabra school, also abandoned the manual method of deaf education. When Jan de la Bat retired in 1925, he was succeeded by his son, G. de la Bat. The younger man had initially planned to do his theological training at Princeton in the USA. However, he changed his plans and went to the Clarke School for the Deaf in Northampton, Massachusetts instead.[7] This was the same school where the King William's Town Dominican sisters had been trained. On his return he continued to build up the school, no longer as a manual school, but now as an oral one.

NG Sending Kerk's Deaf School, Worcester

In 1928, the tenth Synod of the NG Sending Kerk decided to take up a special synodal collection with the view to starting a Deaf school for coloured children. On 1 February 1933, the school was opened in Parker Street, Worcester with its first teacher Izak Februarie.[8] The school employed the oral method of education.[9]

The school had very humble beginnings, but when it was recognised by the state and received a state loan, it was able to purchase land and build more adequate facilities. The pupils and staff moved over to the new school on 20 August 1936. Mrs M.S.

---

7   'Our Deaf and Our Blind: A Brief Record of Work in South Africa,' *The Visit of Helen Keller: Souvenir Programme*, 13–14.
8   Veronica Da Rocha OP, 'A Short History of the Schools for Coloured Deaf Children in South Africa.' Unpublished paper, 1981, 13. Box Education: Deaf education – Wittebome Miscellaneous papers, File: Story of Dominican Schools for the Deaf Cape Town, CDSA, Cape Town.
9   Da Rocha, 'A Short History,' 16.

Taljaard was the first principal until her retirement in 1942. Mr D. du Toit took over and in 1948 he managed to obtain more land and enlarged the school and hostel.

By 1928, all the schools for the deaf in South Africa, both Catholic and Dutch Reformed, used the oral method of deaf education. Most of this arose from the gradual predominance of thinking that it was the superior method of education. Governments and hearing teachers of the deaf were influenced by the events and decisions of the Milan Conference held over 40 years earlier. In South Africa, the Union government passed the Vocational and Schooling Act of 1928 in which it was assumed that the oral method of deaf education was the preferred model in schools for the deaf. New Catholic schools for the deaf were being established that promoted the oral method of deaf education.

From King William's Town to Johannesburg

In 1933, the King William's Town Convent School for the Deaf closed its doors for the last time. It had been in existence for 50 years and in 1934 was transferred to the suburb of Melrose in Johannesburg, its present location. It amalgamated with another small school for the deaf that had been started by the Johannesburg Deaf and Dumb Association. According to the chairman of the Johannesburg Deaf and Dumb Association, Colonel M.C. Rowland, the school had been battling for several years without government assistance. Due to the lack of funds, it had to limit its training until Standard 2.[10] As Colonel Rowland played a vital role in the establishment of the new school in Johannesburg, it is opportune to give a brief biography.

Colonel M.C. Rowland

Colonel M.C. Rowland, born in 1862, was a prominent Catholic layperson in Johannesburg. He was a soldier in the British Imperial Army rising to the rank of Major in 1906. He served in the Union Defence Force until he retired from the military as a Colonel in 1919. Thereafter, he committed himself to charitable works for

---

10   'New School for the Deaf,' *TSC*, 31 January 1934, 1/65, 16/80.

the St Vincent de Paul Society and involvement with the Catholic Federation of the Transvaal.[11]

In 1926, Rowland also gave himself to serving the Deaf community as the chairperson of the Johannesburg Deaf and Dumb Association. He was a founding member of the South African National Council for the Deaf (SANCD) when it was established in 1929 and served as chairperson of this body from 1937–1947. Due to his long-serving commitment to the deaf, when the Johannesburg Deaf Association opened its first old age home for the deaf in Bedfordview it was named the Colonel Rowland Home for the Aged Deaf.[12]

Rowland died in April 1947 at the Frere Hospital in East London and was buried from the pro-Cathedral[13] in Kerk Street, Johannesburg on 11 April 1947. Fr Philip Erasmé OMI presided at the Requiem Mass. Bishop O'Leary OMI was in attendance and seated in the sanctuary.[14]

As we have already mentioned, Rowland was 'largely instrumental in arranging the transfer of the King William's Town School for the Deaf to Melrose.'[15] He later also became chairperson of the school board. It is to this account that we now return.

St Vincent School for the Deaf: A turbulent genesis

The amalgamation of the two schools was not well-received in all quarters. This was not because of dissatisfaction with the oral

---

11 The Catholic Federation was set up by Bishop O'Leary in 1926. The Federation was an umbrella body comprising all Catholic lay societies and sodalities. Its objective was to promote the welfare of Catholics and the church in the Transvaal vicariate. See Joy B. Brain, *The Catholic Church in the Transvaal* (Johannesburg: Missionary Oblates of Mary Immaculate, 1991), 209.
12 'Death of Colonel Rowland,' *TSC*, 23 April 1947, 1/159.
13 A pro-cathedral is a church that is temporarily being used until a Cathedral proper is built. The Church in Kerk Street, Johannesburg was being used at the time. For more information, see Kerk Street Church at catholicjhb.org.za/about/the-cathedral/kerk-street-church.
14 'Death of Colonel Rowland,' 1/159.
15 'Death of Colonel Rowland,' 1/159.

method of deaf education but rather sectarian fears between Protestants and Catholics in South Africa.

While amalgamation was being mooted, parents of the school established by the Johannesburg Deaf and Dumb Association and run by Miss Jessie Davis[16] objected strenuously. The *Rand Daily Mail* ran an article on 17 October 1933, outlining the parents' complaints.[17] Firstly, the parents pointed out that the new school was to be a public school, and they objected that it was going to be 'controlled by a religious institution.' Secondly, they were concerned that the staff of the existing school were going to lose their jobs. Thirdly, they objected that the new teachers coming from King William's Town were from Belgium[18] and they were convinced that they would be unsuitable for teaching South African children. Fourthly, not one of the children to be educated in this new school had parents who were Roman Catholics.[19]

The parents had set up a committee which intended to take their protest to the then-Minister for Education, Mr J.H. Hofmeyr. They wanted to raise their objections but also insisted that if the amalgamation went through, then there had to be a separate hostel for the Protestant children.[20]

---

16   'New School for the Deaf,' TSC, 1/65, 16/80. Also see Arthur W. Blaxall, 'Historical Review,' *The Silent Messenger (TSM)*, April 1952, 2.
17   'Parents to Protest: Deaf and Dumb School Transferred to R.C. Sisterhood,' *Rand Daily Mail*, 17 October 1933. 153/1112 59, KDSA.
18   This was incorrect as the sisters were predominantly of German origin, although some were included later who were South African-born.
19   In his preface to *Totality and Infinity*, 21-23, Levinas explains that human existence that is without an appreciation of infinity or appreciation for 'the face of the other' is to live an existence in a perpetual state of war and conflict. It is to accept Heraclitus' idea that war is at the heart of all reality. Life is about the contest of interested individuals or parties battling for supremacy. War threatens morality and ethics and if it is integral to politics., Rather than war and self-interest, it is love, justice and compassion for others which inaugurates messianic peace and the infinity to which Levinas points. To accept moral or ethical existence is to realise true peace where self-interest is set aside for the good of the other, in this case, the young deaf children, who need to be educated. For more information, see Morgan, *The Cambridge Introduction to Emmanuel Levinas*, 168–169.
20   'Parents to Protest,' 153/1112 59, KDSA.

Not all the parents agreed, however. One parent of a deaf child from Springs, T.A. Chittenden, wrote a letter to the editor of *The Star* on 26 October 1933.[21] She expressed her sincere gratitude and appreciation to the King William's Town sisters for the wonderful tuition given to her son. The sisters had encouraged her son to attend the Wesleyan Church in King William's Town and never tried to force him 'to embrace the Catholic faith if he did not wish to do so.' Chittenden asked everyone involved to look first to the interests of the deaf children and not to bring religious differences into the matter at all.

On Monday 23 October 1933, several Protestant ministers attended the Annual General Meeting of the Johannesburg Association of the Deaf and Dumb, which was chaired by B.C. Vickers, the Mayor of Johannesburg.[22] The ministers expressed their outrage at the decision taken by the committee to hand over the school to the King William's Town Dominican sisters. The committee was accused of 'hoodwinking the public' by agreeing to the amalgamation. The ministers maintained that negotiations had been conducted without the knowledge of the general public or even the parents of the school. Some speakers complained that they only received the news through the press and threatened to withdraw their children from the school.

Colonel Rowland, the chairperson of the Association, responded to the accusations levelled at the committee. He pointed out that he regretted that sectarianism had been brought into the whole matter. He said that when the committee made its decision it did so looking to the best interests of the deaf children. Colonel Rowland said that the committee that made the decision consisted of eight Protestants and two Catholics. The group that was deputed to negotiate with the sisters included no Catholics. He denied that the negotiations had been done in secret without public knowledge. Rowland reiterated that the decision

---

21 'To the Editor of *The Star*,' 26 October 1933. 153/1112 59, KDSA.
22 See 'Deaf and Dumb School, a Lively Meeting, Transfer to R.C. Sisterhood,' *Rand Daily Mail*, 24 October 1933, 153/1112 60, KDSA and 'School for Deaf and Dumb, Sectarian Issue Raised, Strong Criticism of Committee,' *The Star*, 24 October 1933, 153/1112 64, KDSA.

to amalgamate the schools would serve the best interests of the children.

Rowland's response did not satisfy some of the ministers of religion at the meeting and they walked out in protest. Then Dr L. van Schalkwyk, a representative from the Department of Education, explained to the assembly why the Department had agreed to the amalgamation. He stated that 'if any of the parents objected to their children residing in hostels conducted by the sisters, other religious denominations could provide their own hostels if they wished to do so.'[23] He went on to explain that the schools for the deaf in Worcester and King William's Town were conducted by religious denominations but, for educational purposes, they were to be non-denominational. Van Schalkwyk also pointed out 'that for 70 years the English-speaking community has availed itself of the educational facilities provided by the Roman Catholics schools.'[24]

In a letter from Sr Mary Joseph to the Mother General, Sr M. Joseph claimed that Miss Davis, the teacher from the original school, and a parent at the school, Mr Fletcher,[25] had organised the protest. In her report, she mentioned comments from Colonel Rowland that the sisters 'must not have anything to do with Miss Davies. She is out to harm us if she can[26] and is not acting above board.'[27] She said that Mr Walsh, a non-Catholic who supported the amalgamation plans, suggested not to employ Davis as 'she is out against you and, aided by Fletcher, will do all the harm she can in an underhand way.'[28] According to Sr Joseph, the protest began when the association's committee was asked 'how they could dare

---

23   'Deaf and Dumb School: A Lively Meeting,' *Rand Daily Mail*, 24 October 1933, 12.
24   'School for Deaf and Dumb, Sectarian Issue Raised, Strong Criticism of Committee,' *The Star*, 24 October 1933. 153/1112 64, KDSA.
25   Mr J.F. Fletcher was a member of the Plymouth Brethren. See Letter, unknown sister to Mother General, n.d. 153/1112 7, KDSA.
26   Colonel Rowland was himself a prominent Catholic in Johannesburg. More on this contribution to the ministry to the deaf follows later in this chapter.
27   Letter, unknown sister to the Mother General, 3.
28   Ibid, 3.

to hand over their school to the R.C.s.'[29] She also reported that an irate caller phoned her saying: 'You damned Roman Catholics, we are not going to have our children made damned R.C.s also.'[30]

As the Union Education Department, the Johannesburg Association for the Deaf and Dumb and the Dominican sisters had already agreed to the decision, the protest faltered and the plans for the sisters to take over the amalgamated school went ahead. The newly amalgamated school was called St Vincent School for the Deaf. It was named after the Spanish Dominican preacher St Vincent Ferrer, who was purported to have healed a deaf child.[31] It was officially opened and blessed by Bishop O'Leary OMI on 23 January 1934.[32] Fr Laurence Shapcote OP, who attended the official opening, became the first chaplain of the school.

When the school opened its doors, there were 38 pupils and five teachers.[33] Sr Cyrilla Hötzl (1934–1943) continued as principal as she had been previously in the King William's Town School.[34] Jessie Davis was retained as a staff member even though she had been involved in organising the protest. A post was also offered to Miss Holland, Davis' colleague in the previous school. However, Holland declined the offer as she was moving to Ceylon. St Vincent was a government subsidised school meaning that the Department of Education paid the teachers and consequently had a say in the running of the school.

On 11 August 1934, eight months after the school opened, it received a visit from J.H. Hofmeyr, the Minister for the Interior, Education and Public Health. He expressed his pleasure that

---

29   Ibid, 4.
30   Ibid, 2.
31   St Vincent Ferrer OP healed Guillaume de Villiers, a deaf boy. See Stanislaus Hogan, *Saint Vincent Ferrer OP*, (London/New York: Longmans, Green and Company, 1911), 80–81.
32   'New School for the Deaf,' *TSC*, 31 January 1934, 1/65, 16–80.
33   'History/Development of St Vincent School,' *St Vincent School Magazine*, 1999, 5–6. Box EDU29, St Vincent School for the Deaf: School magazines, KDSA.
34   Sr Cyrilla was known as an excellent organiser, leader and administrator. She is credited with laying the foundation for St Vincent's remarkable expansion. She retired from teaching in 1941. For more information on the life of Sr Cyrilla, see 'Sister M. Cyrilla, Deaf School Pioneer,' *TSC*, 21 October 1959, 12/508.

this school for the deaf had been established in Johannesburg because 'until recently there was hardly anything being done in the interior of the Union.'[35] He expressed his hope that the school would have a prosperous future. He emphasised that while the school was getting support from the government presently, it could not depend on that alone. The people of Johannesburg needed to give financial assistance to the school too.

The controversy regarding the establishment of St Vincent School for the Deaf in Johannesburg did not die down immediately. On 13 November 1935, the editor of the Dutch Reformed Church's magazine, *Die Kerkbode*, referred to a letter sent to the magazine from Dominee G. de la Bat, the principal of the School for the Deaf in Worcester.[36] De la Bat complained that pupils that should have been registered at the Worcester School were being encouraged to attend St Vincent School. This was being done in an honest way as the Roman Catholic School was advertising extensively for pupils. Many pupils who should have come to Worcester were going to the Johannesburg school. He said that the Dutch Reformed Church was putting lots of money into extending and developing facilities at the school in Worcester for Afrikaans-speaking deaf children. He said that it was the duty of the Church to make parents aware of this situation especially since the education of the deaf in Roman Catholic schools for the deaf was being done in English and not Afrikaans.

In his comments, the editor supported Dominee de la Bat, saying that it was important to warn all members of the church against sending their children to Roman Catholic schools, be they deaf or hearing schools. He went on to say that 'one needs to ask yourself what the Roman Catholic Church's intention is with regards their establishing big and expensive schools in situations where these needs are already catered for and not really needed.'[37] He concluded that the Roman Catholic Church's objective was to get Protestant children under their influence. In doing so, they

---

35   'Official Visit by Minister: Mr J.H. Hofmeyr at Deaf School,' *TSC*, 15 August 1934, 3/515.
36   'Dowe Kinders van ons Kerk,' *Die Kerkbode*, 13 November 1935, 938. 153/1106 2, KDSA.
37   'Dowe Kinders van ons Kerk,' 938.

would get lifelong support from these children as well as ensure the growth of Catholicism in Protestant countries. He questioned why the Roman Church did not use its resources to improve conditions in their own countries and leave the Protestants to themselves.

Despite the rivalry and competition between Catholics and Protestants, there were also areas of support and collaboration. Just previously in December 1934, Bishop Hennemann of Cape Town complimented Dominee de la Bat and his wife for travelling from Worcester to attend the Dominican-Grimley school concert in St Mary's School hall in Tuin Plein.[38]

> His Lordship told the people that the Principal of the Worcester School for the Deaf had travelled from Worcester and intended returning that night. His sole purpose in coming to Cape Town was to be present at the concert that evening. (Applause.)[39]

There was an ongoing collaboration between all the churches in the SANCD that had been established by Rev. Arthur Blaxall in Bloemfontein in 1929.[40] Delegates from all churches were

---

38 'Concert by Deaf Pupils, Fine Work by the Dominicans,' *TSC*, 5 December 1934, 17/801.
39 'Concert by Deaf Pupils, Fine Work by the Dominicans,' *TSC*, 5 December 1934, 17/801.
40 The decision to start the SANCD was taken at a meeting in Bloemfontein from 25-26 June 1928 of those involved with work among the deaf in South Africa. Present at this meeting were Anglicans Rev. A.W. Blaxall and Mr D.H. Heron-Wright, Rev. G. de la Bat from the Institute for the Deaf in Worcester, a Dutch Reformed school for the deaf, a Christian Brother F.C. McManus representing the Grimley Institute in Cape Town, Mother Mary Alacoque Broderick and Sr Verena Huber representing the King William's Town School, as well as a Miss T.A. Davis from the Johannesburg Deaf School. Two government officials were also present, namely, Dr L. van Schalkwyk from the Department of Education and Dr O.F. Black from the Department of the Interior. There were a further eight delegates from other deaf-related organisations around the country, which included two visitors from Glasgow and London. See *Report of the First Conference of Workers Amongst the Deaf, and the Deaf and Dumb, of South Africa*, held in the Jubileum Hall, Bloemfontein, 25-26 June 1928. 153/1112 102, KDSA.

involved in deaf education in the SANCD throughout its history.[41] This is a wonderful tribute to how having a common project can bring people together, even when they might have strong sectarian views, to work together and to support each other in a shared mission.

Sr Cyrilla continued to run the school until her retirement in 1943. She was succeeded by Sr Verena Huber (1943–1947), who was in turn replaced by Sr Thomasia Knoepfle (1947–1969) as principal. Sr Thomasia was principal for 22 years and left an indelible mark on the school.[42]

Dominican School for the Deaf, Wittebome

Sectarian differences were not the only distinctions in South Africa to seriously affect the education of the deaf. Racial discrimination was always prominent in this society but became more entrenched when segregationist legislation forced conformity on Catholic schools for the deaf.

The Grimley School for the Deaf in Cape Town had, from its earliest years, admitted coloured children to the school.[43] However during the 1920s, the number of coloured children seeking admission to the school continued to grow.[44] Segregation prevailed and in 1931, a new school building was built for the white deaf children and it was decided to build a new school for the coloured children in Wynberg.[45]

In 1937, the Dominican School for the Deaf, Wittebome was established as the first Catholic deaf school for African, coloured and Indian children in South Africa.[46]. Wittebome was a coloured

---

41 A comprehensive history of the SANCD still needs to be written.
42 'Beginning and Development of the School,' 13. 152/1104 43, KDSA. For more information on her life, see 'Sr Thomasia (Luzia) Knoepfle OP: 1904-04-20–1995-10-14,' Necrology Box 37, File 886 (37/886), KDSA.
43 Arthur Blaxall, 'Historical Review,' *TSM*, April 1952, 2.
44 See 'Supplement: New Dominican School for the Deaf, *TSC*, 21 July 1937, i–iv.
45 'Supplement: New Dominican School for the Deaf,' *TSC*, 21 July 1937, iv.
46 No separate Catholic Deaf schools were opened for Indian children. Those that went to Catholic Deaf schools like Suzanne

area approximately 20 kilometres from the Grimley School in the city centre of Cape Town.

When the new school opened its doors, there were 60 children on the roll.[47] The school provided for both academic and vocational training. A hostel that could accommodate 150 boarders was built for those children who travelled from other provinces in the country.[48] In recognising that the school had previously been one, the Union Education Department allowed the Grimley School in Cape Town and the Wittebome School to continue as two departments of the same school. The schools had only one principal in Sister Germaine Lawrence.[49]

The Deaf chaplain in Cape Town

After the death of Monsignor Kolbe in 1934, Fr Gill was appointed the Deaf chaplain in Cape Town. He accepted this ministry with great enthusiasm and dedication until ill-health forced him to return to England in 1942. During his period as chaplain, he conducted many retreats and parish missions for the deaf Catholics in Cape Town. He learnt sign language and taught catechism to the deaf Catholics each month and conducted Masses in sign.[50] When he conducted a retreat at the Cathedral in March 1934, approximately 80 deaf Catholics from all over the Western Cape attended. One young man was so eager to attend the retreat that he walked 24 miles from Belville and back daily. According to an article in *The Southern Cross*, 'Many of them could converse by the modern method of lip-reading so that Fr Gill both spoke the words and translated them by signs.'[51]

The retreat included a visit from Bishop Hennemann who was surprised to see that there were so many Catholic deaf

---

Lombard (neé Barrett), went to the Wittebome School.
47   Da Rocha, 'A Short History,' 9.
48   'Fine New Block of Buildings at Wittebome, Dominican Sisters' Splendid Work for the Deaf,' TSC, 21 July 1937.
49   Da Rocha, 'A Short History,' 9.
50   'Cathedral Mission for the Deaf: Sermons in Sign Language,' TSC, 28 March 1934, 2/194. Also see 'Concert by Deaf Pupils: Fine Work by the Dominicans,' TSC, 5 December 1934, 17/801.
51   'Cathedral Mission for the Deaf,' TSC, 2/194.

people on the Peninsula. He concluded the retreat with a solemn pontifical benediction.

Three years later, Fr Gill led a three-day mission for the deaf at St Mary's parish. Before the start of the mission, he travelled all over the Peninsula 'wandering even on foot through the sands of the Cape Flats in search of his best friends, the deaf and dumb, both Coloured and European.'[52]

Conclusion: Levinas, totality and good conscience

In this chapter we have seen the triumph of the oral method of deaf education over manualism in Catholic schools for the deaf. There was no malicious intention behind it; it was done in good conscience to transform the lives of deaf people, 'to liberate them from their prisons of silence.' Education was a gateway to a better life for the deaf. We saw how some deaf people benefitted from the education they received at school and were able to progress in life. But for Levinas, even actions done with good intentions can be oppressive and function in assimilatory ways or what he called an imperialism of the same. In the case of the schools for the deaf, we see definite moves where the hearing Cabra Dominican sisters, with good intentions and operating from a good conscience, sought to ensure the best education for the deaf children entrusted to their care. They tried to equip them with the skills required to live and find employment in a world of hearing people.[53]

However, in so doing they denied the difference or alterity of these deaf children and drew them into their hearing world. This is what Levinas called totality.

> [Totality or] essence weaves between the incomparables, between me and the others, a unity, a community, and drags us off and assembles us on the same side, chaining us to one another like galley slaves, emptying proximity of its meaning.[54]

---

52 'Mission for the Deaf: Fr T Gill's Splendid Work,' *TSC*, 24 March 1937, 2/214.
53 Levinas, *Collected Philosophical Papers*, 26.
54 Levinas, *Otherwise than Being*, 182.

For Levinas, totality inflicts wounds on those whom it has assimilated but it often does this in good conscience.[55] Acting in good conscience is when 'I am the bearer of a fault which is not reflected in my intentions.'[56]

The Dominican sisters' actions were acts of piety and doing their best but it was also wounding. It was wounding not only in the discipline they exercised over the children but wounding and violent in the way it denied the deaf children the opportunity to learn and study through sign language. As Minister pointed out:

> Much of the ethical force of Levinas's thought comes in the claim that our attempts to persist in being, and be at-home in the world, tasks we carry out in good conscience everyday, make us complicit in the suffering and deaths of unseen, unrecognized others.[57]

Phonocentrism and audism have been identified as violence underpinning the oral method of deaf education. Many of the sisters teaching in these schools for the deaf were unaware or would disagree, that they were operating from totality, acting from self-interest or interestedness. Interestedness, for Levinas, is to think that one is 'the whole' instead of 'a part of a whole.'[58]

The self is just one part of the whole and is not the centre of the world. The teachers can be understood to have acted unjustly, but in good conscience, towards the deaf children to whom they were ministering. They did not see any problem with what they were doing. It was perceived to be pious work, an act of charity.[59] It was lauded by all the hearing government officials, hearing

---

55 Levinas, *Collected Philosophical Papers*, 31.
56 Levinas, *Collected Philosophical Papers*, 32.
57 Minister, *Defacing the Other*, 206.
58 Levinas, *Collected Philosophical Papers*, 26.
59 See Levinas, *Collected Philosophical Papers*, 31: 'The pious soul can, to be sure, suffer from its social guilt, but since this differs from the wrong which *I* commit with respect to *you*, it is reconciled with a "good conscience." Conscience torments the pious conscience only with a secondary torment. One is healed of it after a fashion by charity, the love of the neighbour who knocks at the door, alms given to the poor, philanthropy, or an action undertaken for the first one to come along.'

journalists and all the clerics as God's work, a work from infinity. But this was precisely the problem: the deaf were being chained and forced into accepting a hearing view of the world.

For Levinas, infinity rather than chaining hearing and deaf people on the same side, breaches totality.[60] It exalts alterity and otherness. Infinity or 'the Saying' gives us a 'bad conscience' making us aware of the harm, damage and wounds being inflicted on the Other through our pious – and not so pious – acts.[61] Breaching totality or discovering the need to be otherwise than being is to recognise our guilt and complicity in acting unjustly towards the Other, by diminishing them, reducing them to objects to fit into our, or the self's, way of seeing and living in the world. This 'bad conscience' would make us aware of the ethical relation and help us recognise our responsibility for the Other's good.

---

60 Levinas, *Totality and Infinity*,
61 'My "being in the world" or "my place in the sun," my home – are they not a usurpation of places that belong to the other man (sic) who has already been oppressed or starved by me?' Levinas, *Entre Nous*, 130.

Chapter 7

Totality and the Oral Method of Deaf Education in White and Coloured Catholic Schools for the Deaf, 1928–1969

According to Arthur Blaxall, 'The oral method is the name given to the system of educating the deaf, now all but universal.'[1] The oral method of deaf education was seen, especially after the Milan Conference in 1880, as the modern and scientific answer to the problem of deafness and as the means for deaf people to acquire a spoken language. So, the oral method of deaf education was essentially a hearing discourse on how to help deaf people learn a spoken language by employing the most modern and scientific technologies in assisting in the learning of a spoken language. Learning a spoken language gave deaf children the basic tools they needed to be educated and to integrate into a hearing world

---

1   Arthur W. Blaxall was born in London in 1891. After school he worked in an insurance office where he had his first contact with the deaf and blind in 1910. After the First World War, he studied at Keble College in Oxford and was ordained a priest in 1921. His first assignment was to work as assistant chaplain to the Deaf in Birmingham. He came to South Africa in 1923 and took up duties as a missioner to the deaf in the diocese of Cape Town. He soon recognised that services for the deaf and blind in South Africa were wholly inadequate. He founded the South African National Council for the Deaf in 1928, becoming its first chairperson. In 1934, he was superintendent of the Athlone School for the Blind, Faure, Cape Province. In 1946, he founded the Kutlwanong Deaf and Dumb school in Roodepoort and was on the governing board until 1954. He was proficient in signed English. He also did extensive work for the blind. In 1963, he was arrested for channelling international funding to the Pan-Africanist Congress (PAC) and African National Congress (ANC). After being released he returned to England where he died in 1970. See 'A Well-Deserved Honour,' *TSM*, July 1956, 4. This above quote is from his book entitled *Handicapped: Being Three Short Essays on 1) The Deaf; 2) The Blind; 3) The Doubly-Handicapped* (Pretoria: The Carnegie Corporation Visitors' Grants Committee, 1934).

by finding employment and thereby becoming independent and financially self-supporting. The advocates of this method also actively discouraged and disparaged the use of sign language and manual methods of Deaf education.

In this section, it is important to understand the oral method approach to deaf education to appreciate the challenges that deaf children face and the reaction of deaf adults to this form of education. Before outlining the method of teaching, it is first necessary to understand how being deaf was perceived and understood by the hearing at this time. We will also briefly look at how the deaf children themselves felt about the oral method of deaf and conclude with a reflection on how Levinas can help us understand how the oral method of deaf education functioned as a totality.

What is deafness?

Deafness was understood as the medical condition of suffering from a lack of hearing. It was perceived to be a physical handicap that isolated people from other human beings and imprisoned them in a solitary world of silence.

It was often seen as diminishing the person's ability to function adequately in society and in relationships with other. Mr H.S. Jooste, a hearing social worker, in speaking to ear, nose and throat specialists at a medical conference in Pretoria in 1955 described the experience of deafness for a deaf person as:

> [A] cause of utter isolation from his fellowmen [sic] and from Society. It means an inability to live a full life as a human being and a basic inability to grasp and understand the Society in which he moves and of which he is a part.[2]

In 1959, Mr V.H. Vaughan, from the Union Education Department, speaking at the blessing of the new extension at St Vincent School in Johannesburg, said that deafness was a three-fold handicap. Apart from the absence of hearing and the consequent inability

---

2   H.S. Jooste, 'The Rehabilitation of the Deaf, *TSM*, December 1955, 8.

to speak, 'the third is to my mind the most important, namely, the lack of mental stimulation which is the result of normal conversation between one person and another. This the deaf person misses.'[3] The handicap was understood as the lack of hearing but which resulted in a greater problem, the inability to develop speech. Vaughan's inclusion of the lack of intellectual stimulation arising from deafness, as part of his three-fold handicap understanding of deafness, illustrated that it was a prevalent perception at this time, and not just a coincidence, that deaf people who were not able to speak, were also referred to as dumb.[4] It was earnestly believed that the deaf were imprisoned and 'locked into a world of silence.'[5]

Deafness is understood as a physical lack of being able to hear. This has been referred to as the medical understanding of deafness where hearing is the norm and those who are unable to hear are deviating from the norm.

Hearing deviants

Hearing was taken to be normal and anyone who deviated from this norm was considered deviant or deviate. In a talk, a renowned professor of speech therapy at the University of the Witwatersrand, P de V. Pienaar, referred to the deaf person as a 'hearing deviate.'[6]

The American sociologist Howard Becker identified four types of deviance in social groups. The first is statistical which defines 'as deviant anything that varies too widely from the average.'[7] As redheads are statistically a minority in the USA in comparison to the majority of brunettes, redheads constitute a deviant group. The second common view of deviance is when behaviour is perceived to be pathological or diseased. This medical

---

3	'Deaf School Extension Provided by Pupil's Parents,' *TSC*, 30 September 1959, 12/472.
4	Ibid.
5	Monsignor Desmond Hatton, 'The Deaf to Hear,' *TSC*, 21 November 1962, 5/557.
6	P de V. Pienaar, 'Modern Development in the Field of Audiology,' *TSM*, 29, 1, March 1963, 13–20.
7	Howard S. Becker, *Outsiders: Studies in the Sociology of Deviance* (New York: The Free Press, 1963), 5–8.

analogy is employed to imply that deviance is the product of either a physical or mental illness. When looking at society, deviance can be used in a third sense to distinguish between functional and dysfunctional processes taking place within the society. Fourthly, deviance is used, particularly by Becker, to speak about people who purposely break society's rules.

Paul Higgins developed Becker's idea of deviance as it relates to deaf people. He argued that deaf people were outsiders in a hearing world.[8] Therefore, when speaking of deaf people deviance is understood primarily in the first two senses. Deaf people are a small minority within the overall hearing population and, secondly, they are perceived to suffer from a physical lack of hearing which is understood to constitute a handicap from which they need to be rescued. They are not considered normal in terms of what is normal along the bell curve in relation to an overall population. This was understood as having a negative impact on deaf children.

> In a crowd of hearing children a minority of deaf children disappear or at least take the last place. They have no hope of ever taking a leading part or being counted as important. Their deviation from the normal pattern is constantly brought home to them, and they feel inferior and humbled. Continual dependence on the goodwill and favour of others is draining their self-confidence.[9]

Hearing was considered the normal human state while deafness was regarded as an aberrant deviation from the hearing norm, and therefore a handicap. It was understood as diminishing the deaf person.

This view was so prevalent that the SANCD, established by Rev. Arthur W. Blaxall in 1929, would later use the image of a harp with a broken cord as the emblem for its publication *The Silent Messenger*. As a musical instrument, the harp was defective and

---

8 See Paul C. Higgins, *Outsiders in a Hearing World: A Sociology of Deafness* (London: Sage Publications, 1980).

9 'Schools of Thought at Variance,' *Saint Vincent Quarterly* (SVQ) 9, 3 (1964): 3.

needed fixing by replacing the broken cord. Similarly, deaf people were perceived by the hearing to have a defect that needed fixing.[10] In an editorial, *The Silent Messenger* elaborates: 'The analogy implied here is that of the human being, with special emphasis on the human anatomy and the psychical.'[11]

The school and technology would provide the means to repair the damage and restore the suffering and defective person to wholeness and full humanity. The school became the primary place where the defect was repaired and functioned more as both a clinic and an educational centre.[12]

Deaf children had a defect because they had difficulty hearing and acquiring a spoken language like a 'normal' hearing child. The deaf were handicapped and this needed to be remedied. Remedying the situation was conceived to be impossible without special intervention.

Rehabilitation required

As the deviance was perceived in medical terms – a physical or mental defect – the remedy was seen to be working for the rehabilitation of the deaf child or adult and thereby making them functional in normal society, namely the hearing world. Rehabilitation happened through the early detection of deafness so that the child could be sent to a deaf school to be trained in language acquisition thereby learning to speak and speechread. This was to be accomplished by exploiting, as far as possible, the residual hearing that deaf children had through the provision of hearing aids.

It was understood that the school could remedy this defect only by providing careful training and special education.

---

[10] In fact, the same line of thinking was central to all 'handicapped' people. The theology of disability was developed to contradict this way of thinking about disability. The disabled person was perceived to be a victim of their handicap and needed to be rescued from it by the able-bodied and medical profession.

[11] 'Editorial: Our Emblem,' *TSM*, 33, 4, December 1969, 3.

[12] On the clinical gaze in education, education as therapy and the school as clinic, see Branson and Miller, *Damned for Their Difference*, 113–118, 130–132; 200–202; and 205–206 respectively.

Through the means of this special education, deaf people could be empowered to overcome their handicaps. They would thereafter be able to

> learn something of the wondrous melodies of Nature... the sounds of the flowing stream, the roar of the turbulent sea, the rustle of the leaves in the wind, the crash of the thunder, the music of the human voice.[13]

This was the objective of the oral method of deaf education.

The oral method of education: The remedy for deafness

The key principle of the oral method was to exploit the child's residual hearing. It was believed that very few deaf children were without any hearing at all. Many had some degree of residual hearing. Through the early detection of deafness, the children were fitted with the appropriate technology, like hearing aids, to enhance their residual hearing. In the classroom too, technology like amplifiers and the induction loop were used to boost the children's residual hearing so that they could hear a little more and thereby learn a spoken language just like any other hearing child.

In communication with the child, teachers and parents were encouraged to use ordinary and meaningful conversational exchanges. The child was taught and encouraged to speechread, also known as lip-reading, to assist in comprehending what was being said to them. The children were coached for many hours on how to use their voices for sound production and pronunciation. They were taught the spoken language's grammatical rules and structures.

The use of the natural sign language of the deaf was strictly forbidden in the classroom and the playground. If, at school, any deaf children were caught using signs or 'gestures', as it was referred to, these children were punished. The teachers wanted to

---

13   Monsignor Desmond Hatton, 'The Deaf to Hear,' *TSC*, 21 November 1962, 5/557.

inculcate in the deaf children a greater dependence on the use of their auditory skills rather than their visual skills.

Central to the whole concept of the oral method of education was to prepare the children for life in a predominantly hearing world where they would not receive any preferential treatment in the workplace. Education was primarily geared towards vocational training to equip the deaf child for employment. They had to be equipped to find their place in this world and the starting place was to first acquire the knowledge of a spoken language.

Language acquisition

Deaf people were seen to be imprisoned in a solitary and oppressively silent world, one from which they needed to be liberated. Learning a language was the way to liberate deaf people from their affliction.

> Language is the basic key to education of the deaf child and any means to impart to him this knowledge materially assists him on his long and difficult journey into the land of the hearing. Speech is, of course, but the spoken form of language and together with writing, reading and other visual forms of communication is but a secondary manifestation of language.[14]

Language was the vehicle for thought and knowledge and was primarily acquired by attending a special school for the deaf. The measure of language acquisition was speech. Consequently, deaf children had to learn how to speak correctly so that they could study and learn and find employment in life.

Speech: a manifestation of language

As we have already discussed in Chapter 4, the connection between deafness and speech goes back to Aristotle who wrote that the deaf child is ignorant because he is unable to communicate through speech. Speech was understood as indicating intelligence.

---

14   E.S. Greenway, 'Language the Basic Key,' *TSM*, June 1958, 17.

Those who could not speak had the intelligence of animals rather than human beings. However, in the same way as Aristotle saw women as 'defective males' and this view has had a long history of prejudicial understandings of women in Church and society; so too the deaf have suffered a similar fate in being considered as 'defective hearing people.' This outlook has contributed enormously to the devaluing of sign language and explains why educators of the oral method, over the centuries, have placed so much emphasis on teaching deaf children to speak a spoken language.

The inability to hear sound was therefore correlated to the failure to learn to speak a language, where language meant a spoken language. Without this language, the deaf were understood to be without any means of communication.[15] It was vital to gain knowledge of this language for human growth. However, it was delayed in the deaf, as Sr Thomasia explained:

> Language growth is bound up closely with mental development. This is slow in the deaf. They rarely get a grip of the language until they are 13 years old.[16]

In all this discussion, it is obvious that the hearing and speaking child was determined to be normative, whereas the corollary, being deaf and dumb, was to have a handicap.

Speaking to parents about speech for the deaf, Sr Hermina, a teacher at St Vincent School, said that when parents bring their children to school for the first time, they often ask 'Will my child learn to speak?'[17] In other words, will my child be normal? Central to the oral method of education was to make the deaf child as 'normal as possible' so that the child could function adequately in the hearing world. Speech was considered the mark of normalisation.

---

15   See C. Alan Cook, 'Breaking the Other Sound Barrier,' *Outspan*, 25 November 1955, 106.
16   Cook, 'Breaking the Other Sound Barrier,' 106.
17   Sr Hermina, 'Speech for the Deaf – A Method in the Making,' *SVQ* 9, 2 (1964): 3.

Communicating in a spoken language

The children were thought to be handicapped and thus dependent on hearing people, especially their teachers and parents, to teach them how to communicate in a spoken language so that they could function satisfactorily in a hearing world. Without a spoken language, deaf children were understood not to have a language at all and thus unable to learn and gain knowledge.

According to Sr Hermina:

> We are convinced... that our deaf children need to be taught speech while they are at school, and that on leaving school their speech should be such that it can be understood, not only within their own family but also by others... We claim that deaf pupils have left schools for the deaf, with what may be called satisfactory speech. We have also observed that when the speech elements are mastered well while at school, their speech has actually improved through contact with hearing people.[18]

The learning of a language had to begin from as young an age as possible. There was to be no delay in enabling a young child to learn a language.

Being taught to speak from as young as possible

Learning to speak was a duty that was encouraged from as early an age as possible. Language acquisition is a major challenge for all children in the first three years of life. So, it was for deaf children too. St Vincent School sought to collaborate with parents even before the child was admitted to school. One of the important challenges was that the parents be 'taught to accept their child with all his limitations and residual abilities.'[19]

Instruction in language knowledge needed to start in the home way before the child even attended school.

---

18   Sr Hermina, 'Speech for the Deaf,' 3–15.
19   'St Vincent's School Cracks Isolation of the Deaf Child,' *TSC*, 27 April 1966, 4/196.

> Once severe deafness has been diagnosed no time should be lost in inquiring what should be done at home until the time when the child can get the help of a school for the deaf. The mother will be instructed to use every opportunity for stimulating any slight amount of residual hearing that may be present. We have heard of infants below one year of age being fitted with a hearing aid. The mother will be taught above all to speak close to the child's ears and in such a way that he can see her face and observe, unconsciously of course, the speech movements on her face.[20]

From the age of three or four, some deaf children were accepted into schools for the deaf like St Vincent, Dominican-Grimley and Wittebome. Parents were encouraged to send their children to a deaf school by the age of three years old. 'The consensus... today, is that a child who starts at an early age, gains greater advantages which stand it in good stead in future years.'[21] In a talk to about 150 members of the Catholic Women's League in Cape Town on 11 December 1965, Fr Reginald Cawcutt, the chaplain to the deaf in the Archdiocese, explained that:

> The most important factor was to get a deaf child to school as early as possible, three years being the best... [and that there] be the rule to test for deafness in early infancy. With early training and normal intelligence, it was possible for a deaf child to matriculate and take up a profession.[22]

At other schools for the deaf, it was no different. Sr Thomasia, the principal of St Vincent School, explained that 'children are admitted into the nursery classes from the age of three years and learn to adjust to a completely new environment.'[23] The practice was the same at the Wittebome School, as well as the later

---

20 Sr Hermina, 'Speech for the Deaf – A Method in the Making, *SVQ* 9, 2 (1964): 3-15.
21 L.J. Paolo, 'The Role of the Parent of the Deaf Child,' *SVQ* 10, 1 (1965): 4.
22 'Chaplain Speaks on Work for Deaf at C.W.L. Meeting,' *TSC*, 29 December 1965, 4/616.
23 'St Vincent's School Cracks Isolation of the Deaf Child,' *TSC*, 27 April 1966, 4/196.

established Hammanskraal School and St Thomas School in King William's Town. However, these schools for the deaf for black children only went up to Standard 7 or Standard 8 and never as far as matric. This discrepancy was to be the cause of consternation for black deaf people.[24]

The role of parents in teaching their children to speak

Even when the child was at school, the collaboration between teacher and parent did not end. Parents could not just hand over their responsibilities of educating their deaf child to the school. They had to become proficient in communicating with their child and thus had to play their part in coaching their children to communicate in a spoken language.

It was accepted that the deaf child was not able to learn to speak on their own like a hearing child. The deaf child needed special assistance from both the teacher and parent.

> Your child is deaf and will never be able to appreciate sound as you and I can. As he grows older the sound barrier will assume gigantic proportions, unless someone counteracts the effects of deafness. The child left to himself, is helpless. You and I must come to his rescue with all the resources available. Teacher and parents should work together as a team.[25]

The teacher and parents collaborated to ensure that the child could become more like normal hearing children. This demanded that parents, after school hours, also assume the role of teacher at home.

> First, you must be firmly convinced that you can do a great deal for your child. There are many things which only you can do, nobody else. Having the indispensable faith leave no stone unturned to help your child to be more like other

---

24 We will address this point later in Chapter 8.
25 Interested Teacher, 'A Talk to Parents,' *SVQ* 2, 1 (March 1955): 3.

children... The school is trying to do for your child what an ordinary school does, plus a great deal of what ordinarily he would pick up for himself, at home and outside in the world... If you wish your child ever to compare favourably with hearing children you must be part-time teachers. You must cheerfully, and in a spirit of adventure, assume this extra role.[26]

The collaboration extended to coaching their children into speaking and helping them to improve their vocabulary. The hearing child provided the standard of measure from which many conclusions in deaf education were drawn about the progress of language acquisition of the deaf child.

Talk to your child in a natural and simple way everywhere and at all times ... Try to give him a basic vocabulary to establish contact with yourself and others. Follow the natural method. Take note of the language used by hearing children of the same age and adapt it to your child's needs. Do not treat him as a one-year-old-child is [sic][27] he is two or three years of age. At five or six he is no more a baby, so do not restrict your talk to baby language... At times deaf children surprise one with words and expressions they have picked up in the manner hearing children pick them up.[28]

They were not to treat their children differently from their hearing children. Thus, they were encouraged to have conversations with their children. It was believed that this practice would increase the deaf children's vocabulary and language skills and give them practice in expressing their ideas.

Training in the home went beyond just teaching them vocabulary and language skills. Parents were responsible for instilling discipline in their deaf children and teaching them courteous behaviour and good manners.

---

26   Interested Teacher, 'A Talk to Parents,' 3.
27   Typing error in the original document. It is meant to read 'if' and not 'is'.
28   Interested Teacher, 'A Talk to Parents,' 5–6.

> Parents have a responsibility for their deaf child's general training. You must see that he fits into your family picture, just as the teacher helps him to adjust himself to his school environment. One of the things he must learn is self-control.[29]

They were not to feel sorry for the deaf child and treat him or her any differently than their hearing children. However, there was a warning that the deaf child may not fully understand, and until he or she is sufficiently well educated to grasp abstract ideas, the child may interpret an insistence upon discipline, as cruelty or a lack of love; and may thereby lose the all-important feeling of security, of belonging, of being part of the home.'[30] This was just a phase.

It was more important to realise that the deaf child learnt primarily in a visual rather than in an auditory manner. Therefore, the behaviour that parents modelled was the behaviour that the deaf children copied.

> As your child depends on his [sic] eyes for much of his learning, your own social behaviour sets the example. He patterns his conduct on what he sees in the adults around him.[31]

However, this visual means of learning meant that children learnt language by developing their skills by reading the lips of parents, teachers and other hearing people.

Developing speechreading

The primary way in which parents were encouraged to teach their children language was to instil in them 'the habit of watching lips.'[32]

---

29 See Sr Hermina, 'Home Responsibilities in the Education of Deaf Children,' SVQ 3, 4, (October–December 1957): 13.
30 L.J. Paolo, 'The Role of the Parent of the Deaf Child,' SVQ 10, 1 (1965): 6.
31 Sr Hermina, 'Home Responsibilities in the Education of Deaf Children,' SVQ 3, 4 (October–December 1957): 13.
32 Interested Teacher, 'Talk to Parents,' 7.

> Speechreading, popularly known as lip-reading, is the visible comprehension of what is said by the speaker. Speechreading describes the process more accurately than lip-reading. The lip-reader needs clues apart from those he can gather from the lips. Adults, who depend on lip-reading, will tell you that the facial expression assists a great deal in the interpretation of the lip movements... Deaf persons are expert in deriving meaning from the emotions expressed on the face.[33]

These techniques reinforced those which were employed in the classroom.

> The more language the deaf child has the sooner he will begin to speak... To attract and hold his attention, be it only a passing moment, get him to look at some brightly coloured toy or other interesting object. Slowly move it in various directions to and from your mouth, and also towards him. His eyes will involuntarily follow the movements of your mouth. Or let him feel your breath by blowing on his cheeks, hair or hands. Later you can blow coloured balloons or strips of coloured paper towards him for his amusement. In all these exercises your face must be in the light and your child's face away from strong light.[34]

The purpose of speechreading was to ensure that the deaf child became independent and self-reliant. 'It is learnt more by practice than by set lessons. It takes the place of the listening of the hearing child and is considered the best substitute.'[35]

Speech training

However, speechreading was not enough. It needed to be linked with speech training and voice production.

---

[33] Sr Thomasia, 'Speechreading,' *SVQ* 11, 2 (1966): 3–5.
[34] Sr Hermina, 'Home Responsibilities in the Education of Deaf Children,' *SVQ*, 7.
[35] Sr Thomasia, 'Speechreading,' *SVQ*, 4–5.

> Sense training is an excellent preparation for speech training, when the children have to observe and imitate the minutest details of shapes and movements of the speaker... Most deaf children, even the severely deaf, can laugh aloud, can cry and shout even louder, but to produce voice voluntarily and to shape it into definite speech sounds and words is quite a different matter.[36]

Lip-reading and speech development were not seen as merely the work done in the school classroom. The lack of adequate stimulation and practice at home was viewed askance by teachers at St Vincent School because it engendered 'in the deaf child the wrong attitude towards oral communication.'[37] The advice to parents was to 'arouse in your child a desire to speak.'[38] They needed to realise and be made to understand that speech was a way of getting what they want. The children's success in developing speech depended on their ability to lip-read or speechread.

To become proficient in communicating in a hearing world, it was not only important for deaf children to understand what others were saying but also to know how to speak to hearing people. For this purpose, the deaf child needed good voice production.

> As in all things, the nursery teacher will attend to the first needs first; develop in the child a clear forward voice, open throat and some degree of tongue control until the first simple word emerges after many trials and errors.[39]

This was one of the important contributions that the school made and to ensure good speech it employed the use of modern technology.

---

36 Sr Hermina, 'Speech for the Deaf – A Method in the Making,' *SVQ* 9, 2 (1964): 7.
37 See Sr Hermina, 'Home Responsibilities,' 10.
38 Ibid, 12.
39 Sr Hermina, 'Speech for the Deaf,' 7–8.

Deaf education and technology

After the Enlightenment, with its emphasis on reason and progress, pastoral practice accepted and promoted the new medical knowledge and scientific innovations of the day as integral to the Church's missionary efforts to remedy the ills of the world and as a tool of evangelisation.[40] In ministry to the deaf, the schools relied heavily on modern technological advances to overcome the silent world into which they saw the deaf condemned. The Catholic weekly, *The Southern Cross*, reported in 1948 on a visit from Mrs van Zyl, the wife of the Governor-General, to the Dominican School in Wittebome. The headline read: 'Visit to two Catholic Homes: Mrs van Zyl sees modern Deaf and Dumb methods.' She was accompanied by Bishop Hennemann, the Archbishop of Cape Town, and the parish priest of Wittebome, Mgr J. O'Rourke.

> The programme of welcome included an orchestral item and a most impressive display of the methods of speech-training, showing the highly scientific approach to the problem. This was exemplified further when Her Excellency was shown round the institution and saw the most up-to-date electric apparatus for testing and aiding hearing.[41]

This belief that the oral approach was both modern and scientific was central to the thinking of the educators, teachers and administrators. At St Vincent School in Johannesburg, there was a similar understanding. In 1960, Mr V.H. Vaughan, from the Union Education Department, gave a speech to parents and teachers of St Vincent on the importance of using scientific apparatus in the advancement of education for the deaf.[42]

It was considered vital in the oral method of education that residual hearing is stimulated and developed when the child starts school. This led to the introduction of various technological

---

40   David Bosch, *Transforming Mission: Paradigm Shifts in Theology of Mission*, (Maryknoll: Orbis Books, 1991), 337.
41   'Visit to Two Catholic homes,' *TSC*, 15 September 1948, 6/377.
42   'Deaf School Extension Provided by Pupil's Parents,' *TSC*, 30 September 1959, 12/472.

innovations to assist deaf children make the most use of their residual hearing through amplification or to train them in regulating the sound of their voices.

The most spoken-about innovation was the Coyne Voice Pitch Indicator that was developed in Cape Town.

The Coyne Voice Pitch Indicator

In 1937, Mr A.E. Coyne, a lecturer in engineering at the Cape Technical College, invented and developed the Coyne Voice Pitch Indicator. His wife taught at the Dominican-Grimley School for the Deaf in Cape Town.[43] The instrument was devised to help profoundly deaf children to recognise the pitch of their voices and learn how to regulate it. The pitch of the voice was captured by tuning forks which then lit up a series of coloured lights. The lights rose and fell in relation to the sound emitted indicating the pitch of the voice.

> A little girl who has a naturally high-pitched voice is now able to control it and bring it down to the normal range, and another whose voice for years has been very low has for the first time realised what physical sensation is required in order to raise the pitch, and after three days was able to produce notes four and five tones above her original pitch.[44]

The Coyne Voice Pitch Indicator was not the only technological innovation that was used to assist teachers in the education of deaf children.

Amplifiers, hearing aids and the induction loop system

In the classroom, the hearing aid and amplified sound were integral to teaching in a deaf school. Already back in November 1937, St Vincent School sought to supplement the oral method with what was referred to as the acoustic method. Making use

---

43 'The Coyne Voice Pitch Indicator,' *TSM*, December 1937, 6.
44 'The Coyne Voice Pitch Indicator,' 7. Also see 'Teaching the Deaf to Hear,' *The Star*, 23 August 1946.

of modern technology, the school installed the first group radio hearing aid to be used in South Africa.

> The apparatus consists principally of a microphone for the sister in charge to speak into, and a pair of headphones for each child. The phones are plugged into a transformer and the children can regulate the volume of their phones to suit themselves.[45]

Thus, the acoustic method meant that the classroom was fitted out with various technological aids to assist the teacher in educating the deaf:

> All the children wear hearing aids and there are classroom installations as well as the induction loop systems and special speech-training units in use. To develop sound consciousness highly amplified electronic equipment is used.[46]

Getting deaf children to accept the use of hearing aids seemed to be a challenge. The hearing aids then were heavy as they were attached to an amplifier that was worn around the neck. The children were given these hearing aids as soon as they arrived at school so that they would be able to familiarise themselves with the hearing aids as soon as possible.

> Experience has shown that deaf children will not befriend hearing aids unless they become used to them at a very early age. Therefore, as soon as a child is admitted to the Nursery Class he is fitted with a high fidelity aid. Only the best aids on the market are good enough, for the child will produce the voice and the speech quality he hears through his aid.[47]

---

45 'Radio Teaches the Deaf: Afflicted Children Listen-in, Learn to Speak,' *Sunday Express*, 18 July 1937.
46 'St Vincent's School Cracks Isolation of the Deaf Child,' *TSC*, 27 April 1966, 4/196.
47 Sr Thomasia, 'Report 1960/61,' *SVQ* 6, 1 (March 1961): 2.

In 1961, Mr H. Reichenberg of Westdene Products, a company that sold hearing aids, gave a talk at St Vincent School and explained to parents and teachers that there were essentially three types of hearing aids used in educating the deaf.[48] Firstly, there were specially designed speech training hearing aids for individual tuition. St Vincent had three of these hearing aids and they were used to teach children who were slow in grasping speech and therefore battled with following the lessons in class. Secondly, there were group amplifiers for class teaching. Each child in the class uses headsets similar to those used by pilots and radio operators. The teacher speaks into a microphone which then amplifies the sound to each child in the room. Thirdly, there is the loop induction system. This system did not require the wearing of any heavy headsets. The children's personal hearing aids were able to pick up the sound amplified through a wire that was looped around the classroom. The same system was also operative in the schools for the deaf in Cape Town.

> Today it is her [Sr Alacoque Broderick][49] delight to see the classrooms in Dominican-Grimley School, Cape Town, and in the Wittebome School equipped with the most modern group-hearing-aids including the induction loop system.[50]

The sound perception method

As an extension of the acoustic method, the sound perception method (SPM) was introduced into Catholic schools for the Deaf in the late 1950s.

> This method is used as far as I know by a few schools only, at Cabra in Ireland, a few schools in Australia, the

---

48 See H. Reichenberg, 'Hearing Aids and How They Function,' *SVQ* 6, 1 (March 1961): 10–19.

49 Sr Alacoque Broderick was a veteran teacher of the deaf in the Western Cape. See 'Jubilarian Taught Deaf for 44 Years,' *TSC*, 19 September 1962, 9/453.

50 'Jubilarian Taught Deaf for 44 years,' *TSC*, 19 September 1962, 9/453.

Dominican Grimley School in Cape Town, the Dominican School for the Coloured Deaf, Wittebome, and St Vincent's.[51]

On 5 September 1959, Bishop Boyle of Johannesburg blessed the new Brian Hall at St Vincent School. The school was fitted with the most developed technological aids to teaching the deaf and incorporated a sound perception room.[52]

This was new and innovative and international visitors like Edwin Stevens, a British hearing aid specialist, came to St Vincent school in October 1960 to study the sound perception method. He was impressed by what he saw, saying, 'It is quite remarkable, and there is nothing like this being done in Britain, so far as I know.'[53] The method was teaching the deaf children to perceive or feel the various vibrations and pitches of music or sound 'and to interpret these with different actions, like marching, walking, trotting, running or skipping.'[54]

By 1961, this method had become so successful that Sr Thomasia Knoepfle, the principal of St Vincent School, could report that:

> The acoustic training was intensified by the development of training in Sound Perception. This specific training in rhythm and pitch discrimination has greatly contributed towards an appreciation of sound and aesthetic values. Some time ago the loop system was installed in Brian Hall to enable the teacher to speak to the pupils through a microphone during Sound Perception Lessons. The experiment seems promising and has already created quite a sensation among the teachers.[55]

The method was an adaptation of the Barczy method of teaching speech and language to deaf children. It was introduced into the

---

51   Sr Thomasia, 'The Sound Perception Method,' *SVQ* 9, 4 (1964): 5.
52   'Deaf School Extension Provided by Pupil's Parents,' *TSC*, 30 September 1959, 12/472.
53   'Deaf Children March to Sound of Music: But They Cannot Hear it,' *The Star*, 27 October 1960, 11.
54   'Deaf Children March to Sound of Music,' 11.
55   Sr Thomasia, 'Report 1960/61,' 2.

Sint-Michielsgestel School for the Deaf in the Netherlands, by its director Fr van Uden in 1940.[56] The method encouraged the use and the development of the deaf child's residual hearing. The teacher spoke directly into the deaf child's ear but unlike the SPM, no amplification of any kind was used. The male voice was favoured over the female voice, probably because most deaf children suffer from perceptive deafness with loss of high frequencies.

However, the sound perception method sought to improve deaf children's speech by enabling them to experience highly amplified speech and sounds 'at first through contact feeling and later through resonance feeling.'[57] The contact and resonance feeling was known as the feedback or 'cybernetic principle'. According to Sr Thomasia, 'The cybernetic idea is embodied in all automatic processes in which a principle of feedback operates.[58]

As a result of the feedback, which comes from feeling or 'hearing' music or a person's voice vibrations, deaf children could improve the quality of their own voice production and speech quality. They could gain a greater sense of rhythm which comes through the awareness of sound rather than sight. Thereby the children's speech would improve.

The equipment was required for the SPM to work effectively. It included a Hammond organ which was used because 'it produces strong vibrations and a continuous flow of music as compared with the interrupted sounds of a piano'[59] Music was played on the organ, which was connected to four loudspeakers, and the children were left free to respond to the music in their own way.

> No directions were given during the exercises and the children were free to act and re-act in their own way. They have to pick up patterns and interpret intervals unaided.

---

56 Fr van Uden was responsible for transforming the Sint-Michielsgestel School for the Deaf into an oral school.
57 'Africa's Delegate to US Education of Deaf Congress,' *TSC*, 2 August 1967, 3.
58 Sr Thomasia, 'The Sound Perception Method,' *SVQ* 9, 4 (1964): 5.
59 Thomasia, 'The Sound Perception Method,' 6.

> This trains them to independence, and they are compelled to concentrate on their perceptual powers.[60]

The SPM was introduced for the younger children to train them to distinguish sound from noise and to 'appreciate simple rhythmic patterns and variations in pitch.'[61] The SPM was understood to reinforce the oral method because speech, language and speech reading all benefit as the child learns that pitch and rhythm are central to good speech. This also had the added benefits that:

> improved feeling for rhythm brings about improvement in the deaf child's walk, his balance, his whole bearing and all his bodily movements, a big step in his normalization process.[62]

The children are said to have found the SPM pleasurable and they were eager to attend lessons.

> The children have probably more than once seen a horse galloping, but they have never sensed the rhythm. Sound perception gives them a much clearer concept.[63]

The teacher of SPM had to have musical and rhythmic ability to help the children. She was expected to understand children of all age groups as she was responsible for all the classes. She had to protect her ears too from the loud music during class otherwise she may 'become deaf herself.'[64]

There were many misconceptions and prejudices too. There was an overwhelming trust in the superiority of the sense of hearing over that of seeing.

> It has been proved that the deaf child's vision is more superficial than the hearing child's. This is ascribed to lack of sound experience. Sound perception claims to develop inner focussing and stimulates mental activity.

---

60   Ibid, 7.
61   Ibid.
62   Ibid, 8.
63   Ibid.
64   Ibid, 9.

Chapter 7

> Lack of sound stimulation produces mental lethargy and dreaminess. Vision has not the same rousing effect as hearing. The teacher knows how quickly their attention wanders.[65]

The lack of awareness of sound was also thought to affect the deaf child's concept of space. They were presumed to be afraid of large empty spaces. This was because a hearing child could call out for help if it found itself in a large empty space, the deaf child does not have the same awareness. 'The hearing child knows that he can get help by calling, whereas the deaf child feels he has no contact.'[66]

Breaking the sound barrier

Central to the SPM and the oral approach to deaf education was the desire by educationalists to break through the sound barrier,[67] as the following quote makes clear:

> Movement, dancing, rhythmic activities, enjoying one's own productions, games, healthy competition, manipulation of attractive apparatus, dramatization and the feeling that one can control the situation is of the substance of the Sound Perception Method... We do want to break through the silence surrounding the deaf child.[68]

Thus, technological innovations like the Coyne Voice Pitch Indicator, hearing aids, amplifiers and the induction loop system became important in deaf education. Deaf children needed 'to hear sound in the normal way,'[69] if they were to learn a language as a pathway to knowledge. They needed to discover rhythm and the joy of music which would make 'their carriage, walk and bearing

---

65 Thomasia, 'The Sound Perception Method', 8.
66 Ibid, 10.
67 This was a common perception in the newspaper articles on the deaf schools. 'A "sound-barrier" is being lifted and children at St. Vincent's are being given a language for without language people cannot think.' See Cook, 'Breaking the Other Sound Barrier,' 42.
68 Sr Thomasia, 'The Sound Perception Method,' 10–11.
69 Ibid, 11.

more normal'[70] and their speech more rhythmic and fluent. The focus of the education system was the normalisation of deaf children and overcoming their defect, their lack of hearing.[71]

School psychologists and deaf children

Psychology was also marshalled into providing the testing and supervision required for the normalisation and rehabilitation of the deaf child. Psychological tests were useful for determining the child's intelligence levels but were also to play a part in remedying the effects of the absence of hearing. In 1958, St Vincent School employed a teacher-psychologist as a member of staff.

> It was her duty, in co-operation with the other teachers, to supervise and promote the rehabilitation of every pupil, boy or girl, in making those adjustments which are necessary as a result of the child's handicap. Her delicate task implies a thorough knowledge of each child, and to this end, various tests are carried out and records compiled and studied in respect of each child. Some of her time is devoted also to remedial teaching in subjects in which the children need extra coaching, and her knowledge of, and intimate contact with, the children enable her to attend to problems of behaviour, give vocations guidance and assist in the placement of pupils when schooldays are over.[72]

Being deaf was seen to be the source of psychological problems for the deaf child. This included the lack of full experience. The deaf child's experience was limited by the absence of hearing. Visual experience was one-sided and would never fully 'compensate for the absence of normal auditory experience.'[73] Consequently, the child's thinking and reasoning abilities were limited. The

---

70 Ibid.
71 See Reynolds, *Vulnerable Communion*, 46ff: Thomas Reynolds critiqued this desire to rectify the defects in the disabled and calls this obsession to normalise the disabled or handicapped person: the normalcy cult.
72 'St Vincent's 25 Years Work for Deaf Children,' *TSC*, 1 April 1959, 11/155.
73 'Deaf Children's Problems,' *SVQ* 9,4 (Fourth quarter 1964): 15–16.

psychologist's role was to help the child deal with this deficit of experience.

Secondly, deaf children needed to find a sense of acceptance about their handicap and not resent the hearing. They had to develop 'coping abilities'[74] that would equip them to function well in a hearing world. They needed to avoid developing a complex about being deaf or seeing in the hearing an enemy who was always against them or prejudiced against deaf people. Again, the adjustment required social maturity and this was understood as being able to integrate well into the hearing world.

> For a deaf person, there is nothing more difficult to attain than proper social behaviour. Educationally and economically, by sheer industry and will power he can attain the normal level, but socially he is at a great disadvantage. We must not be blind to this fact. His mere presence in a hearing society does not affect social integration. A good standard of education is a condition for social integration.[75]

Thirdly, the psychologist was employed to help the deaf children to accept their handicap and not use it as an excuse for misconduct or shirking responsibility in life. The children needed to learn acceptable behavioural patterns and not to use their handicaps as an escape from living a disciplined life.

The science of audiology and speech therapy

The provision of hearing aids to deaf children at school meant that the audiologist played an integral part in oral deaf education. They did the ear tests to determine the children's hearing capacity. They also made the ear impressions and prescribed the necessary hearing aid.

There was an industry heavily invested in hearing aid manufacture and which, therefore, had an invested interest in the oral method of education.

---

74   'Deaf Children's Problems,' 15.
75   'Social Maturity,' *SVQ* 10, 1 (First quarter 1965): 8–9.

> Sophisticated hi-fi stereo equipment, said to be the most modern of its kind in South Africa, has been installed in St Vincent's School for the Deaf in Johannesburg to help children with hearing defects to learn to speak... Mr H. J. Reichenberg, director of the company which supplied the equipment, says that a child with impaired hearing who is just learning to recognise and retain sounds is dependent on high-fidelity acoustic amplification. The speech to be learnt must be presented without ambient noise and sound reproduction calls for high levels, the peak values of which must be reproduced without distortion.[76]

Scientific and technological solutions to deafness were seen as eventually resolving the problems experienced by deaf people and equipping them with the ability to function normally within a hearing world.

The superiority of the oral method

The success of the schools was primarily acknowledged by the academic results attained by the various schools. As early as 1948, reports of the successes were recorded in *The Southern Cross* regarding the pass rates at St Vincent School and the Dominican-Grimley School.[77] In 1957, the Chief Inspector of Schools in the Western Cape, M.D.J. Liebenberg, congratulated Dominican-Grimley School for its scholastic achievements as reflected in the school report.[78]

However, alongside school results, the concerts of the schools for the deaf were more visual signs of the success of the oral method. Whenever the mayor of the town, or a government education official attended a school function, there was always a display by the deaf children on how good they were in speaking and lip-reading. Concerts were also organised for parents to see the progress of their children.

---

76   See 'Hi-Fi Helps the Deaf,' *The Star*, 17 December 1971.
77   'Deaf Children Succeed,' *TSC*, 25 February 1948, 2/72.
78   'Work for Deaf Children,' *TSC*, 29 May 1957, 12/268.

Chapter 7

In 1948, in a rendition of *Snow White* for the school concert at St Vincent School for the Deaf the following report in *The Southern Cross* imagined the inner thoughts of some of the hearing audience:

> How could deaf and dumb children give a concert? I suppose it will be a few 'action' items, that is all one can expect. Such were the thoughts of the greater part of the audience at St. Vincent's School for the Deaf recently while they waited for the curtain to rise for the start of a programme of several items. Two-and-a-half hours later as that same audience left the hall one heard on every side, 'Wasn't it marvellous! Who could have believed it? What patience those Sisters must have? I never expected anything like that! Imagine a complete play with over thirty actors and eight different scenes!'[79]

This was not limited to St Vincent School. Similar concerts were held by other schools for the deaf to show the expertise of the deaf children in speaking and communicating through the spoken word.[80] On 18 April 1951, a deaf children's exhibition and entertainment was organised for the gathered guests and parents during the biennial general meeting of the Dominican Schools for the Deaf. The concert was held in St Mary's School Hall in Hope Street, Cape Town. Among the notable guests were Owen Cardinal McCann, the Mayoress Mrs C.O. Booth and the Secretary for Education, Arts and Science, Mr H.S. van der Walt.

> To illustrate the success achieved in training the deaf and dumb child to speak distinctly, one of the senior boys gave a recitation. He spoke quite distinctly with the proper

---

79   'The Deaf Entertain,' *TSC*, 26 October 1949, 2/410.
80   See 'Forthcoming Exhibition at Dominican School for Deaf,' *TSC*, 11 April 1951, 2/170; 'Dominican Work for the Deaf,' *TSC*, 25 April 1951, 12/194; 'Mayor's Tribute to Sisters,' *TSC*, 16 May 1956, 12/240; 'Two Good Things Clash,' *TSC*, 12 September 1956, 12/444; 'At School for the Deaf: "Only Love and Devotion Could Produce Such Wonderful Results."' *TSC*, 4 June 1958, 12/276.

inflection in his voice and putting a great amount of expression into it.[81]

At times, it was the teaching staff rather than the pupils who received the praise. In 1956, after a concert conducted by the deaf children of the Wittebome School, the Mayor of Cape Town, Mr P.J. Wolmarans, said:

> Now, having seen the entertainment provided for us this afternoon, I must say the teachers of the deaf at this school have amply demonstrated what kindness and patience can accomplish. Theirs is a difficult task, but they do have a wonderful reward in seeing the accomplishment of their work in revealing to those who must always live in silence the joy of being useful and of being like other people.[82]

The work of bringing education to the deaf was considered truly miraculous and worthy of the highest praise.

> In a crowded City Hall, the Children's Music Festival of the Dorothy Boxall Young People's Music and Drama Movement was winning tremendous applause. The most moving item of the evening, however, was the performance of the St. Vincent's School for the Deaf percussion band of drums, cymbals, triangles, tambourines and vibraphone[83] ... The children's playing is a miracle of patient teaching, for they have learnt the delight of rhythm by eye ... Their eye for rhythm was sound though they could not hear, and it praised God mightily, indeed.[84]

In 1957, the Dominican-Grimley School had a concert for gathered guests whereby deaf children of varying ages displayed their progress in lip-reading and speaking.

---

81 'Dominican Work for the Deaf,' *TSC*, 25 April 1951, 12/194.
82 'Mayor's Tribute to Sisters: "Unselfish Devotion to Deaf Children",' *TSC*, 16 May 1956, 12/240.
83 'A xylophone type of instrument in which piano-like keys are struck, and the only instrument of the band which gives out a real tune.' See 'Two Good Things Clash,' *TSC*, 12 September 1956, 12/444.
84 'Two Good Things Clash,' *TSC*, 12 September 1956, 12/444.

The seniors took part in an unrehearsed quiz, grasping the normally spoken questions entirely by lip-reading and answering questions just as difficult as those asked on Springbok radio much more promptly and accurately than their unhandicapped elders on the air. Even the loud and clear, 'I do not know' from one of them was loudly applauded, for it was the measure of triumph over a handicap.[85]

On the 25th anniversary of the existence of St Vincent School for the Deaf, *The Southern Cross* reported that the school had educated 270 girls and 330 boys. The most outstanding pupil had been Nigel Pickford, who lip-read his way through Springs Technical College on way to becoming a draughtsman at Daggafontein Gold Mines. He received 'the award for the most outstanding student in the National Certificate section' gaining an 'individual distinction in mathematics and machine construction.'[86]

Securing employment in a hearing world

Sign language was understood as locking up oneself into a deaf ghetto whereas the oral method freed the deaf child so that they could live and work in the hearing world of work. Education provided the skills needed to fit in as a productive member of society and gives the deaf person the opportunity to provide income for his or her family.

---

85 'Work for Deaf Children,' *TSC*, 29 May 1957, 12/268.
86 'St Vincent's 25 Years Work for Deaf Children,' *TSC*, 1 April 1959, 2/146, 11/155. Pickford was grateful to the oral method of education for his success in life. He wrote in a speech: '... when I left school and started working at Anglo American they required me to attend College for my NTC 2 and 3. The teacher at the college did not know for three weeks that he had a deaf person in his class and at the end of the year I came top of 80 hearing students. This story hit the newspaper. I still keep a copy of it with pride. He had reported to my work that I had not been attending college because every time he called out my name I had not responded.' See Nigel Pickford, 'My Years at St Vincents,' Appendix, 465. Sr Macrina Donoghue recorded similar success stories with the 'auditory-verbal approach' in Cape Town too. See Sr Macrina Donoghue, interview conducted by Mark James, 12 July 2016, Cape Town, 446.

This section discusses vocational training for the deaf, job placement and opportunities for the deaf, and prejudice against deaf people in the workplace.

Vocational training in schools for the deaf

The task of the deaf school was understood as empowering the children so that they would have the necessary skills to be employable. A great emphasis was placed on vocational training.

> Vocational training includes the two official languages, mathematics, science, geography, engineering, drawing, trade theory and workshop practice, typewriting and book-keeping.[87]

They were also taught lip-reading and fingerspelling. While the schools sought to give the deaf pupils vocational training, they discouraged parents from removing their children from school and sending them out to work before this training was completed.

> Parents who withdraw their children prematurely are guilty of the same offence as those who postpone sending their children, who are of school-going age, to a nursery. Both types are curtailing their children's education. The children are the losers. It will be increasingly difficult for them to continue their education after they have left school. Deaf children can follow certain courses at Technical Colleges, but these are limited in number. They usually miss the point in oral instruction given by the uninitiated instructor, who is confronted with a large class, and does not realise that one of his pupils cannot lip-read unless he is facing him. Or the tutor cannot be bothered with a handicapped pupil.[88]

Besides the problem of not being able to follow oral courses at a technical college, there was the added problem that:

---

[87] 'St Vincent's School Cracks Isolation of the Deaf Child,' *TSC*, 27 April 1966, 4/196.
[88] 'Editorial,' *SVQ* 1, 5 (March 1954): 1

> the average deaf child at 15 or 16 years of age has not reached a stage of maturity of character and personality that will face up to the strain imposed by a complete change of environment and occupation. Another three years' training would qualify him for his entrance into adult life. Three parties would benefit from such prolonged training, the pupil, the parents and the employer. Moreover, the school would have the satisfaction of having completed its task.[89]

The schools were specialised in vocational discernment for the deaf child too so that the child would be allocated to the most suitable employment. This may not necessarily happen if the child was thrown into a job prematurely.

Gender-based vocational training

In the schools for the deaf during the 1950s and 1960s, the vocational training on offer accorded with the stereotypes of jobs for men and women.

> Past pupils have been successful as draughtsmen, jewellers, engravers, woodcarvers, sheetmetal workers, shopfitters, cabinet-makers, carpenters, plasterers, upholsterers, electricians, plumbers, farriers, hairdressers; one is a fingerprint expert and another studies medical science. Girls have done well as bookkeepers, typists, commercial artists, dressmakers, photographers' assistants and hairdressers.[90]

Just like hearing schools, schools for the deaf strictly divided practical skills into those subjects for boys and those which were considered suitable for girls. It was presumed that the work and skills should be gendered and understood as biologically constituted. Judith Butler has argued that rather than gender being biological constituted and a stable identity and locus of agency, it should be recognised as an identity which is

---

89   'Editorial,' 1.
90   'Editorial,' SVQ 1, 5 (March 1954): 1–2.

'tenuously constituted in time – an identity instituted through a stylized repetition of acts.'[91] Understood in this way, gender is a constructed identity or what Butler called 'a performative accomplishment' which society and even 'the actors themselves come to believe.'[92] Thus Esme Cleall claimed that the role of the school was to ensure that deaf children were 'properly gendered'[93] so that they would be ready to enter a gendered job market and find employment in a gendered workplace.

However, there were some exceptions in jobs which were available for both men and women. In 1955, girls at St Vincent School had the option to be trained in draughting by two women teachers: J. Humphreys and N. Thorpe.[94] In Catholic schools for the deaf, all the schools were co-educational, unlike the hearing schools which, in South Africa, were divided into separate boys' and girls' schools.[95] This brought a different dynamic to the schools, where women, the Dominican sisters, were teaching the boys subjects that were seen patriarchally as the preserve of men.

At St Vincent School, Sr Dosithea, referred to as 'an expert craftsman,'[96] taught boys woodwork, metalwork, fitting and turning, welding, workshop practice, mechanical drawing, how to handle lathes, drills, forges, planers and bandsaws. 'The training she gives them is the same as is given in Government-run technical high schools.'[97] Consequently, the deaf boys at St Vincent School for the Deaf had a different role modelling being

---

91   Judith Butler, 'Performative Acts and Gender Constitution: An Essay in Phenomenology and Feminist Theory,' *Theatre Journal* 40, 4, (December 1988): 519.
92   Butler, 'Performative Acts and Gender Constitution,' 520.
93   Esme Cleall, '"Deaf to the Word": Gender, Deafness and Protestantism in Nineteenth-Century Britain and Ireland,' *Gender and History* 25, 3 (November 2013): 597.
94   'St Vincent's 25 Years Work for Deaf Children,' *TSC*, 1 April 1959, 11/155.
95   Congregations of religious sisters ran schools for the girls and religious brother congregations like the Marist Brothers or Christian Brothers ran schools for boys. In hearing schools, boys were only allowed at Convent schools until Standard 1, now Grade 3. They were then expected to move over to a boys' school.
96   The Man on the Reef, 'This Sister is an Expert Craftsman,' *The Star*, Thursday 20 April 1961.
97   Ibid.

taught by nuns or religious women than those attending hearing schools or other schools for the deaf where the teachers would have been men.[98]

On completion of their education and training, teachers from the Catholic schools for the deaf went out to employers and convinced them to employ the deaf pupils, both men and women, from their schools.[99]

Job placements and opportunities for the deaf

Dr E.D. Cooper, from Cape Town's City Health Department, was very positive about the vocational training of the deaf afforded by the Dominican-Grimley School saying it was in the forefront in equipping deaf persons to be employable and 'thought the time might have come for legislation to foster the employment of the deaf'.[100]

In the schools for the deaf, job placements were often negotiated with businesses for the school-leaving deaf pupils.

> All school-leavers were successfully placed in Engineering and Architectural Draughting, Metal Work, Panel-beating, Blacksmithing, Pattern-making, Welding, office work and Dressmaking respectively. The firms approached have been sympathetic and co-operative. With the progress of time, new types of openings for the deaf, will have to be investigated, and the girls and boys given the necessary vocational training. With this end in view, plans for the expansion of the boys' training centre have been envisaged, and it is hoped they can be carried out during the next financial year. The project does not involve great expenses, but if brought to fruition, will widen the scope of training

---

98   Further research is required to investigate whether or not this had any impact on deaf men's view of gendered roles in the workplace.
99   Ibid.
100 'Nuns Are Up-to-Date in Training the Deaf to Earn a Living,' *TSC*, 24 June 1959, 12/300.

considerably. It would include sheetmetal work, fitting and turning, welding, electric work and upholstery.[101]

The schools also sought to provide the skills required by the job market. They were forward-thinking and enterprising, wanting the best result for their school leavers and ensuring that they had a future. It was not enough to only train deaf people in skills if there were no jobs available for them.

> A review of the conditions prevailing in industry pointed to changes which would ... eventually affect the placement of the deaf boys. It was clear that, in the near future, the woodwork industry would no longer be able to absorb handicapped workers. New avenues had to be explored. There were good prospects in steel and metal work and in engineering and, in 1956, a new department was set up, catering for various branches of the steel and metal industries.[102]

The sisters often kept in touch with their ex-pupils. At St Vincent School, Sr Thomasia was known to visit the factories and offices where deaf school leavers had found employment. In a jewellery workshop, where all the workers were deaf, the owner Mr Max Segal said of them:

> These boys are the salt of the earth. They absorb instructions with surprising intelligence. And no workmen I have met surpass them in diligence – or in loyalty, either. I set great store by these qualities in my boys –who are my friends rather than my employees.'[103]

---

101 Thomasia Knoepfle, 'St Vincent's School, Johannesburg: Report for 1955/56,' *SVQ* 2, 1, (March 1956): 2–3.
102 'St Vincent's 25 Years Work for Deaf Children,' *TSC*, 1 April 1959, 2/146, 11/155.
103 The Man on the Reef, 'Silent Workshop,' *The Star*, 30 August 1962. It is interesting that the owner speaks of adult men as 'his boys'. Among the workers in Segal's workshop was Max Ordman, 36 years of age, who was a South African heavyweight wrestler as well as the Jewish Maccabi wrestling champion; Billy Henschel, a South African welterweight wrestling champion; Robert Wynne, a weightlifter and a very young apprentice jeweller called John Turner, who later joined the Congregation of Mariannhill

Some businesses were happy to take on deaf employees and appreciated their work. They found their dedication commendable. However, this was not always the case.

Prejudice against deaf people in the workplace

In an article on St Vincent School in 1955, Alan Cook highlighted some of the contemporary prejudices towards the deaf that were prevalent at this period. He wrote:

> What did I know about deaf children? As much as the average, I knew, for example, that some people were known as 'deaf and dumb'. The inability to speak always went along with deafness. I had heard about 'mutes' and I always felt that these unfortunate people suffered from mental disturbances as well.[104]

If hearing people thought that deaf people were mentally deficient, they would not be willing to employ them. They would think that the deaf were incapable of doing the type of work done by the hearing. Therefore, the vocational training in the deaf school had to be of a high standard.

> Deafness today should not – indeed must not – carry the stigma, as in bygone days, of mental deficiency or derangement; to let it be known that with proper education and parental guidance, the deaf of today can attain the highest standards of education and conformable communion with their fellowmen.[105]

But even if they were employed, these prejudices could still work against them. There was always the danger that deaf people would be discharged from work if they were perceived to be slack or lazy or did not fit into the work environment. Deaf workers had to be

---

Missionaries (CMM) He dedicated his life to being chaplain to the deaf. See Chapter 16.
104 Cook, 'Breaking the Other Sound Barrier,' 42.
105 L.J. Paolo, 'The Role of the Parent of the Deaf Child,' *SVQ* 10, 1 (1965): 8.

extra vigilant and to work hard to counteract the prejudices of the hearing employer and thereby avoid being dismissed.

> Another consideration in favour of prolonged school attendance is the risk immature deaf children run of being the first to be discharged on work becoming slack. There is the added danger of their being ostracized from a society that demands a certain standard of education and culture.[106]

White schools for the deaf had more resources and were able to give better vocational training than black schools. Among the schools for the deaf, there were many other discrepancies between white and black schools. We will explore this further in the following chapter.

Conclusion: Totality and violence

This chapter presented the oral method of deaf education as it functioned primarily at St Vincent School for the Deaf in Johannesburg although it was similarly applied in other Catholic schools of the deaf. In detail, we have seen how the oral method functioned as, what Levinas called, totality.

> Totality is my way of seeing and living in the world. Economy is a way of talking about the individual self as it is busy with the daily task of living.[107]

This experience Levinas described as nourishment and enjoyment.[108] The self lives by good soup, spectacles and a warm bed.[109] All these things feed life.[110]

However, totality is also understood as the 'whole'. A whole has the sense of completeness, needing nothing more, even perfection. This is where the danger lurks. When a person or an institution seeks itself as 'whole' then the lack is seen elsewhere

---

[106] 'St Vincent's School, Johannesburg: Report for 1955/56,' *SVQ* 2, 1 (March 1956): 2.
[107] Morgan, *The Cambridge Introduction to Levinas*, 102.
[108] Levinas, *Totality and Infinity*, 127–130.
[109] Morgan, *The Cambridge Introduction to Levinas*, 104.
[110] Levinas, *Totality and Infinity*, 110–111.

and in someone or something else. 'Wholes' are beyond criticism or change. 'Wholes' are convinced that the way they do things is correct and they have the truth. 'Wholes' are exclusionary and dismissive of whatever does not form part of the whole. When we have the truth or the answers there is no need to listen or take advice from others. I am wrapped up in my world and this can make me selfish and lacking in compassion for others.

In this chapter, I have tried to illustrate how the oral method of deaf education functioned as a 'whole.' It had the answers to the problems faced by deaf children and it was to train them to speak and converse like hearing people. They did not allow for any alternatives like sign language and punished the children who dared to disturb the 'whole' they had created. They were never willing to learn or listen to the adult Deaf community and those who encouraged the use of sign language. The oral method of deaf education was the answer.

What Levinas' understanding of totality can help us see is how when a method of deaf education operates as a totality there is the danger that it becomes totalitarian. For Levinas, traditional Western thinking is typified 'by the tendency to value unity over multiplicity, identity over difference, sameness over otherness, order over chaos.'[111] Within this framework, it is the one who has power, the self, who would decide what constituted that unity, that synthesis and the self usually did this for reasons of self-preservation and their own good. Self-preservation was privileged at the expense of alterity and the needs of the Other. I use my freedom, my power, to determine what I consider to be good for myself and others like me.

The Dominican sisters were so convinced of the solution they had found they imposed it on the deaf children without ever considering that the means they employed lacked humanity. It was imposed on the children and enforced through corporal punishment.

For Levinas, the true 'whole' experience of living in the world is that human life is comprised of a unity of two different

---

111 Schroeder, *Altared Ground*, 1.

but interrelated dimensions of life: totality and infinity.[112] Everyday life and economic existence is not only about my nourishment and enjoyment but also includes the encounter with the face of the Other. This is the second way where the encounter with the face of the Other is 'a way of being related to another person'[113] and all the other people in a shared world. This shared world is where we interact with countless others who also face us. The Other is represented by the suffering, the vulnerable, or in biblical terms, the widow, the orphan and the foreigner. The Other has needs which call the self's economy or 'whole' into question. It calls for a generous response.[114] This response and taking responsibility for the Other, is what Levinas referred to as hospitality.[115] The face of the Other or infinity breaches the totality of the self's world from its own enjoyment and moving it towards hospitality.

The face of the Other challenges my putting myself first. People are 'human' beings. Being a human being means to recognise that, before or prior to being free to act, I am already responsible for the Other. In summarising Levinas, Morgan explained that 'our responsibility to other persons is what makes our lives good ones. It is not our capacity to act freely and rationally that does so.'

Without things to give and to share from the self's economy means that generosity is not possible. Without the Other, all we have are just things and not gifts or 'giveables' that can be shared.[116] 'This social world is "the whole" that is the venue for justice.'[117] Justice is not just to impose impersonal laws on others but is to act justly and hospitably in relation to the person or persons who face us in daily life.

The second use of totality is linked to the first. It is where the self after encountering the face persists in self-interest or what Levinas termed 'being-persisting-in-being.'[118] The self refuses

---

112 Morgan, *The Cambridge Introduction to Levinas*, 103.
113 Ibid, 107.
114 Ibid, 105.
115 Morgan, *The Cambridge Introduction to Levinas*, 105.
116 Ibid.
117 Ibid, 108.
118 Levinas, *Entre Nous*, xii.

to acknowledge the transcendent face of the Other. The self is consumed by its own economy without reference to the Other or relates to the Other only to grasp, comprehend or assimilate the Other to realise its own needs or economy.

When the self persists in its egoistic pursuits without regard for the Other, it commits murder, it acts violently and in an evil way. 'If I act as if I were a being whose sole concern is with the preservation of my own being (or even with Being), then I commit an evil act.'[119] For Bernstein, Levinas' entire philosophical approach is best understood as developing 'an ethical response to evil,'[120] especially the evils of the twentieth century.[121] This means that one can only become fully human when one responds ethically to the evil being inflicted upon fellow human beings.[122]

Through education, it was believed that deaf people would be able to better integrate into hearing society. They need no longer carry the stigma of being handicapped or worse, having a mental deficiency. Deaf education was the means through which deaf people could be rehabilitated and find their place in a hearing world. What this way of thinking showed is that deaf people were perceived through a totalising optic that saw their alterity as a problem that required rectification.

Deaf people were Other. They were different and 'this difference causes problems.'[123] Deaf people were seen to be the ones that needed changing.[124] There was no awareness that perhaps it was rather hearing people who needed to adjust the totalising and colonising way in which they viewed and interacted with deaf people.

I will now attempt to show how Levinas' philosophy can assist in reflecting on social relations and political systems. Levinas' philosophy is also political thinking.[125] In the following chapter, I will investigate how apartheid in South Africa

---

119 Bernstein, 'Evil and Theodicy,' 265.
120 Ibid, 253.
121 Ibid, 257.
122 Ibid, 263.
123 'Deaf Children's Problems,' SVQ 9, 4 (1964): 16.
124 'Social Maturity,' SVQ 10, 1 (1965): 8–9.
125 See Minister, De-facing the Other, 126–131, 255–269.

corresponded to Levinas' understanding of totality, how it was an 'imperialism of the same'[126] and an act of evil.

---

[126] Levinas, *Totality and Infinity*, 39.

Chapter 8

Catholic Schools for the Deaf and Apartheid, 1948–1968

In 1948, the National Party under Daniel F. Malan edged out General Jan Smuts' United Party in the whites-only general election. The National Party were adamant about instituting a more rigorous form of segregation on South Africa's black population to protect white people from the black majority.[1] Apartheid laws were passed to ensure that white and black people lived separately and only interacted in the workplace where whites were the bosses and blacks were the workers. Whites were privileged under this legislation and black people were disadvantaged in all spheres of life.

When the National Party took control there were only three Catholic schools for the deaf in the country. Two schools catered for white children while the Wittebome School provided education for black[2] deaf children. This was to change with the onset of apartheid and the Nationalist Party's policy of separate development and mother language education.

Catholic Deaf chaplaincies

Chaplains to the deaf were appointed to minister pastorally to the deaf often working in conjunction with the Dominican sisters. The chaplains said Masses for the deaf, taught them catechism, gave retreats to the deaf and offered them the sacramental ministry of the Church. In providing spiritual nourishment to deaf adults, the chaplains ensured that the deaf people were given access to the life of the church.

---

1   For extensive reviews of apartheid, see David Welsh, *The Rise and Fall of Apartheid* (Johannesburg/Cape Town: Jonathan Ball, 2009) and Saul Dubow, *Apartheid 1948–1994* (Oxford: Oxford University Press, 2014).
2   Black will refer to people who are African, coloured and Indian. At the time, the term Non-European was used but it is offensive.

Not all dioceses provided chaplains for the deaf. In fact, initially, only two dioceses appointed chaplains to minister to the deaf. These were the dioceses of Cape Town and Johannesburg.

Father Ernest Green

When Fr T. Gill, the chaplain in Cape Town, returned to England in 1943, the mantle of deaf chaplain was passed onto the newly ordained Father Ernest Green. He was ordained in Rome after completing his studies there.[3] Although born in Johannesburg on 11 May 1915,[4] his family moved to Cape Town in 1918. Green went to school at St Agnes Convent in Woodstock and Marist Brothers in Rondebosch.[5] After school, he worked for a liquor firm for five years before studying for the priesthood at Mungret College, Limerick in Ireland. Two years later he continued his studies at Propaganda Fide College in Rome, where he was ordained on 24 February 1941.[6]

His first assignment was to the Wittebome parish in Wynberg. Thus, began his interest in the deaf. Just like Kolbe before him, he took an interest in the deaf children and learnt sign language and was the school chaplain in 1943.[7] He did not restrict himself to working in the school but, in 1947, established the hostel for 'non-European deaf boys'[8] in Heathfield, Cape Town. The hostel was dedicated to both Bishop Hennemann and Blessed Martin de Porres.[9] The vision behind the hostel was to provide accommodation for deaf men working in Cape Town.

> The hostel has proved a boon, for, after leaving school, the deaf are often easily led astray, because of bad housing conditions and the danger of bad company. Since the

---

3   'Another SA-Born Bishop: Fr Ernest Green Succeeds Bishop Boyle,' *TSC*, 4 May 1955, 1/205.
4   'Bishop Green's Life in Brief,' *TSC*, 2 March 1966, 2/98.
5   'Another SA-Born Bishop,' *TSC*, 4 May 1955, 1/205 and 11/215.
6   'Bishop Green's Life in Brief,' *TSC*, 2 March 1966, 2/98.
7   'Bishop Green's Life in Brief,' *TSC*, 2 March 1966, 2/98.
8   'Another SA-Born Bishop,' *TSC*, 11/215.
9   'Another SA-Born Bishop,' *TSC*, 1/205.

establishment of the Hostel juvenile delinquency amongst the deaf has decreased considerably.[10]

The first seven residents moved in only in 1948 on the feast of Corpus Christi.[11] Their ages ranged from 17-25 and they had various jobs from tailors, shoemakers, gardeners and labourers. It is interesting to note that the only employment on offer for these deaf men were jobs which confirmed that they were to be 'hewers of wood and drawers of water' as envisaged by the apartheid state.[12]

Fr Michael Ramsay OSM: A chaplain at St Vincent

Fr Michael Ramsay was born in London on 30 June 1882.[13] In 1905, Ramsay joined the Anglican Order of the Society of the Sacred Mission. In 1914, he was sent out to work in Modderfontein in the Orange Free State as an Anglican missionary until 1921.[14] He then returned to England and was received into the Catholic Church. Subsequently, he joined the Servite Order in Begbroke near Oxford. He studied for the Catholic priesthood at the Beda College in Rome from 1921[15] until his ordination in the Servite London Church in December 1927 at the mature age of 45.

On 31 March 1928, he came out with Fr Emilio to work in Swaziland.[16] He first worked at St Joseph's mission but was transferred and went on to establish the St Mary's parish in Lobamba in 1929.[17] He worked in Swaziland until his appointment

---

10 'South African Boys Town,' *TSC*, 1 August 1951, 10/368.
11 'South African Boys Town,' *TSC*, 10/368.
12 See Pam Christie and Colin Collins, 'Bantu Education: Apartheid Ideology and Labour Reproduction,' in *Apartheid and Education: The Education of Black South Africans*, edited by Peter Kallaway (Johannesburg: Ravan Press, 1984), 161.
13 '*Elenco dei missionari arrivati in Swaziland a destinatie a questa missione, del principio 1913 al primi di dicembre 1945*', File: OSM 1939–1948. Archives of the Catholic Diocese of Manzini, Eswatini (ACDM).
14 Desmond Hatton, 'Man of Serenity,' *TSC*, 31 December 1969, 5.
15 Fr Barneschi OSM, 'The Catholic Church 54 Years in Swaziland,' 4. File: Paper of historical interest. ACDM.
16 Ibid.
17 Clement Langa, 'Relations Between the First Catholic Missionaries and the People of Swaziland (1914–1955.' PhD diss. (University of South Africa, Pretoria, 2001), 46.

to the Province of the Transvaal in South Africa in November 1937.[18] He stayed first in Heidelberg and then later served as a parish priest in Nigel, South Africa in 1938. During his tenure, he built the parish church in this mining town.[19] In 1947, he was elected vicar provincial of the Venetian Province succeeding Fr Nolan and moved to Kensington, Johannesburg. In 1948, at the age of 66, he was appointed as chaplain to St Vincent School for the Deaf in Melrose, Johannesburg. Being a school committed to the oral method of deaf education, Ramsay unlike his counterpart in Cape Town, Ernest Green, never learnt sign language. He continued in this role until his death on 20 July 1970 at the age of 88.[20]

These chaplains assisted with the work of the schools for the deaf to which we now return.

Two notable South African schools for the deaf

This section focuses on two schools for the deaf, namely the Dominican-Grimley School for the Deaf in Cape Town and the St Vincent School for the Deaf in Johannesburg.

Dominican-Grimley School for the Deaf in Cape Town

When, on 16 March 1951, Helen Keller and Polly Thompson, her assistant and interpreter, visited the Dominican-Grimley School, it was technically still twinned with the Wittebome School. However, it had become a white deaf school committed to the oral method of education. Helen Keller reaffirmed the value of this educational process when, in speaking to the children, she said:

> Well do I understand that things like speech are harder for you because you cannot hear but, believe me, I never was sorry that I learned to speak and your teachers have faith in your ability to acquire speech. I want you to work hard on your articulation, and justify your teacher's belief in your

---

18 'Elenco dei missionary arrivati in Swaziland.'
19 Langa, 'Relations Between the First Catholic Missionaries,' 54.
20 De Vittorio, Luigi M. *Missione Africa* (Rome: Marianum, 2004), 204. This book is in the Archive of the Catholic Diocese of Manzini, Eswatini.

powers. If you do, it will be one of your proudest triumphs; and you will leave a banner for the deaf who follow you.[21]

In delivering the welcome to Helen Keller, *The Southern Cross* reported that one of the senior pupils described as having no hearing at all, said, 'in a clear voice which was heard and understood by all present',[22] that they had learnt so much about Helen Keller and now they had the pleasure to see and talk with her. She expressed the hope that Keller would make South Africa her home.[23]

In 1953, the Dominican-Grimley and the Wittebome schools were formally separated into two different schools. The Dominican-Grimley School remained committed to education using the oral method and it continues to do so to the present day. At the school's regular biennial general meetings, invited dignitaries, as well as many parents, were given displays on the benefits of the oral method. For example, in 1957, a report in *The Southern Cross* recounted that 'before the speeches, deaf children of various ages showed on stage the progress they had made in lip-reading and speaking, by a series of games, tests, exercises and a little play.'[24]

> The seniors took part in an unrehearsed quiz, grasping the normally spoken questions entirely by lip-reading and answering questions just as difficult as those asked on Springbok radio much more promptly and accurately than their unhandicapped elders on the air. Even the loud and clear 'I do not know' from one of them was loudly applauded, for it was the measure of triumph over a handicap.[25]

---

21 'Helen Keller Visits Dominican School for Deaf,' *TSC*, 21 March 1951, 1/133 and 12/144.
22 'Helen Keller Visits,' *TSC*, 12/144.
23 Ibid. Keller had an extensive visit throughout South Africa, visiting not just all the Catholic deaf schools but others too. For her full itinerary, see 'The Visit of Helen Keller to South Africa, 15 March to 22 May 1951, Souvenir programme, 16–17. 152/1104 12, KDSA.
24 'Work for Deaf children,' *TSC*, 29 May 1957, 12/268.
25 'Work for Deaf children,' *TSC*, 12/268.

Deaf children were called handicapped and deviants from the hearing norm. The solution to the problem was seen as teaching deaf children using the most modern methods of training so that they can overcome their handicaps and thereby 'take part in ordinary life.'[26]

In October 1958, Sisters Basil and Michael, former principal and vice-principal of the Dominican-Grimley School, returned from an International Congress on the Modern Educational Treatment of Deafness at Manchester University in England. They had been impressed by a special method of training in 'sound perception' through music. It had been demonstrated at the conference by the pupils of Sint-Michielsgested School for the Deaf in Holland. They planned to introduce this method to their schools in South Africa.[27]

In 1959, at the Dominican-Grimley's biennial general meeting, the pupils of the school put on entertainment for parents and friends. In attendance were also Archbishop Owen McCann, Major P. van der Byl, a member of parliament and Dr E.D. Cooper from the City Health Department.

> Demonstrations, on the school stage before a large audience, included first lessons in lip-reading for three-year-olds (the age from which children are admitted to the school); use of up-to-date instruments for training; and displays of rhythmic movements to music, which the children can feel but cannot hear. Resounding applause greeted such simple actions as a small boy brushing his hair, a little girl skipping, at the unheard, lip-read instructions of their teacher. A youngster playing a small tune on a miniature 'blow organ' received an ovation worthy of an organist giving a recital.[28]

The reason for the applause was explained as the audience appreciating these demonstrations as 'proof that children cut

---

26   'Nuns are Up-to-Date in Training the Deaf to Earn a Living,' *TSC*, 24 June 1959, 12/300.
27   'Cape Town Nuns Plan to Start New Training for the Deaf,' *TSC*, 29 October 1958, 12/528.
28   'Nuns are Up-to-Date,' *TSC*, 12/300.

off from the world by lack of hearing, and thus of speech, were finding a point of contact which would, in time, enable them to take an active part in everyday life.'[29]

The equipping of children for active participation in everyday life was vital for the employment of deaf people. Major van der Byl, in proposing the adoption of the school's biennial report, quoted the situation of two of the school's past pupils who were employed by Cape Town City Council as typists. They were earning the same salaries as 'unhandicapped girls'.[30] In seconding the report, Dr Cooper said he was interested to see 'that commerce was now able to employ some deaf persons and thought the time might have come for legislation to foster the employment of the deaf.'[31]

Through their work and efforts, the Dominican sisters were often commended by visitors like Helen Keller[32], the Archbishop of Cape Town,[33] mayors and mayoresses,[34] and government officials for their patient and selfless service. On 13 May 1963, Dr J.J.P.

---

29   Ibid.
30   Ibid.
31   Ibid.
32   'My heart warmed as you spoke of the noble work which the Sisters are doing in this school, to enable these children to participate in a rightful share of the joy of normal living and I call down a blessing on your labours', Helen Keller. See 'Helen Keller Visits Dominican School for Deaf,' *TSC*, 21 March 1951, 1/133.
33   'Archbishop McCann praised the love and devotion shown by the staff in the great work of helping these children to take their place as useful and wanted members of society. Employers were becoming increasingly ready to take on the handicapped who had been properly trained,' quoted in 'Work for Deaf Children,' *TSC*, 29 May 1957, 12/268. 'He [McCann] paid tribute to the patience and devotion of these Sisters teaching in "the oldest school for the deaf in South Africa,"' quoted in 'Nuns are Up-to-Date in Training the Deaf to Earn a Living,' *TSC*, 24 June 1959, 12/300.
34   'The Mayoress, Mrs. Honikman, said that one could not talk of the Dominican Grimley School without expressing love and gratitude, and that she welcomes the opportunity to pay tribute to 'the miracles accomplished here in this materialistic world … She said that the "demonstration of patience, faith, perseverance and love set by the school is important not only for the children but also for everyone who is sensitive to the problems of our country", quoted in 'Dominican School for Deaf Commemorates Centenary,' *TSC*, 22 May 1963, 1/241 and 2/242.

Op't Hof, secretary to the Department of Education, Arts and Science, commended the work of the sisters in starting the first deaf school, on the occasion of the centennial celebrations for the presence of the Irish Dominican sisters in South Africa, and said:

> This deed of faith has opened up new horizons for those handicapped, and the school has helped them to lead normal lives ... The teaching of deaf children was the most difficult form of teaching and required the highest degree of professional training. It was impossible to over-estimate its value and the help it gave the deaf in adult life, when they would otherwise be isolated by their handicap.[35]

This resonated with the aim of the school, reflected in the school's commemorative booklet specially produced for the occasion, as to equip 'the deaf child morally and intellectually to take his place in the hearing world as a well-adjusted and useful citizen.'[36] The well-adjusted and useful citizen was also to be shaped by the apartheid mentality of separating people into racial categories.

Also speaking at the centenary celebrations, Archbishop Owen McCann of Cape Town said: 'I am proud of this institution because it was the first of its kind in South Africa and from it others have sprung.'[37]

However, under National Party rule, the Cabra Dominican sisters had moved from one school with two departments to three different schools each divided to accord with the racial policies of apartheid. By providing financial support to the cash-strapped schools for the deaf, the government was able to ensure that the church schools complied with the government's racial policies.

Archbishop McCann seemed unaware of how the Church was being forced to play by the government's rules. He complimented the Dominican-Grimley School for its contribution to the well-

---

35 'Dominican School for Deaf,' *TSC*, 1/241 and 2/242.
36 'Its Origin and its Aim,' *TSC*, 22 May 1963, 1/241.
37 By this date the Cabra Dominican Sisters had established the Dominican-Grimley school for whites, the Wittebome school for coloured children and the Dominican School for the Deaf for Africans in Hammanskraal.

being of Cape Town. It was an example of 'civic co-operation and social endeavour, working to the welfare of the country and the people.'[38]

> There is a happy state of co-operation between school and city, and school and the government, and we are grateful for the substantial support accorded to the school by the Department of Education, Arts and Science.[39]

In response to the Archbishop's talk, the secretary of the Department of Education, Arts and Science, Dr Op't Hof, also present at the celebrations, said: 'I trust this partnership between State and voluntary bodies will continue.'[40]

St Vincent School for the Deaf in Johannesburg

St Vincent School for the Deaf was a school for white deaf children from its inception. It was not a private school. It was state-assisted. 'This meant that the Department of Education had a say in the use of teaching methods used at the school. The oral method was officially promoted.'[41] While it had been government policy, it had also been the King William's Town Dominican sisters' policy since the school's inception.[42]

This had implications for the sisters because most of the funding for the school came from the government. As we saw in Chapters 2 and 3, all three Catholic schools for the deaf relied on significant sums of money being given to schools from both government and business. The oral method of deaf education was expensive to maintain as it depended on several specialised teachers of the deaf and those not usually employed at hearing schools like psychologists and speech therapists. There was

---

38   'Dominican School for Deaf,' *TSC*, 1/241 and 2/242.
39   'Dominican School for Deaf,' *TSC*, 1/241 and 2/242.
40   'Dominican School for Deaf,' *TSC*, 1/241.
41   'History/Development of St Vincent School,' *St Vincent School Magazine*, 1999, 5. Box EDU29, St Vincent School for the Deaf: School magazines, KDSA.
42   'The Finger alphabet is not used at all at St Vincent's. The children are taught lip-reading, and in this way, they are able to hold a conversation with almost any one,' in 'Radio Teaches the Deaf,' *Sunday Express*, 18 July 1937.

also expensive equipment that was needed like hearing aids, amplifiers, the induction loop system and special rooms soundproofed for the sound perception method. Class sizes were small so overheads per individual pupil were high in comparison to hearing schools.

There is no doubt that the oral method of deaf education was understood, at the time, as the most effective means by which deaf children could be taught and trained so that they would become functional members of an overwhelmingly hearing world. It was generally held that the oral method would release the deaf from the prison of silence and liberate them so that they could more fully participate in a hearing world.

By acquiring the skills of a spoken language, through patient teaching and the use of modern technological advances, the deaf were released from the grip of ignorance. They were empowered through education to relate to the hearing by speaking as clearly as possible and comprehending what the hearing were saying to them through the means of speechreading or lip-reading. Consequently, they could find employment and attain the financial independence needed to raise a family. Their handicap no longer held them back and they could now be considered normal and fully functional members of society.

Overcoming the handicap and functioning normally

In 1963, at the centennial celebrations of the Dominican-Grimley School, Dr J.J.P. Op't Hof, the secretary of the Department of Education, Arts and Science, one of the guest speakers, referred to the work of the school as a 'great deed of faith'.

> This deed of faith opened up new horizons for those so handicapped, and the school has helped them to lead normal lives.[43]

---

43   Quote from Dr J.J.P. Op't Hof in 'Dominican School for Deaf Commemorates Centenary,' TSC, 22 May 1963, 1/241, 2/242.

In the same speech, Dr Op't Hof neatly summed up the whole intention and objectives of the oral method of deaf education:

> Theoretically, of course, we know that the more fully a deaf person can be habilitated to the human society of which he is an integral part as much as every other citizen, i.e. the more completely he can enter into his community, so as to share in its economic, cultural and spiritual life, the more successfully he has been educated and prepared for life. And since contact between one individual and another is established and maintained chiefly, in many cases almost exclusively, by directly talking to that person, we realise that the ability to speak intelligibly is the only door which can lead him from the isolation imposed on him by his deafness and its many adverse consequences, to a fuller life in relation to his fellowmen.[44]

There is no doubt that the oral method of deaf education that the Dominican sisters gave to the deaf children came from dedicated service by which they sacrificed and cared for 'God's handicapped ones.'[45] They were commended for their patient work[46] and

---

44 Sr Hermina, 'Speech for the Deaf,' *SVQ* 9, 2, 5.
45 See 'New Hostel for the Deaf,' *TSC*, 24 June 1953, 2/292: 'His Lordship [Bishop W.P. Whelan] spoke feelingly of the sacrifice and efforts of the Sisters to care for these deaf children. The care bestowed on them here was not just the patient imparting of knowledge, though in that the Sisters had been wondrfully (sic) successful, but the love and interest that follows from the realisation that they are God's children. Other teachers may take up and try to emulate the work done by the Sisters, but even if they had more financial assistance and greater facilities they would never attain the success that comes to those who dedicate their lives in the service of God's handicapped ones.'
46 See 'Concern Over Schools for Deaf,' *TSC*, 10 June 1953, 2/268: 'Professor Burger, Dean of the Faculty of Education of the University of Cape Town … said that for a number of years he had been bringing large parties of his students to Wittebome to teach them the greatest lesson that any teacher could learn – the lesson of patience. Patience and unfailing love, without which no educational system could be successful, were what the children at Wittebome received from the Dominican Sisters.'

unselfish devotion[47] but being advocates for the oral method came at a cost.

Discouraging the use of sign language

The use of sign language in schools for the deaf was not encouraged. This was assumed to be a primitive form of language development and, therefore, it hampered the children's progress in acquiring language. Consequently, it was forbidden at school and the children were punished if caught signing. This did not stop the children from signing but encouraged to them to engage in public and hidden transcript behaviour as they sought to communicate in their first language.

All manual methods of educating the deaf were thought to be grossly inferior to those of the oral method. Addressing parents of deaf children at St Vincent School in 1957, Sr Hermina said:

> Arouse in your child a desire to speak. Show him by practical examples that speech is a means of getting what we want. Do not respond to your child's signs or gestures, and he will soon abandon them.[48]

Speaking in Port Elizabeth, Mother Nicholas Griffey,[49] the principal of St Gabriel's School for the Deaf in Ireland, argued that the manual or sign system of training and education only

---

47 See 'Mayor's Tribute to Sisters: "Unselfish Devotion to Deaf Children."' *TSC*, 16 May 1956, 12/239: 'The Mayor of Cape Town, Mr. P.J. Wolmarans paid tribute to the "unselfish devotion" of the Sisters and lay teachers who conducted the Dominican School for the Deaf, Wittebome, when he moved the adoption of the report at the annual general meeting last week.'
48 Sr Hermina, 'Home Responsibilities in the Education of Deaf Children,' *SVQ* 3, 4 (1957): 12.
49 For more information on Sr Nicholas Griffey OP and oral education in Ireland, see Leeson and Sheikh, *Experiencing Deafhood*, 67–69.

equipped deaf children to exist in a silent world, 'whereas those who were oral trained grew into more normal adults.'[50]

In response to a question from Bishop Green,[51] Mother Nicholas acknowledged that the deaf 'do usually revert to sign languages when they are together. They are under constant strain, living in a world of sound, and they need to relax when together, as for example, they can in a club for the deaf.'[52] Sign language was acknowledged as important for the deaf to communicate among themselves but was not to be used in the education environment.

Sign language was seen to promote 'ghetto-isation' of the deaf thereby isolating them further from involvement in the hearing world. However, it was also more than just this, sign language was not appreciated as a language. Sign language was perceived to be merely gestural and did not constitute a language. It was assumed that the signs comprised of natural gestures whose meanings were obvious, transparent and self-evident. For this reason, teachers in schools for the deaf advised parents that if they discouraged their deaf children from using signs or gestures, the children would 'soon abandon them.'[53] This did not happen.

Deaf children taught each other sign language

It was precisely at school that deaf children taught each other how to sign. The majority of deaf children are born into hearing families. Jennifer Gillespie remembered that:

> in my family there were none who were deaf. They were all hearing. I was the only deaf one in my family. But I have my

---

50 'Teaching the Deaf: Public Address by Nun from Ireland,' *TSC*, 28 July 1965, 12/360.
51 As we saw in Chapter 5, Bishop Green was a fluent signer. This question raises the unresolved tension in Catholic ministry that existed between the oral method of deaf education among children and the acceptance of sign language in pastoral ministry with adults, as discussed in Chapters 4 and 5. I could find no references to Bishop Green's views on this debate.
52 'Teaching the Deaf,' 12/360.
53 'Home Responsibilities in the Education of Deaf children,' *SVQ* 3, 4 (October–December 1957): 12.

sister who at the age of 13 became hard-of-hearing. I have a brother too who at about 12 also became hard-of-hearing.[54]

Gillespie learnt to sign at school. 'When I was small I used to watch the bigger children sign.'[55] Carmen Kuscus had a similar experience, 'I used to watch the older Deaf children at school … It was the same in the family, I learnt from my older sister.'[56]

Cyril Axelrod remembered:

> [A]t school, I was picking up sign language from the other children in the playground and benefiting from the stimulation and motivation this gave me. For the first time, I could fully understand what people were talking about and I could share my feelings and thoughts with others.[57]

Sign language played a significant role in helping deaf children to learn to understand what was happening around them. Many of them complained about the oral method of education as it favoured those who were hard of hearing. Suzanne Lombard recalled that:

> I finished Standard 7. The teaching wasn't very good. The teachers didn't really encourage the deaf. There was too much focus on the oral method.[58]

> The hard of hearing can manage in school but the deaf not. When the teacher was writing on the board and speaking we couldn't follow. We were not allowed to sign and we had to keep our hands behind our backs. Thus, we failed. We failed school. When we had the opportunity to go outside school we learnt more than inside.[59]

---

54 Jennifer Gillespie, interview conducted by Mark James, 12 November 2015, Cape Town, 404.
55 Ibid.
56 Carmen Kuscus, interview conducted by Mark James, 13 November 2015, Cape Town, 416.
57 Cyril Axelrod, *And the Journey Begins*, (Coleford, Gloucestershire: Douglas McLean, 2005), 34.
58 Suzanne Lombard, interview conducted by Mark James, Cape Town, 13 November 2015, 419.
59 Ibid, 425.

Faith Cronwright confirmed Suzanne Lombard's view that the oral method benefitted the hard-of-hearing more than the profoundly deaf.

> We had a very good teacher Mrs Smith. She taught us well, a very good teacher. She gave us examples, and this helped us understand. It was easier for me because I wasn't fully deaf. For those who were completely deaf, it was more difficult to explain especially when it came to history and geography.[60]

Before the work of linguists like William Stokoe,[61] sign language was not understood to have any structure, grammar or vocabulary that constituted a language. Consequently, the deaf children were discouraged from using signs and told they had to learn a spoken language. Corporal punishment was often the measure meted out to deaf children who were caught signing in the classroom or on the school playground. However, a blind eye was turned to signing in the hostels.[62]

Punishing the use of sign language

Signing during school hours was strictly forbidden. Those deaf children who were caught signing on the playground were often severely punished. This was a common experience in all the Catholic schools for the deaf where the oral method was used. Both Carmen Kuscus, who attended the Wittebome School, and Jennifer Gillespie, who studied at Dominican-Grimley School, recalled that at school they used to hide their signing.[63] In the classroom, they

---

60   Faith Cronwright, interview conducted by Mark James, Cape Town, 16 November 2015, 427.
61   William Stokoe, an American linguist, who argued for American Sign Language has having the same fundamental building blocks of any spoken language and therefore ASL should be recognised as the natural language of deaf people in the United States. See W.C. Stokoe, 'Sign Language Structure,' *Studies in Linguistics: Occasional Papers* 8 (1960) and *Semiotics and Human Sign Languages*, (The Hague: Mouton, 1972).
62   Faith Cronwright, interview conducted by Mark James, Cape Town, 16 November 2105, 426.
63   'We would sign under the trees, or behind a wall where we could not be seen.' Carmen Kuscus, interview conducted by Mark James, Cape Town, 13 November 2015, 416. Jennifer Gillespie,

signed behind their backs to the child seated behind them so that the sister or teacher could not see.[64] Gillespie recalled that 'if they found out we were signing they would hit us on our hands with the ruler.'[65] Nigel Pickford remembered being hit on the hands with a golf stick 'which bruised me so badly that I could not even open a door handle or write.'[66]

James Scott theorised that in situations where people feel dominated or oppressed, there are different responses which he referred to as the public transcript and the hidden transcript. The public transcript is the 'respectable performance' where people say or do things to be seen to be conforming.[67] The hidden transcript, in contrast, is the discourse that subordinate groups develop when they are out of the public eye.

> The hidden transcript of subordinate groups reacts back on the public transcript by engendering a subculture and by opposing its own variant form of social domination against that of the dominant elite.[68]

An example of the relationship between the public transcript and the hidden transcript is that the deaf children were instructed by their teachers to keep their hands behind their backs as a method to ensure that they spoke and did not sign.[69] The deaf children complied, which indicates adherence to the public transcript.

interview conducted by Mark James, 12 November 2015, Cape Town, 403.
64 Jennifer Gillespie, interview conducted by Mark James, 12 November 2015, Cape Town, 403.
65 Jennifer Gillespie, interview conducted by Mark James, 12 November 2015, Cape Town, 403.
66 'The boys got wise and hid the whipping sticks under the teacher's platform. I am sure the sticks are still there today.' See Nigel Pickford, 'My Years at St. Vincents,' A talk prepared for the St Vincent School 75th anniversary celebrations in September 2009, Appendix, 465.
67 James C. Scott, *Domination and the Arts of resistance: Hidden Transcripts* (New Haven/London: Yale University Press, 1990), 45–46.
68 Scott, *Domination and the Arts of Resistance*, 27.
69 'They [the Sisters] would say: "You are not allowed to sign you must be oral!" We had to keep our hands behind our backs and speak.' See Faith Cronwright, interview with Mark James, 16 November 2015, Cape Town, 426.

However, unknown to the teacher or in the classroom when the teacher was not noticing, the children were signing behind their backs to those behind them. This is the hidden transcript. Gillespie said that 'you have to sign behind your back to the children behind you because otherwise the oral, the hearing catch you.'[70] The deaf children were also signing in places where there was less likelihood of being discovered and in so doing were signing behind the teachers' backs.[71]

It would also be helpful to reflect on the children's ways of challenging the power that the sisters had over them. Scott argued that 'by recognizing the guises that the powerless must adopt outside the safety of the hidden transcript, we can, I believe discern a political dialogue with power in the public transcript.'[72] Pickford gave several examples of the guises employed, most of them describing how they could outwit the sisters. He described how after getting beatings by the sisters, 'the boys got wise and hid the whipping sticks under the teacher's platform. I am sure the sticks are still there today.'[73]

There was a power-play taking place between the boys and the school authorities, who in this case were women.

> Senior boys had to get up at 5.30 am for COLD showers (brrr). In Winter when we were woken up for showers we would go to the showers, run the taps on the pretext that we were showering then rush back to bed. The advantage of having female nuns.[74]

The boys also looked to get their revenge on the sisters when the occasion allowed and would not result in expulsion. Pickford related one occasion when this happened.

> Fetes were held every year to fundraise. One morning we were woken at 4 a.m. by the nuns to get rid of rainwater

---

70   Jennifer Gillespie, interview conducted by Mark James, 12 November 2015, Cape Town, 404.
71   Nigel Pickford, 'My Years at St. Vincents,' 465.
72   Scott, *Domination and the Arts of Resistance,*' 138.
73   Pickford, 'My Years at St. Vincents,' 465.
74   Ibid.

that had sagged the canopies. We got underneath one with a broom to push the canopy up and there was one nun who was interfering with us, so we pushed so hard and the rainwater splashed all over her. Due to the weather the Fete was cancelled and a caring man donated £10 000 to the school.[75]

Further research is required on the public and hidden transcripts in schools for the deaf as well as how sign language functioned as an identity marker for the deaf children who often left home at the age of three. What were the other 'arts of resistance' that they developed in response to oralism? I have only been able to provide a few limited insights into these areas which shows that a more extensive social history of schools for the deaf is required.

The internalisation of apartheid by some Dominican sisters

In 1952, Sr Thomasia Knoepfle OP – St Vincent School principal from 1947 to 1968[76] – wrote:

> The European Schools in South Africa adhere strictly to the oral method, whereas the schools for Non-Europeans use also the manual alphabet and conventional signs. There is good reason for this. The Coloured and Native have not the cultural background of the European, and for economic reasons their education is frequently cut short.[77]

This quotation highlights two important aspects to deaf education under apartheid. Firstly, the use of the oral method of education differed between white and black schools. Secondly, various cultural and racial undertones informed the reasons why this discrepancy existed. There were the cultural and paternalistic expressions and then there were the attitudes of white superiority that underlay this.

---

75 Pickford, 'My Years at St. Vincents,' 466.
76 'Taught the Deaf for 37 years,' *TSC*, 22 December 1971, 3.
77 Thomasia Knoepfle, 'Education for the Deaf,' *TSM*, April 1952, 3.

Emmanuel Levinas' understanding of racism and prejudice is that it is a violent denial of the alterity of the face.[78] The Other is reduced to being an object,[79] reduced to a biological attribute, their race or lack of hearing. The Other's uniqueness and singularity, the face, is not recognised. 'They are beings without a face.'[80] The Other is rejected and suffers violence. 'Violence is applied to the thing, it seizes and disposes of the thing.'[81] The racist is caught up in self-interest, in an internal monologue of reason which assumes his way of seeing the world is the only justifiable one. A racist is disobedient to the command 'Thy shall not kill.' Being a racist is to stand accused. 'One has not looked the Other in the face.'[82] This is the way of unredeemed reason, reason which is egocentric.[83] It is a 'philosophy of the Same.'[84] This is what Levinas referred to as 'not thinking.'[85] To think is to act reasonably, it is to recognise the face of the Other that calls the self to responsibility and to act justly.

Apartheid and the Dominican School for the Deaf, Wittebome

There was only one deaf Catholic school that was drastically affected by apartheid legislation, such as the Bantu Education Act and the Group Areas Act. This was the Dominican Deaf School in Wittebome.

> The biggest impact of government legislation on our Catholic deaf schools was the separation of pupils along racial lines. First, in our Cape Town school, the whites were separated from non-whites, to use Apartheid terminology. Then we were forced to split the coloureds from the Africans. Eventually, Indians were not permitted to attend our Wittebome school as schools for Indians

---

78 See Levinas, *Totality and Infinity*, 199 and Levinas, *Entre Nous*, 104.
79 Levinas, *Difficult Freedom*, 8.
80 Ibid.
81 Ibid.
82 Ibid, 10.
83 Minister, *De-facing the Other*, 70.
84 Levinas, *Of God who Comes to Mind*, 31.
85 Levinas, *Collected Philosophical Papers*, 25.

were established in Durban and Johannesburg. We had to conform to government policies as we were totally dependent on state funding.[86]

Since its establishment and separation from the white Dominican-Grimley School in 1937, the Wittebome School provided tuition for both coloured and African pupils. The Eiselen Report,[87] however, recommended that African education fall under the Native Affairs Department and coloured education under Coloured Affairs. This made many in the school uncertain about the school's future prospects. In 1953, Archbishop Owen McCann, at the biennial meeting of the Dominican Schools for the Deaf, confirmed that it meant that 'there will have to be a separation of Africans and Coloureds'[88] at the Wittebome School.

Just before this, the Wittebome School had been administratively separated from the white school in Cape Town. Until 1953, the Cape Town and Wittebome schools were considered by the Department of Education to be two branches of the same school.[89] The principal of the joint school had been Sr Germaine Lawrence. At the beginning of 1953, the Grimley and Wittebome schools were officially separated with the appointment of separate principals for each school. It was also in the same year that the first two coloured teachers joined the previously all-white staff at the school. The school continued to recruit another five coloured teachers the following year.

---

86 Sr Macrina Donoghue, interview conducted by Mark James, 12 July 2016, Springfield, Cape Town, 448.
87 The Eiselen Report emerged from the government commission set up in 1949 under the chair of WMM Eiselen, a lecturer in Anthropology at the University of Stellenbosch. The Commission made recommendations to the Nationalist government on how to revise black education in South Africa. These recommendations were enacted as the Bantu Education Act No. 47 of 1953 and implemented in 1954.
88 'Concern over Schools for Deaf,' *TSC*, 10 June 1953, 2/268.
89 Veronica da Rocha, 'A Short History of the Schools for Coloured Deaf Children in South Africa.' Unpublished paper, 1981, 9. Box Education: Deaf education – Wittebome, Miscellaneous papers, File: Story of Dominican Schools for the Deaf Cape Town: Grimley and general, CDSA, Cape Town.

Three years later, there was still uncertainty about the future of the Wittebome School due to the Group Areas Act. There was a strong possibility that the suburb of Wittebome was going to be re-zoned as a white area. This would create serious complications for the school. However, Archbishop McCann was optimistic, saying at the school's AGM in May 1953: 'I heard today "from a little bird" that the area would remain coloured.'[90] He also confirmed that 'the problem of the African children would seem to be solved by the projected opening of a similar school for deaf African children in the Transvaal.'[91]

Catholic resistance to the Bantu Education Act

At the time of the passing of the Bantu Education Act in 1953, the Catholic Church had 688 state-aided schools and 130 private schools at which 11 361 black students attended. This was about 15% of the black school-going population at that time.[92] The Act meant that all Catholic teacher training colleges for Africans, situated in white areas, were forced to close. Primary and secondary schools were given three options: becoming private schools without government aid; keeping control of the schools but having the government subsidy to pay for teachers' salaries slashed by 75%; or closing the schools and renting out or selling the school buildings.

The Catholic Church refused to hand over its African schools to the government and from 1954 sought to run them without government support. This meant that teachers were forced to accept a 25% drop in their salaries so that the schools could continue. Lay teachers with families were the hardest hit. In 1955, the bishops initiated the Missions Schools Fund, a fundraising drive to keep the African schools financially viable. It was an

---

90 'Mayor's Tribute to Sisters,' *TSC*, 16 May 1956, 12/239.
91 This refers to the establishment of a school for the Deaf in Hammanskraal for the African Deaf.
    'Mayor's Tribute to Sisters,' *TSC*, 16 May 1956, 12/239.
92 Helen Chamberlain, Mercedes Pavlicevic and Brigid Rose Tiernan, 'Catholic Education,' in *The Catholic Church in Contemporary Southern Africa*, ed. Joy Brain and Philippe Denis (Pietermaritzburg: Cluster Publications, 1999), 191.

extensive national campaign in which Catholics were asked to raise funds to support Catholic mission schools.

The Southern Cross, the Catholic weekly newspaper, played an instrumental role in keeping the campaign alive with numerous articles. All Catholics were encouraged to contribute financially and to pray for the success of the campaign. Even the schools for the deaf were roped into the campaign. In one article, Fr Desmond Hatton, a diocesan priest from Pretoria and regular columnist, tells of how deaf pupils started collecting money for the fund at the Grimley-Deaf School in Cape Town:

> One of the boys, Henry de Meillon, was so impressed by the appeal of the Catholic Bishops' Campaign that he brought a Royal Baking Powder money box to the play-room, and without asking anyone for a contribution, pushed his own pennies through the slit – others saw the actions of this practical little man, and the following day it was noticed that no Pepsi-Colas or sweets were purchased in the school's tuck shop, but one by one the boys and girls placed their pennies in the money box... when the box was full the school presented it to the Sister for the Campaign.[93]

Initially, the enthusiasm engendered by the campaign provoked a sense of solidarity among Catholics across racial boundaries. However, it did not have much lasting effect. The financial constraints on African Catholic schools meant that the education standards fell increasingly behind those of the wealthier white Catholic schools.[94] Unfortunately, the Catholic schools were not able to act as a counter-witness to apartheid but became indistinguishable from government schools where large discrepancies existed because of white and black educational standards.

The education crisis of 1954 proved that the Catholic Church was dependent on financial support from the Nationalist government if its schools were to continue. Church leaders sought

---

93 'Deaf Children Give their Pennies,' *TSC*, 5 October 1955, 9/479 and 11/493.
94 Chamberlain, Pavlicevic and Tiernan, 'Catholic Education,' 194.

to cooperate with government departments and implement their policies in exchange for funding to keep the schools going. In this regard, its policy continued as a 'conciliatory approach.'[95] However, the Church began to be more critical, especially under the leadership of Archbishop Denis Hurley OMI. In 1960, Archbishop Hurley, made a cautious but radical call that it was time to establish racial integration in South Africa's Catholic schools.

> Has the time come to make a gesture, even if in many places it can only be a gesture, and state the principle that Catholic schools are prepared to accept any child regardless of race provided the law permits and the fees paid? ... An answer must soon be given to this question if the Church is to be the leader and not the led in its own field of Christian love and justice.[96]

No one dared to consider such a move as yet. However, the situation was very different in 1976.

The racialisation of Catholic Deaf education

As the Dominican sisters at both Cabra and King William's Town were committed to the oral method of education, it was to be expected that these new African schools would also employ the oral method of deaf education.

> In school, the eagerness of these deaf children to overcome their handicap is admirable. They are taught principally by the Oral Method, and great emphasis is placed on reading and writing.[97]

---

95   Garth Abraham, *The Catholic Church and Apartheid: The response of the Catholic Church in South Africa to the first decade of National Party rule 1948–1957* (Johannesburg: Ravan Press, 1989), 86.
96   Denis Hurley, 'School Integration,' *TSC*, 22 June 1960, 5/295.
97   See 'St. Thomas School for the Deaf Bantu Children: Report for the Year 1963/64,' 5. KDSA, Box: Thomas School for the Deaf, 123/373 31.

However, there were clear differences between the white schools for the deaf and their black counterparts.

Firstly, the National Party insisted on mother-tongue education for all groups. This had the effect in dividing the black community into different ethnic and linguistic groups. The Dominican-Grimley School was for whites, Wittebome was for coloureds, St Thomas School was for Xhosa speakers and Hammanskraal was for Tswana children. This meant that the medium of instruction in these schools varied enormously.

> The children at St. Thomas's School, said Mr Maree, would be taught reading and writing in their mother tongue. For communication purposes they would be taught finger spelling and gestures. In cases 'where it can be profitably undertaken,' a little speech training may also be given.[98]

Sign language was permitted in African schools for the deaf, and not in the white schools for the deaf. This enabled the birth of a variety of dialects of SASL.[99]

Secondly, there was a discrepancy in the financial support that the different schools received. Funds were allocated according to race. The white schools for the deaf, just like the white hearing schools, benefitted much more from government subsidies than their black counterparts. This made the starting up of these schools difficult. The government gave the black schools a 50% subsidy but in effect, this was only a reimbursement after the school's expenses had already been paid in full. Sr Michael, from the newly established Hammanskraal school, appealed for support in *The Southern Cross* to assist the new cash-strapped school[100] which was already R30 000 in debt. The Johannesburg diocese had

---

98 'New School for African Deaf is Joint Church-State Effort,' *TSC*, 17 October 1962, 11/503.
99 See Aarons and Akach, 'South African Sign Language,' 1–2. They argue that there is one South African Sign Language but with some variations arising from the differing systems used in the various schools around the country.
100 'These Deaf Children Do Not Even Know They Have Names,' *TSC*, 31 October 1962, 11/527. See also Monsignor Desmond Hatton, 'The Deaf to Hear,' *TSC*, 21 November 1962, 5/557.

already organised a special collection called Efeta Sunday[101] on 26 August and raised R1 289.82 for the school but more was required. In the drive, the example was given of a young boy who arrived at the school without any identification and unable to write or speak his name. The implication is that the sisters were involved in the task of raising the deaf from gross neglect (*il y a*) to a better and humane life.

The Bantu Education Act was an instrument of the Nationalist government, not only to divide and rule but also to maintain white supremacy. Black education was an 'educating for ignorance' to ensure that African people 'carry out automatically the menial and lowly tasks set for them, the hard and dirty work. They were taught not to think, but to obey; not to initiate but to carry out; not to aspire, but to grudge.'[102] Inferior 'Black education' was to remind black people of their inferior status in society. This proved true in schools for the deaf too.

Suzanne Lombard, a pupil at the Dominican School for the Deaf in Wittebome in the late 1960s and early 1970s, said that:

> [T]he education for the whites was better, ours was of a dubious quality. There was no matric and so looking for work without a matric is difficult. Whites got good jobs, they were taught well. They had special classes unlike us. We were not taught well.[103]

The white schools for the deaf offered studies up to matric whereas the black schools only went as far as Standard 7 or 8. This limited the employment opportunities for black deaf adults in comparison to their white counterparts. Job opportunities were more diverse for whites and less so for black deaf people.

---

101   Efeta Sunday was a special collection held in dioceses to support the Catholic schools for the deaf. Efeta is a misspelling of *Ephphatha*, an Aramaic word, used in Mk 7:34 which Jesus used when healing the deaf man. It means 'Be opened.'
102   Pamphlet produced by the Congress of Democrats, *Educating for Ignorance*, 5. Historical Papers Research Archive, University of the Witwatersrand, Box: Federation of South African Women 1954 1963, Collection number AD 1137.
103   Suzanne Lombard, interview conducted by Mark James, 13 November 2015, 423.

Nigel Pickford who attended St Vincent School for the Deaf was appreciative of the sisters who took care:

> [T]o assess their pupils according to their I.Q. and ability for employment after leaving school. They even approached firms to find work for their pupils. They have produced a Professor, Priests, Engineers, Architectural draughtsmen, Staff working with insurance claims and banks, carpenters, welders, panelbeaters, typists. What an amazing range of opportunities.[104]

Pickford became a draughtsman. Jennifer Gillespie who went to the Dominican-Grimley School for the Deaf worked as a typist and later, on computers with insurance companies like Old Mutual and Metropolitan Life, Cape Town City Council and the University of the Western Cape.[105] Suzanne Lombard got her first job sewing in a textile factory and later for an electrical company. Her husband Stephen Lombard trained as a tailor but later went into upholstery work.[106] Faith Cronwright got jobs in factories doing embroidery.[107]

Many white deaf people, not all, had the skills to get white-collar jobs but black people were limited to blue-collar employment in factories. There were also different opinions about the extent to which their schooling equipped them for life outside of school.

Racial and cultural prejudices

Central to the colonising project of the imperialist European powers, who divided the continent of Africa among themselves, was the idea that Europe had the moral duty to conquer and rule Africa because it was racially and culturally superior to the local

---

104 Nigel Pickford, 'My Years at St. Vincents,' 468.
105 Jennifer Gillespie, interview conducted by Mark James, Cape Town, 12 November 2015, 406.
106 Suzanne Lombard, interview conducted by Mark James, Cape Town, 13 November 2015, 419–420.
107 Faith Cronwright, interview conducted by Mark James, Cape Town, 16 November 2015, 428.

black inhabitants. It was the white man's burden and duty to civilise the 'native' through education[108] and industriousness.[109]

Sr Thomasia's comments explaining why white schools for the deaf maintained a strict oral method compared to black schools in which the manual alphabet and signing was allowed, reveal the same prejudices. In thinking that it was the cultural differences between black and white and not economic considerations, government policy and racism that accounted for the different approaches to deaf education between black and white schools for the deaf, she revealed herself as being part of the settler church.

> The settler community looked to the metropole for its identity, values and justification. In the South African settler church the metropoles were: England – as the colonising power; Ireland since a large number of the settler Catholics and clergy came from there and Germany the home of the country for the bishops, clergy and religious of many of the mission dioceses.[110]

In giving voice to the colonial, racial and cultural prejudices of her time, Sr Thomasia revealed that, up until this time, she had never been exposed to the mission church. She had always taught in a white school and never with black children. As a German-born missionary, she had also imbibed the racial and cultural prejudices of white South Africa. There is no indication that Sr Thomasia ever questioned her racialised assumptions. The racial prejudice held by some of the white teachers in the schools for the deaf affected the lives of the black children who were there, as we will see in Chapter 7.

Secondly, Sr Thomasia showed her prejudice against the use of sign language and of fingerspelling in the classroom. The manual approach to Deaf education was thought to be an inferior method when compared with the oral method of education. This revealed her racialised assumption that it was permissible to

---

[108] Stuart Bate, 'One Mission, Two Churches,' 9–10.
[109] Denis, 'A Case of Pastoral Myopia?' 457–458.
[110] Bate, 'One Mission, Two Churches,' 10.

use this sign language approach for black schools because they were more primitive, but not in white schools. This showed an apartheid mentality where it appeared obvious that whites should be educated through the 'perceived' superior form of oral education and that black people should be grateful for the inferior version. Linked to this is the audist assumption that sign language was inferior to the oral method of education.

Thirdly, the idea that whites were culturally more advanced than black people justified in Sr Thomasia's eyes that whites needed to study for the matriculation certificate but not to grant this same privilege to black children. In the 1950s and 1960s, very few white deaf children at Dominican-Grimley and St Vincent graduated with a matriculation certificate. The first deaf person to graduate at St Vincent School was Robert Simmons in 1955. For whites, there was a least the possibility of accomplishing a matric pass if they were able but for black children with a similar aptitude, this was not possible.

Education for the deaf at the Wittebome and Hammanskraal schools for the deaf only went as far as Standard 7. This injustice was perpetuated through the Catholic deaf education system right up until the 1990s.

Complying with apartheid: New black schools for the deaf

Archbishop McCann's public comments, regarding the Wittebome school, raised no voices of protest against the Nationalist government policies. The readiness of the Church to separate the schools into white, coloured and African, shows the extent to which Catholic Church leaders uncritically accepted the government's apartheid policy. The Catholic bishops' response to apartheid policies, like that of Archbishop McCann in Cape Town, highlighted that:

> [T]he English-speaking churches had failed to be more than moderate. Given to verbal protest, they failed to resist.

Trapped within their own history they were predisposed to cautious compromise.[111]

The Catholic Church, like many of the other English-speaking churches, had an ambiguous and ambivalent response to apartheid. The Church denounced apartheid for its anti-Christian character and its adverse effects on the daily lives of black people, but it was also trapped by its dependency and loyalty to the state.[112] The bishops and Church leaders were dependent on state funding for their schools and so were compelled to cooperate with the apartheid policies of the Nationalist government. Consequently, they bowed to government pressure and set up separate schools for the deaf for the different African communities.

Here we discuss two such schools, namely, Dominican School for the Deaf, Hammanskraal and St Thomas School for the Deaf, Woodlands near King William's Town.

Dominican School for the Deaf, Hammanskraal

On 1 April 1962, the Cabra Dominican sisters and pupils moved into the new Deaf school in Hammanskraal[113] near the recently established African seminary called St Peter's. It was the result of 12 years of envisaging, planning and fundraising for this new project. Boner pointed out that in line with apartheid policy, 'the new school served Sotho and Tswana boys and girls and instruction was in the mother tongue.'[114] *The Southern Cross* reported:

> This school for the deaf will cater specially for Sotho pupils but may admit Catholics from other tribes on the Rand, the Free State and Natal. (Xhosa deaf pupils will be admitted

---

111 Charles Villa-Vincencio, *Trapped in Apartheid*, (New York: Orbis Press, 1988), 102.
112 Denis, 'The Catholic Church and Apartheid,' A talk given to the Brazilian Justice and Peace Commission. Unpublished paper, 2014, 3.
113 'Daughter-Foundation of CT Dominican School for Deaf,' *TSC*, 24 January 1962, 12/48.
114 Kathleen Boner, *Dominican Women Speak*, 154.

to another similar school being opened by Bishop Green in King William's Town, also in April).[115]

The school Apostolic Delegate, Archbishop J. McGeough, solemnly opened the school on Sunday 10 June 1962. He was assisted by the Archbishop of Pretoria, Archbishop Garner. In his welcome, Archbishop Garner said:

> It was fitting that the sisters should celebrate the centenary of their arrival in the Cape, and the silver jubilee of their school in Wittebome, by setting up yet another school.[116]

Garner thanked the Department of Education and Training (DET) on behalf of the Dominican sisters for the financial aid given for this new enterprise. He pointed out that, 'The institutions of the Catholic Church had no difficulty in accepting the normal supervision of the state wherever in the world they might be.'[117]

In response, W.W. Bouwer, the inspector of special schools of the Department of Bantu Education, congratulated the sisters and said that the Bantu community was fortunate to have the establishment of such a school. He said that the Department accepted that children would be admitted to the school irrespective of their church denomination. He was confident that the school 'would render great service and that relations with the Department would always be cordial.'[118]

The government provided a 50% subsidy for the school expenses approved by the Department, after such expenses had been paid in full.[119] The remainder of the funds the sisters themselves had to fundraise. It was not easy as the sisters did not have many benefactors in the Transvaal region as both of their schools for the deaf were in Cape Town.

---

115 'Daughter-Foundation,' *TSC*, 12/48.
116 'First Catholic School for African Deaf in Transvaal,' *TSC*, 13 June 1952, 1/277 and 11/287.
117 'First Catholic School,' *TSC*, 11/287.
118 'First Catholic School,' *TSC*, 11/287.
119 See 'These Deaf Children Do Not Even Know They Have Names,' *TSC*, 31 October 1962, 11/527.

Chapter 8

St Thomas School for the Deaf, Woodlands

In 1958, Bishop Ernest Green of Port Elizabeth addressed the local Rotary Club appealing for support so that a Catholic school for isiXhosa-speaking deaf children could be opened in South Africa.[120] There was a need for another deaf school, especially in the Eastern Cape, as the existing schools were packed to the limit. *The Southern Cross* reported that 'Beds are arranged in double tiers to make the most use of available space, [and] capacity has more than been reached.'[121]

It would take another four years before St Thomas School for Deaf Bantu Children opened its doors for the first time on 24 July 1962.[122] Bishop Green had been instrumental in getting funding and government support for the new school. Sr Conrada Förg, who previously had worked at St Vincent School for the Deaf in Johannesburg, was appointed the principal.[123] Sr Guzmana Gfröreis from the King William's Town congregation as well as Sr Agatha Manne OP from the St Martin de Porres congregation[124] were appointed to assist her. It was envisaged that the Dominican sisters of Blessed Martin de Porres would eventually take over

---

120   The other three were Wittebome, Worcester and Kutlwanong in Krugersdorp. See 'Permit to Open School for Deaf African Children Still Awaited,' *TSC*, 12 February 1958, 1/73. In fact, it became the sixth school for the black Deaf because Hammanskraal and another school in Mthatha opened ahead of St Thomas school for the Deaf.
121   'Permit to Open School,' *TSC*, 12 February 1958, 1/73. The other school in the Eastern Cape being referred to is probably the Effata School for the Deaf run by the NG Kerk in Umtata.
122   See 'New School for Bantu Deaf,' *TSC*, 14 March 1962, 12/132 and 'New School for African Deaf is Joint Church-State Effort,' *TSC*, 17 October 1962, 1/493 and 11/503.
123   'New School for Bantu Deaf,' 12/132.
124   The Dominican Sisters of Blessed Martin de Porres were the African and coloured sisters of the King William's Town Congregation who were formed into a separate congregation. The effects of apartheid policies affected the internal workings of religious orders and congregations. For further information, see Margaret Mary Schäffler, 'The Integration of Black and Coloured Sisters in the Congregation of the King William's Town Dominican Sisters of St Catharine of Siena – The Past, the Present and the Future.' Unpublished M.Th. thesis, (University of South Africa, Pretoria, 2002).

the running of the school as well as the school hostel.[125] In 1963, Sr Cecilia Ntlyziwana OP was employed as an additional teacher[126] and Sr Canisia Mangena OP was employed as a school clerk.[127]

The Board of Management of the school consisted of eight members, the Bishop of Port Elizabeth, the parish priest of Woodlands parish, a representative of the King William's Town Dominican sisters, a representative of the St Martin de Porres Dominican sisters, a lawyer and three representatives of the Department of Bantu Education.[128]

The establishment of this new school was proudly proclaimed as a joint Church-state effort. At the opening of the school on 1 October 1962, Mr W. Maree, the Minister of Bantu Education, announced that 'the fact that the government gives a subsidy to the Church is proof of the government's confidence in the Church to carry out its responsibilities towards the children who will be enrolled in this school.'[129] Church initiatives were dependent on the cultivation of a good, also an uncritical, relationship with government because the Church was incapable of financing these schools without state aid.

Consequently, the government could ensure that the Church carry out its education policies in relation to African schools. Education in the mother tongue, a key apartheid language policy, was enforced. At the school's opening, Maree alluded to the fact that the deaf children at St Thomas' School would be taught reading and writing in their mother tongue.

> For communication purposes they would be taught finger-spelling and gestures. In cases 'where it can be profitably undertaken', a little speech training may also be given.[130]

---

125 'St Thomas School for Deaf Bantu Children: Annual Report 1962/63,' 2. 124/374 54, KDSA.
126 'The Annals of St Thomas School for Deaf Bantu Children 1962–1968,' 4. 124/374 55, KDSA.
127 'St Thomas School for Deaf Bantu Children: Report for the Year 1963/64,' 1. 123/373 31, KDSA.
128 'The Annals of St Thomas School for Deaf Bantu Children 1962–1968,' 7–8. 124/374 55, KDSA.
129 'New School for African Deaf,' TSC, 17 October 1952, 1/493.
130 'New School for African Deaf', TSC, 11/503.

The syllabus was also to include simple and practical arithmetic, hygiene, religious instruction, physical education as well as instruction in good social and moral habits. Practical subjects would include gardening, agriculture, woodwork, building, needlework, cane work and home craft.

In 1965, the first male teacher, Mr Mvandaba, was taken on to the staff and Sr Frieda joined the school as vice-principal.[131] She had also previously taught at St Vincent School. In 1967, Sr Agatha left for ministry in the Transvaal and she was replaced by Sr Salesia Nzimande OP.[132] By 1968, the number of staff had increased[133] as the number of children grew from a mere 43 in 1962 to 145 in 1968.[134]

Technological innovations were also made with the introduction of the loop induction system that was introduced for the senior class in 1965.[135]

Apartheid and sign language policy

Under apartheid, education in schools for the deaf for Africans, coloureds and Indians differed substantially from those of white schools for the deaf. The use of sign language and the manual alphabet was considered suitable for African and coloured schools but as an inferior form of education for white schools for the deaf. The apartheid government was also reluctant to spend the requisite financial resources to equip black schools for the deaf as oral schools on par with their white counterparts.

---

131 'Report on the Affairs of St Thomas School for Deaf Bantu Children for the Year 1965/66,' 1. 124/374 67, KDSA.
132 'The Annals of St Thomas School for Deaf Bantu Children, 1962–1968,' 18–19. 124/374 55, KDSA.
133 In the Chairman's report for 1966/67 it was reported that besides the principal and vice-principal, there were ten teachers and five house mothers. See 'Chairman's Annual Report on the Affairs of St Thomas School for Deaf Bantu Children for the Year 1966–1967,' 1. 124/374 68, KDSA.
134 'The Chairman's Annual Report on the Affairs of St Thomas School for Deaf Bantu Children for the Year 1968/69,' 1. 124/374 71, KDSA.
135 'Report on the Affairs of St Thomas School for Deaf Bantu Children for the Year 1965/66,' 1. 124/374 67, KDSA.

Promoting the oral method of education in African schools was not a priority and the acceptance of signing in these schools was permitted. Aarons and Akach[136] have pointed out that in general:

> [S]chools for the white Deaf insisted on oralism, whereas schools for the other races allowed some measure of manualism (in most cases, not a natural signed language, but a mixture of speech and some signs).[137] It is clear that speaking was perceived by the [government] authorities as the prestigious form of language, hence the insistence of oralism in schools for the white Deaf, whereas, based on pigmentation, manualism was permitted increasingly in of other racial groups.[138]

In explaining why Dominican-Grimley School, but not Hammanskraal, even though both were Cabra Dominican schools, was able to adhere to an oral approach to education, Sr Macrina Donoghue explained:

> In the Western Cape, it is only Tygerberg and the Dominican-Grimley school which use the 'auditory-verbal' approach. This is different from the school in Hammanskraal which was forced by the Department of Bantu Education to use sign language and to teach in the medium of Tswana or Sotho.[139]

In many white schools for the deaf, the Dominican sisters, who ran the schools, maintained a cordial relationship with the government officials and political representatives. They invited Department of Education officials, mayors and mayoresses, and other prominent figures to important school events. All this was important for public relations and fundraising for the schools. The

---

136   Aarons and Akach, 'South African Sign Language,' 1–28.
137   The system most commonly used in African schools was known as the Paget-Norman approach.
138   Aarons and Akach, 'South African Sign Language,' 6.
139   Sr Macrina Donoghue, interview conducted by Mark James, 15 July 2016, Cape Town, 445–446.

schools were expensive to run and depended on state funding and generous benefactors.

Levinas, totality and money

For Levinas, being hospitable is a reality that is already happening in our world. We already practice hospitality by being polite and courteous, evident in our everyday actions when we say 'After you, sir!'[140] Thus Levinas can say that 'hospitality, the welcome of the other, cannot be commanded since it is already a fact, *fait accompli*, and indeed the fact of subjectivity.'[141] Going further, we can recognise that this courtesy, this politeness, these actions of a pious soul, [142] this acting from a good conscience can make us think we are fulfilling the command to love our neighbour but, in fact, they can hide an ignorance of others and sometimes even violence towards them.[143]

Providing education for deaf children is an act of hospitality. It is a recognising of the face of the neighbour and extending a generous hand in hospitality. Central to being hospitable is to have something to give the Other. For this money is often required. Money creates sociality where people recognise their interconnectedness.[144] For Levinas, there is an ethical use of money. Money used for the sake of the Other rather than to satisfy one's greed and hunger is a sign of the ethical relation. It can be used for holy or saintly purposes, to breach totality and reach out generously to the Other.

However, money can be used to tie people into a 'totality, since in commerce and transactions man himself [sic] is bought and sold; money is always to some extent wages.'[145] In the previous chapter we saw how totality was also seen in the interests of commercial companies supporting the oral method of

---

140 Levinas, *Otherwise than Being*, 117.
141 Stephen Minister, *Defacing the Other*, 193.
142 Levinas, *Collected Philosophical Papers*,
143 Stephen Minister, *Defacing the Other*, 193.
144 'To recognize the Other is therefore to come to him across the world of possessed things, but at the same time to establish by gift, community and universality.' See Levinas, *Totality and Infinity*, 76.
145 Levinas, *Collected Philosophical Papers*, 45.

education because they have an interest in the selling of hearing aids and the most sophisticated audio equipment to schools. The medical profession had much to gain from the clinical approach to deaf education because there was an economic benefit. The fields of speech therapy and audiology and even psychology flourished under the oral method of deaf education. Rehabilitation was profitable.[146]

In this chapter, we saw how the Dominican sisters in providing education for deaf children were economically dependent on the apartheid state to provide subsidies to pay the teachers. The schools for the deaf were expensive to run and maintain. The sisters were dependent on government grants and subsidies to keep them going. The government had leverage and the Dominican sisters felt they had no choice but to pay the price for these subsidies and that was to ensure that the apartheid policies were implemented in their schools, even if they thought or believed that these policies were unjust and against their Catholic faith. Little to no criticism was expressed by the schools for the deaf against government policies. They adhered to the Nationalist government policies of separating white from black deaf children and establishing separate schools for the different races and ethnic groups. Consequently, when the apartheid government insisted that African children could no longer attend the Wittebome School, the Dominican sisters decided to start a new school for deaf children from the seTswana-speaking community in Hammanskraal. Similarly, Bishop Green opened a school for deaf children from the isiXhosa-speaking community in the Eastern Cape.

Apartheid was a totality. Totality dominates and seeks to 'control' the other – in 'benevolent' or even brutal, racist, murderous and tyrannical ways. Connor pointed out that the falsity of apartheid was thinking that there could not be any constructive social bond between people of different races

---

[146] 'Behind the mask of benevolence is the professional engaged in the human-services market, staking out his particular claim in the fastest-growing sector of our economy.' See Lane, *The Mask of Benevolence*, 77.

and different ethnic groups except for subservience by blacks to whites.[147]

Due to apartheid, there were clear discrepancies in the facilities available for white and black schools for the deaf as well as educational levels. White schools for the deaf like Dominican-Grimley and St Vincent used the oral method for deaf education most ardently. The Wittebome school was also oral but sign language was allowed in the two African schools, St Thomas School for the Deaf in Woodlands in the Eastern Cape and the Dominican School for the Deaf in Hammanskraal. This was only because sign language was disparaged as inferior to the oral method and the apartheid government did not want to give large subsidies to African schools. The white schools taught up to matric but the black schools only taught up to standard seven or eight. This had serious implications for employment opportunities for the black deaf people and showed how apartheid was a system skewed against them.

The education that the Church offered to the deaf children had bought its silence and its complicity in the violence of apartheid's self-interested agenda. It was a compromise. The Catholic schools for the deaf were seen as 'subdued' and 'subservient' to the agenda of the apartheid state and consciously chose not to speak out prophetically against the injustices of apartheid. The Church had tried to resist the apartheid state in 1954 by refusing to hand over its black mission schools to the apartheid government. It failed as a strategy as it was not financially sustainable. The Dominican sisters in the schools for the deaf decided to not challenge the system.

The colonial and racial attitudes of some of the teachers in the schools for the deaf showed that they had internalised the apartheid mentality. They truly thought in 'good conscience,'[148] that it was only natural that white deaf children should receive

---

147   Bernard F. Connor, *The Difficult Traverse: From Amnesty to Reconciliation*, (Pietermaritzburg: Cluster Publications, 1998), 62.
148   'The offense done to others by the "good conscience" of being is already an offense to the stranger, the widow, and the orphan, who, from the faces of others, look at/regard the *I*.' See Levinas, *Entre Nous*, 168.

a better education than black deaf children. They maintained a discriminatory practice in the schools where black schools never offered matric until the early 1990s. While the teachers in the schools for the deaf were subservient to the totality of the apartheid state and its agenda, they had their own audist agenda.

The promotion of the oral method of deaf education like the money received from the state, enabled the sisters to be generous to the deaf children by providing them with an education but one which denied them access to their language and culture. It was an assimilation into the totality of a hearing world. So alongside economic interests, the oral method of deaf education as a totality can also be understood as a way of grasping and understanding of deaf people to a hearing agenda under the subterfuge of effecting a 'hospitable' response. This disguised 'hospitality' or this 'mask of benevolence',[149] hid and obscured the oppressive relations to which deaf people were subjected. The oral method of deaf education prevented them from access to education in sign language. This oppression was linguistic discrimination and oppression.[150]

The next chapter addresses some of the limitations of the oral method of deaf education and its weaknesses. The chapter also shows how some educators were troubled with a 'bad conscience' and encouraged the use of sign language in deaf education. This was the beginning of a return from exile for sign language in the classroom.

---

149   Lane, *The Mask of Benevolence*, 77.
150   Lane, *The Mask of Benevolence*, 84.

Chapter 9

Total Communication, Bad Conscience and Shifts in Deaf Education, 1969–1981

This chapter reflects on the shift in deaf education where Total Communication became seen as the new solution to the failures of the pure oral method of deaf education. In the previous chapter, we saw how African schools for the deaf, since inception, were allowed to use sign language as a language of learning and teaching. Unfortunately, this was not the case in the Catholic schools for the deaf that catered for white and coloured deaf children.[1] During the next ten years, however, some changes did happen at St Vincent School for the Deaf where the use of a combined method in the classroom was unofficially practised even though it was officially disavowed.[2]

These changes were the result of the debate around Total Communication as a new philosophy of education, both internationally and nationally. People across the globe began, in Levinas' terminology, to develop a bad conscience about the oral method of deaf education. This chapter will also show that it was not as revolutionary a philosophy as it was touted to be, even though its long-term effect was to open the door to more revolutionary understandings of Deaf identity and subjectivity.

Alternatives to the oral method of teaching?

In June 1967, the principal of St Vincent School for the Deaf, Sr Thomasia Knoepfle OP, attended a conference in Northampton, Massachusetts on 'The Oral Education of the Deaf Child.' While

---

1 W. van der Sandt, 'Audiology in South Africa,' *TSM*, December 1967, 9.
2 Liguori Töns, interview with Mark James, Johannesburg, 16 December 2016, 434–435.

in the United States, Sr Thomasia took the opportunity to visit and assess the various approaches to deaf education that were prevalent in the country. She managed to visit a total of nine different schools. 'In this way,' she said, 'I had an opportunity to study a good cross-section of various types of schools.' [3] Her comments on her trip were interesting. Firstly, she was impressed by the pure oral schools. After ten years of primary school education, these deaf children were able to apply to study at hearing high schools. Before acceptance, the deaf children had to pass some tests set by the hearing schools.

> I was told that records are on hand to prove that most of the deaf high school pupils in ordinary schools make the grade and integrate with their hearing peers.[4]

While she was complimentary about how they conducted all the lessons orally and were convinced that the pure oral method was justifiable, she was critical when she saw some teachers overdoing oralism.[5] She wrote:

> One teacher spent a whole general science lesson on the oral spelling of vocabulary such as atomic, alchemist, acid, photosynthesis, etc. ... If I had not been ushered out of his classroom I probably would have fallen victim to the temptation of prompting him to resort to the chalkboard to give the children the visual picture of those difficult words.[6]

Secondly, she noted that the supporters of the oral method, in contrast to pure oralism, recognised that not all deaf children had 'the potential for 100% success in oralism.'[7] Some deaf

---

[3] 'All in all I visited nine schools; the Kendall School attached to Gallaudet College, Gallaudet College itself, De Paul Institute at Pittsburgh, Central Institute and St. Joseph Institute at St. Louis, St. Mary's School for the Deaf, Buffalo, Lexington School and St. Joseph School in New York and finally the Clarke School at Northampton.' See Thomasia Knoepfle, 'Visit to the United States', *SVQ* 3, 3 (1967): 2.
[4] Knoepfle, 'Visit', 3.
[5] Ibid.
[6] Knoepfle, 'Visit', 3.
[7] Ibid.

children had very little residual hearing to exploit and never developed fluency in lip-reading. Despite this realisation, the oralists believed that given enough time and using the correct procedures 'every deaf child can learn to speak,'[8] if they had the right motivation.

Thirdly, Sr Thomasia reported on the schools using the combined method, thereby employing a combination of the oral method, fingerspelling and signing.

> These schools feel that at the higher level, quicker and better results are achieved if lip-reading and speech are supplemented by the manual system on the part of both teachers and pupils. They also hold that their pupils would win in the contest for greater happiness.[9]

In discussion with those advocating the combined system, Sr Thomasia said that many argued that the oral method did not help deaf children or adults meet all life's challenges. The oral method had its limits. There were times when deaf people had to resort to the use of pencil and paper to facilitate communication in the outside world, despite their oral training.

While Sr Thomasia reported on the combined method and the arguments used in support of this method, she remained committed to the oral method until she retired as principal of St Vincent School in 1969,[10] and then in 1971 from teaching altogether.[11] She never permitted the use of the combined method or the use of sign language at the school. However, her successor as principal Sr Liguori Töns,[12] started initially as an oralist[13] but gradually came to have a different opinion. Even

---

8   Ibid.
9   Ibid, 4.
10 'Surprise for Sister Thomasia', *The Star*, 25 March 1969.
11 '"Sister Chips" says Goodbye', *The Star* 30 November 1971, 27.
12 Sr Liguori started teaching at St Vincent School in 1954 and became principal in 1969. See Liguori Töns OP, Interview with Mark James, 16 December 2015, Johannesburg, 434.
13 In an article written when she had just become principal in 1970, she upheld all the values of the oral method of education. See Sr Liguori Töns OP, interview with Mark James, 16 December 2015, Johannesburg, 434.

while still a teacher she realised that there were limitations with the oral method. She was much more open to using whatever worked best.[14]

> To me, it was to make contact. If I only talk all the time and they just look at you, then you know that they are not getting what you are saying. For me, the main thing was to be able to communicate with them. Like if you don't know Spanish and you go to Spain ... you have to know that language. For me, it was the same with the hearing impaired. You have to be able to communicate in the way that they can communicate. But officially it wasn't allowed.[15]

So, although the official school policy was strictly an oral approach, there were teachers who used signs as a way to communicate with the children. Sr Liguori remembered that there was no official sign language in the school so she made do with the signs that she knew.[16]

Speaking on 12 May 1970 at an educational meeting of St Vincent School's Parents' Teachers' Association (PTA) on the communication problems a deaf child experienced, even Sr Thomasia, a fervent oralist, accepted that there were times when a teacher 'forgets herself and uses gestures.'[17] Sr Thomasia was quick to point out that she never did because she neither learnt to fingerspell nor to sign. However, this did not mean she was against the use of signs and gestures.

> To combat supplementary methods, i.e. fingerspelling, gestures, signs when there is no alternative to self-expression and communication, is most unpsychological and harmful, and amounts to an infringement of the

---

14 Ibid.
15 Ibid.
16 Sr Liguori Töns OP, interview with Mark James, 16 December 2016, Johannesburg, 434.
17 Thomasia Knoepfle, 'Communication Problems of the Deaf Child,' *SVQ* 5, 6, (Second Term, 1970): 13.

individual's human rights, which in the case of the deaf may be rendered instead of 'freedom of speech, freedom of communication.' No parent, no educator has the right to silence the child, should he indicate that he wants to convey something and cannot find the words for it.[18]

However, the emphasis on spoken language was still seen as primary because the expectation was that as the children grew older, they would be expected 'to substitute words for gestures'[19] in their communication with others. Similarly, there was also 'nothing wrong with fingerspelling'[20] as it did not interfere with correct grammar and language. Despite this, she had harsh words to say to those teachers who approved of using conventional signs in the classrooms. They were committing an 'offence against the oral method.'[21] This was because 'signs mutilate correct language apart from labelling the users as deaf-mutes.'[22] Sr Thomasia was concerned that deaf people were being seen as 'a race apart'[23] and she wanted them to be included as full members of society. For this reason, if deaf people were to fit in and not be considered as people set apart, they had to conform to the demands of the hearing world. Therefore, 'the greater the deaf person's facility in oralism the more successful he will be in being accepted.'[24]

After Sr Thomasia's talk at the PTA, a panel discussion ensued. Three deaf respondents, previously pupils at St Vincent school, namely Cyril Axelrod,[25] Robert Simmons[26] and Alan Mansfield,[27] were allowed to share their thoughts on her talk. Sr

---

18   Knoepfle, 'Communication Problems,' 11.
19   Ibid, 12.
20   Ibid, 13.
21   Ibid, 13.
22   Ibid, 13.
23   Ibid, 16.
24   Ibid, 16.
25   Cyril Axelrod was a candidate for the priesthood at St John Vianney Seminary. Further reflection on Cyril Axelrod will be covered in the next chapter.
26   Robert Simmons was a past pupil and a lecturer at Wits University. See 'The Silent World of Robert Simmons,' 153/1106 25, KDSA.
27   Alan Mansfield had written an article earlier in the year about the need for specially trained psychologists to work with deaf children. He related how as a hard-of-hearing pupil at a hearing

Thomasia's presentation, as we have seen, endorsed her lifelong commitment to the oral method of education.

All three respondents related their own experiences of living as deaf persons in a hearing world. They listed numerous issues that affected them. There was a lack of patience from hearing people in accommodating themselves with "deaf" speech.'[28] Also hearing people did not speak distinctly and slowly when communicating with deaf people. There was a challenge that deaf people faced in lip-reading within groups of hearing people. This meant that deaf people had to improve their oral skills. Equally difficult was the embarrassment that deaf people felt when they misunderstood a question put to them and gave a 'totally irrelevant answer.'[29] They felt foolish and were worried that hearing people may think that they were deficient in intelligence and 'not all there.'[30] Also mentioned was the inability to use the telephone.[31]

Implicit in most of the issues raised was that it was often the deaf who had to accommodate themselves to the dictates of the hearing world. Cyril Axelrod did not agree with this. He felt that hearing people needed to change and adapt themselves to the needs of deaf people. 'Both parties should make efforts to establish satisfactory mutual contacts.'[32] Therefore, when public speeches were made an interpreter should be made available for any deaf people who are present.[33]

---

    school his speech lessons were severely retarded when conducted in the presence of the rest of the class. He was embarrassed and flustered by being corrected in front of other pupils and how he lost confidence. He suggested that if any corrections could be done privately by a psychologist who understood deaf children then it would build up the confidence of deaf children rather than humiliate them. See Alan Mansfield, 'Some Views from the "other side",' *SVQ* 5, 5 (First Term, 1970): 9-11.
28 Knoepfle, 'Communication Problems,' 17.
29 Ibid, 18.
30 Ibid, 18.
31 Simmons made an interesting comment: 'What a boon it would be if someone would invent a "visual" telephone to ease our position.' See Knoepfle, 'Communication Problems,' 18.
32 Ibid, 18.
33 Ibid, 18.

This was a telling comment. Axelrod raised the issue that there was something fundamentally wrong if it was always deaf people who had to adjust to the demands of a hearing world. Why did the hearing not recognise the need to adjust to the needs of deaf people? This view would have enormous implications for deaf education.

Growing appreciation for sign language

In the late 1960s, several voices emerged in South Africa calling for a re-look at the manual methods of education. In March 1968, Nicholas Nieder-Heitmann, the hearing principal of the Kutlwanong School for the Deaf in Rustenburg, stated:

> Those of us who have anything at all to do with the teaching of the Deaf, know very well that in even in schools where actual gesture-language and finger-talk are not officially allowed, gesture-language and finger-talk are practised by scholars, whatever the teaching policy of that school may be.[34]

He pointed out that the deaf themselves communicated easily with one another. They got married, they were good workers, they raised their children and generally were well-adjusted in society. Among themselves, the deaf had no communication problems. The problems only existed in the interaction between deaf and hearing people. Therefore, in deaf education, he said, they should be allowed to use the method of communication which is their own, that of 'gesture-language and lip-reading.'[35]

Even in the Catholic schools for the deaf, as we saw in the previous chapter, sign language was tolerated.

> When growing up, I was staying at boarding school from the age of two. When growing up I was very good at sign language. In boarding school, when sister wanted a meeting with the Deaf children, she would call me to stand in front

---

34 Norman Nieder-Heitmann, 'Guest Editorial: The New Study at Cape Town,' *TSM*, March 1968, 2-4.
35 Nieder-Heitmann, 'Guest Editorial,' 4.

of all the boarders and sign to the other children. When the children responded to sister, I would have to tell the sister what they were saying. I was acting as an interpreter. Whenever anything happened it was always me who was asked to stand up and sign to the others. Other than in the boarding hostel, signing was not allowed in the school.[36]

While signing was forbidden in the classroom, it did not mean that chaplains working with deaf adults did not appreciate sign language. Writing in *The Silent Messenger* in 1969, a deaf chaplain, the Reverend Corfmat spoke in favour of an increased use of the manual method of communication, not just in education, but also in church services. 'Signs have so much ingenuity and beauty.'[37] He recounted the story of two deaf women who told him 'that they were first attracted to their future husbands when they saw them fingerspell and sign so gracefully.'[38] While he considered fingerspelling more accurate and as more grammatical than signing, nevertheless, he appreciated:

> [H]ow pleasant and relaxing it is to watch another who thinks of our Silent Language as an Art and uses it with obvious enjoyment. He or she ... gives life and colour to every conversation, lecture or sermon.[39]

By the beginning of 1970, the whole oral method of education came under greater scrutiny and criticism.

Critiquing the oral method

Various educationalists, especially in the United States, began to express their reservations about the effectiveness of the oral method. Like Axelrod, they also questioned whether it was right that deaf people were always the ones being expected to conform to the demands of a hearing world. One such educationalist, McCay Vernon, wrote articles and books highlighting the

---

36 Faith Cronwright, interview conducted by Mark James, 16 November 2015, Cape Town, 426.
37 R. Corfmat, 'Signs... Signing and Signers,' *TSM*, June 1969, 16.
38 Corfmat, 'Signs,' 17.
39 Ibid.

shortcomings of deaf education. He identified eight 'persistent, pervasive, and unrealistic myths'[40] that were prevalent up to the 1960s and which needed to be dispelled.

The first myth was that deaf children lacked intelligence. He pointed to fifty independent research studies that showed that 'the intelligence of deaf children is distributed in especially the same way as that of nondeaf.'[41] He concluded that 'there is no causal relationship between deafness and IQ. Deaf people are as bright as hearing people.'[42]

The second myth was that 'we have done a good job of educating deaf children.'[43] Studies in the United States again showed that 30% of deaf children leave school at the age of 16 or older functionally illiterate. Sixty percent leave school having only achieved Grade 5 or below and only 5% achieved Grade 10. Most of this 5% group were hard of hearing or were post-lingually deaf.[44] Deaf children lagged behind hearing children concerning reading ability. For Vernon, this indicated that there was something drastically wrong with the education system.[45]

The third myth was that fingerspelling and sign language impair academic achievement. He argued that studies showed that:

> Children who have had and who use fingerspelling and the language of signs do far better in reading, mathematics and academic work in general than do children who have been limited to just 'oral' communication.[46]

---

40   McCay Vernon, 'Myths of the Education,' *TSM*, March 1971, 16–17. Reproduced from the *Maryland Bulletin*.
41   Vernon, 'Myths,' 16.
42   Ibid.
43   Vernon, 'Myths,' 16.
44   Deafness has been divided into two categories: pre-lingual deafness and post-lingual deafness. Pre-lingual deafness is identified as being deaf from birth or before the age of three, that is before the child has acquired a spoken language. Post-lingual deafness is those of have lost their hearing after acquiring a spoken language. For more information, see 'Problems: Prelingual Deafness, Postlingual Deafness,' *TSM*, September 1969, 8.
45   Vernon, 'Myths,' 16.
46   Ibid.

Despite these findings, the education of deaf children continued to be directed by the assumptions of the oral method.

The fourth myth he challenged was that 'sign language will cause deaf children to develop poor habits of expressive language.'[47] Again the research, he believed, showed the contrary opinion. Early exposure to sign language and fingerspelling did not detract from but rather improved the writing ability of deaf children in contrast to those restricted to the oral approach. As we saw in the previous chapter, this view contrasted with the view of Catholic schools for the deaf which insisted on the oral method of education because it promoted a far superior writing ability.[48]

The fifth myth, he identified, was that the use of fingerspelling and sign language have a negative impact on the ability of deaf children to attain speech and lip-reading skills. Vernon contradicted this, arguing that research showed that 'there is no difference in the speech intelligibility of deaf children who used sign language and fingerspelling and those who did not.'[49] Vernon saw Total Communication as a way out of the predicament caused by the prevalence of pure oral methods of education in schools for the deaf. Consequently, he rejected the sixth myth that 'there are people who advocate manualism.'[50] Total Communication was not manualism.

> Those who support the use of a total communication system involving speech, spelling, amplification, sign language, lip-reading, and writing are increasing in number because the factual data indicate total communication to be far superior for deaf children.[51]

Vernon challenged the seventh myth that 'most deaf children can learn auditorially.'[52] Oralists believed this had stopped people from referring to deaf children and that they now referred them

---

47   Ibid.
48   Interview with Sr Siobhan Murphy OP, conducted by Mark James, Cape Town, 12 July 2016, 454–455.
49   Vernon, 'Myths,' 16.
50   Ibid.
51   Ibid, 17.
52   Vernon, 'Myths,' 17.

as being hearing-impaired. He said that this claim was very problematic. This sleight of hand masked the problem.

> They claim that because a child can hear a fog horn or gunshot he is not deaf and that by hanging a hearing aid on him he will learn to understand speech which he cannot hear.[53]

These teachers merely evaded the truth before them that a total aural-manual approach to deaf education was far more helpful to deaf children than the oral method.

The last myth he challenged was that 'all deaf children should be sent away from home for education.'[54] Deaf children should be educated locally in their home areas rather than passing on the responsibility to residential schools situated far from the deaf children's families.

Vernon concluded that the research had shown overwhelmingly that a Total Communication approach to education was far more effective than the oral method and that directors of special education had to now see how they could integrate these findings into their programmes for schools for the deaf.

Total Communication

McCay Vernon advocated that the approach being used by the Maryland School for the Deaf in the United States should be used instead of the oral method. By 1968, the school had introduced a new philosophy of education that was called Total Communication.[55] In many respects, Total Communication was an adaptation of what previously was known as the combined method.

However, rather than just seeing it as a practical solution to the shortcomings of the oral method, Total Communication saw

---

53   Ibid.
54   Ibid.
55   D.M. Denton, 'The Philosophy of Total Communication,' *TSM*, September 1979, 15.

itself as something more positive. It was an approach to education which not only encouraged the use of sign language in conjunction with lip-reading and speech; but advocated this method as far superior to the oral method.

Total Communication in the United States

Throughout the 1970s, Total Communication became more acceptable in American schools for the deaf. By 1975, even the National Association for the Deaf (NAD) in the United States had begun to promote Total Communication.[56] On 5 May 1976, the Conference of Executives of American Schools for the Deaf in Rochester, New York officially adopted the following definition:

> Total Communication is a philosophy requiring the incorporation of appropriate aural, manual, and oral modes of communication in order to ensure effective communication with and among hearing-impaired persons.[57]

Gallaudet University, the Deaf American university, insisted that all new staff at the college attend classes in Total Communication before they were permitted to teach.[58]

Despite growing support for Total Communication, there were still many who criticised this new approach because of its use of sign language. The idea persisted that sign language was not a language, like spoken languages, but mere gesture and a primitive form of human communication, unlike spoken languages.

In 1960, when William Stokoe, professor of linguistics and English at Gallaudet University in Washington DC, proposed the novel but radical idea that the signs deaf people used were a language; he was vilified by educators of the deaf and even staff

---

[56] See Frederick Schreiber, 'Total Communication – As the Adults See It,' *TSM*, September 1975, 14–16. Reproduced from *The Deaf American*. Schreiber was himself deaf.
[57] R.G. Brill, 'Total Communication,' *TSM*, September 1978, 10. Reproduced from *The Maryland Bulletin*.
[58] Frances Parsons, 'Total Communication,' *TSM*, September 1981, 8–9.

at his university.⁵⁹ However, over the years his theory proved itself to be 'an idea that would not go away.'⁶⁰ In comparing the grammatical structure of spoken languages with that of sign language, Stokoe discovered that while spoken languages used sound to convey symbolic meaning, sign languages utilised space. For syntax, sign languages use handshapes, non-manual features (facial expressions) and classifiers. The grammatical structure of sentences differed between English and signed languages. By 1979, Stokoe was arguing that sign language was the deaf person's native or first language and the spoken language was a second one. English and American Sign Language (ASL) are two separate languages with different grammatical structures and syntax.⁶¹

It was not only in the United States that Total Communication was being readily adopted in schools for the deaf, as the preferred philosophy for education, but the same was happening in other countries. By 1977, the Scandinavian countries had adopted Total Communication in their schools,⁶² as had many schools in the United Kingdom and other European countries.

The Fifth World Conference on Deafness held in Copenhagen that year welcomed the shift to Total Communication.

The Fifth World Conference on Deafness

Mrs Beryl Jones and her husband Mervyn⁶³ were delegated by the SANCD to attend the Fifth World Conference on Deafness in Copenhagen, Denmark from 7 to 12 August 1977. On their return, the Joneses highlighted the extent to which Total Communication was being readily accepted worldwide. Beryl Jones said that 'the

---

59   William Stokoe, 'Sign Language Structure,' *Studies in Linguistics: Occasional papers* 8, (1960). For more information on how this idea was received, see William Stokoe, *Language in Hand: Why Sign Came Before Speech* (Washington DC: Gallaudet University Press, 2001), 1.
60   Stokoe used this phrase as the title of the first chapter in his book, *Language in Hand*, 1–16.
61   William Stokoe, 'Sign Language Research: What it Knows and Whither it Leads,' *TSM*, December 1979, 7–11.
62   Beryl Jones, 'Fifth World Conference on Deafness, Copenhagen. August 1977,' *TSM*, November/December 1977, 8.
63   They were the hearing parents of Alan Jones, a past pupil of St Vincent School for the Deaf.

deaf people[64] at this conference were overwhelmingly in favour of "Total communication."[65]

Sign language was being called 'the mother tongue of the deaf' and their preferred mode of communication 'because it was the most natural, comfortable and easy way for them to communicate and to acquire language.'[66]

The call to accept sign language as the mother tongue and natural language of the deaf was a major new development. Before this, the different manual sign systems that were created for education were not those used by the deaf themselves. They were artificially constructed to supplement spoken languages.

The conference took issue that pre-lingually deaf children were getting a raw deal in oral schools. Denying deaf people the right to use sign language was seen as disrespectful. One deaf delegate said, 'The deaf feel like puppets – the Hearing pulling the strings.'[67] The delegate urged the hearing 'experts' in education to take note and comply with the wishes of the deaf so that Total Communication would become acceptable in all schools for the deaf throughout the world.

The voices in support of Total Communication began to grow and develop in South Africa too.

Initial reception of Total Communication in South Africa

One of the first advocates of Total Communication in South Africa was Robert Simmons. In 1971, he was a senior lecturer in anatomy at the University of the Witwatersrand and received the Vista Award for outstanding life achievements. In 1949, he was the first deaf man in South Africa to attain a matriculation pass at St

---

64 Jones reported that 400 people attended the conference from 30 countries from around the world. This number included 100 deaf people. She does not list the countries from which they came. See Jones, 'Fifth World Conference,' 6.
65 Jones, 'Fifth World Conference,' 6–8, 10.
66 Jones, 'Fifth World Conference,' 6.
67 Ibid, 8.

Vincent School. He went on to study anatomy at Wits University and by 1971 was working on his doctoral dissertation.[68]

> He is passionately devoted to the problems of deaf and partially deaf children and to the improvement of educational standards and vocational status of deaf persons in this country.[69]

Already in 1971, he wrote in favour of the Total Communication approach. He encouraged hearing parents of deaf children to use any means of communication to enable them to develop a good grasp of their home language, whether it be English or Afrikaans.

> Please use all means of communication, manual or oral, as long as your children are able to develop a good concept of the spoken language. Do not be ashamed, or pay attention to other people if they remark on your using the sign language, because you will be sure of your triumph one day when your child is able to compete well and equally with his deaf or hearing friends outside the school and home.[70]

His emphasis was on the acquisition of language rather than speech. He argued that sign language was the deaf person's first language whereas English and Afrikaans were secondary languages.[71] Simmons was incredibly well-read and it is very likely that he was versed in the writings of William Stokoe or was at least aware of his thinking.

68　'Robert Michael Thomas Simmons: Winner 1971 Wenner,' *TSM*, December 1971, 22.
69　'Robert Simmons,' 22.
70　Robert Simmons, 'Deaf Education,' *TSM*, March 1972, 24.
71　This argument is possibly influenced by the writings of William Stokoe who argued that sign language was a language and Deaf people's natural language. It is also at the basis of the present debate about the importance of using the bilingual and bicultural method of education for deaf schools. Deaf children need to be taught via two languages – sign language and a spoken language for written work.

Mixed response to Total Communication in South Africa

Initially, there was a mixed response in South Africa to the concept of Total Communication. This section discusses the response of African schools for the deaf as well as that of the Department of Education under which all white schools for the deaf fell.

African schools for the deaf

As was argued in the previous chapter, the use of sign language in African schools for the deaf was already commonplace. So, in these schools, the introduction of Total Communication was not particularly controversial. Instead, it gave theoretical justification for the combined method that was already in place. Up until then, the Paget-Gorman sign system was used in most of the schools. The system was used in conjunction with signs to illustrate the grammatical structure of a spoken language. An additional sign was used to indicate whether the sign was a conjunction, preposition or verb, and in which tense it was being signed. It was an artificially created sign system that was not indigenous to deaf people.[72]

Norman Nieder-Heitmann, the Dutch Reformed principal of the Kutlwanong School for the Deaf in Roodepoort, wanted to use Total Communication in his school instead of the Paget-Gorman method. This spurred him on to start what he called his One-man Committee on the South African Sign Language.[73] Nieder-Heitmann gave a report to the 23rd Biennial Conference of the SANCD on the findings of his 'committee.'[74] He had done a personal survey of 134 specially chosen signs commonly used by deaf people in South Africa. He arrived at these signs by interviewing 180 people in the major cities. He

---

[72] See Charles Chittenden, 'The Paget Gorman Sign System,' *TSM*, June/July 1976, 5.

[73] It is interesting to note that while Nieder-Heitmann spoke about the South African Sign Language he was still advocating Total Communication and not what is now known as SASL.

[74] See Norman Nieder-Heitmann, 'Extracts from the Report of the One-Man Committee on the South African Sign Language at the 23rd Biennial Conference of the SA Council for the Deaf,' *TSM*, March 1977, 14.

wanted to determine their origin and after studying these signs he discovered that roughly speaking 60% were of British (or Australian) origin. Very few signs were of American origin and no signs from the Paget-Gorman sign system were used. This last point was particularly interesting because the Paget-Gorman system had been extensively used in African schools over the previous fifteen years.[75]

However, it was in the white and coloured schools, which were intensely committed to the oral method of education, that the acceptance of Total Communication was met with fierce resistance.

The Department of Education resistance to Total Communication

The South African Department of Education, under which all-white schools for the deaf fell, was staunchly in favour of the oral method of deaf education. In a talk given to the SANCD, a senior department official, Mr K. van der Merwe, said that his department was not in favour of mainstreaming deaf children into hearing schools. Neither was the department going to permit the use of Total Communication at either the primary or secondary school level,[76] even though he had no problem with the use of sign language at the post-secondary school level. While he conceded that there were attractions to the Total Communication approach, such as its affordability when compared with the cost of the oral method, what concerned him was that deaf people constitute a minority group in the country. He was concerned that using an esoteric method of communication like sign language would just further stigmatise deaf people.[77]

Total Communication, he argued, ignored the reality that deaf people lived in a hearing world and, by implication, needed to conform to the demands of this world which the oral method trained deaf people to do. Total communication would just lead to deaf people becoming a minority group and a sub-culture in

---

75 Nieder-Heitmann, 'Extracts,' 14.
76 K. van der Merwe, 'Comment: On the Right Track of Oralism,' *TSM*, December 1975, 12–13.
77 Van der Merwe, 'Comment,' 13.

society. They would become stigmatised as deaf.[78] He was also against sign language because it did not conform to the structure and grammar of the spoken and written languages.[79]

Van der Merwe believed that there were no instant answers or cures to the problem the deaf had in acquiring language, speech and speechreading through the exploitation of their residual hearing. Total Communication was too simplistic a 'solution to a very complex problem.'[80] He was adamant though that the deaf children in the schools under his department would not 'be used as guinea pigs in an experiment of which the final outcome is so uncertain.'[81]

> If the results prove to be better than we know what can be accomplished by the oral method, then, and only then can we reconsider our position regarding how deaf children should first be introduced to deaf education and the acquisition, development and comprehension of oral language.[82]

Until then he wished the schools in the United States good luck because if Total Communication proved to be 'a totally calamitous failure, the disaster would at least be localised.'[83] Van der Merwe did not want any schools under his jurisdiction affected by any fallout that might arise from the premature introduction of Total Communication into schools for the deaf.

Despite some resistance to Total Communication in some quarters, the groundswell of support for this method of deaf education continued to expand. Even the National Council for the Deaf began to discuss the issue.

---

78   Ibid.
79   Van der Merwe, 'Comment,' 13.
80   Ibid, 12.
81   Ibid.
82   Ibid.
83   Ibid.

Chapter 9

The visit of David Denton to South Africa

In July 1979, David Denton from the Maryland School for the Deaf, one of the foremost advocates of Total Communication, was invited out by Norman Nieder-Heitmann[84] to give the keynote address to the SANCD national congress.

In his talk, David Denton emphasised that the philosophy of Total Communication based itself on the view that deaf children would be able to acquire the necessary language skills they needed if they were given the 'opportunity to interact freely with all persons around them and if they were given a symbol system which they could use freely for communication and for language experimentation.'[85] The symbol system, to which he referred, was sign language. For Denton, signing was to be used simultaneously with speaking. Signing reinforced speechreading (or lip-reading) and speechreading, in turn, reinforced the signing, so that better communication would result.[86] This new approach was based on the idea that deaf children listen by watching. At the Maryland School for the Deaf where he worked, Denton said that every staff member was expected to know how to sign while talking.[87] This was both when communicating directly with deaf children but also whenever and wherever they are present.

As background, Denton highlighted that Total Communication was conceived in response to the failure of the traditional oral method of deaf education in the United States. This failure, according to Denton, was brought to the fore by the 1965 Babbidge Report conducted by the United States Department of Health, Education and Welfare.[88] The oral-manual controversy had historically hampered and hindered the proper education of deaf children. Total Communication was an approach to deaf education that overcame the impasse and made the debate irrelevant. Both oral and manual methods were important and

---

84 'Denton Speaks in South Africa,' *TSM*, March 1980, 6–7. Reproduced from *The Maryland Bulletin*, Oct/Nov 1979.
85 David Denton, 'The Philosophy of Total Communication,' *TSM*, September 1979, 15.
86 Denton, 'Philosophy,' 15.
87 Ibid.
88 Denton, 'Philosophy,' 16.

not one more than the other. He also pointed out that Total Communication was a philosophy rather than a method. Total Communication wanted to free up communication between hearing parents and their deaf children so that this could lead to a situation of mutual understanding and acceptance. The deaf child needed to feel accepted in their family of birth and to 'feel free to interact and learn to become a happy, literate and communicating member of society.'[89]

> Because of this humanizing influence of Total Communication, not only upon the child but upon the parents and professionals as well, we have found the bonds of trust between the deaf child, the parents, and the professionals to be growing as never before. This point is dramatized by the remarks of a five-year-old boy whose parents had just learned to sign when he said, 'mommy and daddy are deaf now'.[90]

Total Communication emphasised that deaf children should be introduced to early educational training. This started in the home, in the context of family life, as well as at the pre-school level with training in the acquisition of sign language acquisition rather than speech, as in the oral method. A benefit of Total Communication was that it involved signing and speaking at the same time and so allowed for the use of proper English syntax.[91] Signs presented in this manner reinforced the correct grammatical features of the spoken language.

Alongside oral and manual methods, Total Communication also acknowledged the value of appropriate amplification. This helped with speech and language development. Denton concluded that 'communication is total or multidimensional... one dimension enhancing, reinforcing and enriching the other.'[92]

---

89 Ibid.
90 Ibid.
91 In recent years, this form of signing is called Signed English as the signs support the grammatical structure of English as a spoken language. Sign language has its own grammatical structure employing space rather than sound, classifiers and non-manual features (facial expressions).
92 Denton, 'Philosophy,' 17.

In an interview with *The Maryland Bulletin*[93] on his return to the United States, Denton said that during the eight days he spent in South Africa, he visited some of the schools for the deaf and spent considerable time with deaf adults. He became aware of:

> [T]he subtle feelings of oppression experienced by deaf people, by their parents, and those who work with them regarding communication methods. In the schools I found the students to be literally begging for Total Communication, for the freedom to express themselves in the best way they could. Similarly, the teachers were hungry for information about Total Communication and were asking for the freedom to use the language of signs along with the oral and auditory methods.[94]

He identified that the real problem for the acceptance of Total Communication in South Africa lay with the attitude of those in the Department of Education who upheld the oral method of education.[95] This was an ongoing problem in the white and coloured schools. However, for African schools, and even some Catholic schools, Total Communication alongside written English was accepted as a positive step forward.[96]

His perspective proved to be accurate for Catholic schools for the deaf. It is to these schools that we now turn.

Catholic deaf education and Total Communication

The two white Catholic schools for the deaf, namely, Dominican-Grimley School in Cape Town and St Vincent School in Johannesburg, showed very little interest in Total Communication. They were firmly committed to the oral method of deaf education as was the Wittebome School for coloured deaf

---

93 'Denton Speaks in SA,' 6–7.
94 Ibid, 6.
95 'Denton Speaks in SA,' 7.
96 Sr Siobhan Murphy OP said when she came to the Dominican Deaf School in Hammanskraal in January 1983, Total Communication was already in use. See Sr Siobhan Murphy OP, interview with Mark James, 12 July 2015, Cape Town, 451.

children. The Dominican sisters who ran these schools remained firmly committed to the oral method.

Likewise, the African schools, St Thomas School in Woodlands and the Dominican School in Hammanskraal were oral schools in which fingerspelling and sign language were taught and permitted because the Department for Bantu Education insisted that this be provided. In the school inspector's report on St Thomas School for the Deaf, the inspector stated that the general method of education used in the school is oralism. The basic elements of the oral method, such as lip-reading and speech training, were taught. In his report, he noted that in the previous year, a teacher was given in-service training in speech training and audiometry.[97] 'Fingerspelling, natural gesturing and signs and reading and writing receive due attention,'[98] but in general, he said, the combined method was only used extensively in cases of those deaf children who were slower in learning.

This was not the case with the later establishment of two new Catholic schools, Sizwile School for the Deaf in Dobsonville, Soweto and KwaThintwa School for the Deaf in Inchanga, KwaZulu-Natal, which we will introduce in the next chapter.

Total communication as bad conscience

The concept of Total Communication was not as radical a change or alternative to the oral method as its advocates, like Vernon and Denton, believed it to be. In 1979, at the Fifth Conference on Deafness in Copenhagen, Steve Mathis, a deaf delegate and director of the International Center on Deafness at Gallaudet College admitted that Total Communication was basically 'an oral philosophy.'[99] Fingerspelling and signs merely augment and supplement the oral method.

---

97 'The Chairman's Annual Report on the Affairs of St Thomas School for Deaf Bantu Children for the Year 1968/69,' 2. 124/374 71, KDSA.
98 WW Bouwer, 'Report on Inspection of St Thomas School for Deaf Bantu: March 1970,' 4. 124/374 72, KDSA.
99 Jones, 'Fifth Conference,' 8.

However, Total Communication made the use of sign language in deaf education respectable again. Consequently, with the use of sign language in Deaf education more radical models emerged.

Flourishing of sign language courses and appreciation of sign language

By 1981, one of the effects of the interest in Total Communication in the United States was reflected in more people going on courses to learn sign language. Frances Parsons, the head of languages at Gallaudet College, said: 'We are witnessing today an unprecedented boom in sign language classes springing up everywhere.'[100] A similar phenomenon was taking place in South Africa.

Already in 1978, Alan Jones, a deaf computer programmer and ex-pupil of St Vincent School, teamed up with Norman Nieder-Heitmann, the one-man committee for the study of sign languages, to formulate a dictionary of South African sign language.[101] The dictionary *Talking to the Deaf* was completed and published in 1980. It was used in all the African schools under the DET. In the latter half of 1980, Alan Jones organised his first six-week sign language course which finished just before Christmas. He used the book he co-authored, *Talking to the Deaf*, as the basis for the course. In January 1981, he advertised the next course at the Durban Deaf Club and received the enrolment of 24 students. He then ran two more sign language courses for the Lions in Durban and Pietermaritzburg.[102] His courses were open to people of all races.[103]

Due to his work in teaching sign language, Alan Jones was asked to represent the SANCD at the International Conference

---

100 Frances Parsons, 'Total Communication,' *TSM*, September 1981, 8.
101 'Meet Some of our Deaf: FOYSA Award for Alan Jones,' *TSM*, December 1981, 8.
102 Alan Jones, 'Report on Sign language Courses,' *TSM*, September 1981, 11.
103 Alan Jones, 'International Conference on Sign Language,' *TSM*, December 1981, 14.

on Sign Language Research in England. At this conference, Jones commented on the interpreters' role in communicating the content of the conference to deaf participants that 'was crisp and clear and they used beautiful facial expressions.'[104]

The growing interest and appreciation of sign language opened up deaf people to a different perspective on their place in the world. Previously, they were consistently told that they were expected to conform to the demands of the hearing workplace and the hearing world. Now deaf people were asserting their own identity and rights within society challenging hearing people to learn sign language. In meetings with hearing people, deaf people began to insist that interpreters be made available to ensure that deaf people could participate more fully in public forums on their terms and not those determined by hearing people alone.

Interpreters for hearing people

Employment as interpreters for hearing people who could sign was another spinoff from Total Communication. In the United States, for example, there were an increasing number of employment opportunities for interpreters at hospitals, courtrooms, churches, business meetings and conferences as well as at universities.[105]

Although there were not as many opportunities in South Africa, many hearing people did see the value of learning sign language to assist in the work they were already doing. Alan Jones recounted the story of a social worker working in a law court in Zululand requesting to learn sign language so that she could act as an interpreter for deaf people.[106]

Opening the door to natural sign language

Total Communication was taken on board by a growing number of deaf people. Often Total Communication became a synonym for sign language. Alan Jones and Robert Simmons, both ex-pupils of St Vincent School, promoted the use of sign language

104 Jones, 'International Conference,' 14.
105 Parsons, 'Total Communication,' 9.
106 Jones, 'Report on Sign Language Courses,' 11.

for education and were supporters of the Total Communication approach. This became a door through which deaf people would eventually celebrate the use of natural sign languages in the Church and society.

Levinas, bad conscience and becoming hospitable

In the previous chapter, we saw how totality functioned in the schools for the deaf through the oral method of deaf education. It was a system devised by the hearing to respond to the needs and struggles of deaf people. The oral method of deaf education was devised by hearing people who thought they knew what was best for deaf people –what the hearing thought the deaf needed and therefore wanted. For Levinas, the hearing acted in good conscience. He subverts the normal way we think of acting in good conscience. It showed their self-interestedness. They uncritically assumed that being trained to lip-read and vocalise a spoken language so that they could function effectively in a hearing world would be 'liberating deaf people from the prison of silence.' They never for a moment questioned their own certainties, their own good conscience, their 'benevolent' actions. If they had, perhaps they may found themselves wanting. They never listened to the deaf who were calling for the use of sign language as a means of communication. For Levinas, this illustrates what he meant by the grasping, possessing and comprehending of the Other by the same, or totality, or the imperialism of the same. Hearing people thinking that their view of the world is the whole rather than discovering it was just a part of an even larger whole.

Conclusion

In this chapter, we reflected on Total Communication as a response of teachers at Maryland School. Moved by proximity to the Deaf Other, they began to feel dis-located and uncertain that the oral method of deaf education was the only and right way. They began to recognise that the interests of the deaf other were not being served by the oral method of deaf education. They found themselves under question and wearing new shoes which chafed their consciences.

> The other's face is the revelation not of the arbitrariness of the will, but its injustice. Consciousness of my injustice is produced when I incline myself not before facts, but before the other.[107]

They suffered from what Levinas has referred to as bad conscience. They recognised that they were guilty of indifference to the Deaf Other and being unjust towards the Other. The teachers' bad conscience opened them up to begin to experience the wounds of the deaf children they were teaching.

> The I approached in responsibility is for-the-other, is a denuding, an exposure to being affected, a pure susceptiveness. It does not posit itself, possessing itself and recognizing itself; it is consumed and delivered over, dislocates itself, loses its place, is exiled, relegates itself into itself, but as though its very skin were still a way to shelter itself in being, exposed to wounds and outrage, emptying itself in no-grounds, to the point of substituting itself for the other, holding on to itself only as it were in the trace of its exile.[108]

Having a bad conscience is to realise that one is guilty of usurping someone else's place in the sun.[109] The self's own bad conscience is ironically to have a good conscience where one realises that one is the oppressor of the Other, the cause of the Other's suffering and pain.

For Levinas:

> This is a fear for all that my existing – despite its intentional and conscious innocence – can accomplish of violence and murder.[110] ... What I fear is not my death but that my life, my existence is the reason for another's death, another's hunger and suffering.[111]

---

107 Levinas, *Collected Philosophical Papers*, 57.
108 Levinas, *Otherwise Than Being*, 138.
109 Levinas, *Of God Who Comes to Mind*, 175.
110 Ibid.
111 Ibid.

Denton remarked that the oral method of deaf education was detrimental to the success of the deaf children in the classroom. They are awakened to a problem, they fret and suffer from what Levinas referred to as insomnia, that is, a 'dis-ease' or restlessness where they feel disturbed at the present situation and try to find a more just and loving way of responding to the needs of the deaf children.

> Insomnia, vigilance and wakefulness restlessness of this peace. The subject arising in the passivity of unconditionality, in the expulsion outside of its being at home with itself, is undeclinable.[112]

They are adamant that there is a need to respond and do something about this situation. The bad conscience of the hearing, Denton and members of the Maryland School, caused them to recognise that they were responsible for the deaf. They found themselves elected involuntarily or summoned to do good for them. They want to ensure that the children benefit from their education. They are remorseful of the mistakes made in the past and we saw this in the way that the myths of the success of the oral method were systematically dismantled. 'Identity gnawing away at itself – in remorse. I have not done anything and I have always been under accusation – persecuted.'[113]

In so doing, those advocating the Total Communication approach stumbled upon what Levinas called non-indifference[114] and so they embarked on a campaign to encourage the use of sign language in the classroom to supplement the oral method of education.

Total Communication was proposed as an alternative to the oral method of education. Total Communication opened the door to 'welcoming the Other as hospitality.'[115] Welcoming the Other is an act of generosity, an expression of care for the Other

---

112   Levinas, *Otherwise Than Being*, 139.
113   Ibid, 114.
114   Ibid, 138–139.
115   Levinas, *Totality and Infinity*, 27.

and it is freely given as a gift.[116] It was a move in the direction of hospitality, transcendence and infinity. However, this shift remained with the ambit of the hearing desire to accommodate and assimilate deaf people into a hearing world. The totality of the oral method of education persisted but now it included the use of signed English to supplement the oral method. Total Communication did not provide the full recognition of the Deaf Other's alterity. It was not a breach of totality but rather a compromise. It was a beginning.

Total Communication heralded a new chapter in deaf education providing a change to the oral method that had been a dominant force in deaf education for over 60 years. Yet, Total Communication was neither new nor innovative. It was an adaptation of the combined method of deaf education that had been used in the United States in the previous century. In many respects, it was a variation on the oral method – it was the oral method with a bit of sign language thrown into the mix for good measure. Nevertheless, in giving recognition to the importance of sign language as a tool for education it opened the door to the latent desires among deaf people to learn and study in their natural language.

---

116   Spiros Makris, 'Emmanuel Levinas on Hospitality: Ethical and Political Aspects,' *International Journal of Theology, Philosophy and Science* 2 (2018), 84: 79–96.

Chapter 10

The Use of Sign Language in Catholic Schools for the Deaf, 1982-1994

The tide was turning in Catholic schools for the deaf as the use of sign language slowly became more acceptable.

Following again the two aspects of Catholic deaf ministry, namely deaf education and chaplaincy work, I will attempt to outline the reception Total Communication, as a medium of deaf education, received in the different Catholic schools for the deaf.

During the 1970s, two Deaf priests, Fr Cyril Axelrod CSsR and Fr John Turner CMM, were ordained (see Chapters 13 and 16) ministered in South Africa providing social and liturgical ministry to the Deaf community. A new development was the establishment of Deaf organisations and institutions that lobbied for the rights of deaf people in South Africa. This resulted in a dramatic shift happening among deaf people. The priests promoted Deaf awareness and being proud to be Deaf, which involved Deaf mobilisation. This became evident in both the Catholic Church and in the broader South African society.

It was another step closer to promoting natural sign language as Deaf people's first or indigenous language.[1] In these developments, we will see an incarnation of 'the face signs.'[2]

The Catholic schools for the deaf were slow to come to appreciate the value of sign language. However, during this period several Catholic schools for the deaf began to adopt Total Communication in the classroom. In the first part of this chapter, I will begin with those schools which were the first to use Total Communication and end with those that resisted or grudgingly adopted its use.

Catholic schools that accepted Total Communication as a method of teaching

This section focuses on six Catholic schools that adopted Total Communication as a method of instruction.

Sizwile School for the Deaf, Soweto

In 1978, St Martin Nursery School was the first Catholic school for the deaf to wholeheartedly embrace Total Communication and the use of sign language in the classroom. This was still the case when the school underwent a name change to Sizwile School for the Deaf in 1980. This was a direct result of the school being under the leadership of Fr Cyril Axelrod, a Deaf priest, who was a proponent of Total Communication and sign language in Deaf education.

---

1   The use of the word 'indigenous' for a sign language was used by Peter McDonough in 'Ministry amongst Deaf people' in The Gospel preached by the Deaf: Proceedings of a Conference on Deaf Liberation Theology held at the Faculty of Theology of the Catholic University of Leuven (Belgium), May 19th 2003, edited by Marcel Broesterhuizen, Leuven: Peeters, 2007, 53–69. This use of indigenous language and indigenous culture fits with the debates around the inculturation of the church in relation to African cultures and so may be preferable in the context of Catholic debates.
2   This is my adaptation of Levinas' expression that 'the face speaks.' See Levinas, *Totality and Infinity*, 66. Levinas wrote: 'The face is a living presence; it is expression ... The face speaks. The manifestation of the face is already discourse.'

In an interview with the *Daily News*, Axelrod expressed his preference for Total Communication in schools.

> As a totally deaf person Father Cyril truly believes that a deaf child should be given the opportunity to be taught through 'Total Communication' method which uses speech, lip reading, finger spelling and structured sign language. He thinks that the oral method of education should not be forced upon a deaf child.[3]

He also introduced sign language classes for hearing parents so that they could more easily communicate with their deaf children.

In 1983, when the Brothers of Charity took over the school, under the leadership of Brother Gerard Cox, greater emphasis was given to the oral method of education than had been the case under Axelrod.[4] Brother Cox was trained as an audiologist at Sint-Michielsgested School in the Netherlands. This shift was evident with the building of an audiological diagnostic centre to monitor the pupils' hearing for about R1,2 million in 1988.[5] Funding to the value of R19,7 million was secured for the expansion of the school. Over R11,4 million was provided by the government and the Brothers of Charity raised the remainder. The funds were used for improving the classrooms, building science laboratories and workshops to teach trades as well as improving the hostels.

Nevertheless, sign language at Sizwile was never completely abandoned. On 5 July 1989, the Department of Education and Training funded a literacy training programme for deaf adults at Sizwile School. There were a significant number of deaf adults in Soweto who were illiterate and had never attended school. Some of the teachers at the school were trained to teach literacy to the adults in sign language. In October 1989, 16 out of the 17

---

3   'Give Deaf Responsibility says Priest,' *The Daily News*, Monday, 28 September 1981.
4   Brother Gerard Cox, 'From the Principal's Desk,' in *Year Report: Sizwile School for the Handicapped*, 1. Cyril Axelrod Box – Papers, File 2: Magazines, Redemptorist Archives, Cape Town.
5   'R19,7 Million Growth for Soweto Deaf School,' *TSC*, 27 March 1988, 3.

candidates who had started the programme completed the first two units successfully.⁶

KwaThintwa School for the Deaf

Another Catholic school for the deaf to wholeheartedly embrace education through Total Communication was KwaThintwa School for the Deaf in Inchanga, KwaZulu-Natal. The school was started after Archbishop Denis Hurley OMI of Durban encountered a young deaf boy, Henry Duma, in 1973, near Bergville. As Hurley explained in a letter to Beryl Jones, a friend and the fundraiser for KwaThintwa School:

> The origin of Kwa Thintwa School for the Deaf goes back to a confirmation service that I conducted in a small chapel in the foothills of the Drakensberg mountains to the north of Bergville on 23 September 1973. A hill near the chapel is called Thintwa.⁷ Just before the service began a small boy came running to me, all joy and smiles. I tried to speak to him but after a few moments realised that he couldn't hear. It was hard to reconcile the lively and joyful look on his face with his hearing handicap. I asked the parish priest why he was not in a school for the deaf. He replied that he had tried to get him in but that there were no places available. That experience at Thintwa would not leave me in peace until I had begun investigating the possibility of starting a school for the deaf.⁸

---

6   Henna Opperman, 'Literacy Training for Deaf Adults,' *TSM*, 59, 3, March 1990, 1.
7   The name given to the school KwaThintwa from the Zulu word *wathinthwa* (being touched) refers to the hill but also to Archbishop Hurley feeling touched by the plight of the joyful child with whom he was unable to communicate. See Paddy Kearney, *Guardian of the Light: Denis Hurley, Renewing the Church, Opposing Apartheid*, (Scottsville: University of KwaZulu-Natal Press, 2009), 172.
8   'Beginnings of Kwa Thintwa,' Letter of Archbishop Denis Hurley to Beryl Jones, 4 March 1986. Box 112: Kwa Thintwa School for the Deaf 1985–1988, File 1: Correspondence, Hurley Archives, St Joseph's Theological Institute (SJTI), BIO 11C, Cedara.

Hurley's initial proposal to the DET was turned down. However, in 1978, another opportunity arose when Beryl Jones and Mrs R. Strachan from the SANCD came to see Archbishop Hurley about establishing a pre-school for Deaf children at Umlazi and KwaMashu.[9] After a few years delay, the school was eventually opened on 4 February 1981. Sr Conrada Fögl was the school's first principal. She had previously been principal at St Thomas School for the Deaf in Woodlands.

From the outset, KwaThintwa emphasised that education through sign language, or Total Communication, was the best method of education for deaf children.[10] They insisted that teachers learn sign language and that they attend sign language classes.[11] Sign language classes were also organised and arranged for parents in what became known as the orientation programme.[12]

---

9   Letter, Denis Hurley to Beryl Jones, 4 March 1986, Box 112: KwaThintwa School for the Deaf 1985–1988, File: Correspondence, Hurley Archives, STJI, BIO 11C.

10 Research into South African Sign Language (SASL) has shown that there is no one standardised natural sign language throughout the country. The policies of apartheid have affected sign language in South Africa where Deaf people are divided according to racial and ethnic backgrounds but also by class and geography. According to Penn and Reagan, the divisions among Deaf people are reflected in the number of distinct natural sign languages that were emphasised by the separate schools for the different racial and ethnic groups. See Claire Penn and Timothy Reagan, 'How Do You Sign "Apartheid"? The Politics of South African Sign Language,' *Language Problems and Language Planning* 14, 2 (Summer 1990): 95. Aarons has argued that even though there is extensive racial and regional natural sign language variation in South Africa, Deaf people still understand each other and do not require interpreters. See Debra Aarons, 'South African Sign Language: Changing Policies and Practices,' *Stellenbosch Papers in Linguistics* (1999): 129.

11 "Miss Luvuno holds sign language classes every day except Fridays for all teaching staff." 'Annual Report for the period 1 April 1982 to March 1983,' 12. Box 109: KwaThintwa School for the Deaf 1982–1984, File: Correspondence from January 1982–October 1985, Hurley Archives, SJTI, BIO 11C.

12 'Minutes of meeting with parents – Saturday 24 September 1983 at Kwa Thintwa,' 1, Box 109, File: KwaThintwa School 1984, Hurley Archives, SJTI, BIO 11C.

Even though the school used sign language they employed a speech therapist, Mrs A Grové. She started teaching at the school from 19 July 1982.

> Since she has been here Mrs Grové has helped in teacher training especially in the area of interpretation of audiograms, in etiology of deafness and in the use of hearing aids.[13]

Another innovative development in the school was the appointment of a lay principal of the school after the sudden retirement of Sr Conrada on 4 March 1981 due to ill health.[14] Patrick Mullins was made principal in 1982. He continued in this position until 1996. All the previous Catholic schools still had members of religious congregations as principals.

KwaThintwa was also fortunate to have a Deaf chaplain at the school who conducted Masses and catechetics in sign language. He taught catechism to the Catholic children as an extra-mural activity. In addition, Fr John Turner CMM conducted Masses on the second Sunday of each month as well as every Tuesday at the school. Fr John Turner's participation in the school meant that sign language usage was greatly appreciated. Turner also regularly visited the Dominican School for the Deaf in Hammanskraal.

Dominican School for the Deaf, Hammanskraal

It is not clear when Total Communication was accepted at the Hammanskraal school but it was prevalent when Sr Siobhan Murphy OP arrived at the school in January 1983.[15] The use of Signed English was also being encouraged for use in the

---

13 'Annual Report for the period 1 April 1982 to 31 March 1983,' 8, Box 199, File: Correspondence from Jan 1982 – Oct 1985, Hurley Archives, SJTI, BIO 11C.
14 'Speech for the official opening of Kwa Thintwa School for the Deaf,' 8 October 1983, 3, Box 110, File 2: Correspondence 1975–1979, Hurley Archives, SJTI, BIO 11C.
15 Debra Aarons said that 'schools for the white Deaf insisted on oralism, whereas schools for the other races allowed some measure of manualism.' Aarons, 'South African Sign Language,' 118.

classroom.[16] Although orally trained, Sr Siobhan did not object because she recognised that it was important 'to fit the method to the child and not the child to the method.'[17] She pointed out that some children could only learn through sign language and would never be able to lip-read adequately.[18]

The first attempts to introduce the combined method of education at the school go back to 1968. After a visit to the Kutlwanong Deaf School in Rustenburg on 1 November 1968, Sr Mary Oliver, the principal of the Hammanskraal school, was intrigued to discover that Kutlwanong used the combined method of instruction. Speech, fingerspelling and sign language were all used in the classroom. Hammanskraal still adhered to the oral method of deaf education. So that by 1969, it was reported that a further 20 children had received hearing aids during the year and a portable auditory training unit had been purchased for training to deaf children to use their residual hearing more effectively.[19] Later in 1970, six classrooms were fitted with the induction loop system and amplifiers.[20]

This oral method was conducted in the mother tongue according to government policy. When the school started in 1962, the language medium of instruction was Sesotho. However, in 1969, at the advice of the DET inspector of special schools, Mr W.W. Bouwer, Hammanskraal changed the medium of instruction to Setswana.[21] When Sr Siobhan Murphy became principal in January 1983, she negotiated with the DET to change the spoken language of instruction from Setswana to English.

---

16 Sr Siobhan Murphy OP, interview conducted by Mark James, 12 July 2016, Springfield, Cape Town, 452.
17 Ibid, 451.
18 Ibid.
19 'Annual report 1969/70,' 1. Box 56: Ministry, File: Annual reports 1965–1970, Hammanskraal, CDSA, Cape Town.
20 'Minutes of the meeting of the Board of Management for the Dominican School for Deaf Bantu Children held at the school Hammanskraal, on Wednesday 26th August 1970, at 3,15pm.' Box 5b, File: Board of Management reports, 1962–1970, H/K, CDSA, Cape Town.
21 'Annual Report 1969/70,' in CDSA, H/K Box 5b Ministry, File: Annual reports 1965–1970.

I was able to convince them that English was more important because this meant that they [the Deaf] were more employable if they could communicate with employers, whose first language was English.[22]

This was supplemented with learning to write in good English so that they could more adequately function in a predominately hearing society. Again, much of the focus of the high school was placed on vocational training. The idea of the school authorities was that the deaf children, on completion of their education, would find work in factories or domestic service.[23]

While Total Communication was used in the Sizwile, KwaThintwa and Hammanskraal schools for the deaf, the pace of adopting of Total Communication in some other black schools was much slower.

St Thomas School for the Deaf, Woodlands

In 1970, the inspector's report on St Thomas School stated that 'the general method used is oralism while the combined method is used only for slow children.'[24] In 1985, the school no longer fell under the Department of Bantu Education but was transferred to the Ciskeian Department of Education.[25] By 1987, the oral method of education still predominated in this school. *The Southern Cross* reported that the school possessed 'hearing aids, an FM system and desk aids as well as audiometre [sic] for assessing the degree of hearing of each child.'[26]

However, it lacked a speech therapist. At this time, the school had employed its first African principal, Mr Isaac

---

22 Sr Siobhan Murphy OP, interview conducted by Mark James, 12 July 2016, Cape Town, 451.
23 'Dominican School for Deaf Children brochure 1962 to 1997.' H/K Box: Ministry correspondence, File: H Writings, CDSA, Cape Town.
24 W.W. Bouwer, 'Report on Inspection of St Thomas School for Deaf Bantu: March 1970,' 4, KDSA, 124/374 72.
25 '25 Years of Help for the Deaf,' TSC, 13 September 1987, 5.
26 '25 Years of Help for the Deaf,' TSC, 13 September 1987, 5.

Mvandaba.[27] By 1991, there was a different emphasis at the school when the medium of instruction was changed from isiXhosa to English.[28] Unlike in the past, fingerspelling and signing were no longer forbidden, as Mvandaba reported: 'They use speechreading, what used to be called lip-reading, fingerspelling or any other visual method of communication.'[29]

While some signs were permitted, this approach conformed more with Total Communication than education through natural sign language. This was true too of a new school for the deaf that was opened in an old Dominican convent.

St Martin de Porres School, Port Shepstone

In 1992, the St Martin de Porres Primary School in Port Shepstone, a school originally started by the Newcastle Dominican sisters was renovated and reopened. It was renamed the St Martin School for the Handicapped. The school started with about 200 pupils.[30] It is now run by Polish sisters of the Congregation of Little Servants of Mary Immaculate.

Following the policy of inclusive education, the school includes both deaf and intellectually challenged children. There are separate classes for the two groups. Like the KwaThintwa School before it, St Martin de Porres School for the Handicapped used sign language in the classroom from the outset.

The use of Total Communication as the medium of instruction in Catholic Deaf education became more acceptable, as even a traditionally oral school for the deaf, St Vincent began to adopt its use in the classroom.

---

27   See '25 Years of Help for the Deaf,' *TSC*, 13 September 1987, 5. 'Mr Mvandaba joined the school staff in 1965 with 30 years teaching experience but left to take up a post in industry in 1974 … He returned to the school in 1982 and was appointed principal in 1987. He is an Anglican, and is married, with two sons.' Sheila White, 'School Gives Ears to Deaf children,' *TSC*, 9 June 1991, 7.
28   Sheila White, 'School Gives Ears to Deaf Children,' *TSC*, 9 June 1991, 7.
29   Ibid, 7.
30   'School for Handicapped Reopens,' *TSC*, 25 October 1992, 9.

St Vincent School for the Deaf

As we saw in Chapter 7, when Sr Liguori Töns took over from Sr Thomasia Knöpfle as principal of St Vincent School in 1971, she chose a more pragmatic path. She ignored the use of sign language in the classroom. While a committed oralist, Sr Liguori believed that it was more important to communicate than to adhere to a strict oral method of education even though this was the official policy of the school.

> To me the main thing was to be able to communicate, so whether I used my mouth or my hands, my feet, or never mind my whole body, that was for me the most important.[31]

By the late 1970s, the official policy of the school was still the oral method of education even though some teachers were experimenting with teaching in Total Communication, aided speech or signed English.[32] Deaf house mothers were also being appointed like Sr Bernadette Oelofse OP who could identify with the deaf children and could sign to them. Due to the oral method of deaf education, deaf people could no longer get jobs as teachers and most resorted to becoming house mothers in the residential schools for the deaf. Here they had privileged access to the children who often left home at the age of three. The house mothers had a special role in providing a nurturing environment for the deaf children and they were probably the first deaf adults that many of the children met.

Bernadette Oelofse: The first deaf sister in South Africa

While Axelrod was contemplating his vocation as a Redemptorist novice in 1975, a former Servite sister Bernadette Oelofse, a deaf woman from Port Elizabeth, was also entering the novitiate of the King William's Town Dominican sisters in Brakpan.

---

31   Sr Liguori Töns OP, interview conducted by Mark James, 16 December 2015, Johannesburg, 435.
32   'History/Development of St Vincent School,' *St Vincent School Magazine*, 1999, 5–6, Box EDU44 St Vincent School for the Deaf School magazines, KDSA, Johannesburg.

Sr Bernadette Oelofse (1942–2016) was born, Mavis Elizabeth Oelofse, on 29 December 1942 in North End, Port Elizabeth. She was the only deaf child of four children. Her father was Afrikaans-speaking and a member of the Dutch Reformed Church and her mother was an English-speaking Methodist. She was brought up as a Methodist. On 5 May 1962, seven months before her twenty-first birthday, Oelofse was received into the Catholic Church.[33] A Cabra Dominican sister had given her the necessary instruction in the faith. Oelofse had felt the call to enter religious life and wanted to enter with the Cabra Dominicans. Unfortunately, she was turned down due to being deaf. She then applied to join the Servite sisters in Swaziland and was accepted in 1964. She entered the novitiate in 1965 and was professed on 6 January 1967.[34] There she got involved in missionary work, visiting the sick in hospitals, and women in prison and made home visits to Swazi people at their homesteads. As the Servite sisters were a diocesan congregation, all the sisters joining the congregation were EmaSwati. Oelofse faced increasing difficulties in communicating with her fellow sisters as she could not understand or lip-read SiSwati.

Oelofse remembered that Bishop Green had recommended that she apply to join the King William's Town Dominican sisters.[35] Bishop John Murphy of Port Elizabeth gave her a good recommendation to the King William's Town sisters.[36] Bishop Murphy had also written to Sr Oblata, the Prioress General, requesting that the sisters accept Oelofse into the congregation.[37] After meeting Oelofse, Sr Oblata agreed that she could try her vocation in the congregation.[38]

---

33   Certificate of Baptism, Box 57 File 1153, Necrology, KDSA, Johannesburg.
34   Letter, Sr M Eileen Tsoku OSM to Sr M Oblata, 8 February 1975. Box 57, File 1153, Necrology, KDSA.
35   'Sister Bernadette Oelofse (29 December 1942–5 November 2016),' 1. Box 57, File 1153, Necrology, KDSA.
36   'Letter, Bishop John Murphy to Sister Oblata, 17 January 1975. Box 57, File 1153, Necrology, KDSA.
37   See 'Minutes 1974–1979,' 44. Box 52a: Parktown General Council, Book 506, Johannesburg General Council – Lourdes Convent, KDSA.
38   'Minutes 1974–1979,' 45.

However, before she could start the novitiate, she needed to be dispensed from her vows with the Servite sisters. Bishop Casalini of Manzini granted the dispensation of her temporary vows on 10 January 1975.[39] This resulted in Oelofse being permitted to enter the Dominican novitiate.

On 22 December 1977, Sr Bernadette Oelofse OP made her first profession as a Dominican sister in the St Vincent School chapel in Melrose, Johannesburg. In January 1978, she took up her first, and only, assignment as a house mother to boarders at St Vincent School in Johannesburg.

> For 31 years, I was boarders' mother for the little ones and found it easy to identify with their problems. I could understand their language and give them my care and love.[40]

Throughout her religious life, Oelofse remained the only deaf sister to be accepted into the King William's Town congregation.[41]

Initial reluctance to completely embrace Total Communication

This section discusses the initial reluctance of two specific schools to completely embrace Total Communication, namely, St Vincent School for the Deaf and the Dominican School for the Deaf in Wittebome.

St Vincent School for the Deaf

In her 1982 Principal's Message in the school magazine, Sr Marita Stöcklmayer argued against the official introduction of Total Communication at St Vincent School. She argued that the oral

---

39 'Letter of dispensation for Sister Bernadette Oelofse,' 10 January 1975. Box 57, File 1153, Necrology, KDSA.
40 'Sister Bernadette Oelofse (29 December 1942–5 November 2016),' 1.
41 Sr Bernadette Oelofse OP also remained the only Deaf Sister in South Africa involved in active ministry until her retirement in 2009. After being diagnosed with colon cancer she died on 5 November 2016 in East London. 'Sister Bernadette Oelofse (29 December 1942–5 November 2016),' 1.

method remained the approach that was tried and tested and found to work best.

> We must remember that we are already functioning in a well-defined framework within which we can continually search for ways and means to improve our teaching methods... The Oral Method has proved itself superior over a few centuries now, and by giving our children the best possible opportunities for acquiring language, speech and lip-reading skills, we are doing justice to their problems to the best of our ability. Total Communication may have something positive to offer too but at this point in time it is still unacceptable to us.[42]

Sr Marita argued that the advocates of Total Communication only pointed to its positives and sidestepped the negative drawbacks and limitations of the method. She mentioned that the scientific research done on Total Communication drew their samples from deaf children of deaf parents. However, most deaf children had hearing parents, and this made a big difference. Hearing parents, family members and associates did not have the time to study sign language, she concluded.[43]

Sr Marita's attempt to discourage the introduction of Total Communication into the school, during her tenure as principal, was short-lived. After she retired as principal at the end of 1986, John Perks, the school's first lay principal was appointed in 1987. Under his leadership, from 1987 to 1994, a succession of teachers,

---

42 Sr Marita, 'Principal's Message,' *St Vincent School Magazine*, June 1982, 1–5 in Box Cyril Axelrod papers, File 2: Magazines, Redemptorist Archives, Cape Town. The underlining is in the original text.
43 I have paraphrased her discussion, this is the quote in full: 'It is very easy to imagine that a deaf child signing systematically to its deaf parents (probably not speaking), will be able to improve his own language (and that of his parents) while having improved emotional and social relationships. But where does this leave the hearing parents, or for that matter, the hearing family, associates and friends of the deaf child using T.C.? Can you picture them studying a Manual on Signing of ca 1 200 pages in their spare time?' Sr Marita, 'Principal's Message,' *St Vincent Magazine*, 2. The underlining is in the original text.

who saw the value of sign language, were appointed to work at the school. Consequently, the pendulum swung in favour of the use of sign language as the method of education at St Vincent School for the first time. Among these new teachers was Mrs Claude Goddard who, by 1990, had arranged for deaf pupils to give sign language classes to hearing people interested in learning sign language.[44] This innovative approach meant that the hearing people who attended, according to Goddard, learnt sign language far quicker than any previous group.[45]

In 1992, she took her pupils to see the play *Children of a Lesser God* at the Market Theatre in Johannesburg. The play detailed the relationship between a hearing teacher and his Deaf pupil. The experience of seeing a play that they could follow because it included sign language, even though it was ASL, was eye-opening and affirming for the pupils. 'When the lights went up they conversed in sign language with one another.'[46]

The use of sign language usage even made a national impact. In 1994, Beryl Jones, in a letter to Archbishop Hurley, complimented him on the wonderful contribution made by the St Vincent School teachers who signed for the Deaf community during the televising of Nelson Mandela's inauguration as President of the fully democratic South Africa.[47] The teachers, to whom Jones was referring, were Claudine Storbeck and Kirsty MacIons. They were part of a four-person team brought in by the SABC for the occasion.[48]

Also, a Catholic past pupil of St Vincent, Louis Neethling,[49] became a presenter on the first Deaf TV programme called *Sign-*

---

44 See John Perks, 'Deaf Students Give Signing Lessons,' *TSM*, 59, 6, June 1990, 3 and 'Sign Language Course at St Vincents,' *TSM*, 9/93, September 1993, 8.
45 Perks, 'Deaf Students,' 8.
46 'Deaf Children Thrilled by Play Staged in Sign Language,' *St Vincent School Magazine*, December 1992, 9. Box: Cyril Axelrod Papers, File: Magazines, Redemptorist Archives, Cape Town.
47 Letter, Beryl Jones to Archbishop Hurley, 6 June 1994. AHP, Box 111, File 1: KwaThintwa School, Hurley Archives, SJTI, BIO 11C.
48 'How Did Sign Get Onto Our Screens?' *TSM*, June 1994, 4.
49 'How Did Sign Get Onto Our Screens?' *TSM*, June 1994, 4.

Hear. The programme in sign language first appeared on SABC TV on 15 January 1994.[50]

The use of sign language in the classroom at St Vincent School had become commonplace. So much so that in 1995, Sandy de Araujo, a St Vincent Standard 9 pupil, wrote in the school magazine of that year:

> When you go to a deaf school you want to learn the language of the pupils. The teacher wants to teach the subject but if the teacher only uses Signed English it is a problem for the deaf to remember the work.[51]

Her solution that both teachers and pupils should be able to use signed English and sign language indicated that the use of sign language was no longer outlawed or an issue at St Vincent school.[52] Her essay in the school magazine also displayed a good grasp of written English and showed that it was possible for deaf children to learn through the means of sign language and not necessarily have poor English literacy.

In 1995, Mr Eddie Brown wrote in 'The Headmaster's Report' that 'although Sign Language is the language of the Deaf, Total Communication, as used at St Vincent, is the most effective way of teaching deaf children.'[53] Within two years, it was reported in the press that schools for the deaf were being encouraged to move beyond Total Communication and towards the bilingual approach to Deaf education.[54]

---

50 'TV-Program vir Dowes nou 'n Werklikheid,' *TSM*, February 1994, 8. Louis' father was Mauritz Neethling who had been trained by Fr Cyril Axelrod as a lay minister for the Deaf.
51 Sandy de Araujo, 'Signed English or Sign Language in School,' *St Vincent School Magazine*, 1995, 95.
52 With the appointment of its first Deaf principal, Ingrid Parkin, the school presently promotes a bilingual approach to education. Parkin resigned as principal in 2023 to take up a new post.
53 E.J. Brown, 'The Headmaster's Report,' *St Vincent School Magazine*, 1995, 1–2. Box EDU29 St Vincent School for the Deaf School Magazines. KDSA, Johannesburg.
54 'Learning Favours the Bilingual Approach,' *The Star*, 23 September 1997, 26. The newspaper cutting in 153/1106 28, KDSA, Johannesburg.

Wittebome was another formerly oral school to adopt Total Communication.

Dominican School for the Deaf, Wittebome

The change to Total Communication in the Dominican School for the Deaf in Wittebome was not smooth or easy. Sr Jacinta Teixeira, principal of the school at the time, remembered that there were many tensions between adult past pupils who pressurised the school to change the method of education from the oral method to Total Communication.[55] She favoured the oral method as 'it was important to keep speech alive because the children would be going into a hearing world and they needed speech as a mode of communication.'[56] However, as principal, she felt herself caught in the middle. This debate also divided the staff into two camps, those who wanted the oral method and those who wanted change.[57]

In 1992, the school staff decided to adopt Total Communication in the classroom. This was done even though Teixeira felt it was not realistic as 'we only had a few teachers who could sign.'[58]

One of the positive developments from the use of Total Communication in the classroom was that there was a need for Deaf teachers again.

---

55 Jacinta Teixeira, interview conducted by Mark James, 13 July 2016, Cape Town, 455.
56 Ibid.
57 Ibid, 456.
58 Ibid.

The re-emergence of Deaf teachers[59]

The first Deaf high school teacher to graduate from Wits University in twenty-five years was Lucas Magongwa in 1994.[60] Previously, the only other Deaf person to graduate from Wits University was Robert Simmons, however, he never went into deaf education but continued as a lecturer at the university.

Magongwa was admitted to Wits in February 1989. He had applied first to study at the Transvaal Teachers College of Education, but his application was turned down.[61] At the age of 10, Magongwa contracted meningitis and went deaf. After completing his schooling at Kutlwanong School for the Deaf in Rustenburg, Magongwa considered the possibility of becoming a priest. Fr Cyril Axelrod CSsR had inspired him. He tested his vocation with the Redemptorists but changed his mind and decided to become a teacher instead. He wanted to instil in deaf children a love for learning and he believed that 'a deaf teacher has a better understanding of deaf children as he and his deaf pupils will not find themselves in two different worlds.'[62]

Along with Magongwa at Wits University was another Deaf student, Ingrid Foggit.[63] Both students studied and completed their BEd degrees at Wits with the assistance of interpreters. Wits had developed a department focused on training interpreters.[64] These pioneers prepared the way for more Deaf teachers to be trained and employed in schools for the deaf in South Africa.

---

59   On 25 January 1991, the South African National Council for the Deaf (SANCD) sent a letter to all departments of education requesting that deaf people be trained as teachers. The departments of education felt it was impossible to admit deaf candidates. See 'Training and Employment of Deaf Persons as Teachers,' *TSM*, 60, 8, August 1991, 1–2.
60   Lucas Magongwa is a devout Catholic and lay minister in the St Martin de Porres parish in Orlando West.
61   P. Mosifane, 'Lucas Magongwa, the Road to Success,' *TSM*, 58,11, Nov/Dec 1989, 3.
62   P. Mosifane, 'Lucas Magongwa,' 3.
63   Ingrid Foggit, now Parkin, is not a Catholic. She became the first Deaf principal of St Vincent School for the Deaf from 2010–2023.
64   See Jeffrey Steele, 'Project for Deaf Students at Wits,' *TSM*, May 1994, 4 and 'Deaf Achievers/Dowe Presteerders: Lucas Magongwa,' *TSM*, Nov/Dec 1995, 5.

However, not all the Catholic schools for the deaf moved over to Total Communication.

Dominican-Grimley School for the Deaf, Hout Bay: Faithful to the last

The Dominican-Grimley School for the Deaf remained the only school in the whole country that remained faithful to the oral method of education. This continues to be true even today. The method is no longer referred to as the oral method but the 'auditory-verbal' approach to education.[65] Ever since the 1920s, when education through the means of sign language was replaced by the oral method of education, the school did not experiment with Total Communication. Just like the oral method of education, the central tenet of the 'auditory-verbal' approach was to exploit the residual hearing of the deaf children. Sign language would only be used if the children failed to understand through the 'auditory-verbal' approach.[66] As the only Catholic school for the deaf still committed to the oral approach to education, the school has embraced the use of cochlear implants and actively encourages their use. The auditory-verbal approach teaches children with cochlear implants to speak English and to function as a hearing person. It does not encourage Deaf awareness or the use of SASL. In effect, the auditory-verbal approach is a reformed version of the oral method.

All the other Catholic schools have moved to either a combined or a bilingual approach to Deaf education. It is ironic that the first Catholic Deaf school in South Africa, St Joseph School (later Dominican-Grimley) in Cape Town, which pioneered manual Deaf education in South Africa and employed the first Deaf teachers in South Africa, namely, Brigid Lyne, Anne Marsh, Hannah Farrell and Mrs Hugo, is now the only Catholic school for the deaf still promoting the auditory-verbal method of education. Linked to this is the added twist that the first purely oral Catholic school, St Vincent School, became the first Catholic school to

---

65 Sr Macrina Donoghue OP, interview conducted by Mark James, 12 July 2016, Springfield, Cape Town, 445.
66 Ibid.

adopt the bilingual approach to Deaf education. In 2012, it also became the first Catholic Deaf school to appoint a Deaf principal, Ingrid Parkin. She moved onto a new post in 2023.

Throughout the years of apartheid, the Catholic schools for the deaf remained under the direction and authority of hearing people. In sharp contrast, Catholic Deaf ministry was under the leadership of Deaf pastors and this created a different dynamic among the Deaf laity. Deaf people established Deaf organisations that showed how Deaf people began to shape their own lives and social reality. This was bound to lead to new developments and initiatives as Deaf people took on greater responsibility for evangelisation and social outreach in Church and society. These developments were accompanied by a growing awareness among Deaf adults of their human rights.

Conclusion

We conclude our first section of this book on the history of deaf education in Catholic schools for the deaf. This is an overview of the history and far more research needs to be done to fill in the enormous gaps that exist.

Nevertheless, what has become evident is that the Dominican sisters, both Cabra and King William's Town, in starting their schools for the deaf engaged to some extent in the type of saintly work outlined by Emmanuel Levinas and developed by Edith Wyschogrod. The founders and first teachers of the deaf in South Africa were motivated by the plight of deaf children to start schools for the deaf in Cape Town and King William's Town. The two congregations' approaches to deaf education fell along the fault lines of the two great debates of the day with the Cabra Dominicans adopting the manual method of Deaf education and employing deaf teachers and the King Dominicans opting for the oral method of deaf education and only employing hearing teachers.

In the 1920s, the Cabra Dominicans moved over to the oral method of deaf education and the manual approach fell into disuse in Catholic schools for the deaf. In the modernist views of the period, it was seen as the most effective means by which to equip deaf children to cope in a hearing world. Lip-reading and vocalisation became the order of the day in Catholic schools for the deaf. The use of sign language was forbidden on school property or in the class because it was perceived as hampering the acquisition of lip-reading, vocalisation and good English grammar.

After 1948, the Catholic schools for the deaf had to abide by apartheid government policies as they depended on government funding. The oral method for deaf education persisted in white and coloured schools for the deaf but not the African ones. The apartheid government allocated less money for the African schools for the deaf and therefore also allowed for the use of sign language in the classroom.

While the Dominican sisters sought to uplift the lot of the deaf children they served and they gave their lives for this task, they failed in one crucial aspect. They failed in, what Levinas called passivity and Wyschogrod called self-denial and receptivity to the other. Except for perhaps Mother Dymphna Kincaid who employed a deaf teacher, Bridget Lyne, most of the sisters who taught in the schools for the deaf started from a position of knowing what was best for the deaf children, from a position of power and authority over those children and their parents. They lacked the passivity or recognition that proximity to the deaf child was also placed their commitment and their method of education under question and scrutiny. There was little to no self-appraisal or questioning whether they were doing the right thing. The oral method of deaf education became synonymous with an unquestioned totality.

The service many of the sisters gave was altruistic but did not fully reflect the concern for the other that typified the saintliness and holiness of which Levinas and Wyschogrod spoke. The teacher was always the one in charge commanding the process and seldom considered the need to learn sign language. Those teachers who did learn sign language often learnt it from their pupils which was more in accord with the Levinasian idea of openness to the other. Gradually, however, came with the advent of total communication the use of sign language in the classroom became more acceptable.

In the next section, we will turn to some of the Deaf 'saints' who made their contributions and encouraged the use of sign language within the Church and society. They were responsible for providing resistance to the audist approach that persistently hampered relations between hearing and Deaf people in the Catholic Church in South Africa. It continues to do so even to this day.

Part III

Deaf Saintliness and Prophetic Witness

Chapter 11

Deaf Saintliness

In Part II of this book, we saw how hearing people sought to develop a better world for the Deaf community by providing them with the educational skills they needed to function adequately in a hearing world. Many of those hearing people who engaged in this work, as I attempted to show, did saintly work. They were concerned for the lives of the deaf children they served. Many of them dedicated their whole lives to educating the Deaf community and seeking to provide them with a better life than they had known before. For these efforts, they need to be commended.

Despite the shortcomings of the methods employed, as we have outlined, they honestly, and as Levinas says 'in good conscience,' sought to make the world more hospitable for deaf people. They were engaged in making this a better world. They had concern for their deaf neighbours and believed, not erroneously, that by the oral method of education, the lot of the Deaf community would improve.

However, their greatest drawback was that they forged ahead with what they thought, in good conscience, were in the best interests of the Deaf community and often imposed their phonocentric and audist agenda on that community. They were enamoured by the modernist agenda of progress through technological advancement and did not engage adequately or even at all with those whom they were serving. They were convinced that they had the fulness of truth.

So instead of listening and learning from the Deaf community, many were convinced they knew best. They had the truth and the children were to learn it from them. The saintliness of their efforts as commendable as they were lacked the humility and attentiveness of Levinas' understanding of *hineni* or 'here am I, send me' (Isa 6:9). The missionary approach of these servants of the Church was tainted by knowing and being convinced that they had the truth. The history of the Catholic Church is littered with examples of missionaries who failed to adequately learn from the cultures they evangelised and rather imposed their Christian truth on the people who were subjected to Western colonial power and might.

In the following chapters, our focus shifts from the work done by the hearing in providing education to the Deaf community to the contribution made by Deaf people themselves to show the way to the new world, rather than a better world offered by the hearing. A world that Deaf people envisioned and desired. This new world came to be because certain 'saintly' Deaf men and women sought to show the way to a more prophetic alternative to that which the hearing community was offering. These are their stories.

Chapter 12

Robert Simmons: Doctor in Neurobiology and a Deaf Activist

Robert Michael Thomas Simmons (1931–2007) was born in Johannesburg on 16 September 1931 into a progressive Jewish family. When he was three years old, he was accepted at St Vincent School for the Deaf from where he emerged in 1948 as the first deaf person in South Africa to matriculate.[1] Simmons later became a Catholic.[2]

The Academic

Simmons' love for study meant he was accepted to study for a BSc at Wits University in 1950. With the assistance of Dr Humphrey Raikes, he passed his undergraduate studies in 1955 without the help of an interpreter.[3]

Originally, he had planned to study accountancy to become a chartered accountant. But his father had other plans because he thought his son 'had such a good scientific mind and that it would be pitifully wasted on endless columns of figures!'[4]

After finishing his BSc degree, Simmons found employment as a medical technologist with the South African Institute for

---

1   Marie Viljoen, 'Die Stil Wêreld van 'n Slim Lektor,' in *Foto-Rapport, Bylae tot Rapport*, 13 Mei 1973, 15. KDSA, Box: Johannesburg, St Vincent Convent and School for the Deaf, File: Newspaper cuttings 1933–2004, 153/1106 24.
2   Cyril Axelrod, *And the Journey Begins*, 69.
3   Colin Dangaard, 'The Silent World of Robert Simmons (Deaf and Partly Dumb Teacher), in *Convocation Commentary*, 15. KDSA, Box: Johannesburg, St Vincent Convent and School for the Deaf, File: Newspaper cuttings 1933–2004, 153/1106 25. Also see Simmons, Robert Michael Thomas (1931-2007) available at www.wits.ac.za/alumni/obituaries/obituary-content-by-year. Accessed 6 November 2021.
4   'An address by Dr Robert Simmons,' 45.

Medical Research (SAIMR).[5] He worked there for ten years. At the suggestion of Professor Phillip Tobias he went on to study anatomy and physiology and completed an MSc in neuroanatomy in 1965.[6] This was the same year in which he married May with whom he had been at St Vincent School for the Deaf. They had four children.

He was appointed to the full-time staff of the Department of Anatomy in January 1968 as a qualified scientific assistant and graduate tutor. He was involved in the teaching programmes for second-year students in micro-anatomy and third-year medical BSc students in anatomy. According to the head of his department, Professor Phillip Tobias, he was able to make himself understood by the hearing students and was able to respond to their questions through lip-reading.[7] He also developed charts and diagrams to supplement his teaching methods. At the recommendation of Professor Tobias, he was appointed a lecturer in 1970 and completed his PhD in 1975.

Simmons accomplished this all through lip-reading, the assistance of fellow students and reading books.[8] He loved art and poetry and could speak five languages namely, German, Afrikaans, English, French and Russian.[9] His proud teachers often held him up to others as living proof that the oral method of deaf education worked.

This remarkable man never allowed his 'deafness' to be a barrier to what he sought to achieve. If he could do it then he realised it was also possible for other deaf people too. Being in touch with the events and thinking of Deaf people in the United States and Britain, Simmons became an advocate for Deaf rights and encouraged deaf people not to set the bar too low for themselves. In his talks and writings, Simmons challenged deaf people to recognise their innate and God-given dignity. He

5 Ibid, 46.
6 Viljoen, 'Die Stil Wêreld,' 15.
7 Philip Tobias, 'Memorandum on proposed promotion of RMT Simmons to full lecturer grade,' in Box Biographies, File: Sim. Historical Papers Research Archive, William Cullen Library, University of the Witwatersrand, Johannesburg (HPRA).
8 Viljoen, 'Die Stil Wêreld,' 24.
9 Ibid, 34.

encouraged deaf people to resist attempts to make them conform to the dictates of a hearing world. For Simmons, it was the hearing world that needed to change – not Deaf people.

Deaf activist

In December 1981, Simmons was asked to address the St Vincent School at their Annual Prize Giving. As a past pupil, he was invited to inspire the soon-to-be school leavers and give them advice on how to face life after school. He gave the talk by signing and voicing at the same time.[10]

He started his talk by outlining his personal history telling them that he had studied anatomy at Wits University and eventually qualified with his PhD in 1975. He spoke about the assistance he had received from his mentor Professor Phillip Tobias and from his fellow students at the university, all of whom were hearing. He appreciated what they and his teachers at St Vincent school had done to enable him to achieve.

Then changing tack, he advised the school leavers saying:

> When you go out to earn your living, you will meet people who will display various attitudes towards you when they once discover your handicap. Do not be put off by their attitude of superiority; keep a cool head at all times. Have a strong pair of elbows to push your way through the world. Try not to behave as 'hearing' persons; be yourselves. Do not be ashamed of your deaf friends in public. Have plenty of self-confidence and enthusiasm for life even if you think that you do not possess good speech or excellent English. Do not be ashamed, but proud to be deaf.[11]

He explained that they must be prepared to make friends with hearing people and to encourage them 'to converse with you in sign language.' Sign language, he said, was a gift to the deaf from

---

10 'An Address Given by Dr Robert Simmons (Past Pupil of the School) at the Annual Prize Giving, December 1981,' *St Vincent School Magazine*, June 1982, 44-49. Box: Cyril Axelrod's Papers, File 2: Magazines, Redemptorist Archives, Cape Town.
11 'An Address Given by Dr Robert Simmons,' 47.

God and the deaf should not be ashamed of it. If the hearing people are interested in learning, then one could suggest they start sign language classes.

Simmons' understanding of sign language being a gift from God highlighted the ignorance and apathy of hearing people and the leaders of the Church had about sign language. Hearing people saw deaf and disabled people as handicapped and, therefore, in need of hearing or able-bodied people's charity and benevolence. In no way did they see the deaf and disabled being able to bear gifts to the hearing world.

Sign language for deaf people was the way that deaf people empowered themselves to communicate with each other and the world. It also showed their creativity and resilience in the face of a hearing world which dismissed them as handicapped. Developing upon Emmanuel Levinas' idea that the face of the other speaks,[12] we can say that for Robert Simmons, the face of the Deaf other signs.

This understanding of sign language as a gift from God clarified for Simmons the central importance of education in sign language for Deaf people in South Africa.

Proud to be Deaf

In 1982, two of his articles on Total Communication were published in *The Silent Messenger*.[13] For Simmons, Total Communication was more than just about speech and signing simultaneously and adapting to living in a hearing world. He challenged the idea that deaf people should constantly adapt themselves and 'learn to live in a hearing world.'[14] Instead, he argued that there is another reality for deaf people too: There is a DEAF-WORLD[15] that equally exists, and it has much to offer.

---

12   See Levinas, *Ethics and Infinity*, 87.
13   Robert Simmons, 'Deafness and Total Communication (1),' *TSM*, Nov/Dec 1982, 7, 11 and 'Deafness and Total Communication (2),' *TSM*, March/April 1983, 5–7.
14   Simmons, 'Deafness and Total Communication (1),' 7.
15   DEAF-WORLD is a sign and a concept used in contrast to that of the hearing world. Deaf people experience the world and life in a vastly different way to that of the hearing. DEAF-WORLD

> When the hearing society is willing to accept total communication or sign language as the official language of the Deaf community, conditions can be made possible for deaf persons to shape their own destiny through decision-making involvement in educational, social and government services. Also, the society can make it possible for deaf leaders and their fellows to 'mainstream' themselves in the general public through the use of interpreters as 'communication liaisons' or 'ears' between hearing and deaf communities.[16]

Simmons acknowledged that educators and the hearing community in South Africa had not yet formally recognised sign language. But this does not mean that a deaf person could not change the way that he or she could interact and relate to the hearing world. Rather than allowing the hearing world to determine how a deaf person should live, Simmons asserted his own identity and dignity as a deaf person, saying:

> I have decided to accept the fact that I am profoundly deaf, possessing imperfect but fairly good and rather facile lip-reading. But *never* with the stigma 'deaf and dumb' or 'deaf-mute'.
>
> It is my choice to sign, to think and act as deaf, work for and within the Deaf community. I am proud to be a deaf person in the world of sound, so long shut out to me.
>
> However, deafness does not limit my potentiality and qualifications in doing the same kind of work as my hearing colleagues. Limits, yes; limitations, no.
>
> I shall not accept my limitations because my profound deafness and imperfect speech appear to most people to be a barrier to my ability to communicate with my hearing

---

    also expressed the Deaf self-understanding as a community with its own language and culture. It is capitalised because it is an English gloss (translation) of an American Sign Language (ASL) sign. See Harlan Lane, 'Construction of Deafness,' in *The Disability Studies Reader*, 2nd ed., ed. Lennard Davis (New York/London: Routledge, 2006), 85.

16   Simmons, 'Deafness and Total Communication (1),' 11.

colleagues and students, and also in performing my duties as far as my capability can permit. No longer shall I nod my head in pretended acknowledgement of long-winded conversations or lectures, the context of which I do not grasp at all. If I wish to express my views and opinions at seminars or formal meetings or conferences, I shall request either verbalized or written explanations of only important parts or points of the speech given there.

I shall use sign language to friends in homes, in hotels, in restaurants, in shops and in public transport, and be oblivious to curious stares or perplexed fascination of other people. I shall talk wherever and whenever in my own good voice, as I have always done in the past. But I shall not sit on the fence between hearing and deaf worlds, and pass judgement on people in self-righteousness. Neither shall I dictate to anybody, deaf or hearing, how to lead his/her life, nor whether they wish to use speech or sign language as their own mode of communication. Then, why cannot hearing people let us deaf adults be what we are, and have always been, deaf, and stop trying to tell us to conform to their world, in which we will never be fully accepted. Furthermore, we want to be treated with respect as normal human beings, sans hearing sense, and not be regarded as second-class citizens![17]

In becoming conscious and aware of his dignity and giftedness as a Deaf person, Simmons encouraged and freed other Deaf people to be themselves. He encouraged them not to attempt to emulate hearing people. Simmons was proud to be Deaf and encouraged other deaf people to feel the same way about themselves. This was a significantly different discourse from one which emphasised deaf people adjusting to the hearing world. This discourse was an empowering one, one that emphasised the dignity of Deaf people, people who have a language and culture of their own. It was a discourse which spoke about the gift that Deaf people are, in sharp contrast to the audist discourse that spoke about deaf people as handicapped as lacking hearing and as dependent on

---

17   Simmons, 'Deafness and Total Communication (1),' 11.

hearing benevolence. Simmons encouraged Deaf people to stand up on their own two feet and demand that hearing people learn sign language. This was a revolutionary mindset.

Educationalist

Simmons recognised that the use of sign language in the education of Deaf children was the future. The oral method of deaf education was over. In July 1989, he wrote an article for a conference at Gallaudet University in Washington DC on Deaf education in South Africa entitled: 'The Role of Educational Systems and Deaf Culture in the Development of Sign Language in South Africa.'[18]

In his article, he outlined the diversity of sign languages prevalent in South Africa due to the influences of different schools for the deaf started primarily by a variety of churches. 'The schools developed sign language independently of one another.'[19] He suggested that there was a need to develop a unified SASL for use in all schools for the deaf in the country.

In an address given at the annual general meeting of the Natal Association for the Deaf in 1991, Simmons identified the chief problem for deaf people at the time was not the degree of hearing loss or the best method to prevent deafness:

> BUT the lack of Understanding and easy Communication with the Hearing People. We do not want to ask them to provide us with hearing aids or telecommunications devices straightaway. But to be able to talk with them by means of Manual Communication or even by writing notes. We can give them courses in Sign Language, especially to those who are in closer contact with the Deaf.[20]

---

[18] See Robert Simmons 'The Role of Educational Systems and Deaf culture in the Development of Sign Language in South Africa,' in *The Deaf Way: Perspectives from the International Conference on Deaf Culture*, ed. Carol Erting, Dorothy L. Smith and Robert Johnson (Washington DC: Gallaudet University Press, 1994), 78–84.

[19] Simmons, 'The Role of Educational Systems,' 82.

[20] RMT Simmons, 'What Can the Deaf People Do in the New South Africa?' *TSM*, 60, 8, August 1991, 5. Italics and capitals as they appear in the original article.

Simmons maintained that if deaf people were ever to achieve equal terms with hearing people, they would need to improve their education, and sign language was the key to achieving this. But it also required an attitudinal change among deaf people themselves where they needed to stand together and assert their Deaf rights and desire for equal opportunities with hearing people.[21]

He began to work on this project himself.

Sign language teacher

In February 1993, Simmons started a sign language school at Wits University called the Centre for Deaf Studies.[22] The sign language school offered courses on three different levels for those people desiring to become sign language interpreters or more proficient signers: an elementary level, a 'bilingual level and a level for specialisation for court or hospital interpreters.'[23] It was his way to ensure that the interests of Deaf people be enhanced by more hearing people learning sign language. He also wanted Deaf people to attain higher academic and professional qualifications so that they could enter the fields of medicine, law and business. For this work, Simmons was accepted as an Ashoka fellow in 1994. Ashoka is a non-profit organisation founded by Bill Drayton in 1980 giving recognition to individuals across the globe who were changemakers.[24]

It was Simmons' dream to develop a standardised South African sign language. He had already worked on a SASL Dictionary. However, he realised that while the variations among South African sign languages was a problem for the hearing interpreters, it was not so for the Deaf people themselves.[25] Deaf

---

21 Ibid.
22 Simmons' Centre for Deaf Studies should not be confused with the present Centre for Deaf Studies at Wits which was started by Professor Claudine Storbeck and which focuses on training teachers for schools for the deaf.
23 Robert Simmons, Fellow. Accessed 6 November 2021. Available at http://ashoka.org/cs/fellow/robert-simmons
24 See Ashoka's History. Accessed 6 November 2021. Available at http//ashoka.org/en-us/story/ashokas-history
25 Robert Simmons, Fellow. Accessed 6 November 2021. Available at www.ashoka.org/cs/fellow/robert-simmons

people were readily able to adapt and include new signs in their sign language repertoire.

Sadly, his dream was not to be fully realised in his lifetime as he died peacefully in his sleep on 7 February 2007.[26]

---

26   The information was obtained from the University of the Witwatersrand obituaries. See Simmons, Robert Michael Thomas (1931–2007). Accessed 6 November 2021. Available at http://wits.ac.za/alumni/obituaries/obituary-content-by-year

Chapter 13

Father Cyril Axelrod (1942–): Compassionate Minister Instilling Dignity

A significant shift took place in pastoral care for the Deaf community in South Africa with the priestly ordination of Fr Cyril Axelrod on 28 November 1970. Axelrod was ordained by Bishop Ernest Green in the St Vincent School chapel in Johannesburg. Father Cyril, a convert from Judaism, is the first South African deaf priest to be ordained.

Born in Johannesburg on 24 February 1942 of a Lithuanian mother and a Polish-born father,[1] Cyril Axelrod attended St Vincent School for the Deaf. After completing school, he worked as an accountant for a couple of years before deciding to become a priest.[2] Much to his mother's consternation, he became a Catholic.[3] As part of his studies for the priesthood, Axelrod went to study at Gallaudet University[4] and the Catholic University of America (CUA) in Washington DC before returning to South Africa to complete his theological studies at St John Vianney Seminary in Pretoria in 1969.

Cyril Axelrod was the first deaf Catholic priest to be ordained in Africa and the fifth one ever to be ordained in the

---

1 Cyril Axelrod, *And the Journey Begins*, 10–11.
2 Initially, Cyril had longed to become a rabbi, but this was refused. In the Deuteronomic Code it states that a priest cannot approach the altar if he suffers from a defect or a blemish like blindness, lameness or skin disease (Lev 21:18–20). See Axelrod, *And the Journey Begins*, 55–57.
3 Axelrod was baptised and received into the Catholic faith on 14 August 1965 in Immaculate Conception parish, Rosebank, Johannesburg.
4 Gallaudet University is in Washington DC and is the only university for the Deaf in the United States.

world.⁵ At the time, he was one of only three living deaf priests.⁶ The first to be ordained, as we saw in Chapter 3, was possibly Pedro da Velasquez in the sixteenth century who was taught by the Spanish Benedictine monk, Pedro Ponce de Leon. The second was the French priest Fr Jean-Marie La Fonta (1878–1929) who was ordained in 1921⁷ and then Fr Vincente de Paulo Burnier (1921–2009), a Brazilian from the Archdiocese of Juiz de Fora, on 22 September 1951.⁸ Burnier was deaf from birth and he was inspired to become a priest after reading a book about Fr La Fonta.⁹ The fourth priest was Fr Agustin Yanes Valer (1929–2021). Valer was born in Cuba in 1929 but his family moved to Spain when he was seven months old. He was ordained in 1967.¹⁰

When Cyril applied to join the Diocese of Port Elizabeth under Bishop Ernest Green, a dispensation had to be granted by the Vatican in Rome prior to his ordination, like all the deaf priests before him.¹¹ Before the Second Vatican Council (1962-1965), Canon Law restricted the ordination of any man with a disability. The 1917 Canon Law was still in effect in 1970 and still stated that 'bodily defective men' were unable to be ordained.¹²

The beginnings of Axelrod's ministry

After his ordination Cyril Axelrod was assigned to be chaplain at St Thomas School for the Deaf near King William's Town, teaching

---

5   See 'Deaf Priest One of Only Three in World', *TSC*, 2 December 1970, 5.
6   'Deaf Priest One Only Three in World,' 5.
7   Portolano, *Be Opened*, 102.
8   'Only Deaf-Mute priest,' *TSC*, 2 September 1953, 11/421.
9   Portolano, *Be Opened*, 112.
10   See Cyril Axelrod, 'Fr Cyril's Trip,' *TSM*, June/July 1975, 8; 'The Personal Triumph of One Man!' *The Irish Independent*, 29 July 1971 and 'Benedict XVI Names Deaf Priest "Prelate of Honor",' *Catholic News Agency*, 27 March 2008. Accessed 20 September 2018, https://www.catholicnewsagency.com/news/benedict_xvi_names_deaf_priest_prelate_of_honor
11   See 'Deaf Priest One of Only Three in World,' *TSC*, 2 December 1970, 5.
12   See Canon 827, 2 in S. Woywod, *The New Canon Law*, (New York: Joseph F Wagner, 1918), 197. In this respect, the Catholic Church's teaching prior to Vatican II was no different to that of Judaism.

catechism to the children and saying Mass for them.¹³ He also worked with Fr Donal Cashman for two years as his curate and busied himself learning isiXhosa. Axelrod recalled that:

> The school was run by four Dominican sisters and some dedicated teachers. The three hundred deaf pupils were all Xhosa people. Under the apartheid policy the Government insisted that African languages be used, and so teaching at the school was in their mother tongue, the Xhosa language ... I set to work to learn enough to communicate with the children and teachers, both in Xhosa and in ... sign language.¹⁴

Being one of only three deaf men ordained worldwide, and the first in the English-speaking world meant that Axelrod became well-known internationally. In June 1971, he was invited to Rome to meet Fr de Blais, a member of the Piccolo Mission. This religious congregation was comprised of priests, sisters and deaf lay oblates who were dedicated to serving only the deaf. He also preached to the Italian Deaf community in Rome, Florence, Bologna and Milan for a whole month.¹⁵

Axelrod was also invited to visit schools for the deaf and vocational training centres for deaf boys and girls in Italy. Mr Vittoria Ieralla, the President of the National Education of the Deaf in Italy escorted him. Ieralla was also the first president of the World Federation of the Deaf (WFD) established in 1951. He was himself deaf.¹⁶ On 17 July 1971, they both had a 40-minute private audience with Pope Paul VI at the Vatican.¹⁷ They spoke about how the Deaf could integrate themselves into the Church's mission.¹⁸ For Axelrod, meeting the Pope was one of the highlights of his trip.

---

13   Axelrod, *And the Journey Begins*, 115.
14   Ibid.
15   'Chronology of Cyril Axelrod,' 1, n.d. Box 1 File 5: Fr Cyril Axelrod: Life, Work, Spirituality of the Deaf, Cyril Axelrod Paper,' Redemptorist Archives, Cape Town.
16   Axelrod, 'Fr Cyril's Trip,' 7–9.
17   See Axelrod, 'Fr Cyril's Trip,' 7 as well as the photo and caption in *TSC*, 1 December 1971, 1.
18   Axelrod, 'Fr Cyril's Trip,' 7.

After Italy, Axelrod travelled to Ireland. There he attended the International Catholic Conference for the Religious Education of the Deaf held at St Patrick's Training College, Dublin from 26–31 July 1971. Approximately 120 delegates from fifteen nations from around the world attended the conference.[19] Axelrod had to lip-read his way through all the talks as no provision was made for interpreters.[20]

In her talk to the conference, Sr Nicholas Griffey, the principal of St Mary's School for the Deaf in Cabra, Dublin, noted that only 22% of Catholic deaf children in the United States were practising their faith. This was in sharp contrast to Ireland where 98% of deaf students attended Mass on Sunday and considered their faith an important part of their lives. The low total was attributed to an insufficient number of Catholic schools for the deaf.[21] The conference proposed that every diocese appoint a professionally trained priest to look after the religious education of deaf Catholics.[22] Other concerns raised were that, in light of Vatican II, a catechism for the deaf needed to be developed and that teachers and priests working with the deaf needed to be suitably qualified.

After Ireland, Axelrod went to Paris and attended the Sixth Congress of the WFD held in Paris at UNESCO from 31 July to 5 August 1971. At this conference, he was a representative of the South African National Council for the Deaf.[23] Among 700 deaf

---

19   Axelrod, 'Fr Cyril's Trip,' 8.
20   Axelrod wrote: 'The conference gave me a kind heart by allowing me to take part of the interesting meeting wholly. The speakers show their sympathy and great understanding towards my difficulty to follow the lectures. The[y] spoke quite clearly and considerately so that I took courage to discuss with them at all costs without a bit of frustration or strain.' See Axelrod, 'Fr Cyril's Trip,' 7.
21   This point was made by Sr Nicholas Griffey OP from St Mary's School for the Deaf in Dublin. Sr Griffey was integrally involved in promoting the oral method to deaf education in Ireland (see previous chapter). In fact, Axelrod will challenge this statement. His view was that it was due to lack of sign language being used for Deaf people and them also feeling isolated in hearing churches. See 'More Priests Urged For the Deaf,' *TSC*, 15 September 1971, 5.
22   'More Priests Urged For the Deaf,' *TSC*, 15 September 1971, 5.
23   'Chronology of Cyril Axelrod,' 1.

people from all over the world Axelrod found a deep sense of solidarity among delegates who, even though they were divided by different mother tongue languages, were united by their use of sign language.[24] The main focus of this gathering was to work for the social rehabilitation of the deaf, to share what was being done to overcome deafness and to promote the human rights of deaf people.[25]

After this meeting, Axelrod went to Geneva to attend his third conference. This time the meeting was a gathering of the First Ecumenical Seminar for the Training of Responsible Christian Workers Among the Deaf from 9–26 August 1971. Among the 120 delegates were Catholic priests, Protestant ministers and several social workers. During this meeting, Axelrod met the other two deaf priests who were ordained before him; they were able to share how they approached the spiritual and pastoral needs of deaf people in their respective countries.[26] Before returning to South Africa, he had an opportunity to visit the Sint-Michielsgestedt School for the Deaf in the Netherlands.

Axelrod's international visit to different schools for the deaf in Europe and his attendance at the three conferences gave him, he said: 'a refreshing experience that may encourage me to my practical care for the Deaf more effectively and securely.'[27] It also said it helped him reflect on the work that needed doing in South Africa.

Building up Catholic Deaf communities

While he was chaplain at St Thomas School for the Deaf, Axelrod's contact with the Deaf community throughout the rest of the country was extremely limited. Bishop Ernest Green had envisaged that he should serve the deaf throughout the whole country and not just in the Diocese of Port Elizabeth.[28] Axelrod recollected that:

---

24   Axelrod, 'Fr Cyril's Trip,' 8.
25   Ibid.
26   Ibid.
27   Axelrod, 'Fr Cyril's Trip,' 9.
28   Hatton, 'Deaf Deacon,' 6.

> After my ordination in 1970 Bishop Green proposed to the Bishops' Conference that I would be seconded to service the ministry among the deaf people in the country while I was a diocesan priest for Port Elizabeth. Unfortunately, Bishop Green resigned[29] from the diocese of Port Elizabeth as he struggled to accept himself as a bishop and went back to Cape Town and my plan to work for the country fell apart.[30]

With Green's broader vision of his ministry in mind, Axelrod offered, in 1973, to celebrate the Easter Triduum for the Deaf community in Johannesburg for the first time. Deaf people turned out in large numbers and afterwards encouraged him to return more frequently.[31]

> I was an incardinated priest of Port Elizabeth. So, I couldn't just travel all over. But I asked Bishop John Murphy of Port Elizabeth diocese if I can work in Johannesburg. He wrote a letter to Bishop Boyle to ask him if it could be possible for me to work in Johannesburg. But there was no reply.[32]

Assuming silence was consent, Axelrod moved to Johannesburg the following year and made this his base even though the negotiations between the respective bishops was still unclear.

> I came because I knew many [deaf Catholics] needed my help. I came on my own. I had no formal introduction or acceptance into the Diocese of Johannesburg. I just came because the Bishop didn't communicate. The Bishop was just focused on parishes. You can't work for the deaf and also work in a parish. It is not my responsibility. In the Bishop's mind, I must take a parish. The work for the deaf is outside of parish work. I came on my own accord because

---

29   Bishop Ernest Green resigned as bishop in January 1971. This was a major setback for Axelrod as a newly ordained priest. He lost the support of the bishop with whom he could most easily communicate and had who had always supported him.
30   Cyril Axelrod, personal email to Mark James, 15 March 2015.
31   'Chronology of Cyril Axelrod,' 1.
32   Cyril Axelrod, interview conducted by Mark James, 15 September 2015, Dunnottar, Nigel, 396.

> I was focused on building up the deaf and that they needed my help.[33]

With his arrival in the Diocese of Johannesburg, the establishment and strengthening of Catholic Deaf communities began in earnest. He immediately immersed himself in visiting the deaf population, black and white, spread all over the Reef. He travelled extensively, establishing, developing and sustaining various Deaf communities in different towns and townships in and around Johannesburg and Pretoria.

> For nine months of the year, I spend most of my time ministering to the English-speaking deaf of all denominations in and around Johannesburg where the largest grouping of deaf people is to be found.[34]

He even went to outlying areas like Potchefstroom, Parys, Carolina, Balfour, Pietersburg, as well as travelling to Durban, Pietermaritzburg and Cape Town.[35] When he started, Axelrod worked mostly with the white English-speaking Deaf communities because the Dutch Reformed Church already served the Afrikaans Deaf community. It had a well-established network of hearing pastors who knew sign language and ministered to Dutch Reformed deaf people.[36] They also had schools and had been very involved in Deaf education going back over a century.

Initially, Axelrod's ministry began as being responsible for the English-speaking deaf people in the white community, however, he never restricted himself to this community to the exclusion of the black Deaf community – as we will see later. His approach was extremely ecumenical and he believed it was his task to serve all deaf people regardless of colour or creed.[37] Many non-Catholics attended his Masses and services, especially from those churches that had no chaplain to serve their deaf

---

33 Ibid.
34 Axelrod, 'The Spiritual Care,' 5.
35 Cyril Axelrod, personal email to Mark James, 16 March 2015, 3.
36 'Die Geestelike Versorging van die Dowes,' *TSM*, 46, 3, September 1977, 8–9.
37 Axelrod, *And the Journey Begins*, 141.

congregants. Axelrod also reached out to deaf Jews who sought his help and guidance.[38] Everyone was free to participate in Axelrod's celebrations of the Eucharist without trying to proselytise or convert them to the Catholic Church.

Axelrod's ministry of compassion

Being in Johannesburg meant that Axelrod also became involved with the SANCD. He was asked to write an article for the SANCD's magazine *The Silent Messenger*. Reflecting on his four years of ministry, Axelrod stressed four key aspects: 1) the importance of deaf people's spiritual formation; 2) that deaf people be encouraged to discover their self-respect and autonomy; 3) the importance of sign language for communication with deaf people and its use in the liturgy; lastly, 4) that a spiritual leader had to be a good role model for deaf people.[39]

From his experience, Axelrod saw that the primary task of pastoral ministry to the Deaf was to provide Deaf people with adequate spiritual formation so that:

> [T]he deaf person attain a life of holiness, a life of faith, hope and charity and we must see that he is motivated to appreciate and understand it. We have in the past experience perhaps placed too much emphasis on developing the intellect and not made enough allowance for understanding with the heart affection and love. We have not showed faith as a matter basically of loving and showing love.[40]

For Axelrod, Deaf people needed a personal experience of their faith. Faith should not be presented as something abstract. Instead, it should be a daily encounter with the living and loving God. However, he believed that we cannot love God unless we love other people and they love us. Deaf people needed to experience this love through the interpersonal relationships they had in the

---

38　Ibid, 146–147.
39　Cyril Axelrod, 'Spiritual Welfare and Care for the Deaf,' *TSM*, January 1975, 4–7.
40　Axelrod, 'Spiritual Welfare,' 4.

family. Unfortunately, these relationships had not always been life-giving or affirming experiences, as there was often a lack of adequate communication between deaf children and their parents.

Deaf people also needed to learn how to express their faith and to explain their beliefs to others. But having faith and being loving were not enough. Hope was also required. It was therefore important for ministers and priests to understand that the deaf had something to teach us from their experience of 'not hearing.'

> The deaf must be treated as a person who contributes to the community once his own personality has been developed. We must love the deaf, we must give them courage and hope and our main aim must be to make them independent of us.[41]

From his earliest writings, we also see his concern that Deaf people be empowered and given autonomy. They should not be kept dependent on the hearing or even on a Deaf minister.

For Axelrod, priests and ministers working with the Deaf needed to know how to communicate with the deaf. This required that they know sign language or Total Communication. This was vital. Deaf people needed to know their faith just like hearing people did, so that they could participate in the life of the Church and arrive at a personal union with God. But to do this effectively, those ministering to the Deaf had to know sign language and use it to explain the basic religious concepts and fundamentals of faith. The use of sign language was fundamental to the task of evangelisation and lay at the heart of Axelrod's ministry to the Deaf community. He did not foresee any ministry taking place without sign language.

Finally, the priest or minister had to be a good role model. For Deaf people the basis of faith was not hearing but seeing, as Deaf people are visually focussed.[42] They needed to see their

---

41 Ibid, 5.
42 In promoting the idea that faith for deaf people comes through seeing rather than hearing Axelrod challenged the long-standing position that was attributed to St Augustine who, quoting St Paul, said that faith comes through hearing. We have discussed

priests, ministers and spiritual leaders as good role models that they could follow and emulate.

Ministering in sign language

As we have seen, from the beginning of his ministry Axelrod insisted on the importance of sign language for an effective ministry to Deaf people. When he was at Gallaudet University in the United States, he had to learn ASL[43] and consequently experienced himself becoming 'more confident and independent as an adult deaf man.'[44] While a deacon at St John Vianney Seminary he became known for organising spiritual courses[45] and conducting services in sign language,[46] as well as interpreting and preaching at Masses for the Deaf.[47] Once while talking to his good friend, Robert Simmons, who was also a Jewish convert to Catholicism,[48] Axelrod asked him whether deaf people needed a priest? Simmons responded in the affirmative saying: '[D]eaf people feel excluded and could only really be included if the priest could use sign language.'[49]

For Axelrod, the use of sign language in ministry was about a more profound inclusion of Deaf people into the life of the church. Throughout his ministry, Axelrod promoted the use of sign language in Church liturgy. This was inspiring to both Deaf

	this previously in chapter 3. For Axelrod faith for Deaf people comes from seeing the example of the role models.
43	For more information on the history and nature of American Sign Language, see Harlan Lane, *The Mask of Benevolence: Disabling the Deaf community* (San Diego: Dawn Sign Press, 1999).
44	Axelrod, *And the Journey Begins*, 85.
45	'Spiritual Courses for Deaf People,' TSC, 5 February 1969, 2.
46	'Letter to the Editor from Beryl Jones,' TSM, September 1969, 20.
47	Desmond J. Hatton, 'Deaf Deacon Was Nearly a Rabbi,' TSC, 10 October 1969, 6; 'Interpreting Mass for Deaf,' TSC, 21 January 1970, 3.
48	Robert Simmons had come from a progressive Jewish family. See Axelrod, *And the Journey Begins*, 69.
49	Axelrod, *And the Journey Begins*, 70. Simmons was horrified when Axelrod then inquired whether he (Cyril) could become a priest. Axelrod relates how Simmons 'looked startled and signed wildly, "You must be mad! How can an Orthodox Jew like you become a Catholic priest? Your family would kill you."'

and hearing alike, as Beryl Jones, a non-Catholic but a hearing executive member of the SANCD, wrote:

> On Sunday, 13th July [1969], a special religious service was held in the Roman Catholic Cathedral, Durban, for European deaf (a similar service was held the week before for non-Europeans). Priest[50] Cyril Axeliod [sic], profoundly deaf (an ex-pupil of St. Vincent's School for Deaf) conducted the service ... Of the congregation of about 65 people the majority were deaf. It was the first time I had attended such a service and it was a revelation to me and other hearing people. I think almost every deaf person present knew Priest Cyril and so what he had to say was much appreciated. For once 'the shoe was on the other foot', and I could not understand his message. The deaf lip-read him and fully understood the sign language used to convey his thoughts to them. It was a real joy to realise the deaf were following intelligently, every step of the way. They laughed at his humour and entered fully into the whole service.[51]

In the same letter, Jones admitted that she had come to realise the importance of sign language for the Deaf. She related that her 'profoundly deaf son'[52] even though he 'is a facile lip-reader without the aid of finger spelling or signs he could never follow a sermon or talk with intelligence or understanding.'[53]

This was affirmed by Sheila Eakins, a hearing Catholic, who attended the Palm Sunday Mass celebrated by Cyril Axelrod with a

---

50 In fact, Axelrod was not a priest yet but a deacon.
51 Beryl Jones, 'Letter to the Editor,' *TSM*, September 1969, 20.
52 Alan Jones was a pupil at St Vincent School for the Deaf. As we saw in the previous chapter, Jones was later to assist Mr Norman Nieder-Heitmann – a previous principal of the Kutlwanong School for the Deaf in Rustenburg and who then later worked for the Department of Education and Training – in producing the first sign language dictionary *Talking to the Deaf*. This dictionary is still being used in some schools for the deaf although other dictionaries have been developed. See the photograph of Nieder-Heitmann and Jones working together and comments in 'Opmerking,' *TSM*, November/December 1978; 'Meet Some of Our Deaf: FOYSA Award for Alan Jones,' *TSM*, December 1981, 8.
53 Jones, 'Letter,' 20.

small congregation of about 25 people in Durban in 1974. She was overwhelmed by the evident intimacy and sense of community among the Deaf congregants. Writing as a hearing person experiencing a signed Mass for the first time, she said:

> I noticed how attentive everyone was, following the signs the priest made swiftly and naturally, and lip-reading with serious concentration. Such attentiveness in church would put us to shame. The lessons were read accompanied by mime – waving of the palm, touching the heart to denote love. The reader led them in the repeated response: My God, my God, why have you forsaken me? Then followed the homily, and the appeal to 'accept Jesus as our Saviour, our friend', with Fr Axelrod clasping his wrists to denote the handshake of friendship. The Credo and the Lord's Prayer were said with a feeling of fellowship in which I joined happily; the kiss of peace was full of joy, people stretching across rows of chairs and across the aisle to give hearty signs of friendship – not the self-conscious gestures we so often witness at Mass. And smiling! Their Mass had particular interest for me, because I felt we could borrow much of their simplicity of approach, and so learn that the Mass can be shared happily and with love.[54]

As is evident in the Eakins' account, Axelrod used signs and voiced simultaneously in the liturgy. So much of what was understood to be sign language at this time was called Total Communication.[55] In another context and when speaking about the spiritual welfare and care for the deaf, Axelrod said:

---

54   Sheila Eakins, 'Deaf Jewish Priest Celebrates in Signs,' *TSC*, 26 May 1974, 4.
55   Total Communication is an educational method based on using all forms of communication be it speech, lip-reading or sign language to ensure increased comprehensibility for deaf children. It was used also used outside of the classroom. It is also known as the Combined Method. The type of signing employed by Total Communication is referred to as Signed English as it employs the grammatical structure of English or a spoken language rather than the grammatical structure of natural sign language itself.

Chapter 13

> The deaf must be able to comprehend the way of communication i.e. speech, lip-reading and sign language. The best result is total communication.[56]

Language lies at the heart of any culture and it is no different in the Deaf community. The inclusion of sign language in the liturgy was part of the new developments happening in the Catholic Church after the Second Vatican Council. It became known as inculturation. Axelrod was preparing the way for the inculturation of the Catholic liturgy for deaf people.[57]

New pastoral challenges and additional pastoral ministers (1977–1980)

On 1 February 1976, Cyril Axelrod, after being professed as a Redemptorist, was assigned to the Monastery in Pretoria where he picked up the threads of his work with the Deaf in the dioceses of Johannesburg and Pretoria. The previous year, Axelrod had decided that he no longer wanted to continue as a diocesan priest and applied to join the Redemptorist Congregation. He was accepted and began his novitiate in Bergvliet, Cape Town.[58] During his absence, the ministerial field underwent a substantial shift. On his return, Axelrod had to adapt to new challenges.

Axelrod found himself now confronted with the growth of the establishment of new evangelical churches among the deaf and the arrival of television and preaching in the media. He was

---

56 Axelrod, 'Spiritual Welfare,' 6.
57 There is no indication in his writings that Axelrod was thinking this way himself. Nevertheless, Axelrod's pastoral practice accorded with the five prerequisites for the fruitful inculturation of Christianity in Africa as outlined by the Ugandan theologian, John Mary Waliggo: 1) The existence of a local language by means of which Christianity is communicable to African people. 2) The existence of a local culture with which Christianity is in dialogue. 3) The promotion of a maturing, responsible and actively participating laity. 4) The presence and support of Church leaders who understand and promote the process of inculturation. 5) The development of local research centres for the study of inculturation in African culture. See Waliggo, 'Making a Church That is Truly African,' 26–29.
58 For more information on his reasons and experiences in the novitiate, see Axelrod, And the Journey Begins, 120–134.

to embark on an educational project he had not envisaged, namely the establishment of a nursery school for deaf children in Soweto. He was also to discover that within the Catholic Church he was no longer alone as the only Deaf pastoral worker in South Africa. This shift happened with the profession of Sr Bernadette Oelofse OP, a Deaf Dominican sister, [59] and the ordination of Fr John Turner CMM, a Mariannhill priest.[60]

Establishment of the Christian Deaf Fellowship

A new church called the Christian Deaf Fellowship (CDF) was expanding and growing. It was started originally by Rev. Barrett from the United States,[61] who came out to South Africa and trained local South African deaf pastors like William and Beverley Warmington.[62] These churches were still new and small but were making significant inroads into the white Deaf community. Different churches for the deaf were springing up. They were Bible-based and charismatic with an important emphasis on evangelising others. The pastors were Deaf and celebrated services in sign language. They had been trained in theological colleges for the deaf.

As with many hearing Pentecostal churches the CDF adopted a fundamentalist approach to the reading of scripture and were often hostile to the teachings of the Catholic Church especially relating to Mary and the sacraments.[63] Francois de Villiers remembered that Catholics were criticised for their way of praying too:

> Lots of deaf people don't like Catholics because of parrot prayer. We say the same prayers again and again and don't

---

59 See Chapter 8.
60 See Chapter 16.
61 Cyril Axelrod, interview conducted by Mark James, 15 September 2015, Dunnottar, Nigel, 400. Francois de Villiers, interview conducted by Mark James, 4 August 2016, Edenvale, 461.
62 Francois de Villiers, interview conducted by Mark James, Edenvale, 462.
63 Cyril Axelrod, interview conducted by Mark James, 15 September 2015, Dunnottar, 400; and Francois de Villiers, interview conducted by Mark James, 4 August 2016, Edenvale, 462.

pray from your heart. They don't understand what Jesus has taught about 'Our Father who art in heaven,' but this they called parrot prayer. For me, it is ridiculous.[64]

Some of the English-speaking Deaf, who previously had attended Axelrod's Masses, had never felt comfortable in the Catholic Church. Some were also angry at the way they were treated in the Catholic schools for the deaf.[65] Even baptised Catholics left to join the CDF.[66] The monopoly that the Catholic Church previously had over English-speaking Deaf people, due to its schools for the deaf, was being eroded. Deaf people were making other choices for themselves. This had challenging consequences for Axelrod's ministry to the Deaf community and he had to adapt to changing times. One new area for evangelisation was the broadcast media.

Television and evangelism

In 1977, the benefits of television were being appreciatively lauded by hearing and deaf alike. Television was still very new in South Africa having been introduced the previous year.[67] This new technology had lots of benefits for the deaf and the SANCD were quick to appreciate this. They invited to South Africa a hearing pastor from the United States, Pastor John Stallings, a fluent ASL signer.[68] He was the Mission Director of the CDF in the States. He arrived in February and trained deaf chaplains in South Africa from all churches in how to develop deaf ministry on television. [69] His programmes on SABC, *From the Book*, were incredibly well received among clergy and laity alike.[70] This was probably the first

---

64   Francois de Villiers, interview conducted by Mark James, 4 August 2016, 463.
65   'There was also revenge because of the cruel time when the nuns hit children on the hands and disciplined them.' Francois de Villiers, interview conducted by Mark James, 4 August 2016, Edenvale, 462.
66   Francois de Villiers, interview conducted by Mark James, 4 August 2016, Edenvale, 462.
67   While television was introduced in 1975, extensive programming only began in 1976.
68   'Television for the Deaf?' *TSM*, March 1977, 6.
69   'Television for the Deaf?' *TSM*, March 1977, 6.
70   Many comments were included in the article from individuals and newspapers. See 'Televisie Byna Toeganglik vir Dowes,' *TSM*,

time that sign language had appeared on national television in South Africa. Beryl Jones from Durban wrote:

> Our totally deaf son's appreciation was a joy to behold. His face was a picture and he said, 'I can understand very well.' Very many phone calls, and verbal comments, from hearing as well as deaf people proved without any doubt that both hearing and deaf appreciated the inspiring messages by Pastor Stallings who for 41 years has been a minister for the Deaf. For 16 years he has had a unique TV ministry to the Deaf in U.S.A. We look forward now to Ministers to the Deaf, who are conversant with sign language, bringing God's word to our S. African Deaf community through this medium – speech and sign together.[71]

Cyril Axelrod was equally supportive of this new venture.

> The appearance of Pastor John Stallings on TV brings God's word in speech and sign language was a historical event. I found it very inspiring, and it brings real consolation to the Deaf. I hope it will be recorded on TV from time to time.[72]

Stallings also conducted a series of church services around the country – at the Catholic Deaf hostel in Heathfield, Cape Town; for the Community for the Deaf in Belville as well as in another Dutch Reformed Church in Bosman Street, Pretoria. He also visited St Vincent School for the Deaf in Johannesburg.[73] Axelrod was not able to take up the challenge of doing television programmes for the deaf. Another Deaf priest would do so eleven years later.

Axelrod was not to know that he was soon to be venturing into the area of Deaf education too. Up until now, his ministry had been exclusively focused on pastoral ministry and his only experience of education was the brief period when he was chaplain

---

46, 3, September 1977, 9.
71 'Televisie Byna Toeganlik vir Dowes,' *TSM*, 46, 3, September 1977, 9.
72 'Televisie Byna Toeganlik vir Dowes,' *TSM*, 46, 3, September 1977, 9.
73 'Television for the Deaf?' *TSM*, March 1977, 6.

at St Thomas School for the Deaf in Woodlands. This experience was to prove very formative.

St Martin's Nursery School for the Deaf, Orlando West

In 1978, before leaving for a Redemptorist pilgrimage to the Holy Land, Axelrod was approached by a speech therapist from Baragwanath Hospital in Soweto. She was concerned about the number of deaf children who had been abandoned at the hospital by their parents and for whom no education was being provided. She enlisted Axelrod's assistance.

> I got a phone call message from Baragwanath Hospital. A speech therapist asked me to come and visit. She showed me so many deaf children, of varying ages, staying there and sleeping on the floor. Their parents had brought them to the hospital and then left them there. They didn't take them back home. The speech therapist couldn't cope with all these children. She couldn't teach all of them. She asked me to help.[74]

There was no school for the deaf in Soweto. Axelrod approached Sr Leah, a Notre Dame sister, who was the principal of the school at St Martin's parish in Orlando West.[75] He asked for a classroom so that he could start a school for deaf children. Even though the hearing school was already overcrowded with about a thousand pupils, Axelrod was given the use of a classroom, complete with desks and a blackboard. He divided the classroom into two. One side was for the little children and the other for the older ones.

Sr Conrada Förg, a King William's Town Dominican sister and a teacher at St Vincent School, registered the pre-school with the Department of Co-operation and Training.[76] Axelrod had

---

74 Cyril Axelrod, interview conducted by Mark James, 15 September 2015, Dunnottar, Nigel, 394.
75 'Letter from Cyril Axelrod to Sr Mannes,' 4 July 1988, 1. Box 1 file 3 Correspondence, Cyril Axelrod papers, Redemptorist Archives.
76 'Letter from Axelrod to Sr Mannes,' 4 July 1988, 2.

managed to secure a donation of R25 000 from *Propaganda Fide*.[77] With this money he could pay some of the expenses of the school like the stipends for Mrs Susan Kabane, a retired teacher, and Eugenia Mthembu, a Catholic social worker. On 10 October 1978, the school opened its doors to 40 deaf children.[78] They made a beginning but the biggest challenge was to find the money to keep the school going. Working together as a team, they battled on.

Developing the ministry to deaf adults

Even though Axelrod had just opened a nursery school for abandoned deaf children in Soweto, he was particularly concerned that far more attention was being paid to the deaf child in the school than to deaf adults.[79]

> It must be realised that adults need religious instruction as much as the children if their lives are to be fully integrated. Religious Instruction should not end as soon as the person leaves school. The object of all education is to enable the individual to accept himself as a person endowed with fully human dignity, whether or not he is deaf.[80]

In his ministry which was continuing to grow and expand in white and black areas, Axelrod tried to provide the religious and spiritual instruction that was needed. Initially, he had started with a monthly Mass for the deaf at the Cathedral of Christ the King

---

77 Ibid, 2. *Propaganda Fide* is a Dicastery in the Vatican which seeks to promote the evangelisation of peoples in different countries around the world. They collect money from Catholic church communities around the world and distribute it to mission churches in countries where the church has only been established recently.
78 'Letter from Cyril Axelrod to Sr Mannes,' 4 July 1988, 2. Box 1 file 3 Correspondence Cyril Axelrod Papers, Redemptorist Archives.
79 Cyril Axelrod, 'The Spiritual Care of the Deaf,' 1978? Box 1: Cyril Axelrod papers, File 5: Fr Cyril Axelrod: Life, work spirituality of the deaf, Redemptorist Archives. The report is not dated but it was written before December 1978 as there is a reference to the forthcoming ordination of Fr John Turner CMM. He was ordained priest on 3 December 1978. This article is different from the one previously published as 'The spiritual welfare and care of the deaf'.
80 Axelrod, 'The Spiritual Care,' 6.

in Johannesburg[81] or sometimes at Regina Mundi in Soweto.[82] He would also travel to Hammanskraal for a Mass on the first Sunday of each month.[83] Eventually, he was also doing Masses in Pretoria, Springs and Benoni for white deaf Catholics and in Mamelodi, KwaThema and Daveyton for black Catholics.[84]

> Inevitably, I face the great problems of adapting to the various sign languages which have developed within the various schools for the deaf.[85] However, one sign language is at present being formulated under the supervision of Mr Nieder-Heitmann.[86]

One of the most challenging problems he found in his ministry was that Deaf adults lapsed from the practice of the faith that they learnt at school.

> When the children had finished their education they were plunged into a wide society where they faced the difficulty of obtaining spiritual help because of the communication barrier with their priests and ministers. Most of the deaf were integrated with hearing, participating in their services but being unable to follow and understand the genuine presentation of the service. They then became frustrated.[87]

It was a challenge to get them back to church once they had stopped. But he found that by using sign language in the liturgy and by relying on the assistance of Deaf people in the church community, it could be done.

---

81 Ibid, 3.
82 Cyril Axelrod, personal email to Mark James, 16 March 2015.
83 Axelrod, 'The Spiritual Care,' 3.
84 Cyril Axelrod, personal email to Mark James, 16 March 2015.
85 For a more detailed discussion on variation and regionalisation in SASL, see Aarons and Akach, 'South African Sign Language,' 1–28.
86 Axelrod, 'The Spiritual Care,' 3. Norman Nieder-Heitmann was principal of the Kutlwanong School for the Deaf in Rustenburg and an executive member of the SANCD. He had long argued for the use of sign language in Deaf education. This dictionary is still being used in some schools although other dictionaries have been developed.
87 Axelrod, 'The Spiritual Care,' 2.

> The spiritual care of the deaf began to take a better form when the Deaf community came to encourage one another to attend the services and to enjoy being able to follow them in sign language.[88]

Axelrod also preferred to hold Masses in church or school halls as it proved easier for the deaf to interact during services and socialise afterwards. But just saying Mass using sign language was not enough. He needed to diversify his pastoral approach and so he encouraged the Deaf to participate in Bible study groups on Wednesday evenings. In some groups as many as 20 Deaf people were gathering in homes, meeting with or without the priest or minister, 'to discuss what the passages mean and how they relate to their everyday Christian lives. At the same time, they are helped to understand how the Bible reveals God's presence in us in our daily lives.'[89]

The Deaf youth needed spiritual care too. He recommended the formation of Deaf youth clubs. He saw the need for a residential training programme for Deaf youth, along the lines of the one developed by the Rosebank Union Church in Johannesburg for their Deaf youth. This group met every Sunday afternoon and was organised by the parents of deaf children with the idea of training Deaf Christian youth leaders.[90]

He realised that he could not do all this work alone. He needed pastoral assistants. Initially, Axelrod spoke of training three Deaf lay ministers to assist him in the spiritual care of the deaf, especially when the chaplain was not available.[91] The main criterium for him was that lay ministers needed 'a sound knowledge of the Bible'[92] so that they could lead the community in communion services or Bible study groups. The Second Vatican Council had opened the doors to the training of lay ministers or extraordinary ministers of the Eucharist to assist the priest during Mass or to conduct communion services in the absence of a priest

---

88 Ibid, 3.
89 Ibid, 4.
90 Ibid, 5.
91 Cyril Axelrod, 'The Church Has a Mission to the Handicapped,' TSC, 1 October 1978, 11. The third person is not named.
92 Axelrod, 'The Spiritual Care,' 5.

or deacon.[93] It was Axelrod's great hope that the work started by the Dominican sisters in the schools for the deaf would bear fruit, where adult deaf Catholics would 'be ready for God's call to serve their own community within the Church as a deacon or lay minister or priest.'[94]

His wish was answered with the ordination of Fr John Turner CMM in 1978 but he would have to wait until 1980 when he got two lay ministers, Mauritz Neethling from Springs and Frank de Klerk from Pretoria.[95]

Sizwile School for the Deaf

In 1980, the St Martin's School that Axelrod had started underwent a name change to Sizwile School for the Deaf. It had become a state-aided school with a board of management.

---

[93] The Council of Trent instituted seven orders of priesthood in opposition to the Reformers' denial of the sacrament of Order with their emphasis on the priesthood of all believers and ministry as conferred by the community and not as a sacrament. However, in 1964 the Second Vatican Council passed *Lumen Gentium*, 10, which distinguished between the common priesthood and the ministerial priesthood. Ministerial priesthood or Order was reduced from seven to three orders namely, diaconate, priesthood and episcopacy. In his Apostolic Letter *Ministeria Quaedam* (15 August 1972), Pope Paul VI suppressed the subdiaconate and restored lay ministries. No longer was lector and acolyte conferred through ordination but rather by installation. In doing so, Paul VI permitted that laity could be allowed to exercise these ministries. The cooperation between priest and lay ministers was also affirmed by Pope Paul VI in *Evangelii Nuntiandi* (1975), 73. For more information on the teaching of the church concerning Order, see Jacques Dupuis, ed, *The Christian Faith in the Doctrinal Documents of the Catholic Church*, 6th rev. and enlarged ed. (New York: Alba House, 1996), 671–701.

[94] Axelrod, 'The Church Has a Mission to the Handicapped,' *TSC*, 1 October 1978, 11.

[95] Cyril Axelrod, 'A Time to do More for the Handicapped,' *TSC*, 10 May 1981, 10. Mauritz Neethling is a past pupil of St Vincent School and became an engineer and inventor of gadgets to assist the deaf. See 'Electric Baby-Alarm,' *TSM*, December 1962, 6–7. Mauritz Neethling and his wife Maureen converted to Catholicism and are members of Our Lady of Mercy parish in Springs. Mauritz continued in this ministry until his retirement in 2010. Frank de Klerk was a member of the Monastery parish in Pretoria. Maureen sadly passed away on 17 June 2024.

However, becoming a state-funded school was not without its hazards. The DET insisted that Sizwile School adopt one of the African languages as the school's medium of instruction. This was in line with the government's mother-tongue education policy.

Already from his experiences at St Thomas School for the Deaf, Axelrod recognised how the apartheid policy of mother-tongue education was devised to keep people apart and separate them from each other. In effect, it accentuated tribal and racial differences. The Group Areas Act forced schools for the deaf, just like hearing schools, to separate white deaf pupils from black deaf pupils, as well as the separation of coloureds from Indians and Africans. Mother-tongue education kept Africans divided into various ethnic groups. This was being imposed on schools for the deaf too. This resulted in deaf people from one ethnic group not being 'allowed to make contact with deaf people from other ethnic groups in South Africa.'[96] In an urban context, Axelrod insisted, this was just preposterous and impossible as people from all ethnic groups lived together and interacted daily in the ethnic melting pot that was Soweto.

Axelrod insisted that English be accepted as the medium of instruction. Initially, the officials of the DET refused to change government policy. Due to Axelrod's persistence, they eventually conceded and allowed Sizwile to use English in the classroom.

> I went to the government, [the Department of] Education and Training, and said that in Soweto there are 11 different languages. Which language do we use? I explained this to them. There are so many different languages, which to use? I wanted them to accept English, to have this language alone. They didn't accept at first, but I persisted. Eventually, they agreed with me. Sizwile School was the first to use English because Soweto had so many different languages.[97]

---

96   Axelrod, *And the Journey Begins*, 115.
97   Cyril Axelrod, interview conducted by Mark James, 15 September 2015, Dunnottar, 396–397.

Secondly, he insisted that Sizwile be a day school rather than a residential one. He remembered that at St Thomas School for the Deaf,[98] he had been troubled:

> The biggest shock for me was to discover how isolated the deaf children were from their parents who mostly lived on farms far away. The children were only allowed home for holidays twice a year and usually had little or no communication with their families. So, after a few years, they regarded the school as their home and often did not want to leave at the end of their elementary education as they had little chance of building careers at home. The apartheid policy certainly destroyed family life by forcing deaf children to be separated from their families. It created a communication barrier between parent and children, which meant that the deaf children kept in closer contact with their own deaf peers with whom they could communicate.[99]

Rather than leaving their families and living in a school hostel during term time, attending a day school meant that the deaf children went home every day after school. In this way, the deaf children were kept in regular contact with their deaf or hearing families. Under apartheid, African family life was already under strain due to the migrant labour system.[100] Axelrod wanted deaf

---

98 'Because our pupils are drawn from all over the Cape Province, and indeed, from other Provinces too, it is very difficult to establish personal contact with their parents, as we would wish to do. I was very pleased, therefore, to learn that some of our teachers, in the course of spending their own holidays in some place, take the time to visit the local pupils and their families. They frequently encounter parents with problems and questions to which only a teacher or some other expert can provide the answers.' Quoted from the 'St Thomas School for Deaf Bantu Children. Chairman's Report for the year 1972/73,' 2. 124/374 74. KDSA, Johannesburg.
99 Axelrod, *And the Journey Begins*, 116.
100 For further information on the effects of migratory labour on African family life, see Denis, 'A Case of Pastoral Myopia,' 439–460 and Peter Delius, 'The History of Migrant Labor in South Africa (1800–2014),' *Oxford Research Encyclopedia of African History* (May 2017). Accessed 13 October 2018, www.africanhistory.oxfordre.com/10.1093/acrefore/9780190277734.013.93.pdf

children to experience family life rather than just grow up in an institutionalised boarding school environment. He required that the parents learn sign language that would enhance communication in the home between the hearing parents and their deaf children.[101]

> When I started this day school, I wanted to keep the children with their family. So, I insisted that the parents must learn sign language to communicate with their children. This was the first school to do this. This was the way I tried to fight against apartheid. I did not agree that the children must go away from their families.[102]

For Axelrod, 'apartheid destroyed family life'[103] and he was adamant that it should not affect families with deaf children too.

In 1980, Axelrod attended the Second International Conference for Religious Education of the hearing-impaired in Manchester, England. After this conference, he preached retreats in Ireland and then the United States. While in the United States, however, he was diagnosed with retinitis pigmentosa and had to give up driving.[104] This restricted his ability to travel around South Africa for ministry purposes, as he had done in the past.

Deaf Awareness

During this period, we see Cyril Axelrod becoming more outspoken encouraging the Catholic bishops to take more responsibility for the pastoral care of the deaf and the handicapped. Axelrod was not only concerned with building up institutions for the deaf but also with promoting the human rights of all disabled and handicapped people. He wanted the Church to do more for the handicapped.

---

101 Cyril Axelrod, interview conducted by Mark James, 15 September 2015, Dunnottar, 397. Also see Axelrod, *And the journey begins*, 145.
102 Cyril Axelrod, interview conducted by Mark James, 15 September 2015, Dunnottar, 397.
103 Cyril Axelrod, interviewed by Mark James, Dunnottar, 30 September 2015, 397.
104 Axelrod, *And the journey begins*, 154–155.

Chapter 13

The United Nations declared the year 1981 as the International Year of the Handicapped. Axelrod chose this theme for an article in *The Southern Cross*. Axelrod pointed out that while Pope John Paul II had given his support to the United Nations' call, the Southern African Bishops' Conference (SACBC) had not addressed this issue for the local church. He wrote that as the Church, we need 'to re-examine our attitudes towards our handicapped neighbours and promote their wellbeing in the justice and compassion the Lord so clearly desires.'[105]

For Axelrod, it was not enough to just affirm the rights of the handicapped. The bishops needed to 'ensure a secure place for them in the human community.'[106] He complained that there was enormous ignorance and apathy within the Church and society towards those who were handicapped. Deaf people too needed to be aware of the needs of other people with disabilities. It was not good just to focus on deaf issues to the exclusion of people with disabilities. He expressed his disappointment that the bishops had not shown any interest and had not even appointed a church commission for the handicapped, at either the national or diocesan level. Axelrod exclaimed that 'justice demands that this be remedied.'[107]

Axelrod was a prophet crying out in the wilderness. In calling for the rights of handicapped people to be respected within the Church, he was challenging the bishops and the priests to bring about changes in the Church. However, there was no indication his challenge to the Bishops' Conference was ever heeded. His call was drowned out by the pressing demands of the struggle against apartheid and the challenges bishops faced in the day-to-day administration of their dioceses. They put the concerns of the handicapped, the disabled and the deaf on the back burner and even to this day scant attention is given to disabled and deaf people in Catholic dioceses.[108]

---

105   Fr Cyril Axelrod, CSsR, 'A Time to do More for the Handicapped,' *TSC*, 10 May 1981, 10.
106   Axelrod, 'A Time to do More,' 10.
107   Ibid.
108   In October 2022, Archbishop Dabula Mpako of the Archdiocese of Pretoria established the Office for Ministry to the Deaf

Axelrod was appealing to the conscience of both Church and society to take the needs of the disabled and deaf into account. Not to just view the world from the perspective of the able-bodied and the hearing. Levinas spoke about making totality aware of its bad conscience and calling into question its treatment of the disabled and the deaf.

While the Bishops' Conference was unresponsive, Axelrod ploughed ahead establishing and building up institutions for the ongoing support of the Deaf community.

Bobokweng Deaf Hostel, Hammanskraal

On 29 August 1982, at the invitation of Archbishop George Daniel, the Archbishop of Pretoria, Bishop Green officially opened newly completed buildings[109] called the Bobokweng[110] Centre for deaf working adults. It was situated on the property of the Hammanskraal School. The centre was built to provide accommodation and post-school vocational training facilities for 36 adults. Axelrod was the director of the centre.[111]

Already in 1979, when visiting the Dominican School for the Deaf in Hammanskraal, Axelrod became aware of the needs of ex-pupils of the school. Many of them came from farming areas and had little opportunity to find employment in their home areas once their schooling was complete. Axelrod had already experienced the workings of two other deaf hostels, the Catholic Deaf Hostel in Heathfield, Cape Town which was started by Ernest Green, and the Jewish Hostel in Johannesburg started by his teacher Ralph Hahn.

Bobokweng was envisioned slightly differently from these hostels as the idea was not just to provide accommodation for deaf

---

Community (OMDC) which is beginning to address some of these challenges.
109 In his autobiography, Axelrod wrote: 'Bishop Green officially opened the hostel in 1979 in the presence of government representatives, my cousins and friends.' See Axelrod, *And the Journey Begins*, 149.
110 Bobokweng means 'Place of Progress.' See 'Meet Some our Deaf: Father Cyril Axelrod,' *TSM*, May/June 1982, 7.
111 'Centre for Adult Deaf,' *TSC*, 19 September 1982, 1.

workers seeking employment in Pretoria but to give them skills training too. In describing its function, it was stated that:

> When the deaf complete their elementary education at a school for the deaf, they are sent home without having qualifications. Most of their families live on farms where the deaf cannot make their living. The centre provides them with adult education and a vocational training which enables the deaf to acquire qualifications. The centre also trains the deaf to develop their responsibility of living independently like any hearing person ... This centre aims to help the deaf overcome their feeling of deprivation of the human right to live and work.[112]

With the establishment of both Bobokweng and Sizwile, we see Axelrod putting his theology into practice. For Axelrod, ministering to the Deaf community was not about providing spiritual care but building up institutions that benefitted Deaf people. Not everyone understood or shared his vision.

Sizwile School and conflict with the archbishop

By 1983, the Sizwile School for the Deaf had grown so large there was a need to find alternative premises. The Soweto Council granted land in Dobsonville for the building of a new school for the deaf. Axelrod realised that this was now a venture that he could no longer manage. He approached Archbishop Fitzgerald, the Bishop of Johannesburg,[113] to assist him in finding another religious order, one that specialised in Deaf education, to take

---

[112] 'Meet Some our Deaf: Father Cyril Axelrod,' *TSM*, May/June 1982, 7.

[113] Prior to his appointment as Bishop of Johannesburg, Fitzgerald had been Archbishop of Bloemfontein. When he was moved to Johannesburg, only a diocese under the Metropolitan Archdiocese of Pretoria, he found himself in the position of being the Archbishop Bishop of Johannesburg. Johannesburg became an Archdiocese only in 2010 when Archbishop Buti Tlhagale OMI was also moved to from Bloemfontein to Johannesburg as Bishop in 2009.

over the school.[114] This led to a disagreement between Fitzgerald and Axelrod. The Archbishop wanted Axelrod to continue taking responsibility for the project he had initiated.[115] However, Axelrod believed that this was impossible as he was not qualified to act as principal of the school. This led to an acrimonious dispute between Axelrod and the Archbishop.[116] The situation was partially resolved later that year when the Brothers of Charity agreed to take over the administration of the school.[117]

Brother Gerard Cox, a speech therapist, became principal of the school and a new board of management was appointed.[118] However, Sizwile School only moved from St Martin's Catholic School to its new premises three years later, in April 1986, when the buildings for the new school had been completed.[119] With this move, Axelrod felt excluded and he was never invited to assist in the school again, not even to say Mass for the children.[120]

---

114 Cyril Axelrod, interview conducted by Mark James, 15 September 2015, Dunnottar, 395.
115 Ibid.
116 This conflict led to the breakdown in relationship between Axelrod and Archbishop Fitzgerald. Axelrod's contract as a chaplain to the Deaf community in the diocese of Johannesburg was not renewed by Fitzgerald and he left to work in Cape Town instead. Axelrod felt he was totally misunderstood and what he was trying to do misconstrued. See Cyril Axelrod, interview conducted by Mark James, 395. The situation is reminiscent of some of the conflicts the first black priests experienced when they were involved in ministry. See George Mukuka, *The Other Side of the Story: The Silent Experience of Black Clergy in the Catholic Church in South Africa (1898–1976)*, (Pietermaritzburg: Cluster Publications, 2008).
117 Gerard Cox, 'From the Principal's Desk,' *Year Report: Sizwile School of the handicapped*, 1987, 1. Box 1, File 2 Magazines, Cyril Axelrod papers, Redemptorist Archives.
118 Gerard Cox, 'From the Principal's Desk,' *Year Report: Sizwile School of the handicapped*, 1987, 1. Box 1, File 2 Magazines, Cyril Axelrod papers, Redemptorist Archives.
119 Cox, 'Principal's Desk,' 1.
120 'They didn't recognise my work. They didn't recognise my pioneering work. It was sad ... they pushed me aside.' See Cyril Axelrod, interview conducted by Mark James, 30 September 2015, Dunnottar, 395.

Chapter 13

Axelrod moves to Cape Town

In 1970, Bishop Ernest Green submitted his resignation as Bishop of Port Elizabeth and returned to Cape Town. He resumed his work with the deaf after a short period as the parish priest in Lambert's Bay.

In February 1984, Fr Cyril Axelrod CSsR was transferred to Cape Town to be the novice master of the Redemptorists. Axelrod offered to help Bishop Green in the ministry for the Deaf, but it caused tension between them. Axelrod withdrew the offer as he felt that Green was threatened by his presence.[121]

However, three years later in 1987 Axelrod was appointed as the chaplain to the Deaf community.[122] The Archbishop of Cape Town, Stephen Naidoo CSsR, asked Bishop Green to step down as Green's health was failing.[123] When Axelrod took over as the chaplain, he was discouraged by the state of the deaf hostel that had been handed over to his care. It had not been well managed and there had been hardly any supervision of the hostel for a whole year. No new warden had been appointed after Bishop Green fell ill. Consequently, the hostel had become run down. Axelrod also had other headaches. The Archbishop made it clear that he was not prepared to pay for any repairs to the hostel buildings nor was he willing to support Axelrod's deaf chaplaincy work financially.[124] After ten months of frustration at the lack of

---

[121] Letter, Fr Cyril Axelrod to Sr Mannes OP, 22 August 1984, 2. Box: Cyril Axelrod papers File: Correspondence 1 Redemptorist Archives, Cape Town. According to Axelrod, Bishop Green's Masses were no longer as well attended as when Fr Cyril came to say Mass.

[122] Axelrod was asked to take over the running of the deaf hostel in Heathfield and accepted this responsibility. See Letters, Cyril Axelrod to Sr Mannes OP, 29 June 1986, 11 October 1986, and 1 June 1987. Box: Cyril Axelrod papers, File: Correspondence 1, Redemptorist Archives, Cape Town.

[123] Bishop Ernest Green died and was buried from Corpus Christi Church in Wittebome on 24 March 1988. See 'Hundreds at Funeral of Bishop Green,' *TSC*, 10 April 1988, 7.

[124] Letters, Cyril Axelrod to Sr Mannes OP, 24 June 1987 and 30 July 1987. Box: Cyril Axelrod papers, File: Correspondence 1, Redemptorist Archives, Cape Town.

progress and improvement at the hostel, Axelrod resigned as chaplain to the Deaf in Cape Town in November 1987.[125]

A new idea had been brewing in his mind since he had visited Singapore in 1985 to give retreats. On his return, he began a discernment process to assist him in deciding whether he should respond to a call to work in Far East Asia.[126] He had already started to learn Mandarin.[127] The disappointment and frustrations he experienced first in the Diocese of Johannesburg and then later at the deaf hostel in Cape Town, helped him make up his mind.

On 19 August 1988, Axelrod flew to Hong Kong via Singapore to take up a new apostolate with the Deaf in Hong Kong.[128] Thus ended his ministry to the Deaf in South Africa, although he visited on numerous occasions and has many friends in South Africa, he has not ministered full-time in South Africa again.

After working in Hong Kong and Macau for many years, his eyesight deteriorated and he retired to live in England where social support for the Deaf-Blind is well-developed.[129] On 22 November 2013, Fr Cyril was honoured as an Officer of the Order of the British Empire (OBE) by Queen Elizabeth II in Windsor Castle. The Hong Kong Association for the Blind nominated Fr Cyril for this award due to his untiring and dedicated ministry to the deaf and the blind. Larry Kaufmann, Axelrod's comm-guide,[130] related the story of Fr Cyril saying to Queen Elizabeth, while receiving his OBE, that his disability is a gift from God. 'She replied: "I have

---

125 Letter, Cyril Axelrod to Sr Mannes OP, 24 November 1987. Box Cyril Axelrod papers, File: Correspondence 1, Redemptorist Archives, Cape Town.
126 Letter, Axelrod to Sr Mannes, 1 October 1985.
127 Letter, Axelrod to Sr Mannes, 24 November 1987.
128 Letter, Axelrod to Sr Mannes, 4 July 1988 and 'SA priest off to work in Asia,' *TSC*, 14 August 1988, 12. For more information on his work in South East Asia, see Cyril Axelrod, *And the Journey Begins*, 161–168, and a wonderful tribute to Cyril's work in Hong Kong by Doreen Mui, 'A Legend, an Icon of Hope,' in Cyril Axelrod, *Still on That Journey* (Merrivale: Redemptorist Pastoral Publication, 2021), 117–121. Also see, Portolano, *Be Opened*, 260–263.
129 For more information on Fr Cyril's coming to terms with his being Deaf-Blind, see Axelrod's book: *Still on That Journey*.
130 A comm-guide is a term used for a person who accompanies a Deaf-Blind person as their interpreter, communicator and guide.

no doubt that you have used it for God's glory.'"[131] According to Kaufmann, Axelrod's understanding of his disability as a gift from God goes beyond acceptance but rather suggests 'that God has had a hand in it all; that God has actually gifted Cyril with certain physical conditions that are the exact opposite of what we would consider a gift.'[132] Kaufmann elaborates further:

> In Cyril's case, the gift of disability is ultimately the gift of heart, which in biblical terms symbolizes the *whole* person. Looking at the 'gift of disability' from our own perspective, it is not Cyril's deafness that is a gift to us, or his blindness. It is Cyril himself, the whole person, who is a gift. And his giftedness includes the fact, that he happens to be deaf-blind, and the sort of person which that has made him to be. It is about how his disability has shaped his heart of love. That's the gift.[133]

Presently, Fr Cyril continues to reside in London in the United Kingdom. He has written two autobiographical accounts. *On the Journey* covers his childhood, his decision to become a Catholic and a priest, his life of ministry in South Africa and his move to Macau and Hong Kong. In February 2023, Axelrod celebrated his 80th birthday with the launch of his second autobiography *Still on the Journey*. This book focuses on his experience of being Deaf-Blind and how he continues to minister motivated by this understanding that his disability is a gift from God. Despite his being Deaf-Blind continues to live a full life as a preacher and an artist. He has recently published a new book on his artwork entitled *In Silent Darkness*.[134] Another book is being published where Fr Cyril reflects on his faith journey entitled *Light on the Journey*[135] and how he has been deeply influenced by both Jewish and Christian traditions throughout his life.

---

131   Larry Kaufmann, *Perhaps God: Wisdom Through the Gift of Disability* (Merrivale: Redemptorist Pastoral Publications, 2015), 11.
132   Kaufmann, *Perhaps God*, 12.
133   Ibid, 13.
134   Cyril Axelrod, *In Silent Darkness: Paintings by Deafblind Rabbi-Priest* (Merrivale: Redemptorist Pastoral Publications, 2020).
135   Cyril Axelrod, *Light on the Journey* (Merrivale: Redemptorist Pastoral Publications, 2024).

Chapter 14

Ruben Xulu (1942–1985): Africanising Church Art

The Second Vatican Council, which was called by Pope John XXIII and which ended in 1965, was a major turning point in the history of the Catholic Church in the twentieth century. It was a pastoral ecumenical council with a focus on renewing the pastoral practice of the Church in the modern world. It not only renewed but, at times, also revolutionised Church life for Catholics. Even close to sixty years after the last session ended, the ramifications of this global gathering of Catholic bishops are still reverberating throughout the Catholic world.

One of the effects of the Second Vatican Council was the growing awareness that the Church, in Africa at least, had to move away from being a missionary Church to becoming a truly local African Church.[1] It had to become a Church rooted in the cultural values of the African people and served by local indigenous clergy. This development on the African continent became known as inculturation.

> Inculturation means the honest and serious attempt to make Christ and his message of salvation evermore understood by peoples of every culture, locality and time. It means the reformulation of Christian life and doctrine into the very thought patterns of each people. It is the conviction that Christ and his Good News are even dynamic and challenging to all times and cultures as they become better understood and lived by each people.[2]

---

1 For a brief survey on the reception of Vatican II in the South African church, see Anthony Egan, 'How Vatican II Renewed South African Catholicism – as Perceived by *TSC* 1962–1968,' *Studia Historiae Ecclesiasticae (SHE)* 39, 2 (December 2013):239–257.
2 See John Mary Waliggo, 'Making a Church that is Truly African, in *Inculturation: Its Meaning and Urgency*, ed. John M. Waliggo et al.

Inculturation needs to be distinguished from enculturation, which is a cultural anthropological term similar in meaning to socialisation as it refers to the 'insertion of an individual in his culture.'[3] Many countries in Africa expended great effort on inculturation renewing the Church's liturgical life in the light of African culture and traditions. The participation of the laity in the Church was being encouraged and there were many renewal courses for bishops, priests, religious and laity arising from the decisions of the Council to renew the Church.

Changing the face of the Church after the Second Vatican Council, 1965–1974

In the 1960s and early 1970s in South Africa, inculturation was not an urgent concern for most bishops, priests, religious congregations or the laity.[4] Yet in a corner of the country, in the Catholic prefecture of Ingwavuma, KwaZulu, two unknown Zulu artists were giving an African face to the Catholic Church in South Africa. One of these artists, Bernard Gcwensa (1918–1985) was hearing, the other Ruben Xulu (1942–1985) was deaf. Both Gcwensa and Xulu were lay people, yet they preached through their art. They were doing inculturation before the Second Vatican Council had pronounced on it. Gcwensa was Xulu's artistic mentor but Xulu went further than his mentor by carving images where African themes predominated. It is primarily to the work of Ruben Xulu that we now turn our attention and focus.

Ruben Xulu (1942–1985)

In 1953, Fr Edwin Kinch OSM, an American missionary and Servite priest, was the parish priest of KwaHlabisa in the prefecture of Ingwavuma. While doing home visits he ventured upon the

---

(Nairobi/Kampala: St Paul's Publications – Africa, 1986), 12.

3   Inculturation is the 'process by which the Church becomes part of a culture of a people.' See Ary Roest Crollius, 'Inculturation: Newness and Ongoing Process,' in *Inculturation: Its Meaning and Urgency*, ed. John M. Waliggo et al. (Nairobi/Kampala: St Paul's Publications – Africa, 1986), 34–35.

4   Clement Langa, "The Prayer of the People,' in *The Catholic Church in Contemporary South Africa*, ed. Joy Brain and Philippe Denis (Pietermaritzburg: Cluster Publications, 1999), 310.

Gcwensa homestead. While visiting the family, he was intrigued by a unique doorframe that Gcwensa had made and which adorned the front of the home. He also admired Gcwensa's carvings on different walking sticks that he was selling to support the family.[5] Kinch realised that Gcwensa had talent and invited him to do some carvings of statues of Mary for the Cathedral church at the Catholic mission in KwaHlabisa. This was the beginning of a productive collaboration between Gcwensa and Kinch.

The plight of Ruben Xulu was brought to Fr Kinch's attention in 1961. Ruben Xulu was born on 10 May 1942 at KwaHlabisa in Zululand. As a hearing child, Xulu had been an excellent singer and dancer.[6] In 1949, at the age of seven and while herding cattle, Ruben Xulu had a traumatic experience in the forest from which he never fully recovered. It is not clear what happened, but it resulted in Xulu going deaf and losing his ability to speak. Xulu's family attributed his sudden deafness to an encounter with evil spirits.[7]

In 1957, at the age of fifteen, Ruben went to a hearing school in Mgangatho. Mrs Seraphina Magubane, a teacher at the school, took Xulu under her wing and taught him to read.

> Mrs Magubane told me how she had taught Ruben to read by drawing pictures on the blackboard to illustrate the meaning of words. She would question him by means of signs and he could give her the correct answer.[8]

While still at school, Xulu's artistic talent began to be noticed, especially after he won the annual art competition for black schools in KwaZulu one year.

---

5   Dina Cormick, *Bernard Gcwensa and Ruben Xulu: Christian Artists of Natal*, (Pretoria: Academica, 1993), 12.
6   Cormick, *Bernard Gcwensa and Ruben Xulu*, 23.
7   The family believed that neighbours had cast a 'bewitching spell on Ruben out of jealousy or spite. Ruben Xulu was extremely intelligent but also had a short temper. He was often involved in fights with the neighbours' children. He suffered nightmares for many years after this incident in the forest. See Cormick, *Gcwensa and Xulu*, 24–25.
8   Cormick, *Gcwensa and Xulu*, 26.

In 1960, when Xulu was in Standard 2, the new teacher did not have the patience to give him, a deaf child, the devoted attention he required in class. So Magubane approached Father Kinch and requested that Xulu be placed under the tutelage of the woodcarver at the mission,[9] Bernard Gcwensa. Gcwensa accepted the new apprentice and trained him in woodcarving.

In 1962, Ruben Xulu was baptised a Catholic at the Good Shepherd Mission in Hlabisa.[10] He worked with Gcwensa there for about five years and much of their artwork decorates the Cathedral church.[11] In 1965, Fr Oswin Magrath OP, the Dominican rector of St Peter's Seminary in Hammanskraal, commissioned Gcwensa to carve the chapel doors there.[12] Gcwensa and Xulu worked on them at KwaHlabisa.

In the same year, Kinch was transferred to the parish in St Lucia. Xulu followed him to this new assignment while Gcwensa remained behind in Hlabisa. In St Lucia, Xulu completed many different artworks which are still displayed in the parish church. No longer under Gcwensa's influence, Xulu began to develop his own style. One area where Xulu displayed a different approach to Gcwensa was in portraying Christ as an African man.[13] He also used many different African themes in his work.

In 1971, he accepted a commission to do art for the new church in Matsemhlophe.[14] One of his most famous carvings is in this church. It is a crucifix with the outline of Africa on the face of Christ. Christ was Africa crucified (see Figure 3).

---

9   A doctor advised Ruben Xulu's parents that Ruben could get some assistance at a special school 'where people with "Ruben's type of illness" could get technical tuition.' However, 'the grandfather was adamantly against the idea as he felt it would be like rejecting him [Ruben] as a social outcast simply because of his illness.' See Cormick, *Gcwensa and Xulu*, 25.
10   Ibid, 27.
11   Cormick's book is a visual and textual testament to the artistic abilities of both Xulu and Gcwensa in inculturating the Gospel message within a Zulu context. Cormick, *Gcwensa and Xulu*, 34–43.
12   Cormick, *Gcwensa and Xulu*, 44.
13   Ibid, 8.
14   Ibid, 58–60.

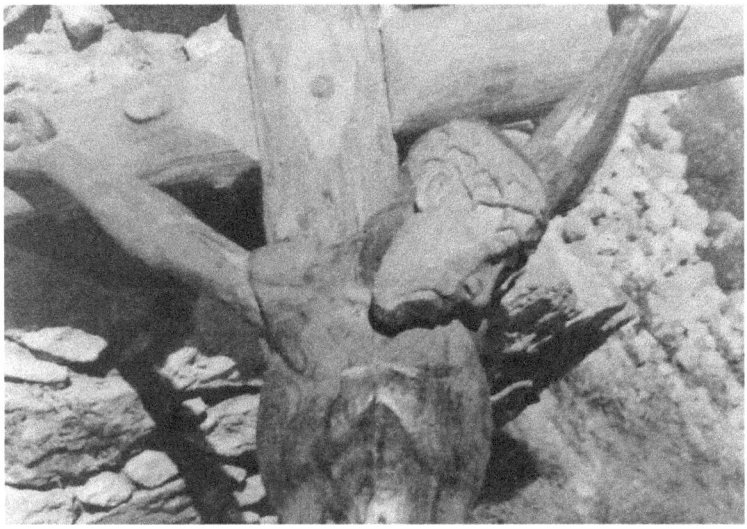

Figure 3: The Xulu crucifix[15]

In one of his earlier works, shown in Figure 4, Xulu portrayed the Madonna and child in contemporary and modern dress with the child Jesus clutching a piece of sugar cane. This highlighted Xulu's appreciation for seeing Christ present and visible in the lives of ordinary people which became much more evident in his later work. This sacramental way of seeing Christ and the sacred incarnate in the life of Zulu people is an extraordinary feature of his work. In a review of Cormick's book, the art historian Elizabeth Rankin and lecturer in Fine Art at the University of the Witwatersrand, wrote:

> Cormick provides us with many examples of the innovative alternatives that Gcwensa and Xulu created. It might be that a work like Ruben Xulu's charming *Mary the Young Mother*, a youthful Zulu woman, barefoot and in a short modern dress and doek, carrying on her hip a lusty toddler who clutches a piece of sugar cane, would seem to some too plebian a

---

15   *TSC*, 13 November 1977, 1. This photograph was on the front page of this issue of *TSC*. The outline of Africa on the Christ's face which was a natural feature of the wood. Permission to reproduce the photograph granted by the editor.

representation of the Mother of God (although there are many 'peasant' Madonnas sanctioned in Western art, in the paintings of Caravaggio and Rembrandt, for example).[16]

Figure 4: *Mary the Young Mother*[17]

Another example of Xulu's ability to bring biblical stories into a Zulu cultural context is evident in one of his sculptures called *Sara Laughing*. Cormick wrote:

---

16 Elizabeth Rankin, 'Book Review: Bernard Gcwensa and Ruben Xulu: Christian Artists of Natal – Dina Cormick,' *Africa Insight*, 23, 4, 1993, 256.
17 Cormick, *Gwensa and Xulu*, 9. Permission to reproduce the photograph granted by Dina Cormick.

> Ruben carved a Zulu Abraham serving his heavenly visitors a traditional Zulu meal ... This is another example of the authentic Africanization of a biblical story at which Ruben excelled. It would be clear to the Zulu people who saw the bas-relief that Abraham had important guests when they noted the selection of meat offered on the platter.[18]

For Rankin, however, the sculpture of the Madonna and child called *Nina weQhawe Sikhulekele*[19] (Mother of the Hero, pray for us) received the greatest praise when she wrote:

> But the image of Mary in traditional Zulu dress, as the principal wife of the chief presenting her firstborn in the guise of a diminutive Zulu warrior in *Nina weghawe sikulekele* (Mother of the Hero) at Njengabantu gives the Madonna all the regal dignity of a medieval Queen of Heaven – in African terms.[20]

Particularly interesting from a theological perspective is that instead of holding a spear with the shield the Christ figure holds a staff with a cross at its head. Jesus is standing with both feet on the snake with his mother's caring and protective hands supporting him (See Figure 5). This highlights that Christ overcomes evil not by violence but by his willingness to offer his life as an act of love by accepting death on the cross for the salvation of all of humanity. His mother stands behind him in loving support.

---

18 Cormick, *Gcwensa and Xulu*, 45.
19 Rankin, following Cormick, used the incorrect Zulu spelling – *Nina Weghawe*. See Rankin, 'Book review,' 256 and Cormick, *Gcwensa and Xulu*, 69.
20 Rankin, 'Book Review,' 256.

Figure 5: Xulu's work depicting the Madonna and child[21]

Growing appreciation for Xulu's art

In 1972 and 1973, Xulu practised his craft extensively in KwaMashu near Durban. In 1974, Xulu moved to Mariannhill where he worked with Sr Johanna Senn and but would go to Seven Oaks often to work with Fr Anton Maier. He did some of his most creative work during this period. At Mariannhill he produced numerous art works of which 60 were sold through the Art Centre. Those purchasing his works were no longer restricted to KwaZulu-Natal but now orders came from the whole country

---

21   Cormick, *Gcwensa and Xulu*, 69. Permission granted to reproduce the photograph was granted by Dina Cormick.

and even internationally.[22] Xulu was not one to stay in one place for a long time – travelling between Mariannhill, KwaHlabisa and Seven Oaks. Fr Maier commissioned him to sculpture eight works for the Seven Oaks parish including an extraordinary Easter candle stand with Jonah emerging from the whale's mouth (Figure 6).[23]

Figure 6: Easter candle stand with Jonah emerging from the whale's mouth[24]

From being an unknown artist from KwaHlabisa, Xulu began to make a name for himself. His art was increasingly being seen as a significant contribution to the Africanisation or inculturation of the Catholic faith in KwaZulu.

---

22 Cormick, *Gcwensa and Xulu*, 114–124.
23 Ibid, 66–71, 124.
24 Ibid, 66. Permission to reproduce the photograph was granted by Dina Cormick.

At an art exhibition at the Mariannhill Art Centre in November 1977, he won first prize for his paschal candle stand with an Exodus theme which depicted Moses leading the children of Israel from Egypt through the Red Sea to the promised land (Figure 7).[25]

Mr Reuben [sic] Xulu's carved cypress-wood paschal candlestick titled Israel's Way to Light is about 1,75 m tall and features 19 figures climbing upwards in a spiral towards the Light of Christ, the Easter candle.[26]

Figure 7: Ruben Xulu standing next to his carving of the Easter candle stand [27]

25 Cormick, *Gcwensa and Xulu*, 69.
26 'Deaf Artist Takes First Prize,' *TSC*, 13 November 1977, 12.
27 Ibid. Permission to reproduce the photograph was granted by the Editor of *TSC*.

Chapter 14

From a Christian perspective, this exodus journey is akin to the journey of faith from slavery to sin, through the waters of baptism and renewal, to come into full knowledge of the light of Christ. Xulu tells this Easter tale with vivid detail and links it with the Exodus account.

Challenging hearing prejudices

Ruben Xulu challenged Catholic understandings of how Christ should be portrayed in art and promoted greater inculturation in the Catholic Church. As Xulu became recognised for his artwork, he also began to assert his dignity as a Deaf person in his personal life and challenged hearing people's perceptions of deaf people.

Brother Florian Langmann CMM, a carpenter in Mariannhill, told Cormick the story of how Xulu, when he was working in Mariannhill around 1975, challenged hearing attitudes that deaf people were backward. At this time, deaf people were still referred to as deaf and dumb.

> [Ruben] had gone to the carpentry shop to collect a piece of wood for a commissioned carving. The men working in the carpentry shop had treated Ruben's inability to speak with a little scorn. However, a few weeks later when Ruben carried back to the workshop the finished carving, he went right up to the men and put it down in front of them as if to say, 'There, take a look! I am somebody!'[28]

Through his art, Xulu demanded respect from the hearing community. He was not prepared to be treated in a scornful or paternalistic way. He was deaf but not dumb. He was a gifted artist. Through his art, he was claiming not only his identity as Zulu and African but also as Deaf.

Xulu died in tragic circumstances in Mariannhill. After being involved in an argument with a hearing man in a shebeen, he was

---

28   Cormick, *Gcwensa and Xulu*, 26.

discovered later stabbed to death outside the convent house on the morning of 14 December 1985.[29]

Evaluation of Xulu's contribution to social change

Ruben Xulu was one of the first Catholic African artists in South Africa to use African themes extensively in his artwork. In doing so he gave an African face to Christianity in Catholic Churches throughout KwaZulu-Natal. Unfortunately, insufficient attention has been given to reflecting on the theological thought that underpinned so much of the art created by Gcwensa and Xulu. They are still to this day under-appreciated both within the Church and without.

James MacDonald writing about Xulu's work in his doctoral dissertation emphasised that Xulu and Gcwensa were among a notable number of African artists who countered 'in some measure the engrained cultural bias of a European-styled Christianity.'[30] Nevertheless, Macdonald criticised Xulu for displaying an ambivalent attitude towards his art because he regularly asked his patrons 'whether the Christ, the Madonna be done as black or white.'[31] Consequently, he concluded that Xulu's work was a 'brokered undertaking driven by the sociological and theological agendas of liberal, white and for the most part foreign missionaries.'[32] Macdonald also concluded that because Gcwensa and Xulu's artwork was so poorly received by several local congregations and priests, their Africanising of Christianity was contested and not readily appreciated.[33]

---

29 This was the sad end to a brilliant deaf sculptor who, with Bernard Gcwensa, challenged the Eurocentric conceptions of Christian art and prepared the way for a greater appreciation of African depictions of Christ, the saints and Christian symbols. See Cormick, *Gcwensa and Xulu*, 3, 75 and 'Deaf Artist Dies Violently,' *TSC*, 12 January 1986, 1.

30 James Macdonald, 'Tracing the Passion of a Black Christ: Critical Reflections on the Iconographic Revision and Symbolic Redeployment of the Stations of the Cross and Passion Cycle by South African Artists Sydney Kumalo, Sokhaya Charles Nkosi and Azaria Mbatha.' Unpublished MA thesis (University of Cape Town, 2016), 5.

31 Macdonald, *Tracing the Passion*, 33.

32 Ibid.

33 Ibid.

This assessment is extremely prejudicial towards Xulu in particular. Underlying this argument is the assumption that Xulu was merely pleasing his benefactors and did not really know his own mind. Unfortunately, the research into Xulu started in earnest only after his death. There are no records of any attempts to interview him and to get his understanding of his work. That Xulu was deaf was a contributing factor as to why no enquiry was ever attempted.

A more sympathetic reading of Xulu's willingness to please his benefactors was that his art was his livelihood. He depended on the money he earned from his work to support himself. He had no other source of income, and so the willingness to please the customer made for good business sense rather than a sign of a character flaw or a desire to fulfil other people's agendas.

Be that as it may, it is vitally important to recognise that Xulu worked primarily within a Church context rather than a political one. The impact of his work needs to be assessed in relation to the impact he made within the Church and secondarily to the political reality.

MacDonald has correctly pointed out that his work was not well received in some quarters of the Church. In making sense of similar experiences in the Church, African theologian, Xolile Keteyi argued, in his incisive book *Inculturation as a Strategy for Liberation*, that Christianity came to Africa with the European settlers and the economically exploiting and civilising agendas of colonisation.[34] Apartheid was itself an extension of this colonising project. African cultures were seen as inferior to Western cultures and so needed to be replaced by the imposition of Western values and cultural norms. In this regard, culture was never neutral but a contested terrain and a site of struggle.[35] In resisting foreign domination and Western cultural values, black people in South Africa 'have always used their culture as a way of holding onto their souls.'[36] The use of art, theatre and music was instrumental

---

34   Xolile Keteyi, *Inculturation as a Strategy for Liberation: A Challenge for South Africa*, (Pietermaritzburg: Cluster Publications, 1998).
35   Keteyi, *Inculturation as a Strategy for Liberation*, 22–24.
36   Ibid, 27.

'to tell the story of their trauma and pain; to proclaim their aspirations and affirm their humanity.'[37]

That some congregations and priests did not appreciate Xulu's work can be seen as a prophetic contribution this artist made. In this regard, Xulu, and Gcwensa to an extent, made an enormous contribution to challenging African people to see that Christianity was not antagonistic towards African cultures but rather embraced them. There was an African way of being Christian. In the African parishes where Xulu's works were displayed, people began to recognise that the Catholic faith was not just another 'European import' but rather a vehicle for acknowledging the intrinsic worth and value of their African cultures and ways of life but also a way to resist the exploitative and oppressiveness of the Western colonial agendas.

For Keteyi, inculturation is the way through which Christianity should propagate itself, liberating itself from the limitations inherent in both the transmitting and receiving cultures and thereby freeing the Gospel to be a renewing and re-evangelising agent in all cultures.[38]

> Inculturation has to show that Christianity is not a universalism that finds a home everywhere, rather it is a concreteness that must be universalized.[39]

Art can make a world of difference to people's mental frames of reference and change the way they see themselves, their lives of faith and their own cultures. Both Ruben Xulu and Bernard Gcwensa's artwork decorated the chapel doors of the St Peter's seminary for African priests in Hammanskraal. Ruben Xulu worked on the Stations of the Cross in the chapel and this undoubtedly influenced the African students who studied at the seminary.[40]

---

37 Ibid, 28.
38 Ibid, 40.
39 Ibid, 41.
40 In 1972, the seminarians at St Peter's were instrumental in forming the St Peter's Old Boys' Association to call for a black rector and more black staff at the seminary. The students were also involved in the establishment of the Black Consciousness

Using Keteyi's idea of inculturation as a strategy for liberation we can have another look at Xulu's artwork through this prism. It is relatively easy to interpret Xulu's image of the suffering Christ on the cross where his face bears the imprint of the African continent (Figure 3)[41] as a sign of his identifying the suffering Christ with the suffering of African people. However, can we not see the face of the suffering Deaf (South) African Christ crucified by phonocentrism and audism too?

Similarly, Xulu's work on the Easter candle stand (see Figure 5) shows African people on the move from the Exodus of oppression towards the liberty promised by the light of Christ.

> Liberation is a process, a movement from victim to subject, from promise to fulfilment. It is not only a movement forward but also an opening up of new possibilities that are qualitatively different and better than what the present is. As such it is a process that is future-oriented which leads to new ways of being community.[42]

Is it legitimate to interpret his carving not only as the journey of African Christians but all black South Africans being liberated from the oppression of apartheid and moving into becoming a new community of the liberated? Considering that Xulu was both African and Deaf, could his work also not speak of the liberative force at work within the Deaf community too?

Can the photograph of Ruben Xulu standing next to his carving of the Easter candle stand[43] not be seen as a tribute to Deaf

---

Movement and the South African Students' Organisation (SASO) on campus. For more information, see George Sombe Mukuka, 'The Impact of Black Consciousness on the Black Clergy and their Training from 1965–1981.' Unpublished M.Th.thesis (University of Natal, Pietermaritzburg, 1996) and Philippe Denis, 'Seminary Networks and Black Consciousness in South Africa in the 1970s,' *South African Historical Journal* 62, 1 (March 2010): 162–182.

41 Interestingly, this also happened to be the first full-colour photograph ever printed by the Catholic weekly. See *TSC*, 13 November 1977, 1.
42 Keteyi, *Inculturation as a Strategy for Liberation*, 48.
43 'Deaf Artist Takes First Prize,' *TSC*, 13 November 1977, 12. In the photograph, Ruben Xulu, the Deaf sculptor, stands next to his work of art that took first prize.

(South) African people as the crucified victims of a hearing world? They are a people who have been called forth in exodus, from the darkness of racist, audist and phonocentric oppression into the wonderful light of a new South Africa where Deafhood and Deaf Gain can flourish. This is the new land where sign language, Deaf culture and the Deaf community are appreciated and respected as contributing to the fulness and variety of human society and Christian life.

Chapter 15

Lindsay Moeletsi Dunn (1959–): Black Consciousness and Challenging Racism and Audism in a Catholic School for the Deaf

Introduction: The rise of Black Consciousness

The Second Vatican Council took place at a time of growing nationalism on the African continent and many African countries were gaining independence from their colonial rulers. Political life in South Africa was not exempt. After the banning of the ANC and PAC, first white and then more so black university students formed the backbone of internal resistance to apartheid.[1] By 1971, Black Consciousness was a prominent feature of political life in South Africa. Steve Biko, a militant black activist and a founder of the Black Consciousness Movement, encouraged black people to recognise their inherent dignity as black people and stand up for their rights. He urged them to reject and resist the white colonial mindset that was being imposed on them to keep them feeling inferior to whites. His famous statement: 'Black man you are on your own', encapsulated this new shift in political life in South Africa. Black Consciousness was a direct rejection of the apartheid policies, especially Bantu Education, which sought to keep black people from regarding themselves as the equal of whites and resigning themselves to an inferior position in society.

Biko wanted black people to have confidence in themselves, their African cultures and in their languages. He rejected the paternalism that was inherent in apartheid and believed that black people had to take control of the struggle for their own freedom.

---

[1] See Julian Brown, *The Road to Soweto* (Johannesburg, Jacana Media, 2016), 20–61.

Biko's militancy had an enormous effect on the struggle against apartheid, which culminated in the Soweto Uprising in 1976.

The spark to these protests was the education policy of introducing Afrikaans as a medium of instruction in township schools by conservative Bantu Education officials like Andries Treurnicht.[2] The imposition of Afrikaans was rejected by students and gave rise to a whole new militancy among the youth of South Africa to work for a new dispensation in South Africa. This influenced raising the awareness of deaf pupils too.

Lindsay Dunn and the August 1976 Wittebome School protest

In Cape Town, a group of school pupils at the Dominican School for the Deaf in the suburb of Wittebome identified with the Soweto protests in an equally dramatic way. In August 1976, black pupils at the school staged a protest against the racist attitudes held by some of the teachers towards their pupils. This virtually unknown event sowed the seeds for Deaf empowerment, autonomy and human rights in South Africa.[3]

---

2   In 1982, Andries Treurnicht later broke away from the National Party and formed his own Conservative Party in opposition to the Tricameral Parliament reforms being introduced by President PW Botha. See Saul Dubow, *Apartheid 1948–1994* (Oxford: Oxford University Press, 2014), 203.

3   Most of the details of this event are the recollections of one person, Lindsay Moeletsi Dunn. Faith Cronwright and Suzanne Lombard alerted me to this event. However, they were vague about the specific details of what transpired during the protest. As there was no archival material relating to this topic, it was not possible to verify all aspects of Dunn's testimony. There is one thing that is without dispute: this event shaped the lives of Lindsay Moeletsi Dunn, Faith Cronwright, Suzanne and Stephen Lombard. It set them on their life paths asserting the dignity of Deaf people. We will investigate this further in chapter 17. There is need for further research on this topic as well as the resistance offered by deaf pupils against hearing domination in schools for the deaf. Despite these shortcomings it was necessary to include this protest in this book as it brings to light a relatively unknown event of anti-apartheid resistance history. It also highlights the value of the oral history approach to data collection.

In August 1976,[4] Standard 7 pupils of the Dominican School for the Deaf in Wittebome staged a sit-in protest. 'We had a two-week sit-in where we attended class but folded our arms and did nothing and said nothing.'[5] Similar to the events in Soweto on June 16, the protest at the Wittebome School erupted spontaneously. 'The irony was that we acted spontaneously as we did not have sufficient information to know how to stage a political resistance activity.'[6] Lindsay Moeletsi Dunn, one of the participants of the boycott, remembers the spark that ignited the pupils' fury. He recounts that Sr Jane (previously known as Fabian), the boys' hostel matron, slapped one of the girls, Jennifer Hess, 'for taking a short-cut through the boys' hall to the playground.'[7] She was 'our "Hector Pietersen!"', Dunn recalled.[8]

'During the breaks, we would sing freedom songs such as *We shall Overcome* in sign language gathering at the playground at the space that Sr Fabian used to sell candy/snacks to us.'[9] Another pupil, Faith Cronwright recalled singing songs during the protest.[10]

Dunn assumed leadership of the sit-in protest because he was 'the most familiar with the Black Consciousness Movement

---

4 Dunn could not remember the exact date. He was 'certain that it was around August 1976 after we had returned from the holiday (if we done that before the winter holidays, I believe we would have been kicked out and not expected to return).' See Lindsay Moeletsi Dunn, personal email to Mark James, 27 April 2018, 472.
5 Lindsay Moeletsi Dunn, personal email to Mark James, 27 April 2018, 472.
6 Ibid.
7 Ibid, 469. In schools for the deaf, the Dominican Sisters taught boys and girls in the same school often from the age of three to eighteen. Inappropriate conduct and interaction between boys and girls in the hostels, especially in the high school, was to be avoided. Strict rules existed in the schools to keep the boys and girls separated from each other outside of the classroom and mealtimes. They were often rigidly enforced. See Cleall, '"Deaf to the Word",' 597.
8 Lindsay Moeletsi Dunn, personal email to Mark James, 21 April 2018, 469.
9 Lindsay Moeletsi Dunn, personal email to Mark James, 27 April 2018, 473.
10 Faith Cronwright, interview conducted by Mark James, 16 November 2015, Heathfield, Cape Town, 427.

and had read the Heinemann African Writers series,'[11] including 'banned materials related to the American Civil Rights movement and the African National Congress.'[12] Dunn was influenced by the writings of Steve Biko but he also grew up in Clermont township outside Pinetown in KwaZulu-Natal in a family with struggle credentials. Dunn's mother 'is Elizabeth Marie Mkame,[13] an iconic figure in Clermont Township especially and in the eThekwini (Durban) region in general.'[14] As a result, Dunn grew up rubbing shoulders with families who were then part of the ANC underground. 'Dr Diliza Mji,[15] for instance, was a family doctor, Phumzile Mlambo-Ngcuka[16] a very close family friend, Thulani Gcabashe,[17] and others who became prominent in the post-apartheid government were all families I had grown up with.'[18]

---

11   Billy Masetlha, a SASM activist in Soweto and a member of the Soweto Students' Representative Council (SSRC) in 1976, remembered reading the African Writers' Series. See interview with Billy Maseltha reproduced in Baruch Hirson, *Year of Fire, Year of Ash, the Soweto Revolt: Roots of a Revolution?* (Cape Town: BestRed, 2016), 331.
12   Lindsay Moeletsi Dunn, personal email to Mark James, 27 April 2018, 473.
13   Elizabeth Mkame is presently an activist for the aged and a member of Age Demands Action (ADA). She is a board member of the Muthande Society for the Aged. Previously, she worked for the Diakonia Council of Churches in Durban for many years. For more information, see the link http://www.helpage.org/blogs/elizabeth-mkame-25201/how-nelson-mandela-inspired-me-as-an-older-person-820/ Accessed 21 July 2018.
14   Lindsay Moeletsi Dunn, personal email to Mark James, 27 April 2018, 471.
15   Diliza Mji was formerly a President of SASO, presently he is the founder and chair of Busamed Hospital Group. See www.sahistory.org.za/people/diliza-mji and www.africaoutlookmag.com/outlook-features/busamed-hospital-group
16   Phumzile Mlambo-Ngcuka was Deputy President under President Thabo Mbeki (2005–2008) but is currently the United Nations Under-Secretary-General and Executive Director of UN Women (2013–). See www.unwomen.org/en/about-us/directorate/executive-director/ed-bio and www.sahistory.org.za/people/phumzile-mlambo-ngcuka. SA History incorrectly state that she was born in Claremont in Durban instead of Clermont near Pinetown. Accessed 8 August 2018.
17   Thulani Gcabashe is presently chair of the board of directors for Standard Bank. See www.standardbank.com/pages/StandardBankGroup/web/directors.html. Accessed 8 August 2018.
18   Lindsay Moeletsi Dunn, personal email to Mark James, 21 April 2018, 469.

During the sit-in, Dunn recalled that one of the teachers, Mrs N.Y. Hebbert, 'asked us who she could talk to as it was obvious, we were protesting something.'[19] Dunn volunteered and gave Mrs Hebbert the list of demands that the pupils had formulated. He also explained to her why they were protesting. 'Mrs Hebbert was furious when she heard that Jennifer Hess was slapped by the boys' matron.'[20] She personally delivered the pupils' list of demands to the principal. As Dunn recounts:

- They demanded that all students be given an education equal to that given to students at St. Augustine's (the hearing school next door to the Deaf school).
- They demanded that the choice of academic or vocational education beyond Standard 6 be made by students themselves.
- They demanded more social integration among girls and boys so that they could learn the proper social etiquette/behaviours expected of them in adulthood.
- They demanded that instruction be in Sign Language in all classes.
- They demanded an end to what they considered to be abuse by school authorities – they saw it as discipline but argued that they were never given a fair say and were punished without the right to present a defence.[21]

Faith Cronwright's memory of why they boycotted was because she and others wanted to go on to get their matriculation certificate.[22] Suzanne Lombard (née Barrett) concurred that they boycotted because they wanted to get their matric and because they wanted more use of sign language in classes at school.[23] The pupils were stonewalled by the principal who did not respond to their demands. Both Lombard and Cronwright said that they were very disappointed with the decision of the school authorities to

---

19 Lindsay Moeletsi Dunn, personal email to Mark James, 27 April 2018, 472.
20 Ibid.
21 Lindsay Moeletsi Dunn, taken from a personal email to Mark James, 21 April 2018, 469.
22 Faith Cronwright, interview conducted by Mark James, 16 November 2015, 427.
23 Suzanne Lombard, interview conducted by Mark James, 13 November 2015, 425.

refuse their request.[24] Dunn was more scathing in his response: 'It was Sr Winnock who was apparently assigned to "investigate". This really was giving Sr Winnock powers to scare us and threaten us with expulsion if we did not name the ringleaders who started this.'[25]

The Dominican sisters refused to entertain any of the demands and the protest and sit-in ended to the dissatisfaction of the pupils. Dunn remembered that 'after the school closed for the summer holidays in December, we were told we were not coming back and there would not be a Standard 8 class to come to.'[26] Faith Cronwright and Suzanne Lombard left school to find employment. As Cronwright recalled:

> At age 16, we had to finish and leave school ... I wanted to study further but my family were poor. They couldn't afford for me to study further and pay for it themselves. So, I had to go out and look for work.[27]

Lombard returned home to Ladysmith in KwaZulu-Natal. Dunn went to study for his matric at Bechet Senior Secondary School in Sydenham, Durban. He earned his matric in 1979 without the aid of any interpreters.

> An Indian classmate who became my buddy throughout my time at Bechet, David Naicker allowed me to copy his notes in class. My hearing aid was not enough for me to understand anything in class, so it was pretty much useless.[28]

---

24 See Faith Cronwright, interview conducted by Mark James, 16 November 2015, Cape Town, 427; and Suzanne Lombard, interview conducted by Mark James, 13 November 2015, Cape Town, 425.
25 Lindsay Moeletsi Dunn, personal email to Mark James, 27 April 2018, 472.
26 Ibid.
27 Faith Cronwright, interview conducted by Mark James, 16 November 2015, Cape Town, 427.
28 Lindsay Moeletsi Dunn, personal email to Mark James, 27 April 2018, 472.

Chapter 15

The implications of the Wittebome protest

The events at Wittebome School were largely inspired by the events of June 16. Dunn pointed out that pupils at the school for the deaf came from all over the country and 'so many were aware of the protests, boycotts and police abuse.'[29] A certain portion of the students were also politicised. Dunn remembered that two of their teachers, Mrs Hebbert and Mrs Arendse, were 'instrumental in exposing us to knowledge that stimulated our inquisitive minds.'[30] In class they discussed and debated political issues of national and international interest from newspaper articles in the *Cape Argus* and *Cape Times*.

This was not the case in all the classes. Dunn recalled a few clashes and ideological disputes he had with Sr Amata in the catechism classes.[31] Having read the writings of Steve Biko, Dunn objected to ideas of racial privilege and that black people 'ought to be grateful to white people for what they have done for us.'[32] When Dunn took exception to something that Sr Amata said in class, pointing out that denying black people 'equality and liberty was nothing to be grateful for,'[33] he would be sent to Mr van der Berg, the shoe-making instructor, to receive a caning for his 'cheeky retorts.'[34] Other deaf students were also conscious of the injustices of apartheid and the racism prevalent in the school. Few, however, were as brave as Lindsay Dunn to challenge the teachers head-on.

This indicates that the protest was not as spontaneous as has been asserted. Firstly, there were no doubt frequent indignities, like attitudes of racial superiority, racism and the extensive use of corporal punishment, that had irked the deaf pupils. These indignities and injustices kept on accumulating and mounting up until the final straw, the slap suffered by Jennifer

---

29 Ibid, 473.
30 Lindsay Moeletsi Dunn, personal email to Mark James, 21 April 2018, 469.
31 Ibid.
32 Lindsay Moeletsi Dunn, personal email to Mark James, 27 April 2018, 472.
33 Lindsay Moeletsi Dunn, personal email to Mark James, 21 April 2018, 470.
34 Lindsay Moeletsi Dunn, personal email to Mark James, 27 April 2018, 470.

Hess, caused them to protest. Secondly, there were possibly also pupils like Dunn who, having read the writings of Steve Biko or influenced by other family members who supported Black Consciousness, refused to accept the injustices in the school any longer. They would have actively encouraged other students to challenge these injustices. Thirdly, there was the influence of the June 16 uprising itself. Deaf pupils were aware that pupils in Soweto, and by this time also in the Western Cape, were protesting against the injustices of apartheid's Bantu Education. It is no surprise that the deaf pupils at Wittebome decided it was time they did something similar in their school and organised the sit-in protest.

But it was not only racial prejudice and injustice that affected the deaf pupils; they also suffered under added prejudices. These were more directly related to the experience of being deaf and being educated orally rather than through the means of sign language. This other system of discrimination has come to be known as audism.

Uncovering audism at the Wittebome School

In the list of demands set before Sr Basil by the protesting pupils, we can see their rejection of what later came to be known as audism – even though the word 'audism' was not in common usage in South Africa in 1976. The first demand, for example, challenged the idea that deaf people are inferior to hearing people. The pupils demanded an education equal to the neighbouring hearing schools in Wittebome, which all offered matric. Implicit in this demand is the question of why hearing children could study for a matriculation certificate but not deaf children. The deaf pupils were able to discern that they were discriminated against because of being deaf. Many of the teachers at the schools for the deaf never questioned government policies regarding deaf children.

This policy was also racially discriminatory. White schools for the deaf like Dominican-Grimley in Cape Town and St Vincent School for the Deaf in Johannesburg offered schooling up to matric for their deaf pupils. At that time, very few if any, black deaf pupils would have been aware that white deaf pupils were able to study for their matric. Back in 1976, there was no contact between whites and blacks even in Catholic schools for the deaf.[35]

White schools for the deaf were given more substantial subsidies that allowed for the purchase of expensive electronic equipment to enhance the residual hearing of their pupils. However, this was not the case in the black schools. The Nationalist government was not prepared to provide education to black pupils up to matric. Schools for the deaf for black pupils only went up to Standard 7 or Standard 8.

The second demand for the right to choose their own future vocational stream, academic or technical as well as the third demand to have greater interaction between boys and girls in the school indicated that the deaf pupils wanted to have a say in how their lives were shaped at school. They wanted a say in how they should be educated. They did not want to be treated paternalistically. The pupils at the Wittebome School wanted a say in the important areas of their lives both as Black and as Deaf people.

The fourth demand for the use of sign language as the medium of instruction in all classes was a direct challenge to the audist approach to education which insisted that deaf children should learn to speak a spoken language and learn lip-reading. This demand goes to the heart of Deaf identity and Deaf culture and the idea that Deaf people have a right to determine the language in which they should be educated. Sign language, for many centuries, was not considered a language but was dismissed, in a derogatory way, as merely primitive gestures.

It was only in the 1960s that linguist William Stokoe, from Gallaudet University in the USA, was able to prove that sign languages had a grammatical structure comparable to any spoken language. Rather than utilising sound, sign languages

---

35   Faith Cronwright, interview conducted by Mark James, 16 November 2015, 430.

utilise space for communication by using hand movements and facial expressions.[36]

Dunn summed it up when he said that 'we had enough experience to understand that the oral method was not effective as a mode of communication in a classroom or on the playground.'[37] The demand to the staff of a school for the deaf that was totally committed to the oral method of deaf education as the most sophisticated, scientific and modern means of education was more than likely seen as proof that the deaf pupils did not understand what was good for them. It was no doubt rejected by teachers as a retrogressive step.[38] It was only with the new democratic South Africa that sign language was fully accepted for the education of Deaf children. South Africa started the roll-out of a South African Sign Language (SASL) curriculum in 2015.[39] In the 2023 SONA address, President Cyril Ramaphosa announced that SASL was recognised as South Africa's twelfth official language.[40]

---

36   For information on the sign language structure, see William Stokoe, 'Sign Language Structure,' *Studies in Linguistics, Occasional papers* 8 (1960) and *Semiotics and Human Sign Languages* (The Hague: Mouton, 1972).
37   Lindsay Moeletsi Dunn, personal email to Mark James, 21 April 2018, 471.
38   'When I went to the school in 1979, oral was the method used in the school ... Sign language was not allowed in the classroom. This was very strict rule in 1979 and most of the Sisters in the school were in favour the Oral/Aural method of teaching. In the hostel the use of signing was discouraged, but it was used by the pupils.' Jacinta Teixeira, interview conducted by Mark James, 13 July 2016, 458.
39   The rollout for Grade R to Grade 3 started in 2015, see 'SA Sign Language added to curriculum,' *Cape Argus*, 1 December 2014. Accessed 9 August 2018, www.iol.co.za/news/south-africa/western-cape/sa-sign-language-added-to-curriculum-1788756. Grade 12 students write the first SASL exams in November 2018, see 'Education Dept Preparing for SA's First Sign Language Exams, *The Citizen*, 23 June 2018. Accessed 9 August 2018, www.citizen.co.za/news/south-africa/1961863/education-dept-preparing-for-sas-first-sign-language-exams
40   See 'Following the recognition by the Department of Basic Education in 2108 of South African Sign Language as a home language and the recommendation by the Parliamentary Constitutional Review Committee that it be the twelfth official language, we are now poised to finalise the matter,' in 'SONA 2020: Read President Cyril Ramaphosa's full speech,' 13 February 2020. Accessed 22 March 2020, www.iol.co.za/news/

The fifth demand criticised the use of corporal punishment. Under apartheid, corporal punishment was permitted in all schools – hearing and deaf. This was not particular to schools for the deaf. It was permissible to discipline children by caning or hitting them on the hands with rulers. However, the significant difference in oral deaf schools was that any deaf child, caught signing in class or on the school playground, was punished by being hit on their hands or fingers with a stick or ruler. This was done to repress the use of sign language so that the deaf child would be compelled to practice speaking and lip-reading during school hours.

Corporal punishment was used so that the teacher in the school environment could re-assert their power and authority over 'cheeky' and misbehaving children. This use of corporal punishment was an exercise of power of the hearing over the deaf, even to the extent where deaf children internalised their 'inferiority' and the audist agenda. Genie Gertz referred to this internalised sense of inferiority as 'dysconscious audism.'[41]

> Dysconscious audistic Deaf people unwittingly help to continue the kind of victimized thinking that they are responsible for their failure. Such thinking enables hearing people to continue pathologizing Deaf people.[42]

In some instances, some deaf people who underwent the oral method of education went through life believing that hearing people were more intelligent than deaf people. They seldom questioned the inadequacy of the oral method of education that was used in deaf schools.

At play too, was the internalised racism of some of the Irish Dominican sisters. According to Dunn, this is precisely the source of the conflict he had with the school administration.[43] As Irish immigrants many of them had grown up in a country that had

politics/sona2020-read-president-cyril-ramaphosas-full-speech-42675302

41 See G. Gertz, 'Dysconscious Audism: A Theoretical Proposition,' in Bauman, *Open your Eyes*, 219–234.
42 Gertz, 'Dysconscious Audism,' 223.
43 Lindsay Moeletsi Dunn, personal email to Mark James, 472.

only recently been liberated from English colonial oppression. Despite this, some sisters had internalised the colonial and racist attitudes of white South Africans.[44]

Due to signing being forbidden in the classrooms or the playgrounds of schools for the deaf, signing went underground. The Deaf people interviewed reported that they signed 'behind our backs', 'out of sight of their teachers like behind a wall' or in the hostels.[45] Nevertheless, the pupils at oral schools for the deaf were aggrieved by this practice. It was perceived as a means of suppressing deaf children's legitimate use of sign language at school and as a tool for education.

The emergence of a 'Deafhood' consciousness

The pupils' five demands indicate an outright rejection of racism and audism. It was an expression and desire for nascent Deafhood. In 2003, Paddy Ladd proposed the idea of 'Deafhood' as an alternative to the use of the word 'deafness.' Deafhood is Deaf people's 'way of being in the world, of conceiving the world and their place within it in both potentiality and actuality.'[46] Deaf identity was not to be understood negatively as those people who lack hearing but rather positively as those who share a common way of being-in-the-world through their language and culture. This way of life is different from that of hearing people. Sign

---

44 At the beginning of 1976, the Cabra Dominican Sisters decided to open all their white schools to children of other races. This was in open defiance of apartheid legislation at the time. For more information on the 'Open Schools' movement, see Pam Christie, *Open Schools: Racially Mixed Catholic Schools in South Africa, 1976–1986*, (Johannesburg: Ravan Press, 1990) and Jude Pieterse and Robyn Picas, *The Open Schools Era: 1976–1986*, (Johannesburg: Marist Brothers, 2020). None of the Cabra schools for the deaf were opened: 'We were not able to take black pupils or join in with the Open Schools' policy of the private Catholic schools and defy government. Our schools being, what we now call "public schools on private property", were 100% dependent on government subsidies to keep going.' Macrina Donoghue, interview conducted by Mark James, 12 July 2016, 447.

45 Depending on the school, a blind eye was turned to the use of sign language in the hostels. See Faith Cronwright, interview conducted by Mark James, 16 November 2018, 427.

46 Ladd, *Understanding Deaf Culture*, 81.

language is at the heart of Deaf identity and is Deaf people's natural language. Those who use sign and identify themselves as belonging to Deaf culture are Deaf whereas those who lack hearing are deaf.[47] Consequently, Ladd talked about Deafhood as 'a process by which Deaf individuals come to actualize their Deaf identity, positing that those individuals construct that identity around several differently ordered sets of priorities and principles.'[48]

Deafhood prevents the victimisation of Deaf people in a predominantly hearing world. Rather, Deafhood empowers Deaf people and changes their consciousness of themselves as people deserving of respect and imbued with dignity. As a result, Deaf people relate differently to the hearing world. Central to this new identity is the role of sign language. Reflecting on his experience at school, Lindsay Dunn wrote years later:

> The Irish Sign Language, which was used at my school, afforded me an opportunity to engage in dialogues regarding racism and audism and how these twin vices affect my life. My subsequent immersion into this world and new consciousness was almost parallel with the Black Consciousness Movement of my generation, which culminated in our rejection of the perceived inferiority of black people as a race. I was now rejecting this perceived inferiority of myself as a deaf person ... Rather than internalizing negative stereotypes of my experiences under a brutal apartheid regime and an ignorant hearing world, I found liberation and hope that there was a very important place for me in this world.[49]

Deaf people are bonded together through sign language and Deaf culture. They want to be respected in their alterity. They want to

---

47 Deaf people with a lower case 'd' refer to those who went deaf later in life and those who attended oral schools and either do not know how to sign or refuse to sign. Deaf with the uppercase 'D' refers to people who adopt the Deaf identity and culture and who use sign language. They seek to assert their dignity as being Deaf, not deaf.
48 Ladd, *Understanding Deaf Culture*, xviii.
49 Lindsay Dunn, 'The Burden of Racism and Audism,' in Bauman, *Open Your Eyes*, 242.

be acknowledged as a linguistic and cultural minority within the hearing world and to determine what is best for themselves.

Racism, audism and the Wittebome protest

Under apartheid, whites thought they knew what was best for black people. The colonial mentality made white people think they were not only superior to black people but could also make decisions for them. Steve Biko challenged these paternalistic attitudes not just among the white supporters of apartheid but also against white liberals and the Left who thought they could speak and act on behalf of the oppressed black majority.

> I am not sneering at the liberals and their involvement. Neither am I suggesting that they are most to blame for the black man's plight. Rather I am illustrating the fundamental fact that total identification with an oppressed group in a system that forces one group to enjoy privilege and to live on the sweat of another, is impossible. White society collectively owes the blacks so huge a debt that no one member should automatically expect to escape from the blanket condemnation that needs to come from the black world. It is not as if whites are allowed to enjoy privilege only when they declare their solidarity with the ruling party. They are born into privilege and are nourished by and nurtured in the system of ruthless exploitation of black energy.[50]

Black Consciousness, for Steve Biko, was an expression of group pride and 'the determination of the blacks to arise and attain the envisaged self.'[51] Black people needed to rally together in solidarity around the cause of their oppression, namely 'the blackness of their skin'[52] and rid themselves of this oppression and servitude imposed upon them by white racism.

---

50 Steve Biko, *I Write What I Like* (Johannesburg: Picador Africa, 2004), 71.
51 Biko, *I Write What I Like*, 74, 101.
52 Ibid.

Linking Biko's thinking to that of Emmanuel Levinas' understanding of proximity can help us take this reflection further. For Levinas, proximity is the encounter with the face of the Other that challenges the self. The encounter with the Other calls the self to give account, to become responsible. This is to realise that, in proximity to the Other, the self is called into question, the totality of self-interest is breached, and is already judged to be unjust. According to Levinas, 'In every social encounter, whether violent or benign, the other person stands as other than the self, as a *no* to the I.'[53]

As Levinas said, 'the face resists possession, resists my powers. In its epiphany, in expression, the sensible, still graspable, turns into total resistance to the grasp.'[54] The resistance of the face breaches totality, not as a force, but as an authority, a plea and a command that 'Thou shall not kill.' Ethical resistance is a call or a summons to the self to responsibility. 'The face of the other in its precariousness and defencelessness is for me the temptation to kill and the call for peace, the "Thou shalt not kill."'[55]

The young students' resistance to the authority of their teachers showed their ethical asymmetry when they call the teachers to account. They do it not from a position of power but rather vulnerability and what Levinas called height, a moral or ethical transcendence, that calls their teachers' attitudes and actions into question and shows them to be unjust. The teachers 'win' the contest by the assertion of their power, their intransigence and their unwillingness to listen to 'cry of the little ones.' They see only rebellion, disobedience and disorder. They do not see the injustices they have committed or perpetuated like their racist and audist attitudes and behaviour.

Integral to the protest, as outlined in the demands made by the pupils, was criticism and active resistance to the white Dominican sisters' 'benevolence' and 'altruism'. The sisters were convinced that they knew what was best for the young black

---

53 Morgan, *The Cambridge Introduction to Emmanuel Levinas*, 69.
54 Levinas, *Totality and Infinity*, 197.
55 Emmanuel Levinas, *Alterity and Transcendence* (London: The Athlone Press, 1999), 141.

deaf children. They were also unaware of their racial prejudices and that they were operating from a perspective of power. In the context of apartheid, integral to the assertion of power was the belief that whites were superior to black people. Whites expected black people to acknowledge and appreciate what was being done for them.

Although the deaf pupils were resisting the racism of apartheid and poor education like their contemporaries in Soweto and the Western Cape, they also realised that they were protesting against the oral method of deaf education. They protested by maintaining spoken silence and sang their freedom songs in sign language. This was a clear rejection of the system of oralism which insisted upon lip-reading and vocalising a spoken language. One of the demands was to have education in sign language but again these demands were pushed aside and the emphasis of the Dominican principal was to instil law and order. This was a preoccupation of the apartheid state too.

Consequently, it is not surprising that the protest fizzled out after two weeks. It led to no immediate changes at the school. At least, the seeds of change were at hand. Deaf people were showing that they were taking their liberation into their own hands. They wanted to enjoy the same rights and privileges of hearing people both in Church and society. However, the days of the oral method of Deaf education, like apartheid, were numbered. The oral method persisted in the school for another 15 years and apartheid for another 18 years. The Dominican sisters failed in their compassionate responsibility to their Deaf neighbours whom they were called to serve.

Dunn's present occupation and writings

After leaving school, Dunn went to the United States to study at Gallaudet University in Washington DC. After graduating, he remained on as a lecturer. He is presently dedicating his life to enhancing the lives of Black Deaf people by exposing injustice, prejudice, racism and audism in all manifestations within society. He has written extensively on these subjects and is an activist for

Chapter 15

the dignity of Black Deaf people in the United States and across the globe.

Chapter 16

Fr John Turner CMM (1945–2013): Pastor and Teacher

John Turner was born in Johannesburg on 25 August 1945. Unlike Axelrod, Turner was a cradle Catholic. He was hard of hearing and attended St Vincent School for the Deaf in Johannesburg. After completing his schooling, he went to work as a jeweller for Max Segal.[1] A few years later he felt the call to priesthood and entered the novitiate of the Mariannhill Missionaries in KwaZulu-Natal. His novice master was Fr Urs Fischer CMM. He studied at St Joseph's Scholasticate at Cedara near Pietermaritzburg and was ordained to the diaconate at Mariannhill Monastery on 12 March 1978[2] and then to the priesthood by Bishop Ernest Green on 9 December 1978.[3]

Early ministerial life

After his ordination, John Turner was sent to be curate to Fr John Driessen CMM, the parish priest in Umzinto. Driessen was very interested in working with the deaf. Together they developed an integrated ministry for both hearing and Deaf within the parish. This was new and innovative and had not been tried before. The celebration of the Eucharist was integrated, hearing and deaf together. When Driessen said Mass, Turner would interpret by signing the spoken word to the Deaf people in Church. They also used visual aids, like pictures and sketches to make the message clear to both hearing and Deaf people.[4] This was instructive to

---

1 'Silent Workshop,' *The Star*, 30 August 1962, 6.
2 'A Priest for the Deaf,' *TSM*, June 1978, 9.
3 'SA Deaf Honour Bishop Today,' *TSC*, 29 June 1980, 8.
4 John Driessen CMM, interview conducted by John Turner CMM, posted on 12 May 2012. Accessed 2 August 2014, www.deafcatholicchurch.mariannhillmedia.org and www.youtube.com/watch?v=Md4eB1qMrr4

both groups. The hearing and the deaf were able to appreciate one another's gifts and differences.

From his base in Umzinto, John Turner started making monthly visits to Durban and Pietermaritzburg to visit the deaf people in these cities and celebrate the Eucharist with them. Turner was also an excellent catechist and would teach the deaf about the Catholic faith after the Eucharistic celebration. He also got to know Deaf Catholics in Zululand and so his mission extended to the whole of Natal.

Collaboration with Cyril Axelrod

As the first two Deaf priests in South Africa, Cyril Axelrod and John Turner sought to work together. In 1980 or 1981, they conducted an Easter retreat together at Red Acres, Cedara in KwaZulu-Natal. Axelrod remembered that:

> One of our unforgettable ministry experiences together was a retreat during Easter weekend at Cedara. John and I worked together. We had such an impact among the Catholic and non-Catholic deaf people. It focussed on the drama of Holy Thursday, Good Friday and Easter vigil. It was such a powerful experience, but it never came again.[5]

Axelrod expressed regret that he and John Turner were never able to collaborate again. He attributed this to the differences between himself and Fr John Turner.

> There was a difference between myself and Fr John. It is what? My work with the deaf is broad. My focus was on human and social development. I built up a school and worked in different places. Fr John basically said Mass. That's all. His approach was narrow, whereas mine was broader.[6]

---

5 Cyril Axelrod, personal email to Mark James, 15 March 2015.
6 Cyril Axelrod, interview conducted by Mark James, Dunnottar, 30 September 2015, 401.

Francois de Villiers remembered that the differences between Turner and Axelrod also stemmed from the fact that Turner felt that Axelrod was too liberal in his interpretation of Catholicism and his pastoral outreach. Turner, on the other hand, was much more traditional.[7] Axelrod continued to minister to deaf Catholics, including the Deaf people who had left the Catholic Church whereas Turner ministered primarily to the faithful Catholics.

Nevertheless, the needs of the Deaf around the country were so extensive that they decided it would be better to divide the work.[8] John Turner concentrated on the Deaf community in KwaZulu-Natal and later expanded to the kingdom of Swaziland. Cyril Axelrod focused on Johannesburg, Pretoria, the Eastern Cape and later Cape Town.

Within five months, pastoral ministry to the deaf in South Africa lost two signing priests, Bishop Green, who passed away, and Cyril Axelrod, who left Cape Town to work with the Deaf communities in Macau and Hong Kong. This meant that Fr John from Mariannhill remained the only signing priest working with the deaf in South Africa.

Saying Mass and teaching catechism at KwaThintwa

In 1981, Fr John Turner became pastorally involved in the KwaThintwa School for the Deaf in Inchanga, receiving a stipend for his work from the Archdiocese of Durban.[9] He said Mass at the school every second Sunday of the month as well as every Tuesday before lunch. On the other Sundays, the children attended the parish Masses at Inchanga parish and a teacher interpreted for the children. Fr John's other commitments included teaching catechism to the children, especially the First Holy Communion

---

7   Francois de Villiers, interviewed by Mark James, Edenvale, 4 August 2016, 463-464.
8   Ibid, 460.
9   'I would like to say a sincere thank-you for your interest in the Deaf people of Natal as well as Kwa Thintwa Deaf School at Inchanga. Thank-you also for your kind financial help to me for the Apostolate for the Deaf.' See 'Letter from Father John Turner CMM to Archbishop Hurley,' 8 June 1982, see Hurley Archives, SJTI, BIO 11C.

class each Thursday. Turner used Total Communication in his interaction with the children.

Turner was a born teacher. Archbishop Hurley, writing about him in his annual school report for 1983/84, said: 'His [Fr Turner's] ingenuity in using signs, fingerspelling and illustrations is bearing gradual fruit and we are grateful for his interest and dedication.'[10]

Turner excelled in explaining Catholic dogma and teachings in such a way that deaf people were able to appreciate the depth of the Catholic faith. In his sermons he always used illustrations and he was not averse to transforming the sanctuary into a classroom. He would set up a blackboard or use newsprint and coloured koki pens to draw pictures or write up concepts. As Francois de Villiers describes:

> He always brought a blackboard with him and would draw a picture of the relationship between people and the Spirit. It was always very interesting. He would write down a list of the good and a list of the bad. He would explain the relationship between them. He would explain why this is good and why this is bad. I can't remember all he said but the way he was teaching us, it was excellent. I used to enjoy his sermons. Every time he came to Johannesburg to say Mass we used to always come to his church because we knew that church was going to be brilliant and enjoyable.[11]

British theologian Wayne Morris who worked with Deaf communities in the United Kingdom observed that 'sermons are rarely if ever monologues in Deaf churches.'[12] Turner's approach bore witness to this. His sermons were interactive and informal without being chaotic. When the space allowed it, Turner would often get Deaf people to sit in a semi-circle at Mass so that they

---

10   'Annual report 1 April 1983–31 March 1984,' 17, Archbishop Hurley's Papers, Box 109, File: KwaThintwa School 1984, Hurley Archives, SJTI BIO 11C.
11   Francois de Villiers, interview conducted by Mark James, Edenvale, 4 August 2016, 460.
12   Wayne Morris, *Theology with Words: Theology in the Deaf Community* (Aldershot, Hampshire: Ashgate, 2008), 127.

could more easily interact during the sermon, especially when someone made a comment or asked a question.[13] He knew how to make people relax and celebrate together.

> One time before he started Mass he came out of the sacristy and saw deaf people sitting in church. He looked around and saw that they were all looking very serious. They didn't look happy. He said: 'No, the people are too serious. They should be happy.' He decided to tell one joke before Mass started. He told the joke and we all laughed and laughed. When he saw people laughing, he said: 'That's better, now we can start the Mass.' He had a lovely sense of humour.[14]

At the reading of the Gospel, Catholics make the sign of the cross on their foreheads, mouths and hearts. Turner added the sign of the cross on each hand too. Deaf people's hands were used for speaking. In these ways, Turner attempted to inculturate the Catholic Mass and to make allowances for Deaf culture and experience within the liturgy.

When Fr Turner first started in ministry, he was open to working with Deaf people from other churches and religions. In 1983, both he and Cyril Axelrod served on the SANCD's Spiritual Welfare Committee[15] ministering to Deaf people regardless of their faith. John Turner was also a long-standing member of the Natal Association for the Deaf based in Durban.[16]

Later in his life, however, Turner became less open to other Deaf Christians, especially when he perceived that the Deaf Christian Fellowship (DCF) and similar churches were drawing Catholics away from their faith and encouraging them

---

13 Morris observed that in deaf churches 'visibility is crucial and determines the arrangement of furniture.' Morris, *Theology Without Words*, 126.
14 Francois de Villiers, interview conducted by Mark James Edenvale, 4 August 2016, 461.
15 Letter, Beryl Jones to Archbishop Hurley, 12 September 1983. Archbishop Hurley's Papers, Box 109 File: KwaThintwa School 1984, Hurley Archives, SJTI, BIO 11C.
16 See 'Fifty-Six Years of Service to the Deaf,' *TSM* 59, 7, July 1990, 2 and 'News from Natal,' *TSM* 61, 7, July 1992, 3.

to join, what he saw as, fundamentalist churches. Even though he disagreed with this, he was never confrontational.

> He was very humble. He never showed off. There were lots of deaf people with the wrong beliefs who told Fr John what he must do, and he would say: 'Oh, Oh!' but he knew that they were talking rubbish. It was a waste of time to argue about small things that were not important. Also, what I see as a clear picture from Fr John, he tried to get the Deaf people to focus on the holy Mass, but Deaf people are blind. They can't see anything there. They see the tabernacle, they see the candles, the table, but it means nothing to them. It is because they are distracted. He never wanted to fight and show off what it meant. If they said –what they said –it was fine. He always kept himself humble. But if people were interested then he would encourage them, support them, continue to explain what the Catholic faith means.[17]

In 1984, Fr John formed the 'A-Team'[18] with his brother Brian Turner[19] and Debbie Eaton.[20] They travelled together as a pastoral team visiting Catholic Deaf communities throughout South Africa, Zimbabwe, Swaziland and Botswana providing catechetical, pastoral and spiritual care.

> He went to Zimbabwe once because petrol was cheap but he never went again because of financial problems. Most of the time he travelled around South Africa, to Swaziland and Mozambique. In South Africa, he went to Hammanskraal, Cape Town, Port Elizabeth and Johannesburg. He came to

---

17   Francois de Villiers, interview conducted by Mark James, Edenvale, 4 August 2016, 462.
18   This is a reference to a popular American TV series about a group of ex-Special Forces soldiers who became mercenaries that was screened on SABC-TV from about 1985–1991. Another indication of Turner's sense of humour.
19   Brian Turner's primary task was to be the A-Team driver.
20   Debbie Eaton helped with catechetical instruction. Debbie Eaton had been a pupil at the Dominican school for the deaf in Wittebome and had wanted to become a religious sister. However, she could not find a congregation willing to accept her. She had declared private vows and her consecration to virginity before Archbishop Hurley on 14 December 1991.

Johannesburg lots of times. He also went to Rustenburg to the school for the deaf in Rustenburg and he would say Mass there. He invited us to join with him and he was very good at getting people in the community to work together. Sometimes there were problems with understanding each other because of the different sign languages but otherwise things went very well.[21]

The 'A-Team' produced catechetical resources for the Deaf and used the latest technology when ministering to the Catholic Deaf communities that they served. Turner's sermons were videotaped and distributed among Deaf communities all over South Africa and Swaziland. He also developed a successful ministry on television doing *Thy Kingdom Come* programmes on SABC in sign language.[22] Turner's success in this ministry fulfilled a challenge to which Axelrod, eleven years previously, had not been able to respond.[23]

When Turner was not travelling, he stayed at the Mariannhill monastery and transformed an old house into a chapel for the Deaf community called *Ephphatha*. This recalled the words Jesus spoke to the deaf man when he prayed and healed him, saying: 'Be opened' (Mk 7:34).

Turner became an accomplished preacher to deaf people. He had a wonderful technique of contextualising his preaching and being able to use current events to make a theological point. In his chapel, he developed a series of sermons based on the three-year cycle of Sunday readings which he videoed onto DVDs. These he distributed to Deaf people all over the country so that they could have a sermon in signed English available for them every Sunday. Turner serialised the book, *The Joy of Being Catholic*, a basic catechism written by Bishop Oswald Hirmer, onto DVD.

---

21 Francois de Villiers, interview conducted by Mark James, Edenvale, 4 August 2016, 460. Also see www.deafcatholicchurch. mariannhillmedia.org. Accessed on 15 February 2014.
22 See 'Sermon for Deaf on TV,' *TSC*, 7 June 1987, 1 and 'Deaf Sign Language on TV tonight,' *TSC*, 17 April 1988, 1.
23 See Chapter 12 on Pastor Stallings and his television ministry in sign language.

Bringing the Church to the Deaf people of God

Turner had a gift for making the Catholic Church accessible to Deaf people. His teaching style was simple but profound. In some respects, John Turner developed a Deaf inculturation in his style of saying Mass and making Deaf people feel at home in the Church. He took Deaf culture seriously and made the faith accessible to the Catholic Deaf Community. When people could not come to Mass, Turner, together with the 'A-Team', went out to tend to the scattered flock all over South Africa and Swaziland, bringing them the good news and the sacraments.

However, as Turner's health declined, the number of trips around the country declined until his sudden and untimely death on 17 June 2013. He was buried in the Mariannhill cemetery on 25 June 2013, aged 67 years old.

Just before Turner's death, the Congregation of Mariannhill Missionaries sent Fr Lufeyo Mpaha CMM, a newly ordained priest, to the University of the Witwatersrand to study SASL and Deaf Education. Mpaha continues the ministry established by Fr John Turner.

Chapter 17

The Deaf Community of Cape Town: Sign-Deaf Space as Breathing Spaces for Prophetic Ministry

Deafhood can be characterised as the process that Deaf people experience as they become aware of their innate dignity and identity as a community of people with their own language and cultural traditions. Central to the development of this sense of Deafhood and cultural identity is sign language. In the chapters on the lives of Robert Simmons, Cyril Axelrod and Lindsay Moeletsi Dunn, there was an attempt to highlight the early pioneers, at least in the Catholic Church, who promoted Deafhood in South Africa. Integral to this was to make Deaf people proud of their Deaf culture and sign language and to conscientise them so that they did not acquiesce to being marginalised. Some Deaf people in the Western Cape took up the baton and made their contribution to the transformation of Church and society.

During the 1980s, the United Democratic Front (UDF) mobilised and organised diverse groups of people, across various racial, class and political affiliation boundaries, into an organisation to oppose apartheid. 'People's power' provided an overall strategy to mobilise and unite people, thereby building the organisation, and also providing the political education necessary to resist the apartheid government.[1]

This chapter shows how within the Deaf community, the institutional and organising of Deaf people into different Deaf organisations accounted for a significant shift in strategy too. It provided breathing spaces for Deaf solidarity and community which made Deaf people more aware of their human rights and their sense of Deafhood. In building up a participatory

---

1   Jeremy Seekings, *The UDF: A History of the United Democratic Front in South Africa, 1983–1991*, (Cape Town: David Philip, 2006), 174.

organisation, Deaf women were also empowered. All the actions undertaken pointed to a prophetic response to the divisiveness of apartheid where a marginalised group found ways to point to a new future for themselves but also for the country.

The Deaf Community of Cape Town

In Cape Town, a Deaf NGO was started with a strong local flavour. Faith Cronwright recalled that the first time that the establishment of the Deaf Community of Cape Town (DCCT) was mooted as a Deaf initiative was after one of the Masses held on the third Sunday of every month:[2]

> I came to the Mass on the THIRD SUNDAY regularly and socialised with the Deaf. After one of the Masses, Stephen [Lombard] asked us: 'What problems do the Deaf have and what do they need?' We reflected on the social problems affecting Deaf people. Father Cyril said we need to start a group and build it up to help Deaf people ourselves. We didn't know how to do this. So, he helped us and we tried.[3]

As a consequence of this discussion, in 1987, this group of past pupils of the Wittebome School, with the assistance of Fr Cyril Axelrod CSsR,[4] started DCCT. Axelrod had recently been transferred to Cape Town after leaving Johannesburg. Cronwright remembered that 'Fr Cyril planted a seed and told us we must carry on and so it grew and developed from there.'[5]

From the outset, the DCCT was concerned with the grassroots upliftment of deaf people in the Western Cape regardless of race, religion or creed. The founding members of DCCT were all Deaf. They were Stephen Lombard, Wilma

---

2   The Third Sunday Mass was held on the third Sunday of every month. In sign language became known as THIRD SUNDAY. It is capitalised to indicate that this is a gloss or a direct translation of a sign into English.
3   Faith Cronwright, interview conducted by Mark James, 15 November 2015, Cape Town, 428.
4   Ibid.
5   Faith Cronwright, interview conducted by Mark James, 15 November 2015, Cape Town, 429.

Newhoudt,[6] Suzanne Lombard, Faith Cronwright and Sue Bruce.[7] Interestingly, three of the five founders – Faith Cronwright, Stephen and Suzanne Lombard – had been involved in the Wittebome School protest in August 1976.

DCCT was possibly the first organisation of Deaf people serving other Deaf people. Most of the other deaf organisations like the SANCD and Deaf Equal Awareness Foundation (DEAF) had hearing people in prominent leadership positions.

Stephen Lombard was appointed the administrator of DCCT and Faith Cronwright worked as his secretary. They identified the needs of deaf people in the Western Cape and began to develop programmes that could respond to these needs.

> We developed programmes and projects for Deaf people. The organisation had mothers' groups, women's groups, a literacy programme – Adult Basic Education and Training (ABET), audiology, and computer training.[8]

The following year, Fr Cyril left to minister to the deaf in Hong Kong[9] and Wilma Newhoudt went to study at Gallaudet University in Washington DC for a social work degree.[10] That DCCT not only survived but continued to grow and flourish after the departure of Axelrod and Newhoudt is testament to the leadership that remained behind.

After the departure of Fr Cyril Axelrod for Asia, Fr Peter John Pearson was appointed chaplain to the Deaf. He worked closely with Mr Nick Bruce, who was a teacher at St Joseph's Marist School in Rondebosch.[11] While hearing, nevertheless, he was fluent in sign language as Sue Bruce his wife was Deaf. Sue was involved

---

6   Wilma Newhoudt was the only non-Catholic founder of DCCT. She was the daughter of a Protestant pastor. See Nick Bruce, 'Deaf Cape Student Graduates in US,' *TSC*, 2 August 1992, 2.
7   Faith Cronwright, interview conducted by Mark James, 15 November 2015, Cape Town, 429.
8   Ibid.
9   'SA Priest off to Work in Asia,' *TSC*, 14 August 1988, 12.
10 Faith Cronwright, personal email to Mark James, 1 April 2018.
11 'Sign Language Easter for Cape Deaf,' *TSC*, 24 April 1988, 12 and 'Letter, Axelrod to Sr Mannes,' 28 April 1988.

in DCCT's women's group and later the sewing group. Bruce was studying for the permanent diaconate. He was eventually ordained deacon by Archbishop Lawrence Henry in Bergvliet, Cape Town on 21 September 1991.[12]

By 1990, Stephen Lombard and Faith Cronwright continued as director and secretary respectively but Nick Bruce was included as the financial administrator of DCCT. He was also asked to manage and administer the Deaf hostel in Heathfield.[13] Under Lombard, Cronwright and Bruce's leadership, various projects were developed by DCCT and implemented throughout the Western Cape. The work of DCCT started initially on helping Deaf people find employment and cope in the workplace as many misunderstandings were happening in the workplace between hearing and deaf people.[14] By 1993, following the visit of a BSL teacher Judith Collins[15] who taught five sign language teachers, DCCT also set up the Sign Language Teaching project to teach hearing people sign language.[16]

The organisation also started literacy classes for the Deaf in Khayelitsha and Langa and helped Deaf people deal with accessing disability grants and maintenance payments. DCCT also helped Deaf people deal with marital and family conflicts and they offered counselling for HIV and AIDS, alcoholism and drug addiction.

12   'Deacon to the Deaf Ordained,' *TSC*, 6 October 1991, 3.
13   'SA Deaf Priest off to Work in Asia,' *TSC*, 14 August 1988, 12.
14   Faith Cronwright explained about some of the challenges that Deaf people experienced at work. '[W]hen hearing people make fun of you or laugh at Deaf people, the Deaf people can get very angry and want to fight. We always explain to the hearing people that you talk, and we sign, and explain that you must not just laugh ... You need to explain and say if you want to learn sign language, fine. We can teach them sign language, basic sign language so it makes it easy to communicate.' In another example, Cronwright said that '[If] Deaf people are working as seamstresses and they need to communicate with someone else they have to stop their work in order to speak to other people. Now a hearing person will ask them: "Why you stopping work?" but not understand that they must stop in order to communicate. So, hearing people need to understand how to communicate with Deaf people.' See Faith Cronwright, interview conducted by Mark James, Cape Town, 16 November 2015, 432.
15   'Sign Language Expert Teaches in South Africa,' *TSM*, 61, 7, July 1992, 3.
16   'Deaf Community of Cape Town Annual Report, 1993,' 3.

Central to the developments was the establishment of a women's support group in July 1993. It was to function as a support group for Deaf women where they could freely express their feelings and experiences. Many had domestic or work-related problems which they were able to discuss and they could share their struggles. Together they formulated ways to accompany and assist each other. Twenty-one women originally participated in these meetings of which seven were elected to act as an executive committee. It was empowering Deaf women to take the initiative themselves.[17]

One of these actions that they undertook as women in DCCT was to protest about the lack of accommodation for women at the Deaf hostel. When Bishop Green founded the hostel in 1947, it only provided accommodation for Deaf men. Jennifer Gillespie remembered that:

> [O]nly men stayed here under Bishop Green. No women were allowed ... Then one of the women began to moan and moan that there needs to be a building for women too. When Bishop Green left, they built one for the women.[18]

After the renovations were completed, there was accommodation for about twelve women and twenty men.[19]

Another initiative arising from the women's group was the establishment of a sewing project. Unemployed Deaf women were taught to sew and to produce bags and children's clothing as a way to generate income for themselves. It later developed into a self-sustaining project that generated income to supplement DCCT's work.

But they realised that they also had a responsibility to affirm the dignity of Deaf people by encouraging all Deaf people

---

17 Members of the Women's group travelled to the United States in 1994 to attend the graduation of Wilma Newhoudt from Gallaudet University in Washington DC with a MA in social work. See 'Deaf Woman Attains Master's Degree in the USA,' *TSM*, 7/94, July 1994, 6.
18 Jennifer Gillespie, interview conducted by Mark James, 12 November 2015, Cape Town, 410.
19 Ibid.

to appreciate themselves, their language and their culture. DCCT's mission was not only to address people's social needs but their spiritual ones too.

The THIRD SUNDAY as a Sign-Deaf space

Alongside the community development work, the micro-enterprise projects, the literacy and the sign language classes, DCCT kept up the tradition of the THIRD SUNDAY Mass started in 1940 by Father Ernest Green. Green was an accomplished signer and always signed the Mass in the Corpus Christi parish church in Wittebome where he was parish priest. Later when Fr Green left to become bishop of Port Elizabeth, the venue for the Mass was moved to St Joseph's Marist Brothers' College in Rondebosch, then to the Bastion in Newlands and eventually to its present home at the Deaf hostel in Heathfield.

The THIRD SUNDAY was a time for expressing one's faith by attending the church service. It was also to socialise and to receive information about Deaf events and happenings in the Western Cape. It was a time for community-building. It was predominantly, what sociologist Marion Heap called, a Sign-Deaf space but it was a Sign-hear space too.[20] There is a qualitative difference between the two spaces. Sign-hear spaces are spaces where Deaf people respond to living in a hearing world, where they interact with hearing people and adapt themselves to the hearing person's ability or inability to sign. In contrast, 'Sign-Deaf spaces were about creating spaces of communality and solidarity, spaces as DCCT expressed it, where people "felt" that they "belonged" and could identify with "other deaf people."'[21]

DCCT was a space where Deaf people could be themselves with other Deaf people. Heap quotes from an attendee she interviewed:

---

20   Marion Heap, 'Crossing Social Boundaries and Dispersing Social Identity: Tracing Deaf Networks From Cape Town,' Unpublished PhD diss. (Stellenbosch: University of Stellenbosch, 2003), 92, 142.
21   Ibid, 128.

'I go to meet friends', explained Jane. For Jane, a staunch Baptist on other Sundays of the month, Third Sunday was not about being Catholic, nor strictly about worship. 'It's like being at a family wedding' was how my mother, who often accompanied me, described the ambience.[22]

It was a space that cultivated and nurtured Deafhood.[23] In this space, sign language as first language predominated and the social ties and relationships between Deaf people were deepened and celebrated in liturgy and in community life. News was shared, relationships deepened and so the Deaf network was enhanced. It was more than just a network of friends and Deaf people.

The THIRD SUNDAY as a counter-witness to apartheid

In this Sign-Deaf space, friendships developed across racial, denominational and religious divides.[24] It was not, and still is not, limited to Catholics. As Faith Cronwright recounts: 'DCCT had all the different races of Deaf people. They were all integrated and mixed together, Muslims, white, black and coloured. It was fine.' [25]

The THIRD SUNDAY provided a space where the crossing of the boundaries of race, age, religion or denomination was experienced, where friendships and bonds of cooperation were established. Within the context of apartheid South Africa, this was an attempt to realise a non-racial, non-sexist, non-sectarian and non-audist community where different people were drawn together through sharing a desire to celebrate and work for the good of the Deaf community. Sign language and Deaf culture proved to be the glue that drew this community of peace together and kept it bonded.

---

22 Ibid, 125.
23 This is indicative of a growing emphasis on Deaf Gain which celebrates the gains of being Deaf, for Deaf people themselves and for church and society. It is a sign of a post-audist perspective which is a moving beyond the hearing and Deaf divide. See Guy McIlroy, *The Implementation of SASL*, 24.
24 Heap, 'Crossing Social Boundaries,' 41–145.
25 Faith Cronwright, interview conducted by Mark James, 15 November 2015, Cape Town, 431.

The THIRD SUNDAY as a prophetic, ethical and messianic space

DCCT reflected what the philosopher Emmanuel Levinas has called prophetic eschatology or the eschatology of messianic peace.[26] This community pointed beyond the society and Church in which it found itself and inspired people to live from a new and transformed vision of life. For Levinas, a prophetic eschatology is life that overflows and breaches the history of war among peoples. This state of war arises from self-interest, which for Levinas, gives rise to competitive and violent relations between people. Where a person recognises his or her responsibility for the suffering neighbour, they change from being a self-for-itself or self-interested ego to becoming dis-interested and a responsible self or a self-for-the-other or what he calls 'to be *otherwise than being.*'[27]

People are obligated to one another and called upon to act for the good of the suffering one. We are not isolated individuals concerned with personal salvation but a people journeying together and responsible for one another. For Levinas, people who recognise that they are responsible for their neighbour live ethically and prophetically. They display their true humanity because they recognise that they are not solitary individuals but people already in relation to others. Even the language they speak, the culture and religions they practice, pre-existed them. They received them from others and they were not of their own creation. Likewise, people who recognise their true humanity are those who see that they are responsible not only for themselves or their loved ones but primarily for the suffering other, that is, one's neighbour.

For Levinas, what is of concern is not my death but the death of my neighbour. Consequently, in proximity to the suffering other, the self needs to be a neighbour by offering even the bread destined for one's own mouth.[28] This is the practice of justice and, where justice as an ethical relation to the neighbour reigns,

---

26 Levinas, *Totality and Infinity*, 22–24.
27 Levinas, *Otherwise than Being*, 4.
28 Levinas, *Otherwise Than Being*, 74.

an eschatological community of peace and hope is born. For Levinas, the eschatological is the 'beyond of history' that draws people out of the history of contestation, violence and war, and inaugurates a new and different future, where people live their full responsibility to the needs of the suffering of the world.[29]

In theological terms, this is what Christians refer to as a sign of the reign of God breaking into human history. Organisations and Christian social movements that respond to the suffering of marginalised people and work to overcome the 'globalisation of indifference',[30] are referred to, by American theologian Kevin Ahern, as 'structures of grace.'[31] By working for social justice and social transformation, these social movements enable people to experience God's grace in their lives.

The THIRD SUNDAY as a breathing space

In his later writings, Levinas used the image of human breathing as a way of understanding the ethical relation where one recognises one's responsibility for one's neighbour. He wrote:

> In human breathing ... we have to already hear the breathlessness of an inspiration that paralyzes essence, that transpierces it with an inspiration by the other, an inspiration that is already an expiration.[32]

The THIRD SUNDAY was a space where Deaf people could be themselves to breathe freely and inspire one another as we saw above in the attempts to build friendships beyond the divisions imposed by apartheid. It was a space for communality and solidarity 'where people "felt" that they "belonged" and could identify with "other deaf people".'[33] This Sign-space was a creative space, a compassionate space, one in which they could relax and live as a sign language people despite their differences

---

29 Levinas, *Totality and Infinity*, 23.
30 Pope Francis, *Evangeli Gaudium*, 54.
31 See Kevin Ahern, *Structures of Grace: Catholic Organizations Serving the Global Common Good*, (Maryknoll, NY: Orbis Books, 2015), 125–142.
32 Emmanuel Levinas, *Otherwise Than Being*, 180.
33 Heap, 'Crossing Social Boundaries,' 128.

determined by society and religion. As we have already seen, they came together as fellow human beings in prophetic contradiction to the separating ideology of apartheid regardless of race or class.

It was a prayerful space where they praised God together in sign language despite religious differences. It was a space within which friendships were enhanced, cultural ties and bonds strengthened and an opportunity for the most vulnerable within the community to articulate their needs and challenges.

In this sense, DCCT pointed to a new reality for the Deaf community where to use Levinas' words, their breathing 'transpierces' the injustices of the present and inspires an expiration, that is, a movement outwards responding to the needs of the most vulnerable. This was visible in all the social programmes that DCCT embarked upon. Breathing and expiration is the saintly work that transforms life as it reaches out to those who are vulnerable and marginalised in society and in church.

Theologically, the breathing, prophet and ethical space DCCT provided was space for the breaking through or breathing of the Holy Spirit upon the community. It was a moment where heaven and earth met. This is the breaking in of the reign of God, or as Levinas says more philosophically, it is the trace or means by which God comes to mind. A graced moment of ethical transformation for the Deaf community in the Western Cape where the history of war, hatred and division, so commonplace in human relations, was at least momentarily overcome.[34]

DCCT – A community of hope always in need of reform

Levinas is also quick to point out that at the level of the political, the search for justice is always a continual search for a better justice, a more lasting peace.[35] It does not last forever as the political reality of life is constantly shifting. Nevertheless, for Levinas, the political needs to always recognise that it is in debt to the ethical relation. The political or justice is always an

---

34   Levinas, *Totality and Infinity*, 23.
35   Wright, Hughes, Ainley, 'The Paradox of Morality,' 177-178.

approximation of the ethical. The political is always a work in progress. The eschatological community of peace never wins the battle once and for all. For Ahern, even structures of grace are made up of fragile people, they are never perfect and are in constant need of reform and change.[36]

But change is not always change for the better when tensions and divisions between people reassert themselves. As Cronwright pointed out:

> Only later did Deaf people split into different groups. The leaders came and took the Muslims away, the black Deaf people also moved away, and even the whites. Before this we were all together.[37]

Even within DCCT, the inner dynamics among the leadership of the organisation became strained. In 1994, Deacon Nick Bruce resigned from his positions as assistant chaplain and financial administrator/fundraiser for DCCT. Bruce had been influential in DCCT. He was instrumental in securing funding from the Energos Foundation,[38] for the women's self-help sewing project and a feeding scheme.[39] He had set up a Deaf burial fund and arranged the Christmas party every year for Deaf children.

There are contrasting opinions as to why Bruce resigned from DCCT.[40] However, his departure meant that the complete administration of DCCT was now in the hands of Deaf people. The only hearing person involved in DCCT was the chaplain, Fr Mark Foster, who had been appointed by Archbishop Lawrence Henry to succeed Fr Peter John Pearson. Foster was assisted

---

36 Ahern, *Structures of Grace*, 38.
37 Faith Cronwright, interview conducted by Mark James, Cape Town, 16 November 2015, 431.
38 Faith Cronwright, personal email to Mark James, 1 April 2018. See 'News from Affiliates,' *TSM*, 2/94, February 1994, 5.
39 Faith Cronwright, personal email to Mark James, 1 April 2018.
40 Various reasons are given for Bruce's departure from DCCT due to 1) personality clashes, 2) his being too controlling of Deaf people, and 3) financial irregularities and mismanagement. Nick Bruce and his wife Sue later emigrated to New Zealand. Faith Cronwright, personal email to Mark James, 1 April 2018.

by an interpreter when conducting pastoral activities on the Third Sunday.

With the resignation of Nick Bruce, the Deaf people involved in DCCT were able to take the organisation in the direction that suited them. The changes at DCCT began to impact Deaf organisations within South Africa, particularly the SANCD which, since its inception in 1928, was administered by hearing people on behalf of the Deaf community. South Africa was undergoing political change and Deaf people's perceptions of themselves were also changing.

DCCT's contribution to the transformation of the SANCD into DeafSA

By the early 1990s, DCCT was the only Deaf organisation with an elected Deaf leadership as well as being established as an organisation 'by the Deaf for the Deaf.'[41] Marion Heap writes, 'During the early 1990s, history placed DCCT strategically for the "crossing" from apartheid to post-apartheid.'[42]

The SANCD, established in 1927, was essentially a hearing organisation that sought to lobby the government on deaf issues and to do charitable work for deaf people. Faith Cronwright highlighted one of the problems Deaf people had with the SANCD:

> The SANCD had mainly hearing people in the office. The Deaf used to go to their Observatory offices to ask for help and assistance in finding work. But what they saw they didn't like because SANCD did not really help the Deaf community. If they went on their own, they couldn't get jobs. Some would go but not understand what was being said to them because the SANCD people were hearing. The SANCD people did not know sign language at all. They were hearing and couldn't understand the deaf people's signing,

---

41 Heap, 'Crossing Social Boundaries,' 145.
42 Ibid.

so they kept saying: 'What are you saying? What are you saying?' It wasn't easy.[43]

In the 1980s, it began to employ Deaf people to work for the organisation but only got its first Deaf president, Nico Beaurain, and vice-president, Kobus Kellerman, in September 1991.[44] The SANCD and its provincial affiliates were essentially a white and hearing organisation working for the deaf. Stephen Lombard from DCCT was one of three Deaf people elected to the executive as the representative for the Western Province.[45]

With the changes taking place in South Africa, the SANCD was seeking to gain re-admission from the WFD, an affiliate of the United Nations.[46] Its membership had been revoked due to apartheid. Before re-admission, the WFD insisted that the SANCD comply with its policies. Consequently, the SANCD set about amending its constitution and undergoing a name change.

The SANCD first spoke about a name change and affirmative action, that is the employing of more Deaf people, at its Biennial Council Meeting held on 26 and 27 October 1993.[47] The historic name change to the Deaf Federation of South Africa (DeafSA) took effect on 29 June 1995.[48] The constitutional change made the organisation more democratic and representative of the nine provinces of South Africa.[49] Both the change of name and the changes in the constitution enabled DeafSA to reaffiliate to the WFD.[50]

In the same year, Wilma Newhoudt, a DCCT founder-member, was offered a job with DeafSA as a social worker.[51] She

---

[43] Faith Cronwright, interview conducted by Mark James, Cape Town, 16 November 2015, 429.
[44] 'Deaf to Play Increasing Role in Council affairs,' *TSM*, 60, 9, September 1991, 1, 4.
[45] Ibid.
[46] Heap, 'Crossing Social Boundaries,' 145.
[47] See 'Looking Towards the Future' *TSM*, 10/93, October 1993, 6 and 'SANCD Policy on Affirmative Action,' *TSM*, March 1995, 5.
[48] 'The SANCD's New Name,' *TSM*, July 1995, 5.
[49] Ibid.
[50] 'DeafSA to Attend Congress in Vienna,' *TSM*, July 1995, 2.
[51] In 1993, Newhoudt had returned to Cape Town to work at DCCT after completing her studies in Social Work in Gallaudet

later became the first Deaf director of DeafSA in the Western Cape.[52] Stephen Lombard[53] as the Western Cape representative and Lucas Magongwa[54] as the North West representative were both on the executive committee of the SANCD when it was transformed into DeafSA.[55] Catholics were involved in the process of transforming DeafSA, like DCCT before it, into an organisation of the Deaf for the Deaf. It was no longer an organisation of the hearing that 'benevolently' worked for the deaf. Consequently, DeafSA had become both a social development office for the Deaf community in South Africa but also a lobby organisation for Deaf rights in South Africa. It challenged hearing people to work with the Deaf community rather than on their behalf. This change of preposition has a long and painful history.

DeafSA continues to be influential in campaigning for bilingual Deaf education and sign language to be accepted as the twelfth official language of the country. The president of DeafSA is presently Bruno Druchen who had formerly been a member of a Catholic Deaf youth group in Durban established by Fr John Turner CMM.[56] In 1999, Wilma Newhoudt-Druchen became the first Deaf person to become a member of Parliament in South Africa.[57]

University in Washington DC.
52   Heap, 'Crossing Social Boundaries,' 145.
53   Stephen Lombard was on the SANCD Executive Committee from 1991, see 'Deaf to play increasing role in Council affairs,' *TSM*, 60, 9, September 1991, 1,4; 'SA Nasionale Raad vir Dowes: Nuwe Komitees,' *TSM*, 10/93, October 1993, 2 and 'Biennial Council Meeting/Tweejaarlikse Raadsvergadering,' *TSM*, Nov/Dec 1995, 1–4.
54   This was the first time that Lucas Magongwa's name appears as a delegate of North West. See 'Biennial Council Meeting/Tweejaarlikse Raadsvergadering,' *TSM*, Nov/Dec 1995, 1–4.
55   The implementation of the new constitution of DeafSA took place at the Biennial Council meeting on 26 and 27 October 1995 at Technikon SA. See 'Biennial Council Meeting/Tweejaarlikse Raadsvergadering,' *TSM*, Nov/Dec 1995, 1–4.
56   Before becoming director of DeafSA, Druchen trained as an actor. He is married to Wilma Newhoudt. See 'Bruno Druchen Acts in America,' *TSM*, 61,6, June 1992, 1 and 'Bruno Off to America Again,' *TSM*, July 1994, 6.
57   Heap, 'Crossing Social Boundaries,' 169. Also see Jacinta Teixeira, interview conducted by Mark James, 13 July 2016, Cape Town, 395.

Chapter 17

Breathing, justice and religion

In Part III, we have seen how deaf people themselves created breathing spaces for themselves or others in the Church, which seriously impacted upon the lives of people in both Church and society. We have traced the steps of Robert Simmons, Fr Cyril Axelrod, Lindsay Moeletsi Dunn and Fr John Turner, and seen how DCCT and DeafSA created new spaces for deaf people.

In speaking about DCCT, Marion Heap spoke about the establishment of Sign-spaces where Deaf people could be themselves. As we have seen, DCCT was a community where Deaf people did not have to conform to hearing expectations but created spaces where they could be free to sign and live in a way of their own choosing. Sign-space was a breathing space where Deaf people could be themselves, as a signing people and interact with each other without fear of judgement or criticism. They could breathe freely and inspire one another. Sign-space was therefore a creative space, a compassionate space, and a political and cultural space. It was a space in which to relax and to celebrate together. It was a holy space in which the Holy Spirit breathed and moved. It was a prophetic and transcendent space pointing to a reality where heaven meets earth, a place pointing to messianic peace, an eschatology.

For Levinas, 'breathing is the transcendence in the form of opening up.'[58] This is the task of Christian and Catholic ministry to an opening up to the Deaf community and to offer justice to Deaf people by engaging in a transformed conversation within society and the Church between Deaf and hearing beyond the violence of racism and audism. This is the prophetic and transcendent dimensions of the ethical relation.

Within the Catholic Church's Deaf ministry, the establishment of DCCT in 1987 and its subsequent development and struggles highlighted the movement towards the Deaf way of being in the world, namely Deafhood. Deaf people took charge of their organisations and used their skills and the organisation's resources to improve the lives of ordinary Deaf people in the

---

58   Levinas, *Otherwise than Being*, 181.

Western Cape. In bringing together Deaf people from a wide range of backgrounds, by including various groups of people like Catholics, Protestants, Muslims, Africans, whites, and coloureds into one organisation, DCCT were able to point to a messianic peace. They pointed to a life in a community beyond apartheid, beyond race, beyond class, beyond Christian denomination and beyond religious creed. It was an anticipation of a new relationship among people. It is a sign of how God comes to mind. DCCT continues this work even to this day thirty-eight years later.

DCCT briefly had a taste of this messianic peace when Deaf people came together without regard for colour, ethnicity, class, religion or Christian denomination. This peace breaks into our world as surprisingly new and gratuitous, which was exactly how the early disciples experienced Christ's resurrection. We seek to move beyond being to a new world of love and justice for all of humanity and creation.

Part IV

Conclusion and the Way Forward

Chapter 18

Conclusion

The power of saintly witness to a new world

This book has been dedicated to reflecting on the history of how Deaf people developed a prophetic ministry to the Deaf community and how this prophetic stance calls us to a different way of seeing holiness, saintliness, spirituality and mission. Following Levinas, prophetic ministry and the saintly life is a call to transcend the limited horizons of the preoccupations of the self and to respond with compassion and concern for the needs of our suffering and marginalised neighbours. Included in Christian life and ministry, alongside the worship of God, is the practice of justice and hospitality towards others. It is about creating a community with others and not just the like-minded, by sharing our lives, including our money and resources with them. It is about living with a troubled conscience, recognising in humility and distress, that we have often arrived too late. It is seeking to live the holy and saintly existence of care for others and to follow Jesus' commandment: 'Love one another as I have loved you. No one can have greater love than this, to lay down one's life for one's friends' (Jn 15:12–13).

Emmanuel Levinas' prophetic philosophy awakens us to our responsibility for the stranger, the enemy and the neighbour. Jesus' parable of the Good Samaritan (Lk 10:29–37) is the illustration of the other who is a stranger, enemy and neighbour to the one left for dead by the roadside. In responding to the suffering of the wounded Jewish man lying along the roadside and in seeking to alleviate this suffering, the Samaritan showed his compassion by 'haemorrhaging' for the Jewish man's wounds.[1] The Samaritan becomes a hostage to the man's suffering and cannot but help his enemy in his suffering.[2] He helps him by

---

1 Levinas, *Otherwise Than Being*, 74.
2 Ibid, 117.

offering hospitality and paying the innkeeper to care for him. In this way, the Samaritan shows himself to be one of the just who, through his care and concern for the other, helps us understand, in Levinas' understanding, how 'God comes to mind.' For Christians, Jesus is the compassionate one who in substitution pulls us out of the ditches of life, into which we have fallen, and reveals through his prophetic act of death on the cross that he is truly the Son of God.

This is an important challenge that Christian faith and spirituality can become yet another means through which we become comfortable and preoccupied with our own well-being, security and safety – forgetting that the Christian life is primarily about dying to self and rising in Christ. Christ himself through the kenotic act of emptying himself of divinity, became humble, and gave his life on a cross for our sakes. His life was not focused on his own well-being but on the well-being of the suffering and the marginalised of his time and of all times. We are called to follow his pattern of his dying and rising, as a result of our baptism, when we seek to incarnate in our times, that self-giving love, that care for other people, that charity which Jesus displayed in his life. The example of the martyrs and saints who have gone before us is a testament to that new world that Jesus inaugurated through his death and resurrection. By attempting to live a holy or saintly life ourselves, we point eschatologically beyond our present times to the kingdom of the unthematizable God, the God beyond our manipulations, the truly transcendent One.

In the first part of this book, we saw how the institutional Church in Mother Dymphna and Sister Stephana stumbled upon the suffering of deaf children and felt compassion for their suffering. They could have passed them by, like the biblical Pharisee and the Levite, but these sisters felt the responsibility of proximity. They exercised non-indifference. In educating deaf children, these sisters and the deaf lay women who also contributed, responded, like the Samaritan, with enormous generosity and hospitality. This was a just act and one which demonstrated a Samaritan-style saintliness.

However, this illustrious history of service and ministry was also fraught with misconceptions between hearing and deaf people that hampered the effectiveness of this mission. In the school for the deaf in Cape Town, the conflict between Sr Thecla Kolbe and Hanna Marsh illustrated the difference in perceptions between hearing and the deaf about how deaf children should be educated. Marsh objected to Sr Thecla being appointed principal of the school as she did not know sign language. This was indicative of later and more widespread dissatisfaction among deaf people with the quality of the education they received when the oral method became the predominant means of deaf education. Deaf teachers were no longer employed and sign language was banned from the classroom and repressed through the administering of corporal punishment for offences.

But Levinas reminds us that this call to empty oneself of self and open one's heart in compassion is not just a once-off event but is passivity, that is, a continual calling into question of one's assumptions and perspectives. It is a kenotic process of unlearning, of being undone, of attentiveness and learning from the other. It means sitting at the feet of the other just as Mary of Bethany sat at the feet of Jesus and learned from him (Lk 10:39).

This ongoing process of passivity and learning from the other was where the Dominican sisters' ministry to the deaf began to falter and lose its prophetic edge. Even though there was a great willingness in the Cabra School for the Deaf in Cape Town to employ Deaf teachers, they too migrated to the use of the oral method of deaf education. In the 1920s, the Dominican sisters of both congregations were convinced, in good conscience, that in this oral method, they had found the answer to solving the 'deaf problem' and liberating the deaf children from their prisons of silence. They applied the oral method of deaf education rigidly and sometimes without compassion, thus failing to listen to the calls from the Deaf community to revise their strategy. They imposed what Levinas has called an 'imperialism of the same.' Deaf children were to learn in the manner of hearing children rather than in a manner more appropriate to Deaf people's true needs and thinking.

However, in the 1970s, some educators, teachers and even school principals in the United States, Europe and South Africa began to realise that the oral method was not the panacea they had hoped it was. They recognised that there was value in using sign language in the classroom and began to adopt a combined method of education called Total Communication. This meant the use of both oral and manual methods of education in the classroom. It was a step in the right direction but was also ineffective in improving the education of deaf children.

The more radical shift to the use of natural sign languages in the classroom and the Church did not originate, unlike Total Communication, from hearing educators and clergy, but from Deaf people themselves. It was a Deaf initiative. This is the focus of the second part of the book. They were the agents of change within Church and society. It is outside the scope of this book to detail the entire history of how this transformation took place. I have limited myself to the Catholic contributors to this process. Each person and group selected to some extent or other to engage in what Glenn Morrison has called a Trinitarian praxis of radical self-giving.[3] Being a Christian, a person-in-Christ, is to be one committed to the way of Christ in his self-emptying and self-giving love for humanity and for all of God's creation or what Levinas called passivity and substitution. Through the Holy Spirit, the divine breath, we find ourselves drawn into an eternal Trinitarian relationship where we emulate the Trinitarian love of Father, Son and Holy Spirit through a holy and saintly praxis of self-emptying and self-giving for our neighbour, for all others, even our enemies. Morrison writes: 'To resemble God reflects a journey of growing more and more into the likeness of God, responsible for everything and everyone... There are no limits to responsibility and love.'[4]

The Spirit provides 'breathing space' for us to anticipate the Trinitarian relationship (*perichoresis*) of generous self-giving love, compassion and mercy for a broken world. But more importantly, to open up new relationships, a new relationality, and a new world. These 'saintly' models opened up this new world

---

3   Morrison, *A Theology of Alterity*, 210–254.
4   Morrison, *A Theology of Alterity*, 211.

where sign language as well as African culture and experience forged new relationships and a different relationality within both Church and society.

Audism and the oral method of deaf education was an attempt at creating a 'better world' for deaf people[5] as apartheid was an attempt to impose the 'better world' whites foresaw for themselves on black people. Both attempts were inherently self-referential and self-interestedness. They did not create an openness to the new relationality that can arise when people are willing to open their hearts to other persons, feel their pain and even haemorrhage with them. When we incarnate in our own bodies the tears, sufferings, the joys and hopes of people, when we welcome them in hospitality or lament and cry out for justice, we encounter the gift of this other. We are reconfigured by responding to them and so a new world becomes possible.

This is what is traced in the academic achievements of Dr Robert Simmons and his activism for the Deaf community. Sign language was the means to free Deaf people from the shackles of inferiority that the oral method instilled within many of them. He reminded them that they should be 'Proud to be Deaf.'

The artistic work of Ruben Xulu, a black and Deaf artist, opened a new breathing space for a truly African Catholicism and Christianity.

The Deaf ministry to the Deaf community was radically transformed by the work of the first two Deaf priests, Fr Cyril Axelrod CSsR and John Turner CMM, as well as the first Deaf sister Bernadette Oelofse OP. The church became a 'breathing space,' a 'hospitable home' where Deaf people could worship God in Sign and in culturally appropriate ways.

Deaf pupils like Lindsay Moeletsi Dunn, Faith Cronwright and Suzanne Lombard (neé Barrett) among others stood up against the injustices of racism and audism in 1976. We saw how this inspired them to continue to work later in life for the good of the Deaf community in South Africa and even beyond our shores. They created 'breathing spaces' for inspiration, and wonder, for

---

5   I thank Glenn Morrison for this insight.

a new imagination to develop among the Deaf community where they could bring a little more goodness into the world. Through a growing appreciation of the value of sign language, Deaf awareness and Deafhood developed among Deaf people. Through organisations like DeafSA, Deaf people called for the successful adoption of SASL as the twelfth language and that the bilingual and bicultural method of Deaf education be promoted in the post-apartheid society.[6]

Saints and prophetic witnesses transform the Church and society

Through their acts of saintly piety, these Deaf people pointed to what true religion and faith is – the journey of people responding to the needs of others in a bent, distorted and broken world and thereby revealing their faith in a God of compassion and mercy who calls people into anticipating a new world of love, justice and peace. They remind the Church that its task is not primarily concerned with the maintenance of present membership or the performing of pious acts in good conscience. Rather it is about responding compassionately to the suffering neighbour in our midst.

The Church is faithful to its task when it moves beyond concern with personal salvation and ecclesiastical self-interest and instead opens up to a radical self-giving; a generosity and gift of self for the good of the neighbour. Christian ministry is the summons to do good and to move beyond the confines of one's own world even to the point of self-sacrifice, to 'expire' and to bleed or 'haemorrhage' for the good of the Other.

This religion, for Levinas, is always embodied as prophetic spirituality, in a way of life, a saintly way of living.[7] A saint, for Levinas, is 'the person who in his being is more attached to the

---

6   Bilingual education is Deaf education where the medium of instruction is in the natural sign language and a spoken language like English is used as a written language. For more information on the bilingual approach, see Wilna Opperman, 'Bilingualism – a New Trend in Deaf education,' *TSM*, 1/94, January 1994, 1–2.
7   Levinas, *Otherwise than Being*, 149.

being of the other than to his own.'[8] It refers to those who live in a dis-interested way.[9] The spirituality of justice and peace is the fundamental path to discovering our true humanity and is the primary path of spirituality as a way to the 'God who comes to mind' as we draw closer to our suffering neighbour.

This is an opening up to all of humanity and creating breathing spaces for all unrecognised people. It is important to recognise the value of Deaf breathing spaces. The Deaf community need a space in the Church to be themselves and to feel at home. An inclusive Church will allow Deaf people space and the opportunity to celebrate the Eucharist together in sign language. Deaf people can join with the hearing in integrated Masses and celebrations especially when there is an interpreter available. However, interpreted Masses and celebrations are not sufficient to constitute an inclusive faith community. These occasions remain dominantly hearing celebrations where the Deaf community is an invited guest. Greater hospitality will mean that Deaf signed singing, Deaf lectors and acolytes may be permitted in these joint celebrations. Occasionally, perhaps hearing people may be free to attend Deaf celebrations especially the sacraments of initiation. But more importantly, Deaf people need to have the opportunity to celebrate their faith together as a community. The appointment of a priest who can sign is vital for the viability and spiritual sustenance of these Deaf communities. An inculturated Deaf liturgy is a necessity for a vibrant Deaf community to experience the church as their home too. There is much that we can learn from the ministries of both Fathers Cyril Axelrod and John Turner.

The way forward

The purpose of this book was to reflect on the ministry of the Catholic Church and call for a change of perspective. I hope it will be like a new pair of shoes that will chafe the consciences of hearing Catholics so that they recognise their misconceptions about Deaf people. People in the church need to be more open to Deaf people and those with disabilities in parishes, and so to

---

8   Wright, Hughes and Ainley, 'The Paradox of Morality,' 172.
9   Levinas, *Alterity and Transcendence*, 171.

learn from them how to be a more inclusive Church. This may even mean that they begin to learn sign language to ensure better inclusion of Deaf people in the Church.

There are still several challenges which could be considered for more effective pastoral outreach to Deaf people and people with disabilities. The leadership of the Church is the responsibility of each bishop in his diocese. For a more effective ministry, bishops could evaluate what is being done in their dioceses regarding this ministry. The appointment of priests to serve these communities would be welcome, but also the development of policy with regard to meeting the needs of these communities is equally important. Deaf people require access to interpreters and visual aids to facilitate participation. For people with physical disabilities, however, church access is a major challenge. Bishops are instrumental in encouraging seminaries to hold special training for seminarians in developing pastoral sensitivity and skills in meeting the needs of the Deaf and the disabled.

Parish priests could assist the work of chaplains for the Deaf by developing an inclusive parish community that respects the needs of the Deaf and the disabled within the parish. Parish priests could help with the empowerment of Deaf people in the parish by introducing or allowing for interpreted Masses in their parishes. Priests could learn sign language so that they could communicate with their Deaf parishioners without the aid of an interpreter. Deaf people should be encouraged to become lectors and interpreters engaged to do the voicing. Similarly, Deaf people could become acolytes in the parish. Including Deaf people in these ministries would be a prophetic sign acknowledging that the Deaf can share in the ministry of the church and not just be recipients of ministry.

There is also a desperate need to have Deaf priests who can minister to Deaf people. There is a need to consider a diocese's openness to encourage Deaf men and women to become priests or to enter religious life. Having Deaf priests and religious sisters in a community with the hearing will be more possible in a post-audist world where Deaf people and hearing people become more bilingual.

As I have attempted to illustrate, the hearing thought they knew better than the Deaf what would be good for them. If this was an isolated incident one might be more forgiving. However, it seems to be symptomatic of uncritical human thinking or totalising thinking. Whites thought they knew what was best for blacks, the rich knew what is best for the poor, the educated knew what is best for the illiterate, and so we could go on. We need to empty ourselves of self, become listeners and learn from those who speak to us from their positions of marginalisation and vulnerability. Only then will we be able to find the breathing spaces, the places where all people will flourish and benefit.

'May your unthematisable kingdom come.'

Bibliography

Primary sources

Oral sources

Fr Cyril Axelrod CSsR, interview conducted by Mark James, 20 September 2015, Dunnottar, Nigel.

Jennifer Gillespie, interview conducted by Mark James, 12 November 2015, Heathfield, Cape Town.

Carmen Kuscus, interview conducted by Mark James, 13 November 2015, Heathfield, Cape Town.

Suzanne Lombard, interview conducted by Mark James, 13 November 2015, Heathfield, Cape Town.

Faith Cronwright, interview conducted by Mark James, 16 November 2015, Heathfield, Cape Town.

Sr Liguori Töns OP, interview conducted by Mark James, 16 December 2015, Hyde Park, Johannesburg.

Sr Macrina Donoghue OP, interview conducted by Mark James, 12 July 2016, Springfield, Cape Town.

Sr Siobhan Murphy OP, interview conducted by Mark James, 12 July 2016, Springfield, Cape Town.

Sr Jacinta Teixeira OP, interview conducted by Mark James, 13 July 2016, Springfield, Cape Town.

Francois de Villiers, interview conducted by Mark James, 4 August 2016, Edenvale.

Manuscript sources

Archbishop Denis Hurley Archives: St Joseph's Theological Institute (BIO 11C)

Box 109: Archbishop Hurley Papers: KwaThintwa School for the Deaf 1982–1984

Files: KwaThintwa School 1984

Correspondence from January 1982–October 1985

Box 110: Archbishop Hurley Papers: KwaThintwa School for the Deaf

Files: Correspondence 1980–1981

Correspondence 1975–1979

Box 111: Archbishop Hurley Papers: KwaThintwa School for the Deaf

Files: KwaThintwa School

Correspondence

Box 112: Archbishop Hurley Papers: KwaThintwa School for the Deaf 1985–1988

Files: Correspondence

DEH KwaThintwa

Box 113: Archbishop Hurley Papers: General correspondence KwaThintwa Staffing

Files: KwaThintwa/Inchanga HS

Mandla Cele

KwaThintwa: Staff matters

Box 114: Archbishop Hurley Papers: Minutes KwaThintwa School

Box: Bantu Education Act 1954

File: Interview with SACBC delegation with Dr Verwoerd 2 Sept 1954.

Archive of the Archdiocese of Cape Town, Cape Town (ACT)

Box 299: Deaf community

Files: Educational facilities for Deaf children

Dominican School for Deaf

Principal's reports

SANCD Biennial reports

Archive of the Catholic Diocese of Manzini, Eswatini (ACDM)

De Vittorio, Luigi M. Missione Africa (Rome: Marianum, 2004).

'Elenco dei missionari arrivati in Swaziland a destinatie a questa missione, del principio 1913 al primi di dicembre 1945',

File: OSM 1939–1948.

Fr Barneschi OSM, 'The Catholic Church 54 years in Swaziland,' 4.

File: Paper of historical interest.

Archive of the Diocese of Port Elizabeth, Port Elizabeth (APE)

Box: St Thomas School for the Deaf, Woodlands

Box: King Dominicans

Box: Bishop Green: Correspondence to priests 1943–1960

Cabra Dominican Sisters Archive, Cape Town (CDSA)

Grimley School for the Deaf

Box I: Education: Deaf education – Grimley

Files: Grimley School correspondence

Applications and appointments of teachers (1907–1912)

Biennenial reports, 1943–1963.

Biennenial reports, 1969–1971

Brochure for celebration of centenary, 1973

Miscellaneous: Hout Bay property, 1966–1973

Dominican Grimley School, inspectors' reports, 1893–1901 and 1973.

Box II: 1993–2011

Dominican School for the Deaf, Hammanskraal

Box: Ministry

Files: Board of management reports, 1962–1970

Annual reports, 1965–1970.

Hammanskraal

Box: Ministry correspondence

File: H writings

Dominican School for the Deaf, Wittebome

Box: Deaf education – Wittebome, miscellaneous papers

Files: Story of Dominican Schools for the Deaf, Cape Town: Grimley and general

Wittebome and general

Box: Deaf School Wittebome, 2003–2010

File: Photos and newspaper cuttings

Box: St Dominic's Convent, Wittebome

Files: Convent history and some events, 1937–1875
School for the Deaf, 1937–1982

Catholic History Bureau, Johannesburg (CHB)

Box: Dominicans 182 OP Convent Schools

Files: St Vincent School for the Deaf
Various School magazines

Box: The Irish Dominican Sisters and their missions

Files: Irish Dominican Sisters, Cape Town
Saint Vincent School for the Deaf

DeafSA Archive, Johannesburg:

The Silent Messenger: 1937–1947
1954–1995

Historical Papers Research Archive, University of the Witwatersrand, Johannesburg (HPRA):

Box AB1363 C51.1–51.17 CPSA Archbishops, Records – C, Clergy A-B

File: AB1363/C51.13 CPSA Archbishops of Cape Town
Clergy: Blaxall, A.W.

Box: Federation of South African Women 1954–1963,

Collection number: AD 1137

King William's Town Dominican Sisters Archive, Johannesburg (KDSA)

Sacred Heart School, King William's Town

Box 1, Book 18: Annals 1897–1903; 1905–1906

St Vincent School for the Deaf, Johannesburg

Necrology: Box 19, File 349 Sr Gisella Greissl OP

        Box 20, File 376 Sr Cyrilla Hötzl OP

        Box 26, File 606 Sr Verena Huber OP

        Box 37, File 886 Sr Thomasia Knoepfle OP

        Box 57, File 1153 Sr Bernadette Oelofse OP

Box 52a Johannesburg General Council – Lourdes Convent

File: 506 Minutes: 1974–1979

Box 150 Johannesburg St Vincent Convent and School for the Deaf

Files: 1087 Annals 1934–1971

        1088 Annals 1971–1995

        1089 General notes 1984–1987

        1090 Historical sketch Annals 1953–58

        1091 Visitations 1936–1991

        1092 Council meetings 1940–1963

Box 151 Johannesburg St Vincent Convent and School for the Deaf

Files: 1093 Community meetings 1950–1959

        1094 Community meetings 1964–1971

        1095 Minutes of community meetings 1972–1980

        1096 Council meetings 1980–1992

        1097 Council meetings 1974–1984

        1099 School brochure: St Vincent for Deaf

        1101 Community meetings 1988–1995

        1100 Correspondence: Property

Box 152 Johannesburg St Vincent Convent and School for the Deaf

File: 1104 Brochures, programmes, magazines 1934–2009

Box 153 Johannesburg St Vincent Convent and School for the Deaf

Files: 1105 School documents

        1106 Newspaper cuttings 1933–2004

        1112 Documents related to move of Deaf school to Johannesburg

Box Edu 27 Johannesburg St Vincent School for the Deaf, Melrose

File: Quarterly magazines 1956–1971/School information magazines

Box Edu 28 Johannesburg St Vincent School for the Deaf, Melrose

File: Quarterly magazines 1964–1972

Box Edu 29 Johannesburg St Vincent School for the Deaf, Melrose

File: School magazines 1981–2001

St Thomas School for the Deaf, Woodlands

Box 124: King Williams Town Woodlands Maria Hilf Convent Mission

School for the Deaf: White School: Xhosa School: Farm

Files: 374: Annual Reports, School Reports 1925–1986

375: Correspondence 1906–1995

Box 126: King Williams Town Woodlands Maria Hilf Convent Mission

School for the Deaf: White School: Xhosa School: Farm

File: 376: History of Property

Redemptorist Archive, Cape Town (RA)

Cyril Axelrod box: Papers (materials collected by Sr Mannes OP)

Files: Newspaper cuttings

Magazines file

Correspondence file 1

Correspondence file 2

Fr Cyril Axelrod: Life, work, spirituality of the Deaf

Gallaudet College file

Newspaper articles

The Southern Cross

Fr William Leeson, 'Pioneer Work for the Deaf: Nuns First in the Cape to Care for Mutes,' 25 March 1931, 12/260.

'New School for the Deaf,' 31 January 1934, 1/65 and 16/80.

'Cathedral Mission for the Deaf: Sermons in Sign Language,' 28 March 1934, 2/194.

'Official Visit by Minister: Mr JH Hofmeyr at Deaf School,' 15 August 1934, 3/515.

'Concert by Deaf Pupils: Fine Work by the Dominicans,' 5 December 1934, 17/801.

'International Board for Africa?' *The Southern Cross*, 24 February 1937, 11/147.

'Mission for the Deaf: Fr T Gill's Splendid Work,' 24 March 1937, 2/214.

'Fine New Block of Buildings at Wittebome, Dominican Sisters' Splendid Work for the Deaf,' 21 July 1937, 2/540.

'Death of Colonel Rowland', 23 April 1947, 1/159.

Mary Singleton, 'Monsignor Kolbe,' 7 January 1948, 6/6.

'Deaf Children Succeed,' 25 February 1948, 2/72.

'Visit to Two Catholic Homes,' 15 September 1948, 6/377.

'The Deaf Entertain,' 26 October 1949, 2/410.

'Helen Keller Visits Dominican School for Deaf,' 21 March 1951, 1/133 and 12/144.

'Forthcoming Exhibition at Dominican School for Deaf,' 11 April 1951, 2/170.

'Dominican Work for the Deaf,' 25 April 1951, 12/194.

'South African Boys Town,' 1 August 1951, 10/368.

'First Catholic School for African deaf in Transvaal,' 13 June 1952, 1/277 and 11/287.

'New School for African Deaf,' 17 October 1952, 1/493 and 11/503.

'Concern Or Schools for Deaf,' 10 June 1953, 2/268.

'Only Deaf-Mute priest,' 2 September 1953, 11/421.

'Another SA-born Bishop: Fr Ernest Green Succeeds Bishop Boyle,' 4 May 1955, 1/205 and 11/215.

'Mayor's Tribute to Sisters: "Unselfish Devotion to Deaf children,"' 16 May 1956, 12/239.

'Two Good Things Clash,' 12 September 1956, 12/444.

'Work for Deaf Children,' 29 May 1957, 12/268.

'Permit to Open School for Deaf African Children Still Awaited,' 12 February 1958, 1/73.

'At School for the Deaf: "Only Love and Devotion Could Produce Such Wonderful Results,"' 4 June 1958, 12/276.

'Cape Town Nuns Plan to Start New Training for the Deaf,' 29 October 1958, 12/528.

'St Vincent 25 Years Work for Deaf Children,' 1 April 1959, 2/146 and 11/155.

'Nuns Are Up-to-Date in Training the Deaf to Earn a Living,' 24 June 1959, 12/300.

'Deaf School Extension Provided by Pupil's Parents,' 30 September 1959, 12/472.

'Sister M. Cyrilla, Deaf School Pioneer,' 21 October 1959, 12/508.

Denis Hurley, 'School Integration,' 22 June 1960, 5/295.

'Daughter-Foundation of CT Dominican School for Deaf,' 24 January 1962, 12/48.

'New School for Bantu Deaf,' 14 March 1962, 12/132.

'Jubilarian Taught Deaf for 44 years,' 19 September 1962, 9/453.

'New School for African Deaf is Joint Church-State Effort,' 17 October 1962, 1/493 and 11/503.

'These Deaf Children Do Not Even Know They Have Names,' 31 October 1962, 11/527.

Monsignor Desmond Hatton, 'The Deaf to Hear...,' 21 November 1962, 5/557.

'Its Origin and its Aim,' 22 May 1963, 1/241.

'Dominican School for Deaf Commemorates Centenary,' 22 May 1963, 1/241 and 2/242.

'Teaching the Deaf: Public Address by Nun from Ireland,' 28 July 1965, 12/360.

'Chaplain Speaks on Work for Deaf at C.W.L. meeting,' 29 December 1965, 4/616.

'Bishop Green's Life in Brief,' 2 March 1966, 2/98.

'St Vincent School Cracks Isolation of the Deaf Child,' 27 April 1966, 4/196.

'Africa's Delegate to US Education of Deaf Congress,' 2 August 1967, 3.

'Spiritual Courses for Deaf People,' 5 February 1969, 2.

Desmond Hatton, 'Deaf Deacon was Nearly a Rabbi,' 1 October 1969, 6.

Desmond Hatton, 'Man of Serenity,' 31 December 1969, 5.

'Interpreting Mass for Deaf,' 21 January 1970, 3.

'Deaf Priest One of Only Three in World,' 2 December 1970, 5.

'More Priests Urged for the Deaf,' 15 September 1971, 5.

'Taught the Deaf for 37 Years,' 22 December 1971, 3.

Sheila Eakins, 'Deaf Jewish Priest Celebrates in Signs,' 26 May 1974, 4.

Photo: Crucifix by Ruben Xulu, 13 November 1977, 1.

'Deaf Artist Takes First Prize,' 13 November 1977, 12.

Cyril Axelrod, 'The Church Has a Mission to the Handicapped,' 1 October 1978, 11.

'SA Deaf Honour Bishop Today,' 29 June 1980, 8.

Cyril Axelrod, 'A Time to do More for the Handicapped,' 10 May 1981, 10.

'Centre for Adult Deaf,' 19 September 1982, 1.

'Deaf Wood Artist Dies Violently,' 12 January 1986, 1.

'Sermon for Deaf on TV,' 7 June 1987, 1.

'25 Years of Help for the Deaf,' 13 September 1987, 5.

'R19,7 Million Growth for Soweto Deaf School,' 27 March 1988, 3.

'Hundreds at Funeral of Bishop Green,' 10 April 1988, 7.

'Deaf Sign Language on TV Tonight,' 17 April 1988, 1.

'Sign Language Easter for Cape Deaf,' 24 April 1988, 12.

'SA Priest off to Work in Asia,' 14 August 1988, 12.

Sheila White, 'School Gives Ears to Deaf Children,' 9 June 1991, 7.

'Deacon to the Deaf Ordained,' 6 October 1991, 3.

Nick Bruce, 'Deaf Cape Student Graduates in US,' 2 August 1992, 2.

'School for Handicapped Reopens,' 25 October 1992, 9.

Photo: Ruben Xulu, 13 June 1993, 1.

The Silent Messenger

'The Coyne Voice Pitch Indicator,' December 1937, 6.

Arthur W. Blaxall, 'Historical Review,' April 1952, 2.

Thomasia Knoepfle, 'Education for the Deaf,' April 1952, 3.

H.S. Jooste, 'The Rehabilitation of the Deaf,' December 1955, 4–7.

'A Well-Deserved Honour,' July 1956, 4.

E.S. Greenway, 'Language the Basic Key,' 27, 10, June 1958, 17.

'Electric Baby-Alarm,' 29, 1, December 1962, 6–7.

P. de V. Pienaar, 'Modern Development in the Field of Audiology,' 29, 1, March 1963, 13–20.

W. van der Sandt, 'Audiology in South Africa,' 31, 4, December 1967, 7–10.

Norman Nieder-Heitmann, 'Guest Editorial: The New Study at Cape Town,' 32, 5, March 1968, 2–4.

R. Corfmat, 'Signs… Signing and Signers,' 33, 2, June 1969, 16–17.

'Problems in Deafness,' 33, 3, September 1969, 8–9.

'Letter to the Editor from Beryl Jones,' 33, 3, September 1969, 20.

'Editorial: Our Emblem,' 33, 4, December 1969, 3.

McCay Vernon, 'Myths of the Education,' March 1971, 16–17.

'Robert Michael Thomas Simmons: Winner 1971 *Wenner*,' December 1971, 22.

Robert Simmons, 'Deaf Education,' March 1972, 24.

Father Cyril Axelrod, 'The Spiritual Welfare and Care for the Deaf,' January 1975, 4–7.

Cyril Axelrod, 'Fr Cyril's Trip,' 42, 11, June/July 1975, 7–9.

Frederick Schreiber, 'Total Communication – As the Adults See it,' 43, 11, September 1975, 14–16.

K. van der Merwe, 'Comment: On the Right Track of Oralism,' December 1975, 12–13.

Charles Chittenden, 'The Paget Gorman Sign System,' June/July 1976, 5.

'Television for the Deaf?' March 1977, 6.

Norman Nieder-Heitmann, 'Extracts from the Report of the One-Man Committee on the South African Sign Language at the 23rd Biennial Conference of the SA Council for the Deaf,' 46, 1, March 1977, 14.

'Die Geestelike Versorging van die Dowes,' 46, 3, September 1977, 8–9.

'Televisie Byna Toeganglik vir Dowes,' 46, 3, September 1977, 9.

Beryl Jones, 'Fifth World Conference on Deafness Copenhagen. August 1977,' 46, 4, December 1977, 6–8, 10.

Father C. Axelrod, 'Spiritual Welfare of the Deaf,' 47, 5, March 1978, 4–5.

'A Priest for the Deaf,' 47, 6, June 1978, 9.

Bibliography

R.G. Brill, 'Total Communication,' 47, 3, September 1978, 10.

'Opmerking,' November/December 1978, 6.

Denton, D.M. 'The Philosophy of Total Communication,' 48, 3, September 1979, 15–16, 18.

'Denton Speaks in South Africa,' March 1980, 6–7.

Frances Parsons, 'Total Communication,' 50, 3, September 1981, 8–9.

Alan Jones, 'Report on Sign language Courses,' 50, 3, September 1981, 11.

'Meet Some of Our Deaf: FOYSA Award for Alan Jones,' 50, 4, December 1981, 8.

Alan Jones, 'International Conference on Sign Language,' 50, 4, December 1981, 14.

'Meet Some Our Deaf: Father Cyril Axelrod,' May/June 1982, 7–8.

Robert Simmons, 'Deafness and Total Communication (1),' Nov/Dec 1982, 7, 11.

Robert Simmons, 'Deafness and Total Communication (2),' March/April 1983, 5–7.

P. Mosifane, 'Lucas Magongwa, the Road to Success,' 58, 11, Nov/Dec 1989, 3.

Henna Opperman, 'Literacy Training for Deaf Adults,' 59, 3, March 1990, 1.

John Perks, 'Deaf Students Give Signing Lessons,' 59, 6, June 1990, 3.

'Fifty-Six Years of Service to the Deaf,' 59, 7, July 1990, 2.

'Training and Employment of Deaf Persons as Teachers,' 60, 8, August 1991, 1–2.

Robert Simmons, 'What can the Deaf People do in the New South Africa?' 60, 8, August 1991, 5.

'Deaf to Play Increasing Role in Council Affairs,' 60, 9, September 1991, 1, 4.

Laurie Davids, '200 Deaf on March for Rights,' *Sunday Times*, 8 September 1991. Reproduced in 60, 10, October 1991, 7.

'Bruno Druchen Acts in America,' 61, 6, June 1992, 1.

'News From Natal,' 61, 7, July 1992, 3.

'Sign Language Expert Teaches in South Africa,' 61, 7, July 1992, 3.

'Sign Language Course at St Vincents,' 9/93, September 1993, 8.

'SA Nasionale Raad vir Dowes: Nuwe Komitees,' 10/93, October 1993, 2.

'Looking Towards the Future,' 10/93, October 1993, 6.

Wilna Opperman, 'Bilingualism – a New Trend in Deaf Education,' 1/94, January 1994, 1–2.

'News from Affiliates,' 2/94, February 1994, 5.

'TV-Program vir Dowes nou 'n Werklikheid,' 2/94, February 1994, 8.

Jeffrey Steele, 'Project for Deaf Students at Wits,' 5/94, May 1994, 4.

'How did Sign Get Onto our Screens?' 6/94, June 1994, 4.

'Deaf Woman Attains Master's Degree in the USA,' 7/94, July 1994, 6.

'Bruno off to America Again,' 7/94, July 1994, 6.

'SANCD Policy on Affirmative Action,' March 1995, 5.

'DeafSA to Attend Congress in Vienna,' July 1995, 2.

'The SANCD's New Name,' July 1995, 5.

'Biennial Council Meeting/Tweejaarlikse Raadsvergadering,' Nov/Dec 1995, 1–4.

'Deaf Achievers/Dowe Presteerders: Lucas Magongwa,' Nov/Dec 1995, 5.

Saint Vincent Quarterly

'Editorial,' 1, 5, March 1954, 1–2.

The Interested Teacher, 'A Talk to Parents,' 2, 1, March 1955, 3–9.

Thomasia Knoepfle, 'St Vincent School, Johannesburg: Report for 1955/56,' 2, 1, March 1956, 1–5.

Sr Hermina, 'Home Responsibilities in the Education of Deaf Children,' 3, 4, October–December 1957, 10–14.

Sr M. Thomasia, 'Report 1960/61,' 6, 1, March 1961, 1–4.

H. Reichenberg, 'Hearing Aids and How They Function,' 6, 1, March 1961, 10–19.

Sr Hermina, 'Speech for the Deaf – A Method in the Making,' 9, 2, 1964, 3–15.

'Schools of Thought at Variance,' 9, 3, 1964, 1–4.

Sr Thomasia, 'The Sound Perception Method,' 9, 4, 1964, 3–12.

'Deaf Children's Problems,' 9, 4, 1964, 15–16.

L.J. Paolo, 'The Role of the Parent of the Deaf Child,' 10, 1, 1965, 3–8.

'Social Maturity,' 10, 1, 1965, 8–9.

Sr Thomasia, 'Speechreading,' 11, 2, 1966, 3–5.

Thomasia Knoepfle, 'Visit to the United States,' 3, 3, 1967, 2–14.

Alan Mansfield, 'Some Views From the "Other Side",' 5, 5, 1970, 9–11.

Thomasia Knoepfle, 'Communication Problems of the Deaf Child,' 5, 6, 1970, 13.

St Vincent School Magazine

'An Address Given by Dr Robert Simmons (Past Pupil of the School) at the Annual Prize Giving, December 1981,' June 1982, 44–49.

Sr Marita, 'Principal's Message,' June 1982, 1–5.

'Deaf Children Thrilled by Play Staged in Sign Language,' December 1992, 9.

E.J. Brown, 'The Headmaster's Report,' 1995, 1–2.

Sandy de Araujo, 'Signed English or Sign Language in School,' 1995, 95.

'History/Development of St Vincent School,' 1999, 5–6.

The Star, Johannesburg

T.A. Chittenden, 'To the Editor of *The Star*,' 26 October 1933.

'School for Deaf and Dumb, Sectarian Issue Raised, Strong Criticism of Committee,' 24 October 1933.

'Teaching the Deaf to Hear,' 23 August 1946.

'Deaf Children March to Sound of Music: But They Cannot Hear It,' 27 October 1960, 11.

The Man on the Reef, 'Silent Workshop,' 30 August 1962, 6.

Robin Hood, 'At St. Vincent's Her Spirit Found Liberation,' 15 July 1964, 33.

'Surprise for Sister Thomasia,' 25 March 1969.

'"Sister Chips" Says Goodbye,' 3 November 1971, 27.

'Hi-fi Helps the Deaf,' 17 December 1971.

'Learning Favours the Bilingual Approach,' 23 September 1997, 26.

Other newspapers and magazines

'Parents to Protest: Deaf and Dumb School Transferred to R.C. Sisterhood,' *Rand Daily Mail*, 17 October 1933.

'Deaf and Dumb School, a Lively Meeting, Transfer to R.C. Sisterhood,' *Rand Daily Mail*, 24 October 1933, 12.

'Radio Teaches the Deaf: Afflicted Children Listen-in, Learn to Speak,' *Sunday Express*, 18 July 1937.

C. Alan Cook, 'Breaking the Other Sound Barrier,' *Outspan*, 25 November 1955, 42–45, 106.

'Obituary: Sr Gisella Greissl,' *The Silver Star*, 1957, 130.

'The Personal Triumph of One Man!' *The Irish Independent*, 29 July 1971.

'Give Deaf Responsibility Says Priest,' *The Daily News*, Monday, 28 September 1981.

'Inspiring Sportsman Passes Away,' *The Springs and Brakpan Advertiser*, 25 May 2001.

Newspaper articles online

'Benedict XVI Names Deaf Priest "Prelate of Honor",' *Catholic News Agency*, 27 March 2008. Accessed 20 September 2018, www.catholicnewsagency.com/news/benedict_xvi_names_deaf_priest_prelate_of_honor

'Education Dept Preparing for SA's First Sign Language Exams,' *The Citizen*, 23 June 2018. Accessed 9 August 2018, www.citizen.co.za/news/south-africa/1961863/education-dept-preparing-for-sas-first-sign-language-exams

'SA Sign Language Added to Curriculum,' *Cape Argus*, 1 December 2014. Accessed 9 August 2018, www.iol.co.za/news/south-africa/western-cape/sa-sign-language-added-to-curriculum-1788756.

'SASL Soon to Become 12th Official Language,' *Cape Argus*, 28 July 2017. Accessed 7 August 2018, www.iol.co.za/capeargus/news/sasl-soon-to-become-the-12th-official-language-10522103

'SONA 2020: Read President Cyril Ramaphosa's Full Speech,' 13 February 2020. Accessed 22 March 2020, www.iol.co.za/news/politics/sona2020-read-president-cyril-ramaphosas-full-speech-42675302

Email correspondence

Doreen Hayhurst, DeafSA, personal email to Mark James, 20 September 2014.
Cyril Axelrod, personal email to Mark James, 13 March 2015.
Cyril Axelrod, personal email to Mark James, 15 March 2015.
Cyril Axelrod, personal email to Mark James, 16 March 2015.
Lindsay Moeletsi Dunn, personal email to Mark James, 21 April 2018.
Lindsay Moeletsi Dunn, personal email to Mark James, 27 April 2018.

Private collections

Deaf Community of Cape Town Annual Report, 1993 – Faith Cronwright.
'My Years at St Vincents' – Nigel Pickford.

Secondary sources

Published books and journal articles

Aarons, Debra and Philemon Akach. 'South African Sign Language: One Language or Many? A Sociolinguistic Question.' *Stellenbosch Papers in Linguistics* 31 (1998), 1–28. https://doi.org/10.5774/31-0-55

Abraham, Garth. 'The Catholic Church and Apartheid, 1948–1957.' Unpublished MA thesis, University of Natal, Durban, 1984.

————— *The Catholic Church and Apartheid: The Response of the Catholic Church in South Africa to the First Decade of National Party Rule 1948–1957.* Johannesburg: Ravan Press, 1989.

Ahern, Kevin. *Structures of Grace: Catholic Organizations Serving the Global Common Good.* Maryknoll, NY: Orbis Books, 2015.

Akach, Philemon. 'Application of South African Sign Language (SASL) in a Bilingual-Bicultural Approach in Education of the Deaf.' Unpublished doctoral diss., University of the Free State, South Africa, 2010.

Aronowicz, Annette. 'Translator's Introduction,' in Emmanuel Levinas, *Nine Talmudic Readings*. Bloomington and Indianapolis: Indiana University Press, 1990.

Axelrod, Cyril. *And the Journey Begins*. Coleford, Gloucestershire: Douglas McLean, 2005.

————— *In Silent Darkness*. Merrivale: Redemptorist Pastoral Publication, 2020.

————— *Still on That Journey*. Merrivale: Redemptorist Pastoral Publication, 2021.

————— *Light on the Journey*. Merrivale: Redemptorist Pastoral Publication, 2024.

Bate, Stuart C. 'One Mission, Two Churches,' in *The Catholic Church in Contemporary Southern Africa*, edited by Joy Brain and Philippe Denis. Pietermaritzburg: Cluster Publications, 1999, 5–36.

————— 'The Church Under Apartheid,' in *The Catholic Church in Contemporary Southern Africa*, edited by Joy Brain and Philippe Denis. Pietermaritzburg: Cluster Publications, 1999, 151–186.

Bauman, H-Dirksen, ed. *Open Your Eyes: Deaf Studies Talking*. Minneapolis/London: University of Minnesota Press, 2008.

Bauman H-Dirksen and Joseph Murray, eds. *Deaf Gain: Raising the Stakes for Human Diversity*. Minneapolis: University of Minnesota Press, 2014.

Bauman, Zygmunt. *Postmodern Ethics*. Oxford: Blackwell, 1993.

Becker, Howard S. *Outsiders: Studies in the Sociology of Deviance*. New York: The Free Press, 1963.

Bernstein, Richard J. 'Evil and the Temptation of Theodicy,' in *The Cambridge Companion to Levinas*, edited by Simon Critchley and Robert Bernasconi. Cambridge: Cambridge University Press, 2004, 252–267. https://doi.org/10.1017/CCOL0521662060.012

Bialystok, Lauren. 'Being Your Self: Identity, Metaphysics, and the Search for Authenticity.' Unpublished doctoral diss., University of Toronto, Canada, 2009.

Biko, Steve. *I Write What I Like*. Johannesburg: Picador Africa, 2004.

Blaxall, Arthur W. *Handicapped: Being Three Short Essays on 1) the Deaf; 2) the Blind; 3) the Doubly-Handicapped*. Pretoria: The Carnegie Corporation Visitors' Grants Committee, 1934.

Boner, Kathleen. 'The Irish Dominicans and Education in the Western Cape (1863–1892).' Unpublished MA thesis, University of South Africa, Pretoria, 1976, 150–183.

––––– 'Dr FC Kolbe: Priest Patriot and Educationalist.' Unpublished doctoral diss., University of South Africa, Pretoria, 1980.

––––– *Dominican Women: A Time to Speak*. Pietermaritzburg: Cluster Publications, 2000.

Bonney, Nathan David. '*A Figure of Rhetoric: Holiness, Hyperbole and Embodied Subjectivity in the Later Writings of Emmanuel Levinas.*' Unpublished doctoral diss., University of Toronto, Canada, 2020.

Bosch, David. *Transforming Mission*. Maryknoll: Orbis Books, 1991.

Boynton, Eric and Martin Kavka, eds. *Saintly Influence: Edith Wyschogrod and the Possibilities of Philosophy of Religion*. New York: Fordham University Press, 2009. https://doi.org/10.5422/fso/9780823230877.001.0001

Brain, Joy. *The Catholic Church in the Transvaal*. Johannesburg: Missionary Oblates of Mary Immaculate, 1991.

––––– 'Charitable Works and Services,' in *The Catholic Church in Contemporary Southern Africa*, edited by Joy Brain and Philippe Denis. Pietermaritzburg: Cluster Publications, 1999, 97–123.

Branson, Jan and Don Miller. *Damned for their Difference: The Cultural Construction of Deaf People as Disabled*. Washington DC: Gallaudet University Press, 2002.

Broesterhuizen, Marcel. 'Faith in Deaf culture.' *Theological Studies* 66, 2, (June 2005), 304–329. https://doi.org/10.1177/004056390506600204

––––– 'Pastoral Ministry with the Deaf: From Care For the Hearing Impaired to Deaf Ministry,' in *The Gospel Preached by the Deaf: Proceedings of a conference on Deaf Liberation Theology, Faculty of Theology at the Catholic University of Leuven (Belgium), May 19, 2003*, edited by Marcus Broesterhuizen. Leuven: Peeters, 2007, 1–11.

Brown, Julian. *The Road to Soweto: Resistance and the Uprising of 16 June 1976.* Johannesburg: Jacana Media, 2016. https://doi.org/10.1515/9781782047605

Brown, William Eric. *The Catholic Church in South Africa: From its Origins to the Present Day.* London: Burns and Oates, 1960.

Bruce, Scott G. 'The Origins of Cistercian Sign Language.' *Cîteaux: Commetarii cistercienses*, 52 (2001), 193–209.

Burggraeve, Roger. 'The Ethical Meaning of Money in the Thought of Emmanuel Levinas.' *Ethical Perspectives* 2, 1 (1995), 13–16. https://doi.org/10.2143/EP.2.2.563064

----- 'Violence and the Vulnerable Face of the Other: The Vision of Emmanuel Levinas on Moral Evil and our Responsibility.' *Journal of Social Philosophy* 30, 1 (Spring 1999), 29–45. https://doi.org/10.1111/0047-2786.t01-1-00003

Butler, Judith. 'Performative Acts and Gender Constitution: An Essay in Phenomenology and Feminist Theory.' *Theatre Journal* 40, 4 (December 1988), 519–531. https://doi.org/10.2307/3207893

----- 'Precarious Life,' in *Radicalizing Levinas*, edited by Peter Atterton and Matthew Calarco. Albany: SUNY Press, 2010, 3–19.

Castiglione, Savino. 'Deaf People in the World: Between the Past and the Present.' *Dolentium Hominum* 73 (2010), 13–15.

Catherine of Siena. *The Dialogue.* London: SPCK, 1980.

Chalier, Catherine. 'Levinas and the Hebraic Tradition,' in *Ethics as First Philosophy: The Significance of Emmanuel Levinas for Philosophy, Literature and Religion*, edited by Adriaan T. Peperzak. New York/London: Routledge, 1995, 3–12.

Chamberlain, Helen, Mercedes Pavlicevic and Bridget Rose Tiernan. 'Catholic Education,' in *The Catholic Church in Contemporary Southern Africa*, edited by Joy Brain and Philippe Denis. Pietermaritzburg: Cluster Publications, 1999, 187–212.

Christiaens, Tim. 'Aristotle's Anthropological Machine and Slavery: An Agambenian Interpretation.' *Epoché: A Journal for the History of Philosophy* 23,1 (Fall 2018), 239–262. https://doi.org/10.5840/epoche201881127

Christie, Pam. *Open Schools: Racially Mixed Catholic Schools in South Africa, 1976–1986.* Johannesburg: Ravan Press, 1990.

Cleall, Esme. '"Deaf to the Word": Gender, Deafness and Protestantism in Nineteenth-Century Britain and Ireland.' *Gender & History* 25, 3 (November 2013), 590–603. https://doi.org/10.1111/1468-0424.12027

Cochrane, James P. *Servants of Power: The Role of the English-Speaking Churches in South Africa, 1903–1930*. Johannesburg: Ravan Press.

Cohen, Richard. 'Foreword,' in Emmanuel Levinas, *Otherwise Than Being or Beyond Essence*, Pittsburgh: Duquesne University Press, xi–xvi.

Comaroff, Jean and John Comaroff. *Of Revelation and Revolution: Christianity, Colonialism and Consciousness in South Africa*, vol. 1 and 2. Chicago: Chicago University Press, 1991. https://doi.org/10.7208/chicago/9780226114477.001.0001

Connor, Bernard F. *The Difficult Traverse: From Amnesty to Reconciliation*. Pietermaritzburg: Cluster Publications, 1998.

Cormick, Dina. *Bernard Gcwensa and Ruben Xulu: Christian Artists of Natal*. Pretoria: Academica, 1993.

Critchley, Simon. 'Five Problems in Levinas' View of Politics and the Sketch of a Solution to Them,' in *Radicalizing Levinas*, edited by Peter Atterton and Matthew Calarco. Albany: SUNY Press, 2010, 41–53.

Critchley, Simon and Robert Bernasconi, eds. *The Cambridge Companion to Levinas*. Cambridge: Cambridge University Press, 2004.

Deferrari, Roy Joseph, ed. *The Fathers of the Church*, vol. 2. Washington DC: The Catholic University of America Press, 1947.

––––– *The Fathers of the Church*, vol 35. New York: Fathers of the Church, 1957.

De Gruchy, John W. *The Church Struggle in South Africa*, 2nd ed. Grand Rapids: Wm. B. Eerdmans; and Cape Town: David Philip, 1986.

De Gruchy, John W. and Charles Villa-Vicencio, eds. *Apartheid is a Heresy*. Cape Town: David Philip/Guildford: Lutterworth Press, 1983.

Davis, Colin. *Levinas: An Introduction*. Cambridge: Polity Press, 1996. https://doi.org/10.2307/j.ctvpj740w

Denis, Philippe. *The Dominican Friars in Southern Africa: A Social History 1577–1990*. Leiden: Brill, 1998. https://doi.org/10.1163/9789004320017

───── 'The Ethics of Oral History,' in *Oral History in a Wounded Country: Interactive Interviewing in South Africa*, edited by Philippe Denis and Radikobo Ntsimane. Scottsville: University of KwaZulu-Natal Press, 2008, 63–84.

───── 'Seminary Networks and Black Consciousness in South Africa in the 1970s.' *South African Historical Journal* 62,1 (March 2010), 162–182. https://doi.org/10.1080/02582471003778417

───── 'The Christian Response to Apartheid in South Africa,' A talk given to the Brazilian Justice and Peace Commission. Unpublished paper, 2014, 1–12.

───── 'Memory and Commemoration as a Subject of Enquiry for African Christianity Scholars.' *Studia Historiae Ecclesiasticae* 41, 3 (2015), 4–22. https://doi.org/10.25159/2412-4265/450

─────Abbot Pfanner, the Glen Grey Act and the Native question.' *South African Historical Journal* 67, 3 (2015), 271–292. https://doi.org/10.1080/02582473.2015.1094122

─────The Authorship and Composition Circumstances of the Kairos Document.' *Journal of Theology for Southern Africa* 158 (July 2017), 4–19.

─────A Case of Pastoral Myopia? The South African Church's Ambiguous Response to the Erosion of Family Life in the Early Years of the Migrant Labor System.' *International Journal of African Historical Studies* 50, 3 (2017), 439–460.

Derrida, Jacques. *Of Grammatology*. Baltimore: Johns Hopkins University Press, 1976.

Dressler, Hermigild, ed. *The Fathers of the Church*, vol 4. Washington DC: The Catholic University of America Press, 1947.

Dubow, Saul. *Apartheid 1948–1994*. Oxford: Oxford University Press, 2014.

Dupuis, Jacques, ed. *The Christian Faith in the Doctrinal Documents of the Catholic Church*, 6th rev. ed. New York: Alba House, 1996.

E A F. 'What did St Augustine say?' *American Annals of the Deaf* 57, 1 (January 1912), 108–120.

Egan, Anthony. 'How Vatican II Renewed South African Catholicism – As Perceived by *The Southern Cross* 1962–1968.' *Studia Historiae Ecclesiasticae* 39, 2 (December 2013), 239–257.

Eaglestone, Robert. *The Holocaust and the Postmodern*. Oxford: Oxford University Press, 2004. https://doi.org/10.1093/acprof:oso/9780199265930.001.0001

----- 'Postcolonial Thought and Levinas' Double Vision,' in *Radicalizing Levinas*, edited by Peter Atterton and Matthew Calarco. Albany: SUNY Press, 2010, 57–68.

Erting, Carol, Robert Johnson, Dorothy L. Smith and Bruce D. Snider, eds. *The Deaf Way: Perspectives from the International Conference on Deaf Culture*. Washington DC: Gallaudet University Press, 1994.

Fitzgerald, Sarah and Janice Andrew, eds. *Open Minds Open Hearts: Stories of the Australian Catholic Deaf Community*. Lidcombe, NSW: CCOD, 1999.

Fleisch, Brahm. 'State formation and the Origins of Bantu Education,' in *The History of Education Under Apartheid 1948–1994: The Doors of Learning and Culture Shall be Opened*, edited by Peter Kallaway. Cape Town: Maskew, Miller and Longman, 2002, 39–52.

Gibbs, Robert. 'Jewish Dimensions of Radical Ethics' in *Ethics as First Philosophy: The Significance of Emmanuel Levinas for Philosophy, Literature and Religion*, edited by Adriaan T. Peperzak. New York/London: Routledge, 1995, 13–24.

Gouws, Mariette. *All for God's People*. Queenstown: King William's Town Dominican Sisters, 1977.

Gracer, Bonnie L. 'What the Rabbis Heard: Deafness in the Mishnah,' in *Jewish Perspectives on Theology and the Human Experience of Disability*, edited by Judith Abrams. Binghamton, NY: Haworth Press, 2006, 85–99.

Guenther, Lisa. '"Nameless Singularity": Levinas on Individuation and Ethical Singularity.' *Epoché: A Journal for the History of Philosophy* 14, 1 (Fall 2009), 167–187. https://doi.org/10.5840/epoche200914128

Hand, Sean, ed. *The Levinas Reader*. Oxford: Basil Blackwell, 1989.

Heap, Marion. 'Crossing Social Boundaries and Dispersing Social Identity: Tracing Deaf Networks from Cape Town.' Unpublished doctoral diss., University of Stellenbosch, South Africa, 2003.

Heath, Malcolm. 'Aristotle on Natural Slavery.' *Phronesis: A Journal for Ancient Philosophy* 53, 3 (2008), 243–270. https://doi.org/10.1163/156852808X307070

Higgins, Paul C. *Outsiders in a Hearing World: A Sociology of Deafness.* London: Sage Publications, 1980.

Hirson, Baruch. *Year of Fire, Year of Ash, the Soweto Revolt: Roots of a Revolution?* Cape Town: BestRed, 2016. https://doi.org/10.5040/9781350251243

Hodgson, Kenneth W. *The Deaf and their Problems: A Study in Special Education.* London: Watts and Co, 1953.

Hogan, Stanislaus. *Saint Vincent Ferrer OP.* London/New York: Longmans, Green and Company, 1911.

Humphries, Tom. 'Audism: The Birth of a Word,' in 'Talking Culture and Culture Talking,' in *Open your Eyes: Deaf Studies Talking*, edited by H-Dirksen Bauman. Minneapolis/London: University of Minnesota Press, 2008, 35–41.

Hull, John M. 'Open Letter from a Blind Disciple to a Sighted Saviour,' in *Borders, Boundaries and the Bible*, edited by Martin O'Kane. London: Sheffield Academic Press, 2002, 154–177.

Jackson, B. Darrell. 'The Theory of Signs in St Augustine's *De doctrina christiana.*' *Revue d'Etudes Augustiniennes et Patristiques* 15, 1–2 (1969), 9–49. https://doi.org/10.1484/J.REA.5.104162

James, Mark. 'Deaf as Other: A Levinasian Reading of the History of Deaf Ministry in the Catholic Church in South Africa from 1948 to 1994.' PhD diss. (University of Kwazulu-Natal, Pietermaritzburg, 2019).

––––– 'Christian Ministry, the Philosophy of Emmanuel Levinas and the Deaf Community,' *Journal of Theology for Southern Africa* 167 (July 2020): 43-61.

Kallaway, Peter. ed. *Apartheid and Education: The Education of Black South Africans.* Johannesburg: Ravan Press, 1984.

Kaufmann, Larry. *Perhaps God: Wisdom Through the Gift of Disability.* Merrivale: Redemptorist Pastoral Publications, 2015.

Kavka, Martin. 'Humanizing Philosophy of Religion: On Language in Levinas and Sellars,' *Journal for Cultural and Religious Theory* 14, 2 (Spring 2015), 225–240.

Kearney, Paddy. *Guardian of the Light: Denis Hurley, Renewing the Church, Opposing Apartheid*. Scottsville: University of KwaZulu-Natal Press, 2009.

Keteyi, Xolile. *Inculturation as a Strategy for Liberation*. Pietermaritzburg: Cluster Publications, 1998.

Key, William, ed. *Eye-Centered: A Study on the Spirituality of Deaf people with Implications for Pastoral Ministry*. Silver Spring, MD: National Catholic Office for the Deaf, 1992.

Kral, Andrej. 'To Hear or Not to Hear: Neuroscience of Deafness,' in *Deafness*, edited by Andrej Kral, Arthur Popper and Robert Fay. New York: Springer, 2013, 1–15. https://doi.org/10.1007/2506_2013_1

Ladd, Paddy. *Understanding Deaf Culture: In Search of Deafhood*. Clevedon: Multilingual Matters, 2003. https://doi.org/10.21832/9781853595479

Landon, Edward. *A Manual of Councils of the Holy Catholic Church*, vol II. Edinburgh: John Grant, 1909.

Lane, Harlan. *When the Mind Hears: A History of the Deaf*. New York: Random House, 1984.

───── *The Mask of Benevolence: Disabling the Deaf Community*. San Diego: Dawn Sign Press, 1999.

───── 'Construction of Deafness,' in *The Disability Studies Reader*, 2nd ed., edited by Lennard Davis. New York/London: Routledge, 2006, 79–92.

Langa, Clement. 'The Prayer of the People,' in *The Catholic Church in Contemporary South Africa*, edited by Joy Brain and Philippe Denis. Pietermaritzburg: Cluster Publications, 1999.

───── 'Relations Between the first Catholic Missionaries and the People of Swaziland (1914–1955.' Unpublished doctoral diss., University of South Africa, Pretoria, 2001.

Lategan, Laetus, Linus Vanleare and Roger Burggrave. *Vulnerable Responsibility – Small Vices for Caregivers*. Bloemfontein: SUN Press, 2019.

Leeson, Lorraine and Haaris Sheikh. *Experiencing Deafhood: A Snapshot of Five Nations*. Dublin: Interesource Group Publishing, 2010.

Levinas, Emmanuel. *Totality and Infinity: An Essay on Exteriority.* Pittsburgh: Duquesne University Press, 1969.

– – – – – *Ethics and Infinity: Conversations with Philippe Nemo.* Pittsburgh: Duquesne University Press, 1985.

– – – – – *Time and the Other.* Pittsburgh: Duquesne University Press, 1987.

– – – – – *Difficult Freedom: Essays on Judaism.* Baltimore: The Johns Hopkins University Press, 1990.

– – – – – 'Reflections on the Philosophy of Hilterism.' *Critical Inquiry* 17 (Autumn 1990), 63–71. https://doi.org/10.1086/448574

– – – – – *Collected Philosophical Papers.* Dordrecht: Kluwer Academic Publishers, 1993.

– – – – – *Beyond the Verse: Talmudic Readings and Lectures.* Bloomington, Indiana: Indiana University Press, 1994.

– – – – – *Nine Talmudic Readings.* Bloomington, Indianapolis: Indiana University Press, 1990.

– – – – – *Entre Nous.* New York: Columbia University Press, 1998.

– – – – – *Of God who Comes to Mind.* Stanford, California: Stanford University Press, 1998.

– – – – – *Otherwise than Being or Beyond Essence.* Pittsburgh: Duquesne University Press, 1998.

– – – – – *Alterity and Transcendence.* London: The Athlone Press, 1999.

Lewis, Hannah. *Deaf Liberation Theology.* Aldershot: Ashgate, 2004.

Lingis, Alphonso. 'Translator's Introduction,' in Emmanuel Levinas, *Collected Philosophical Papers.* Dordrecht: Kluwer Academic Publishers, 1993, VII–XXXI.

MacDonald, James. 'Tracing the Passion of a Black Christ: Critical Reflections on the Iconographic Revision and Symbolic Redeployment of the Stations of the Cross and Passion Cycle by South African artists Sydney Kumalo, Sokhaya Charles Nkosi and Azaria Mbatha.' Unpublished MA thesis, University of Cape Town, Cape Town, 2016.

Makris, Spiros. 'Emmanuel Levinas on Hospitality: Ethical and Political Aspects.' *International Journal of Theology, Philosophy and Science* 2 (2018), 79–96. https://doi.org/10.26520/ijtps.2018.2.2.79-96

Maree, Lynn. 'The Hearts and Minds of People,' in *Apartheid and Education: The Education of Black South Africans*, edited by Peter Kallaway. Johannesburg: Ravan Press, 1984, 148–159.

McCabe, Herbert. *Law, Love and Language*. London: Sheed and Ward, 1968.

McDonough, Peter. 'Ministry amongst Deaf People,' in *The Gospel preached by the Deaf: Proceedings of a conference on Deaf Liberation Theology held at the Faculty of Theology of the Catholic University of Leuven (Belgium), May 19th 2003*, edited by Marcel Broesterhuizen. Leuven, Paris, Dudley MA: Peeters, 2007, 53–69.

McIlroy, Guy. 'Deaf Identities: A Range of Possibilities.' Paper presented at the Deafness and Mental Health conference, Worcester, Cape Town, De La Bat Institute for the Deaf, August 2005.

⸺ 'The Implementation of South African Sign Language (SASL) and Sign Bilingualism in a School for the Deaf Interpreted Through the Identity Metaphors Used by School Leadership (SMT) and Teachers.' Unpublished doctoral diss., University of the Witwatersrand, Johannesburg, 2017.

McKeon, Richard, ed. *The Basic Works of Aristotle*. New York: Random House, 1941.

Minister, Stephen. *De-facing the Other: Reason, Ethics, and Politics After Difference*. Milwaukee: Marquette University Press, 2012.

Molteno, Frank. 'The Historical Foundations of the Schooling of Black South Africans,' in *Apartheid and Education: The Education of Black South Africans*, edited by Peter Kallaway. Johannesburg: Ravan Press, 1984, 45–107.

Morgan, Michael. *The Cambridge Introduction to Emmanuel Levinas*. Cambridge: Cambridge University Press, 2011. https://doi.org/10.1017/CBO9780511921551

Morris, Wayne. *Theology Without Words: Theology in the Deaf Community*. Aldershot, Hampshire: Ashgate, 2008.

Morrison, Glenn. 'The (Im)possibilities of Levinas for Christian Theology: The Search for a Language of Alterity,' in *Responsibility, God and Society: Theological Ethics in Dialogue: Festschrift Roger Burggraeve*, edited by J. de Tavernier, J.A Selling, J. Verstraeten and P. Schotsmanet. Leuven: Peters, 2008, 103–122.

───── *A Theology of Alterity: Levinas, von Balthasar, and Trinitarian Praxis.* Pittsburgh: Duquesne University Press, 2013.

───── 'Practical Theology from the Heart: Becoming Children of God.' *Compass: A Review of Topical Theology* (Spring, September 2016), 30–34.

Mukuka, George. *The Other Side of the Story: The Silent Experience of Black Clergy in the Catholic Church in South Africa (1898–1976).* Pietermaritzburg: Cluster Publications, 2008.

Murphy, Charles M. 'Action for Justice as Constitutive of Preaching of the Gospel. What Did the 1971 Synod Mean?' *Theological Studies* 44, 2 (1983), 298–311. https://doi.org/10.1177/004056398304400206

Naicker, Linda. 'The Role of Eugenics and Religion in the Construction of Race in South Africa.' *Studia Historiae Ecclesiasticae* 38, 2 (December 2012), 209–220.

Neuman, W. Lawrence. *Social Research Methods: Qualitative and Quantitative Approaches*, 4th ed. Boston: Allyn and Bacon, 2000.

Nolan, Albert. 'Structures of Sin.' *Angelicum* 84 (2007), 625–637.

Pascal, Blaise. *Pensées and Other Writings.* Trans. Honor Levi. Oxford: Oxford University Press, 1995.

Penn, Claire. 'Signs of the Times: Deaf Language and Culture in South Africa.' *The South African Journal of Communication Disorder*, 40, (1993), 11–23. https://doi.org/10.4102/sajcd.v40i1.652

Penn, Claire and Timothy Reagan. 'How do you Sign "Apartheid"? The Politics of South African Sign Language.' *Language Problems and Language Planning* 14, 2 (Summer 1990), 91–103. https://doi.org/10.1075/lplp.14.2.02pen

Peperzak, Adriaan, ed. *Ethics as First Philosophy: The Significance of Emmanuel Levinas for Philosophy, Literature and Religion.* New York and London: Routledge, 1995.

───── 'Transcendence,' in *Ethics as First Philosophy: The Significance of Emmanuel Levinas for Philosophy, Literature and Religion*, edited by Adriaan T. Peperzak. New York/London: Routledge, 1995, 185–192.

Perpich, Diane. 'Levinas, Feminism and Identity Politics,' in *Radicalizing Levinas*, edited by Peter Atterton and Matthew Calarco. Albany, NY: SUNY Press, 2010, 21–40.

Pieterse, Jude and Robyn Picas. *The Open Schools Era: 1976–1986.* Johannesburg: Marist Brothers, 2020.

Portolano, Lana. *Be Opened! The Catholic Church and Deaf Culture.* Washington DC: Catholic University Press, 2021. https://doi.org/10.2307/j.ctv1chs9w2

Rankin, Elizabeth. 'Book Review: Bernard Gwensa and Ruben Xulu: Christian Artists in Natal – Dina Cormick.' *Africa Insight* 23, 4, 255–256.

Raymond of Capua. *The Biography of St Catharine of Sienna.* Dublin: James Duffy and Co, n.d.

Reagan, Timothy. 'Language-in-Education Policy in South Africa: The Challenge of Sign Language. *African Education Review* 4, 2, 26–41. https://doi.org/10.1080/18146620701652663

Reynolds, Thomas E. *Vulnerable Communion: A Theology of Disability and Hospitality.* Grand Rapids: Brazos Press, 2008.

Rose, M. Lynn. 'Deaf and Dumb in Ancient Greece,' in *The Disability Studies Reader*, 2nd ed., edited by Lennard J. Davis. New York/London: Routledge, 2006, 17–32.

Sacks, Oliver. *Seeing Voices: A Journey Into the World of the Deaf.* London: Picador, 1990.

Said, Edward W. *Orientalism.* New York: Vintage Books, 1994.

Schäffler, Margaret Mary. 'The Integration of Black and Coloured Sisters in the Congregation of the King William's Town Dominican Sisters of St Catharine of Siena – The Past, the Present and the Future.' Unpublished M.Th thesis, University of South Africa, Pretoria, 2002.

Schroeder, Brian. *Altared Ground: Levinas, History and Violence.* New York/London: Routledge, 1996.

Scott, James C. *Domination and the Arts of Resistance: Hidden Transcripts.* New Haven: Yale University Press, 1990.

Seekings, Jeremy. *The UDF: A History of the United Democratic Front in South Africa, 1983–1991.* Cape Town: David Philip, 2006.

Seidenspinner-Nunez, Dayle, ed. *The Writings of Teresa de Cartegena.* Cambridge: D.S. Brewer, 1998.

Senghas, Richard J. and Leila Monaghan. 'Signs of their Times: Deaf Communities and the Culture of Language.' *Annual Review of Anthropology* 31 (2002), 69–97. https://doi.org/10.1146/annurev.anthro.31.020402.101302

Simmons, Robert. 'The Role of Educational Systems and Deaf Culture in the Development of Sign Language in South Africa.' *The Deaf Way: Perspectives From the International Conference on Deaf culture*, edited by Carol Erting, Dorothy L. Smith and Robert Johnson. Washington DC: Gallaudet University Press, 1994, 78–84. https://doi.org/10.2307/jj.4688148.20

Simmons, William Paul. 'The Third: Levinas' Theoretical Move From An-Archical Ethics to the Realm of Justice and Politics.' *Philosophy and Social Criticism* 25, 6 (1999), 83–104. https://doi.org/10.1177/019145379902500604

Steinberg, Sheila. 'Sign Language as the Bridge Across Deaf Boundaries: A South African Experience.' *Communicatio* 24, 1 (1998), 59–66. https://doi.org/10.1080/02500169808537845

Stokoe, William C. 'Sign Language Structure.' *Studies in Linguistics: Occasional Papers* 8 (1960).

————— *Semiotics and Human Sign Languages*. The Hague: Mouton, 1972.

————— 'Sign Language Research: What it Knows and Whither it Leads.' *The Silent Messenger* (December 1979), 7–11.

————— *Language in Hand: Why Sign Came Before Speech*. Washington DC: Gallaudet University Press, 2001.

Storbeck, Claudine. 'Bilingual Education for the Deaf in South Africa – Can it work?' *South African Journal of Communication Disorders* 47 (January 2000), 51–59. https://doi.org/10.4102/sajcd.v47i2.978

Swinton, John and Harriet Mowat. *Practical Theology and Qualitative Research*. 2nd ed. London: SCM Press, 2016.

Tijsseling, Corrie and Agnes Tellings. 'The Christian's Duty Toward the Deaf: Differing Christian Views on Deaf Schooling and Education in 19th Century Dutch society.' *American Annals for the Deaf* 154, 1 (2009), 36–49. https://doi.org/10.1353/aad.0.0078

Topolski, Anya. *Arendt, Levinas and a Politics of Relationality*. London/New York: Roman and Littlefield International, 2015.

Bibliography

Tosh, John. *The Pursuit of History: Aims, Methods and New Directions in the Study of Modern History*, 2nd ed. London/New York: Longman, 1991.

Tracy, David. *Plurality and Ambiguity: Hermeneutics, Religion and Hope*. Chicago: University of Chicago Press, 1987.

Van Cleve, John V. and Barry A. Crouch. *A Place of their Own: Creating the Deaf community in America*. Washington DC: Gallaudet University Press, 1989. https://doi.org/10.1097/00003446-198908000-00024

Vanier, Jean. *Made for Happiness: Discovering the Meaning of Life with Aristotle*. London: Darton, Longman and Todd, 2001.

Veling, Terry A. *For you Alone: Emmanuel Levinas and the Answerable Life*. Eugene, OR: Cascade Books, 2014.

Volf, M. *Exclusion and Embrace: A Theological Exploration of Identity, Otherness and Reconciliation*. Nashville: Abingdon Press, 1996.

Waliggo, John Mary. 'Making a Church that is Truly African,' in *Inculturation: Its Meaning and Urgency*, edited by A. Roest Crollius, J.M. Waliggo and T. Nkéramihigo. Nairobi/Kampala: St Paul's Publications, Africa, 1986, 11–30.

Weber, Max. *Economy and Society*, edited by G. Roth and C. Wittich. Berkeley: University of California Press, 1978.

Welsh, David. *The Rise and Fall of Apartheid*. Johannesburg/Cape Town: Jonathan Ball, 2009.

Wirzba, Norman. 'From Maieutics to Metanoia: Levinas's Understanding of the Philosophical Task.' *Man and World* 28 (1995), 129–144. https://doi.org/10.1007/BF01278941

Worsnip, Michael. *Between the Two Fires: The Anglican Church and Apartheid*. Pietermaritzburg: University of Natal Press, 1991.

Woywod, Stanislaus. *The New Canon Law: A Commentary and Summary of the New Code of Canon Law*. New York: Joseph F Wagner, 1918.

Wright, David. *Deafness: A Personal Account*. London: Allan Lane/The Penguin Press, 1969.

Wright, Tamra, Peter Hughes and Alison Ainley. 'The Paradox of Morality: An Interview With Emmanuel Levinas,' in *The Provocation of Levinas: Rethinking the Other*, edited by Robert Bernasconi and David Wood. London, New York: Routledge, 1988, 168–180.

Wyschogrod, Edith. *Saints and Postmodernism: Revisioning Moral Philosophy*. Chicago and London: The University of Chicago Press, 1990.
– – – – – *An Ethics of Remembering: History, Heterology, and the Nameless Others*. Chicago and London: The University of Chicago Press, 1998.
Zahn, Gordon C. *German Catholics and Hitler's Wars: A Study in Social Control*. New York: Sheed and Ward, 1962.

Articles on the Internet

Ashoka USA. 'Ashoka's History'. Accessed on 6 November 2021, www.ashoka.org/en-us/story/ashokas-history
– – – – – 'Fellow Robert Simmons.' Accessed on 6 November 2021, www.ashoka.org/cs/fellow/robert-simmons
Bauman, H-Dirksen. 'Listening to Phonocentrism with Deaf Eyes: Derrida's Mute Philosophy of (Sign) Language.' *Essays in Philosophy* 9, 1 (2008), 2. Accessed on 7 September 2018, https://doi.org/10.5840/eip20089118
– – – – – 'Reframing the Future of Deaf Education: From Hearing Loss to Deaf-Gain.' Talk given to the Canadian Hearing Society, 8. Accessed on 30 November 2022, https://www.chs.ca/sites/default/files/uploads
Bauman, H-Dirksen and Joseph M. Murray, 'Reframing: From Hearing Loss to Deaf Gain,' transl. from ASL by Fallon Brizendine and Emily Schenker. *Deaf Studies Digital Journal* 1 (Fall 2009), 3. Accessed on 30 November 2022, http://dsdj.gallaudet.edu
– – – – – 'Deaf Studies in the 21st Century: "Deaf-Gain" and the Future of Human Diversity,' in *The Oxford Handbook of Deaf Studies, Language, and Education*, vol. 2, edited by Marc Marschark and Patricia Elizabeth Spencer. Oxford Handbooks Online, September 2012. Accessed on 30 November 2022, https://doi.org/10.1093/oxfordhb/9780195390032.013.0014
Bell, Alexander Graham. 'Memoir Upon the Formation of a Deaf Variety of the Human Race.' Paper presented to the National Academy of Sciences, New Haven, Connecticut, 13 November 1883. Accessed on 20 February 2018, https://archive.org/details/cihm_08831

Bibliography

Berke, Jamie. 'Samuel Heinicke, Father of Oral Education.' Accessed on 11 February 2018, https://www.verywell.com/samuel-heinicke-oral-education-1046549

Compelling Truth. 'How do Exegesis and Eisegesis Differ.' Accessed 12 October 2024, www.compellingtruth.org/exegesis-eisegesis.html

Cyfko, James. 'Levinas and the Significance of Passivity in the Christian Religious Experience.' *Open Theology* 4 (2018), 511–519. Accessed on 15 May 2019, https://doi.org/10.1515/opth-2018-0040

Deaf History. 'Milan Conference 1880.' Accessed on 25 March 2013, https://deafhistory.eu/index.php/component/zoo/item/1880

D' Emilio, Frances. 'Vatican to Open Archives on World War II-Era Pope Pius XII.' *Crux* 4 (March 2019). Accessed 23 May 2019, https://cruxnow.com/vatican/2019/03/04/vatican-to-open-archives-on-world-war-ii-era-pope-pius-xii/

Enerstvedt, Regi Theodore. *The Legacy of the Past II: The Development of Education for the Deaf.* Dronninglund: Nord Press, 1996. Accessed on 28 June 2015, www.folk.uio.no/regie/litteratur/index.htm

Ericksen, Robert P. 'German Churches and the Holocaust: Assessing the Argument for Complicity.' The Raul Hilberg Memorial Lecture, The University of Vermont, 15 April 2013, 17. Accessed on 29 October 2018, www.uvm.edu/sites/default/files/media/HilbergLectureEricksen.pdf

Gcabashe, Thulani. 'Biographical Information.' Accessed on 8 August 2018, www.standardbank.com/pages/StandardBankGroup/web/directors.html

Gulliver, Mike. 'Bede's St John Less a Healer More a Teacher?' Accessed on 7 September 2018, https://mikegulliver.com/2016/10/21/bedes-st-john-less-a-healer-more-a-teacher

Janks, Hilary. 'Language and the Design of Texts.' *English Teaching: Practice and Critique* 4, 3 (December 2005), 97–110. Accessed on 4 May 2019, http://education.waikoto.ac.nz/research/files/etpc/2005v4n3art6.pdf

Lettman, Reinhard. 'Introduction to Three Sermons in Defiance of the Nazis by Bishop von Galen.' The Church in History Information Centre. Accessed on 5 November 2018, www.churchinhistory.org/pages/booklets/vongalen(n).htm

Mkame, Elizabeth. 'Biography.' Accessed on 21 July 2018, http://www.helpage.org/blogs/elizabeth-mkame-25201/how-nelson-mandela-inspired-me-as-an-older-person-820/

McIlroy, Guy. 'Sign Bilingualism in South Africa, Moving Towards Dynamic Bilingualism?' Paper presented to the International Symposium of Bilingualism 9: Singapore, 11 June 2013. Accessed 7 August 2018, www.academia.edu/3739205/Paper_for_ISB9_Sign_Bilingualism_in_South_Africa_moving_towards_dynamic_bilingualism

McIlroy, Guy and Claudine Storbeck. 'Development of Deaf Identity: An Ethnographic Study.' *Journal of Deaf Studies and Deaf Education* 16, 4 (Fall 2011), 494–511. Accessed on 8 September 2018, https://doi.org/10.1093/deafed/enr017

Mji, Diliza. 'Biographical information.' Accessed 21 July 2018, www.sahistory.org.za/people/diliza-mji and www.africaoutlookmag.com/outlook-features/busamed-hospital-group

Mlambo-Ngcuka, Phumzile. 'Biographical Information.' Accessed on 8 August 2018, www.unwomen.org/en/about-us/directorate/executive-director/ed-bio and www.sahistory.org.za/people/phumzile-mlambo-ngcuka

Moore, Michael Edward. 'The Spirit of the Gallican Councils, AD 314–506.' *Annarium Historiae Conciliorum* 39 (January 2007), 10. Accessed on 8 September 2018, https://doi.org/10.30965/25890433-0390102002

National Association of the Deaf, Accessed 6 December 2024, http://nad.org/resources/early-intervention-for-infants-and-toddlers/

Pope Gregory the Great. 'Homily on Mark 7:31–37.' Accessed on 8 September 2018, https://thedivinelamp.wordpress.com/2011/08/22/sunday-august-28-pope-st-gregory-the-greats-homily-on-mark-731-37/

Pope Paul VI. Apostolic Letter, *Ministeria Quaedam* (15 August 1972). Accessed 5 November 2018, www.ewtn.com/library/papaldoc/p6minors.htm

––––– *Evangelii Nuntiandi* (8 December 1975). Accessed 5 November 2018, www.vatican.va/content/paul-vi/en/apost_exhortations/documents/hf_p-vi_exh_19751208_evangelii-nuntiandi.html

Bibliography

Reagan, Timothy, Claire Penn and Dale Ogilvy. 'From Policy to Practice: Sign Language Developments in Post-Apartheid South Africa.' *Language Policy* 5, (2006), 187–208. Accessed on 15 September 2108, https://doi.org/10.1007/s10993-006-9002-y

Steinfels, Peter. 'Emmanuel Levinas, 90, French Ethical Philosopher.' *The New York Times*, 27 December 1995, 1. Accessed on 3 May 2019, www.nyti.ms/29iQumz

St Joseph Institute for the Deaf. Accessed 5 November 2018, www.csjcarondelet.org/educational-institutions/

University of the Witwatersrand. Obituary, 'Simmons, Robert Michael Thomas (1931–2007).' Accessed on 6 November 2021, www.wits.ac.za/alumni/obituaries/obituary-content-by-year

WFD (World Federation of the Deaf). 'Our Mission, Our Values, Our People.' Accessed on 20 February 2018, https://www.wfdeaf.org/who-we-are/our philosophy/

Wyschogrod, Edith and Carl Raschke. 'Heterological History: A Conversation.' *Journal for Cultural and Religious Theory* 1, 2 (2000). Accessed on 2 May 2019, www.jcrt.org/archives/01.2/wyschogrod_raschke.shtml

www.ingramcontent.com/pod-product-compliance
Lightning Source LLC
Chambersburg PA
CBHW071732150426
43191CB00010B/1546